An Intro

Put together a book like this, and you ca⌐   ⌐y did you did it?

Well, why not? With the dimensions ⌐. ⌐⌐. p⌐⌐⌐⌐. ⌐⌐⌐⌐ ⌐⌐⌐⌐⌐⌐⌐⌐, there can be no doubt that interest in other countries' football is on the increase. Five years ago, for example, the thought of English-language TV coverage of German league football matches in the U.K. was laughable. Today, it's taken for granted.

Our native tongue is blessed with a healthy number of football reference books and yet even the best provide only a superficial level of information on what goes on outside the English-speaking world. Admittedly, league tables and results are decipherable in just about any language, but there's a lot more to the game than just a bunch of numbers.

Information on German football—particularly information which extends beyond the top echelons of play—is difficult to come by, even in Germany. That's why I wanted to put together this book. Some details were easier to find than others, though, and in the end the desire to complete this project overtook the desire to unearth every last piece of information. Sharp-eyed readers will note the absence of round-by-round East German Cup results, and top scorers for some leagues. Should there be a need for a revised edition of this book, those of you able to provide these particulars know where to send them.

For those who find this publication failing to meet their expectations, I offer two excuses. First, I am not a German football expert. I have not grown up with the game and have no childhood memories of the sport upon which to draw. My home is not filled with shelves of books on the subject, and I have not spent long hours downing glasses of *Weissbier* in the company of German sports historians. My trips to the continent to watch German matches are woefully infrequent; I wasn't even able to visit a German library to assist with the research for this book.

Second, I do not write football books for a living. I hold no professional relationships with sportswriters, nor am I able to employ assistants to help me plow through reference books. What you hold in your hands is simply the product of countless long nights in front of a word processor, armed with stacks of facts and whatever inspiration cups of tea and listening to old Crusaders records can provide.

Football may be football all over the world, but the history of the game reads differently in each country. The fact that the Bundesliga is played where English is not the principal language should not make it any less interesting, only perhaps more enigmatic. I hope this book will serve to enlighten you the way putting it together has enlightened me.

Dave Wangerin
November 1993

Acknowledgements

Football being a team game, it's fitting that putting together this book has been a team effort. A lot of people played a part in getting this book into your hands, and I'm grateful to them all. You know who you are.

Teams have their superstars, though, and my *Elfmeter* associate Derek Megginson definitely deserves the award for Player of the Season. His versatility knows no bounds: writer, information-provider, translator, proof-reader, motivator, all-around indispensable assistant. That this book was completed at all is a tribute to Derek's hard work as much as mine. Perhaps one day I'll even get to meet him.

Providing the dazzling wing play was Peter Schimkat, who gave the proverbial 110% in providing me with the more esoteric particulars and a German's view of the manuscript. Perhaps one day I'll get to meet him, too.

The rest of the team also displayed an impressive array of talents. In particular, I am indebted to Alexander Graham, Hardy Grüne, Gordon McCreath, and Andrew Wallace for their assistance with facts and figures. Others provided information which ultimately could not be used in this project, but their endeavours are nevertheless appreciated.

And to my wife Nicola, supplier of more tea and sympathy than anyone has a right to expect, and left to fend for herself for much of the past year: my heartfelt apologies. At last, it's finished.

The Fussball Book

© David Wangerin 1993

First published in Great Britain by David Wangerin, 16 Mallory Road, Perton, Staffordshire WV6 7XN.

ISBN 0-9522452-0-5

All rights reserved. No part of this publication may be reproduced, stored in a retrieval system, or transmitted in any form, or by any means, without the prior permission in writing of the publisher, nor be otherwise circulated in any form of binding or cover other than that in which it is published, and without a similar condition including this condition being imposed on the subsequent purchaser.

This book was produced using the Ami Pro 3.0 word processing package.

Printed and bound in Great Britain by Catford Copy Centre, London.

Whilst every effort has been made to ensure the information contained in this book is accurate, the publisher accepts no liability for any errors or omissions.

Roots of the Bundesliga

Writing a statistical history of German football which begins with the year 1963 may be kind of like playing one side of a record without ever playing the other. But many would argue that the game's modern era began in earnest with the formation of the Bundesliga, and it is this milestone which has been chosen, rightly or wrongly, as the starting point for this book.

It may seem incredible that Germany, one of the most powerful footballing nations on earth, did not have a professional national league until thirty years ago. But when one considers how for many centuries the German nation had been fragmented, and that for 35 years after the Second World War it was split in two, perhaps this is not too surprising. Though German football did not have a unified First Division until the formation of the Bundesliga, a championship to determine the national *Deutscher Meister* had been contested on a regular basis as far back as 1903, when VfB Leipzig's name was the first engraved on the championship plate. Entrants for the competition were drawn from the various regional leagues which operated across the country, with clubs like Phönix Karlsruhe and Viktoria Berlin crowned national champions in the early years.

The German F.A., the *Deutscher Fussball Bund* (DFB), was founded in 1900. Even during its infancy, there had been a great deal of discussion about forming a national league, but not until the 1920s were any concrete proposals put forward. These always seemed to be of secondary importance, however, when compared to the continuing debate about professionalism.

For many years, the German F.A. had insisted that all clubs remained scrupulously amateur. The normal length of a ban for any player caught receiving "payments" was six months, as the national goalkeeper Willibald Kress once found to his cost. Bans of up to three years for serious offences were not uncommon. But the progressive clubs in the west of Germany continued to push for the legalisation of professionalism and made no secret of the fact that they wanted the entire system overhauled. Each time, however, their proposals were met with apathy or antagonism from the other areas of the country. In the early 1930s, an Extraordinary General Meeting of the DFB was called to decide on the introduction of professional football. But after Hitler seized power, the political situation became unstable and the idea was shelved. In the late thirties there were again definite proposals to form a *Reichsliga* but the outbreak of war put paid to these plans.

In the 1950s—and in particular after West Germany's World Cup triumph in 1954—there were renewed proposals from clubs in the Ruhr district and neighbouring areas for a national West German league. But once again, the other regions voted against them. As with Brazilian football today, each regional association resented handing over its power and authority to a national body. So the German championship continued to be decided by an end-of-season playoff—long after East Germany had developed its own national *Oberliga*.

Still, the pressure for change continued to be applied, and soon it came to be acknowledged that many of the country's top teams were furtively offering compensation of one sort or another to players in order to maintain a competitive edge. In some cases, players were promised easy "jobs" by wealthy businessmen with links to a particular club. The whole concept of "amateurism" was coming under serious threat, and with the revenue being generated by huge crowds for the top matches, a lot of money was available to the dishonest.

The first real breakthrough came in 1960, when the Saarland representative proposed a "reduction in the number of clubs fielding professional teams," and a working party was set up to study the whole footballing system.

The 1961 Annual General Meeting of the German F.A. presented the breakthrough that the progressive clubs had been waiting for. The DFB accepted in principal the idea of forming a *Bundesliga* and at the following year's AGM on Dortmund on July 28, 1962, the clubs voted 103-26 to develop a national league. Amongst the decisions taken were:
- that the proposed Bundesliga would consist of not more than sixteen clubs;
- that only those clubs already in one of the five *Oberligen* could apply to join;
- that sporting criteria should take precedence over economic and other factors;
- that the league would consist of five clubs from the Oberliga South, five from the West, three from the North, two from the Southwest, and one from Berlin;
- that full-time professional players would finally be allowed.

Forty-six clubs applied to join the Bundesliga. The steering committee designed a system which evaluated the clubs' performances over the past twelve years, whilst giving greater weight to the most recent finishes. Newspapers soon took to publishing a number of rather speculative calculations, all of which were strenuously denied by the DFB—perhaps because no set formula really existed.

In north Germany, there was little doubt that Hamburg SV, who had won the last nine Oberliga North championships, and Werder Bremen, the eternal runners-up, would be invited to participate in the new league. The third spot, though, was up for grabs, with little to choose between Eintracht Brunswick,

Hanover 96, VfL Osnabrück, Holstein Kiel, and St. Pauli. In the end, Brunswick's third-place Oberliga finish probably swung the decision in their favour.

In Berlin, Hertha BSC faced stiff competition for a place with local rivals Tasmania 1900. Tasmania had been the more successful side in the Oberliga Berlin in recent years and were financially more stable. But Hertha got their 1962-63 season off to a dream start. Halfway into the season, as the selection process heated up, they were ten points clear of Tasmania.

In the west, it was assumed that the three strongest sides in recent seasons—1.FC Cologne, FC Schalke 04, and Borussia Dortmund—would be accepted. Had the Bundesliga been formed a few years earlier, there is little doubt that Rot-Weiss Essen would also have been included, but they had since fallen into the Second Division. Meanwhile, city rivals Schwarz-Weiss Essen had been heading in the opposite direction, and as the selection process began, were well in touch with the Oberliga West leaders. But as relative newcomers to the top flight, their recent playing record couldn't compete with the likes of Preussen Münster and Alemannia Aachen, two clubs who seemed more likely to complete the western line-up.

There was, though, a slight complication. With Münster in the Westphalian wilderness, Aachen virtually in Belgium and the three other sides too strong to leave out, the densely-populated lower Rhine area would be excluded from the new league. If the Bundesliga was to be a true national league, it was logical to include a representative from this region. So there was hope for Schwarz-Weiss Essen—until they fell apart in the latter part of the season. The darkness over the *Niederrhein* was lifted, though, thanks to an inspired performance from a little-known outfit from Duisburg called Meiderich SV. They finished third in the Oberliga behind Dortmund and Cologne, and stood an excellent chance of filling the void.

In the southwest, there wasn't much to choose between the region's top four clubs. 1.FC Saarbrücken and 1.FC Kaiserslautern seemed the likeliest two teams to be admitted, but in recent years small-town Borussia Neunkirchen and FK Pirmasens had staked their claim with a string of consistently impressive finishes. Consequently, the DFB was expected to make their decision about this region's representatives at the latest possible date.

Five places were reserved for clubs from the Oberliga South, and there was little doubt that the playing records of 1.FC Nuremberg, Eintracht Frankfurt, Kickers Offenbach, VfB Stuttgart, and Karlsruhe SC had earned them the right to play in the Bundesliga. The city of Munich, then, seemed destined to be left out, with Bayern having occupied a place near the top of the Oberliga only since the start of the decade, and city rivals TSV 1860 foundering in recent years.

The Munich problem fuelled the fire for advocates of an eighteen-team rather than a sixteen-team Bundesliga. With TSV and Bayern both in contention for the title, it seemed possible that an Oberliga champion would be excluded from the new league. Or perhaps, with Stuttgart having started their season so atrociously, a place was still there for the taking.

Stuttgart eventually straightened themselves out to finish sixth—but Munich 1860 won the league. The unfortunate club to lose out would be Offenbach, in spite of the fact that unofficial measurements rated them as the second best side in the region. But Offenbach suffered from being very near geographically to Frankfurt—a very handy explanation for the DFB in denying them Bundesliga status.

At a meeting on January 11, 1963, the first batch of clubs were informed that they had been officially accepted as founder members of the Bundesliga. They were: 1.FC Cologne, Borussia Dortmund, and Schalke 04 from the West; Hamburg SV and Werder Bremen from the North; Eintracht Frankfurt and 1.FC Nuremberg from the South; 1.FC Saarbrücken from the Southwest; and Hertha BSC from Berlin.

The decision to include Saarbrücken at this early stage raised a few eyebrows, particularly amongst supporters of southwestern clubs Pirmasens, Neunkirchen, and Kasierslautern, who felt Saarbrücken had hardly demonstrated any superiority on the pitch. The DFB pointed out that Saarbrücken was the biggest city of the four, with more convenient motorway connections than the likes of Pirmasens, and at the time of the decision, 1.FC Saarbrücken were top of the table (although not by much; eventually they drifted out of the top four, and missed out on the playoff for the national championship). Kaiserslautern wound up winning the Oberliga Southwest, while Neunkirchen pipped Pirmasens for second place and performed well in the playoffs, only just missing out on an appearance in the final.

The nine clubs selected had seven months to prepare for the Bundesliga, which was to kick off in August. This gave them what must have been a considerable advantage. (Indeed, Dortmund went on to win the last fragmented German championship in the spring of 1963.) At the same meeting, fifteen clubs had their applications rejected, including Borussia Mönchengladbach and Bayer Leverkusen. Two other clubs, Wuppertal SV and Sportfreunde Saarbrücken, withdrew from contention. With twenty clubs contesting the remaining seven places in the new league, a bitter struggle began. But proposals to increase the size of the new league to eighteen or even twenty clubs were ultimately rejected.

On May 6, 1963—just three and a half months before the start of the new league—the committee reached their final decision and announced the remaining seven Bundesliga clubs: VfB Stuttgart, Karlsruhe SC and TSV 1860 Munich from the south; Preussen Münster and Meiderich SV from the west; Eintracht Brunswick from the north, and 1.FC Kaiserslautern from the southwest. All thirteen of the clubs left out by the decision immediately launched appeals, but each was unsuccessful. Kickers Offenbach and Alemannia Aachen even took the DFB's decision to court. Both claimed geographical considerations had unfairly taken precedence over performance on the pitch. But there was a certain inevitability that some clubs would suffer the misfortune of being in the wrong place at the wrong time.

It's interesting to think how the course of German football might have been altered had the DFB's selection criterion been different. Perhaps Hamborn 07 or Westfalia Herne would have finished strongly in the inaugural Bundesliga season, and gone on to win the Bundesliga a few years down the road. Maybe the names Schwaben Augsburg or VfR Mannheim would mean more to a German fan today than Werder Bremen or VfB Stuttgart. Who knows—European football might even have been littered with regular appearances from Viktoria 89 Berlin or Wormatia Worms. And, had their original applications been declined, maybe few outside of Germany would ever have heard of 1.FC Kaiserslautern or Eintracht Frankfurt.

But the summer of 1963 was not a time to reflect—it was a time to look ahead. And on August 24, the Bundesliga kicked off.

1963-64

First Cologne

Once the decision had been made as to who was invited to play in the Bundesliga, speculation shifted toward which team would prove the strongest. Of the five old regional leagues, the south and west were generally acknowledged as the most competitive, so their champions, TSV 1860 Munich and 1.FC Cologne—the "first football club of Cologne"—were naturally rated amongst the favourites. Also tipped were Borussia Dortmund, winners of the 1963 national championship playoffs, and Hamburg SV, champions of the north for the past nine consecutive years.

Of these teams, only Cologne got off to a winning start, with 19-year-old Wolfgang Overath scoring his club's first Bundesliga goal in a 2-0 win at Saarbrücken. On the first day of the season, each of the eight matches attracted gates of 30,000 or more. In mid-September there was a crowd of 85,411 to see Hertha Berlin play host to Cologne. The visitors won 3-0 and opened up a gap at the top of the league by collecting eleven points from their first six matches.

There was also interest—at least amongst statisticians—as to who would score the first goal in the new Bundesliga. Fifty-eight seconds into Borussia Dortmund's match at Werder Bremen, Timo Konietzka was assured of his place in the annals of German football history with his goal for Borussia, who went on to lose, 3-2. Unfortunately, no film or television footage exists of this historic event—suggesting, perhaps, that for all the interest in the new league shown by the general public, the media were lagging behind.

No players were sent off on the inaugural day, but it was not long until Meiderich's Helmut Rahn gained this dubious honour, for a foul on Hertha's Harald Beyer. Rahn was one of three players in the league who had figured in West

Germany's World Cup win of 1954, the others being Cologne skipper Hans Schäfer and Nuremberg's 38-year-old inside-right Max Morlock.

Whilst on the subject of firsts, the first *Trainer* to be sacked was Herbert Widmeyer of Nuremberg, after only nine games. He never took charge of a Bundesliga club again. The first match to be postponed was Stuttgart against Schalke in January, because of a frozen pitch. The first penalty kick was awarded to Kaiserslautern, in their opening day clash with Frankfurt, with Jürgen Neumann converting it in the 38th minute. And the first Bundesliga footballer to break his leg was Nuremberg's Reinhold Gettinger, 55 minutes into the match with Eintracht Brunswick in December.

It was also not long before the first instances of crowd trouble and hooliganism occurred, most notably in the form of a Cologne fan who ran onto the pitch to hit a linesman after a 1-1 draw with Frankfurt in February. The DFB was quick to mete out its punishment, and the Müngersdorf Stadium was closed for one game. Cologne nevertheless won that match, 4-1 over Brunswick in Wuppertal.

It soon became apparent that Cologne were head and shoulders above every other team in the league. The club was superbly organised from its President right down to the ball-boys. *Trainer* Georg Knöpfle, a 59-year-old disciplinarian, and his coach "Tschik" Cajovski prepared the players thoroughly and professionally. In their fifteen home games, *die Geissböcke* (the Billy-goats) dropped only six points, their lone defeat being a shock 3-1 loss to bottom club Saarbrücken.

As Cologne edged towards the title, they introduced another teenager to the team, Wolfgang Weber. Both Weber and Overath were in such good form they were summoned by national team manager Helmut Schön for their full international debuts this season. Throughout their long careers, they remained loyal to the club, Weber making 356 Bundesliga appearances and 53 for West Germany, and Overath 409 and 81.

Cologne wrapped up the championship with three matches remaining, but the fight for the runners-up spot lasted right until the end. Meiderich finished second with a goal average 0.08 better than Frankfurt. Had the later system of goal difference been used, Frankfurt would have finished second. At the bottom, 1.FC Saarbrücken came last by some distance, but the other relegation spot was not decided until the penultimate match. Preussen Münster were relegated after losing 4-2 at Werder Bremen, whilst Hertha BSC Berlin won at home to Munich 1860 3-1 before 55,000 to stay up. Münster have the notorious distinction of being the only founder member of the Bundesliga to have played just one season there.

German football may have been nationalised at First Division level, but at other levels it remained provincial. The Second Division was represented by five regional leagues from the north, south, west, southwest, and Berlin. The novelty of the Bundesliga captured the bulk of the nation's attention, and regional play took something of a back-seat, with some parts of the country left trailing in the Bundesliga's wake. Devoid of a First Division entry, the city of Ludwigshafen found itself with three Regionalliga Southwest entries—Phönix, TuRa, and SC, each of whom finished comfortably in mid-table yet struggled for support. At the end of the season, Phönix and TuRa merged to form Südwest Ludwigshafen.

No fewer than five Second Division teams managed to score over a hundred goals in Regionalliga play. FK Pirmasens of the Südwest racked up 128 goals whilst conceding only 49—and still wound up finishing second. Attacking football was the order of the day, with even relegated Sportfreunde Siegen managing to find the net 69 times in their 38 Regionalliga West matches. The top two finishers in the west, south, southwest, and north *Regionalligen* joined the champion of Berlin in a playoff for promotion. Hanover 96 and Borussia Neunkirchen finished at the top of their respective groups to earn a place in the following season's Bundesliga.

The sixteen Bundesliga clubs automatically qualified for the new-look West German Cup. They were joined by sixteen amateur clubs who had done well in the regional cup competitions: four each from the north, west, and south, three from the southwest, and one from Berlin. Frankfurt gained some consolation for their disappointing league form with a good cup run. They reached the final but, on a sweltering August afternoon, were well-beaten by Munich 1860, Wilfried Kohlars and Rudi Brunnenmaier scoring the goals. The real cup sensation, though, was Altona 93 of Hamburg, who knocked out Mönchengladbach, Meiderich and Karlsruhe before bowing out to 1860 in the semifinal.

In East Germany, a national first division, the Oberliga, had been introduced some fourteen years earlier, with Vorwärts Berlin and Wismut Karl-Marx-Stadt dominating play in the late fifties and early sixties. Clubs were constantly being re-named, merged, or in some cases transported to completely different cities—although Wismut Karl-Marx-Stadt, previously known as Wismut Aue, had continued to play their home matches in their old city. This season it was the city of Leipzig's turn to undergo the latest "reorganisation." The Rotation and Lokomotive clubs merged to form a supposedly top-class SC Leipzig, replete with the best players, whilst Chemie were re-founded by grass-roots support after an absence of nine years. But things did not go exactly as planned. The supposedly pedestrian Chemie won the League, whilst SC could finish no better than third.

At international level, West Germany tried four different goalkeepers before deciding on Hans Tilkowski. The low point of the season was undoubtedly a defeat by Algeria, one which would repeat itself in more critical circumstances nineteen years later. East Germany's national team, which had played Mali and Guinea the season before, continued to make journeys down international football's lesser-travelled roads. They lost 3-0 to Ghana, but beat Burma 5-1 before a crowd of 40,000 in Rangoon. They also achieved their highest-ever international score by beating Sri Lanka 12-1 in Colombo, with seven different players appearing on the scoresheet. The West Germans did not enter the year's European Nations Cup, but East Germany made it to the last sixteen before losing 5-4 on aggregate to Hungary. Meanwhile the East German Olympic team—a kind of "B" team—won the bronze medal at the Tokyo games.

Although there were some good results for German club sides in the European competitions, the Bundesliga had yet to prove itself as one of Europe's strongest professional leagues. Borussia Dortmund made it to the semifinal of the European Cup, with a memorable 5-0 win over Benfica on the way, but were eliminated by AC Milan. In the Cup Winners' Cup, there was an epic tussle between Hamburg and Barcelona, with a 4-4 draw in Spain and a 0-0 draw in Germany necessitating a third match in Lausanne, which HSV won 3-2. But Lyon put Hamburg out in the following round.

Bundesliga

Club	P	W	D	L	Goals	Pts
1. 1.FC Cologne	30	17	11	2	78-40	45
2. SV Meiderich	30	13	13	4	60-36	39
3. Eintracht Frankfurt	30	16	7	7	65-41	39
4. Borussia Dortmund	30	14	5	11	73-57	33
5. VfB Stuttgart	30	13	7	10	48-40	33
6. Hamburg SV	30	11	10	9	69-60	32
7. TSV 1860 Munich	30	11	9	10	66-50	31
8. FC Schalke 04	30	12	5	13	51-53	29
9. 1.FC Nuremberg	30	11	7	12	45-56	29
10. Werder Bremen	30	10	8	12	53-62	28
11. Eintracht Brunswick	30	11	6	13	36-49	28
12. 1.FC Kaiserslautern	30	10	6	14	48-49	26
13. Karlsruhe SC	30	8	8	14	42-55	24
14. Hertha BSC Berlin	30	9	6	15	45-65	24
15. Preussen Münster	30	7	9	14	34-52	23
16. 1.FC Saarbrücken	30	6	5	19	44-72	17

Top Scorers

Seeler (Hamburg SV)	30
Konietzka (Borussia Dortmund)	20
Brunnenmeier (TSV 1860 Munich)	19
Huberts (Eintracht Frankfurt)	19
Matischak (FC Schalke 04)	18
Emmerich (Borussia Dortmund)	16
Thielen (1.FC Cologne)	16
Strehl (1.FC Nuremberg)	16
Dörfel (Hamburg SV)	15
Höller (VfB Stuttgart)	15
Müller (1.FC Cologne)	15

Bundesliga Promotion Playoffs

Qualifying Round: Wuppertal SV v FK Pirmasens (0-2, 1-2); Pirmasens qualify for playoffs

Group One	P	W	D	L	Goals	Pts
1. Borussia Neunkirchen	6	4	0	2	9-7	8
2. Bayern Munich	6	3	1	2	12-7	7
3. Tasmania 1900 Berlin	6	2	2	2	12-9	6
4. St Pauli	6	1	1	4	8-18	3

Group Two	P	W	D	L	Goals	Pts
1. Hanover 96	6	5	0	1	15-6	10
2. Hessen Kassel	6	3	0	3	11-12	6
3. Alemannia Aachen	6	2	0	4	10-13	4
4. FK Pirmasens	6	2	0	4	10-15	4

Regionalliga Berlin

Club	P	W	D	L	Goals	Pts
1. Tasmania 1900 Berlin	27	21	4	2	73-22	46
2. Tennis Borussia Berlin	27	19	4	4	73-22	42
3. Wacker 04 Berlin	27	15	4	8	52-45	34
4. SV Spandau	27	13	7	7	63-41	33
5. Blau-Weiss Berlin	27	9	5	13	37-55	23
6. Hertha Zehlendorf	27	11	2	14	46-47	22
7. Reinickendorf Füchse	27	8	5	14	31-46	21
8. SV Berlin 92	27	6	7	14	28-49	19
9. BFC Südring	27	7	3	17	36-64	17
10. SC Union 06 Berlin	27	4	3	20	23-71	11

Hertha Zehlendorf two points deducted
Promoted: Viktoria 89 Berlin
Regionalliga Playoff: SC Gatow v BFC Südring (1-1, 0-2); Südring remain in Regionalliga

Regionalliga North

Club	P	W	D	L	Goals	Pts
1. FC St Pauli	34	21	9	4	87-35	51
2. Hanover 96	34	22	5	7	78-27	49
3. Arminia Hanover	34	18	9	7	73-44	45
4. FC Altona 93	34	21	2	11	82-46	44
5. Holstein Kiel	34	18	7	9	72-48	43
6. VfL Osnabrück	34	16	7	11	56-52	39
7. VfB Oldenburg	34	16	6	12	63-50	38
8. ASV Bergedorf	34	13	9	12	65-65	35
9. VfL Wolfsburg	34	14	6	14	50-61	34
10. VfR Neumünster	34	12	9	13	56-61	33
11. Victoria Hamburg	34	9	11	14	49-71	29
12. TuS Bremerhaven 93	34	9	10	15	48-48	28
13. VfV Hildesheim	34	10	8	16	40-53	28
14. VfB Lübeck	34	11	5	18	59-78	27
15. SV Friedrichsort	34	7	10	17	46-85	24
16. Concordia Hamburg	34	8	7	19	39-62	23
17. VfL Oldenburg	34	6	11	17	36-69	23
18. SV Barmbek-Uhlenhorst	34	5	9	20	40-84	19

Top Scorer: Haecks (St Pauli), 36 goals

Regionalliga North Promotion Playoffs

Preliminary Round: Olympia Wilhelmshaven v Leu Brunswick (2-2, 2-7); Leu Brunswick qualify for playoffs

Group One	P	W	D	L	Goals	Pts
1. Göttingen 05	6	4	1	1	9-5	9
2. VfL Pinneburg	6	4	1	1	11-7	9
3. Kilia Kiel	6	3	0	3	12-10	6
4. SV Blumenthal	6	0	0	6	2-12	0

1963-64

Group Two	P	W	D	L	Goals	Pts
1. Rasensport Harburg	6	5	1	0	14-6	10
2. VfL Bad Oldesloe	6	3	1	2	12-8	7
3. SV Meppen	6	1	2	3	7-14	4
4. Leu Brunswick	6	1	1	4	10-15	3

Regionalliga South

Club	P	W	D	L	Goals	Pts
1. Hessen Kassel	38	22	5	8	116-61	55
2. Bayern Munich	38	22	8	8	115-61	52
3. Kickers Offenbach	38	21	8	9	96-66	50
4. Schwaben Augsburg	38	19	11	8	77-56	49
5. SSV Reutlingen	38	19	9	10	76-61	47
6. VfR Mannheim	38	18	9	11	68-50	45
7. Schweinfurt 05	38	17	9	12	82-55	43
8. TSG Ulm 46	38	20	2	16	73-74	42
9. SpVgg Fürth	38	14	11	13	68-61	39
10. FC Freiburg	38	14	9	15	58-61	37
11. SV Waldhof	38	15	6	17	56-60	36
12. ESV Ingolstadt	38	12	11	15	61-81	35
13. Bayern Hof	38	12	9	17	61-64	33
14. Kickers Stuttgart	38	12	9	17	54-74	33
15. 1.FC Pforzheim	38	12	9	17	51-75	33
16. FSV Frankfurt	38	13	5	20	69-85	31
17. SpVgg Neu-Isenburg	38	11	5	22	49-80	27
18. Borussia Fulda	38	8	10	20	53-77	26
19. BC Augsburg	38	10	5	23	48-90	25
20. Amicitia Viernheim	38	8	6	24	47-86	22

Top Scorer: Jendrosch (Hessen Kassel), 34 goals
Promoted: SV Darmstadt 98, Wacker Munich

Regionalliga South Promotion Playoffs

Club	P	W	D	L	Goals	Pts
1. FC Emmindingen	5	4	0	1	11-6	8
2. VfR Heilbronn	5	2	1	2	5-6	5
3. FV Ebingen	5	2	0	3	9-12	4
4. SV Schwetzeingen	5	1	1	3	10-11	3

As Emmendingen had clinched promotion, the final round was not played.
Also Promoted: Wacker Munich, SV Darmstadt 98

Regionalliga Southwest

Club	P	W	D	L	Goals	Pts
1. Borussia Neunkirchen	38	25	10	3	106-32	60
2. FK Pirmasens	38	27	5	6	128-49	59
3. Wormatia Worms	38	25	8	5	85-41	58
4. FSV Mainz 05	38	20	7	11	82-57	47
5. Eintracht Trier	38	16	11	11	72-68	43
6. Saar 05 Saarbrücken	38	15	12	11	78-52	42
7. VfR Kaiserslautern	38	16	10	12	65-54	42
8. Spfr Saarbrücken	38	17	6	15	81-62	40
9. Phönix Ludwigshafen	38	15	10	13	58-56	40
10. SC Ludwigshafen	38	17	6	15	66-64	40
11. TuS Neuendorf	38	16	7	15	84-73	39
12. TuRa Ludwigshafen	38	14	9	15	64-54	35
13. SV Völklingen	38	11	13	14	65-74	35
14. SV Weisenau	38	11	12	15	60-77	34
15. VfR Frankenthal	38	12	8	18	55-77	32
16. BSC Oppau	38	13	6	19	49-71	32
17. Phönix Bellheim	38	11	5	22	67-99	27
18. TSC Zweibrücken	38	8	7	23	50-96	23
19. ASV Landau	38	6	5	27	39-110	17
20. SV Niederlahnstein	38	6	1	31	37-123	13

Top Scorer: Kapitulski (FK Pirmasens), 31 goals

Regionalliga Southwest Promotion Playoffs

Club	P	W	D	L	Goals	Pts
1. Germania Metternich	4	2	2	0	6-3	6
2. Viktoria Salzbach	4	1	1	2	4-5	3
3. Eintracht Bad Kreuznach	4	1	1	2	4-6	3

Regionalliga West

Club	P	W	D	L	Goals	Pts
1. Alemannia Aachen	38	27	5	6	105-37	59
2. Wuppertal SV	38	19	4	5	66-36	52
3. Fortuna Düsseldorf	38	21	8	9	85-50	50
4. TSV Marl-Hüls	38	20	8	10	56-41	48
5. Viktoria Cologne	38	19	7	12	77-53	45
6. Westfalia Herne	38	17	10	11	69-63	44
7. Rot-Weiss Oberhausen	38	16	10	12	68-58	42
8. Borussia Mönchengladbach	38	17	7	14	71-47	41
9. Duisburg SpV	38	13	13	12	54-55	39
10. Rot-Weiss Essen	38	13	12	13	70-64	38
11. Arminia Bielefeld	38	14	10	14	65-74	38
12. Bayer Leverkusen	38	13	9	16	62-62	35
13. Schwarz-Weiss Essen	38	13	8	17	60-71	34
14. Sportfreunde Hamborn 07	38	12	10	16	49-71	34
15. STV Horst-Emscher	38	11	9	18	56-75	31
16. SpVgg Herten	38	12	7	19	55-79	31
17. VfB Bottrop	38	11	8	19	53-68	30
18. Spfr Siegen	38	9	11	18	69-85	29
19. TuS Duisburg 48/99	38	9	4	25	47-88	22
20. Lünen SV	38	5	8	25	41-101	18

Top Scorer: Martinelli (Alemannia Aachen), 33 goals
SpV Duisburg became Eintracht Duisburg

Regionalliga West Promotion Playoffs

Qualifying Round: Eintracht Gelsenkirchen v SC Dortmund 95 (2-2, 1-1, 2-0); Gelsenkirchen qualify for playoff

Club	P	W	D	L	Goals	Pts
1. SpVgg Homberg	2	1	1	0	4-3	3
2. Eintracht Gelsenkirchen	2	1	0	1	8-1	2
3. Schlebusch SV	2	0	1	1	3-8	1

1963-64

Third Division Champions
Baden (Nordbaden): SV Schwetzingen
Baden (Südbaden): FC Emmendingen
Bayern: Wacker Munich
Berlin: Viktoria 89 Berlin
Bremen: SV Blumenthal
Hamburg: VfL Pinneberg
Hessen: SV Darmstadt 98
Mittelrhein: SV Schlebusch
Niederrhein: SpVgg Homberg
Niedersachsen: Hanover 96 (Am.)
Rheinland: Germania Metternich
Saarland: Viktoria Sulzbach
Schleswig-Holstein: VfL Oldesloe
Südwest: Eintracht Bad Kreuznach
Westfalen: Eintracht Gelsenkirchen
Württemberg: VfB Stuttgart (Am.)

West German Cup
First Round
1.FC Cologne 3, 1.FC Nuremberg 2 aet
1.FC Kaiserslautern 2, Wuppertal SV 0
1.FC Saarbrücken 6, Tennis Borussia Berlin 1
Eintracht Brunswick 3, VfL Osnabrück 0
Eintracht Gelsenkirchen 0, SV Duisburg 2
Eintracht Trier 1, Hanover 96 1 aet (0-4)
FC Altona 93 2, Borussia Mönchengladbach 1
Hamburg SV 1, SpVgg Fürth 1 aet (1-2 aet)
Kickers Stuttgart 0, Phönix Ludwigshafen 3
Preussen Münster 1, Karlsruhe SC 3
SV Meiderich 1, Hertha BSC Berlin 2 aet
TSV 1860 Munich 2, Borussia Dortmund 0
VfB Stuttgart 2, SSV Reutlingen 2 aet (4-0)
VfL Wolfsburg 0, Eintracht Frankfurt 2
Werder Bremen 0, Schalke 2
Wormatia Worms 2, Hessen Kassel 3

Second Round
1.FC Cologne 3, Hanover 96 0 aet
1.FC Saarbrücken 2, Eintracht Brunswick 1 aet
Eintracht Frankfurt 6, Hessen Kassel 1
FC Altona 93 2, SV Duisburg 1
Hertha BSC Berlin 4, SpVgg Fürth 3
Karlsruhe SC 2, VfB Stuttgart 1
Phönix Ludwigshafen 1, FC Schalke 04 2
TSV 1860 Munich 4, 1.FC Kaiserslautern 2

Quarterfinals
1.FC Saarbrücken 1, TSV 1860 Munich 3
Eintracht Frankfurt 2, FC Schalke 04 1
FC Altona 93 2, Karlsruhe SC 1
Hertha BSC Berlin 4, 1.FC Cologne 2

Semifinals
Eintracht Frankfurt 3, Hertha BSC Berlin 1
FC Altona 93 1, TSV 1860 Munich 4 aet

Final
in Stuttgart
TSV 1860 Munich 2, Eintracht Frankfurt 0

West German Internationals
28/9/63 in Frankfurt 3-0 v Turkey
3/11/63 in Stockholm 1-2 v Sweden
29/12/63 in Casablanca 4-1 v Morocco
1/1/64 in Algiers 0-2 v Algeria
29/4/64 in Ludwigshafen 3-4 v Czechoslovakia
12/5/64 in Hanover 2-2 v Scotland
7/6/64 in Helsinki 4-1 v Finland

East German Oberliga
Club	P	W	D	L	Goals	Pts
1. Chemie Leipzig	26	13	9	4	39-20	35
2. SC Empor Rostock	26	13	7	6	40-23	33
3. SC Leipzig	26	12	8	6	33-28	32
4. SC Karl-Marx-Stadt	26	10	9	7	31-29	29
5. ASK Vorwärts Berlin	26	10	6	10	45-36	26
6. SC Motor Jena	26	10	6	10	43-35	26
7. Motor Steinach	26	8	9	9	30-36	25
8. SC Dynamo Berlin	26	9	6	11	35-34	24
9. Lokomotive Stendal	26	9	5	12	31-34	23
10. Wismut Aue	26	7	9	10	23-32	23
11. SC Aufbau Magdeburg	26	7	9	10	25-38	23
12. Motor Zwickau	26	7	8	11	37-41	22
13. SC Chemie Halle	26	8	6	12	24-35	22
14. SC Turbine Erfurt	26	4	13	9	23-38	21

Top Scorers
Backhaus (Lokomotive Stendal) 15
Bauchspiess (Chemie Leipzig) 13
P Ducke (Motor Jena) 13
Steinmann (Karl-Marx-Stadt) 13
Drews (Empor Rostock) 10
Hall (Dynamo Berlin) 10
Frässdorf (Vorwärts Berlin) 10
H Müller (Motor Jena) 10
Queck (Motor Steinach) 10
Kleiminger (Empor Rostock) 9
Vogt (Vorwärts Berlin) 9

Second Division (Staffel North)

Club	P	W	D	L	Goals	Pts
1. SC Neubrandenburg	30	19	7	4	89-37	45
2. TSC Berlin	30	19	5	6	75-31	43
3. Vorwärts Cottbus	30	18	4	8	57-36	40
4. SC Cottbus	30	17	6	7	50-31	40
5. Motor Dessau	30	16	4	10	55-44	36
6. Stahl Eisenhüttenstadt	30	14	7	9	61-47	35
7. Dynamo Schwerin	30	11	8	11	44-45	30
8. SC Potsdam	30	9	11	10	41-47	29
9. Turbine Magdeburg	30	11	6	13	47-58	28
10. Vorwärts Neunbrandenburg	30	6	15	9	36-41	27
11. Vorwärts Rostock	30	10	6	14	47-51	26
12. Einheit Greifswald	30	9	8	13	35-42	26
13. Dynamo Hohenschönhausen	30	9	7	14	41-53	25
14. Motor Köpenick	30	6	10	14	35-42	22
15. Motor Wolgast	30	6	7	17	32-62	19
16. SC Frankfurt/Oder	30	2	5	23	25-103	9

Promoted: Aktivist Brieske-Ost, Empor Neustrelitz

Second Division (Staffel South)

Club	P	W	D	L	Goals	Pts
1. Dynamo Dresden	30	20	9	1	57-14	49
2. SC Einheit Dresden	30	14	8	8	49-35	36
3. Wismut Gera	30	12	11	7	49-43	35
4. Dynamo Eisleben	30	11	10	9	41-30	32
5. Motor Weimar	30	13	6	11	47-41	32
6. Fortschritt Weissenfels	30	12	8	10	47-46	32
7. Stahl Riesa	30	9	13	8	28-30	31
8. Aktivist K.M. Zwickau	30	11	7	12	41-43	29
9. Motor Bautzen	30	11	7	12	35-38	29
10. Motor West Karl-Marx-Stadt	30	9	10	11	27-31	28
11. Vorwärts Leipzig	30	8	11	11	37-36	27
12. Motor Eisenach	30	10	7	13	42-45	27
13. Chemie Zeitz	30	8	9	13	29-39	25
14. Stahl Eisleben	30	6	12	12	22-42	24
15. Stahl Lippendorf	30	7	9	14	32-42	23
16. Chemie Wolfen	30	6	7	17	25-47	19

Promoted: Motor Wema Plauen, Chemie Riesa, Motor Rudiseleben

East German Cup Final
in Dessau
Aufbau Magdeburg 3, SC Leipzig 2

East German Internationals
4/9/63 in Magdeburg 1-1 v Bulgaria
19/10/63 in Berlin 1-2 v Hungary (ECQ)
3/11/63 in Budapest 3-3 v Hungary (ECQ)
17/12/63 in Rangoon 5-1 v Burma
12/1/64 in Colombo 12-1 v Sri Lanka
23/2/64 in Accra 0-3 v Ghana

European Cup
First Round
Lyn Oslo v Borussia Dortmund .... (2-4, 1-3)
Dinamo Bucharest v Motor Jena .... (2-0, 1-0)
Second Round
Benfica v Borussia Dortmund .... (2-1, 0-5)
Quarterfinals
Dukla Prague v Borussia Dortmund .... (0-4, 3-1)
Semifinals
Borussia Dortmund v Inter Milan .... (2-2, 0-2)

Cup-Winners' Cup
First Round
Hamburg SV v US Luxembourg .... (4-0, 3-2)
Motor Zwickau received a bye
Second Round
Barcelona v Hamburg SV .... (4-4, 0-0, 2-3)
Motor Zwickau v MTK Budapest .... (1-0, 0-2)
Quarterfinals
Hamburg SV v Olympique Lyon .... (1-1, 0-2)

Fairs Cup
Group One
1.FC Cologne v La Gantoise .... (3-1, 1-1)
1.FC Cologne v Sheffield Wednesday .... (3-2, 2-1)
Group Seven
Hertha BSC Berlin v Roma .... (1-3, 0-2)
Quarterfinals
Roma v 1.FC Cologne .... (3-1, 0-4)
Semifinals
Valencia v 1.FC Cologne .... (4-1, 0-2)

1964-65

Bald is beautiful

If the public reaction to the inaugural Bundesliga campaign was measured by the following season's attendance figures, then the arrival of the new national league had been an unqualified success. Gates for the second season would increase by a further 1,800 per match to an average of 26,934—a figure which even today has never been exceeded. With attacking football in abundance, and the first Bundesliga campaign demonstrating the open, competitive nature of play, fans eagerly awaited the second season.

Werder Bremen's wily 62-year-old *Trainer* Willy Multhaup was unhappy with his club's tenth-place finish in 1964 and decided to make three major signings: striker Klaus Matischak—affectionately known by fans as "Zickzack"—from Schalke 04, centre-half Heinz Steinmann from relegated Saarbrücken and fullback Horst-Dieter Höttges from Borussia Mönchengladbach of the Regionalliga West. Höttges was to stay with Bremen fourteen years, and it was indeed the dramatic improvement in Bremen's defence which was the key to their rise to the top of the table and their first-ever German championship.

With Günter Bernard performing reliably in goal, sweeper Helmut Jagielski organising from the back and skipper Arnold Schütz leading by example, Werder remained undefeated at home all season. Their away form was patchy, but a vital 2-1 win over Kaiserslautern at the Betzenberg opened up a five-point gap over their pursuers which proved decisive.

As Werder returned home from their final match in Nuremberg, having taken both points in a 3-2 win, 100,000 people lined the streets of Bremen to greet them. The carnival atmosphere was heightened by the appearance of Max Lorenz and Matischak, their heads shaved bald from a bet they had made.

Defending champions Cologne had to settle for second place, although they could take some comfort from having beaten the new *Meister* 4-2 at home early in the season. Their form dipped slightly after the two-week winter break, and with six matches to go they discovered themselves in fifth place. Despite rallying, they found the gap too wide to close.

Bremen's triumph was somewhat overshadowed by off-the-field events in Berlin, where Hertha, disadvantaged by their isolated geographical position, tried to stave off the threat of relegation by making illegal extra payments to their players. A DFB investigation established this beyond doubt, and Hertha were expelled from the Bundesliga at the end of the season. But because this would leave West Berlin without a team in the Bundesliga, the DFB controversially invited Tasmania 1900 Berlin to take their place. Although Tasmania had only narrowly been edged out by Hertha to qualify for the original Bundesliga in 1963, the champions of the Berlin Regionalliga for the current season were in fact Tennis Borussia, who naturally were incensed at the decision.

It also emerged that Hertha's financial records for the previous season were not a true reflection of their financial status. Had this revelation come to light before the Bundesliga had begun, it is doubtful that Hertha would have been invited into the league at all—and Tasmania would have almost certainly have gone in their place. The decision to replace Hertha with Tasmania had perhaps come two seasons too late.

Two clubs who would go on to become the most successful in the history of the league won their respective *Regionalligen* to gain entry in the Bundesliga. Bayern Munich scored an amazing 146 goals in the Regionalliga South to qualify for the promotion playoffs. Borussia Mönchengladbach came top of the Regionalliga West and were placed in the other playoff section. Both clubs finished first in their group to join the Bundesliga.

Newcomers Hanover 96 made a successful debut in the Bundesliga, leading the league in attendance. An average gate of over 40,000 helped them to climb to fifth place—to date the highest finish the club has known. The luckiest teams of the season were Karlsruhe and Schalke, who finished bottom yet were not relegated, because the DFB had decided to extend the Bundesliga from 16 to 18 teams. That sort of good fortune eluded Karlsruhe *Trainer* Kurt Sommerlatt—he was given the sack shortly after his team lost 9-0 at Munich 1860. The five goals scored in that match by Rudi Brunnenmaier would help him to the Bundesliga goalscoring title. Sommerlatt's successor, Helmut Schneider, would last only nine months. Hertha's Jupp Schneider, Kaiserslautern's Günter Brocker, Duisburg's Rudi Gutendorf, and Stuttgart's Kurt Baluses were also replaced before season's end.

Alemannia Aachen, runners-up to Mönchengladbach in the Regionalliga West, enjoyed a memorable season in the West German Cup. They reached the semifinal, where they met Schalke—who had nearly gone out in the first round to second-division Schwaben Augsburg—and won a thrilling encounter 4-3 after extra time, watched by a capacity crowd of 32,000 in Aachen's Tivoli Stadion. After 53 minutes Schalke had found themselves 3-1 up, but Aachen fought their way back into the match to force extra time, where Christian Breuer's goal proved decisive.

But it was Dortmund, conquerors of Nuremberg in the other semifinal, who took the trophy. Two early goals—the first from the ageing "Aki" Schmidt, who beat

Alemannia's offside trap, and the second a 25-yard blast from Lothar Emmerich—settled the outcome before a crowd of 55,000 in Hanover.

The 1964-65 season couldn't end soon enough for FC Emmendingen of the Regionalliga South. They managed to take just four points out of a possible 72, and despite scoring a credible 41 goals they conceded a less admirable 158, or over four a match. The club finished twenty points adrift of their nearest rivals at the bottom of the league. Not surprisingly, this was the last time Emmendingen would appear at Second Division level.

The Regionalliga Berlin season saw its ten clubs split into two groups, with the top five clubs playing each other again to determine the champion, and the bottom five clubs settling the relegation issue. But nothing was as it seemed. In light of Hertha's financial misdemeanours and Tasmania's good fortune, Tennis Borussia's first-place finish had a hollow ring to it. And no clubs wound up being relegated, owing to the decision to expand the league to sixteen teams.

In Europe, Cologne reached the quarterfinal of the European Cup and played two goalless draws with Liverpool, necessitating a playoff in Rotterdam which was drawn 2-2 after extra time. Penalties being a later contrivance, Liverpool went through—on the toss of a coin. The Cup-Winners' Cup Final featured a German representative, with Munich 1860 needing a third match in Zurich to get past Torino in the semifinals. In the final at Wembley, though, two second-half goals from Alan Sealey gave the cup to locals West Ham United. The Fairs Cup proved to be something of a disaster for German sides, in particular for Dortmund, who lost 10-1 to Manchester United on aggregate. Bundesliga sides were coming close to winning a European trophy, but nearly ten years since the start of European club competition the Germans were still without a trophy.

At the end of the East German season, each football club was required to become a separate entity from its local sports club. This resulted in nine out of the fourteen clubs changing their names, some more significantly than others. SC Empor Rostock, for example, became FC Hansa Rostock. Motor Jena were renamed Carl Zeiss Jena, SC Leipzig were altered to Lokomotive Leipzig, Aufbau Magdeburg were now 1.FC Magdeburg, and Turbine Erfurt changed to Rot-Weiss Erfurt. Vorwärts Berlin, who missed out on this cosmetic surgery for the time being, captured their fourth East German championship in seven years, finishing five points clear of Motor-cum-Carl Zeiss Jena. But gates had slumped to an average of 9,712, which would prove to be the lowest figure for twenty years to come.

Aufbau Magdeburg retained the East German Cup, once again needing a last-minute winner to triumph in the final. The previous June, a 90th-minute winner from Hermann Stöcker had beaten SC Leipzig 3-2 in Dessau. This time, an 89th-minute penalty from Günter Hirschmann gave Aufbau a 2-1 win over Jena in Berlin. But the East German Cup Final could not be counted amongst the world's great footballing spectacles. A mere 12,000 had turned up for the Dessau final, and only 25,000 were in attendance in Berlin. Nevertheless, Magdeburg would be the last club to retain the cup until fourteen years later, when under their new name they would repeat the achievement.

The East German national team played only three matches this season, the highlight being a 1-1 draw against Hungary in Leipzig, where 105,000 saw Eberhard Vogel score the only goal of the match.

Bundesliga

Club	P	W	D	L	Goals	Pts
1. Werder Bremen	30	15	11	4	54-29	41
2. 1.FC Cologne	30	14	10	6	66-45	38
3. Borussia Dortmund	30	15	6	9	67-48	36
4. TSV 1860 Munich	30	14	7	9	70-50	35
5. Hanover 96	30	13	7	10	48-42	33
6. 1.FC Nuremberg	30	11	10	9	44-38	32
7. SV Meiderich	30	12	8	10	46-48	32
8. Eintracht Frankfurt	30	11	7	12	50-58	29
9. Eintracht Brunswick	30	10	8	12	42-47	28
10. Borussia Neunkirchen	30	9	9	12	44-48	27
11. Hamburg SV	30	11	5	14	46-56	27
12. VfB Stuttgart	30	9	8	13	46-50	26
13. 1.FC Kaiserslautern	30	11	3	16	41-53	25
14. Hertha BSC Berlin	30	7	11	12	40-62	25
15. Karlsruhe SC	30	9	6	15	47-62	24
16. FC Schalke 04	30	7	8	15	45-60	22

No clubs were relegated this season; the Bundesliga was expanded to eighteen teams for the following season.

Top Scorers

Brunnenmeier (TSV 1860 Munich)	24
Konietzka (Borussia Dortmund)	22
C Müller (1.FC Cologne)	19
Strehl (1.FC Nuremberg)	16
Brungs (Borussia Dortmund)	14
Seeler (Hamburg SV)	14
Gerhardt (FC Schalke 04)	12
Grosser (TSV 1860 Munich)	12
Madl (Karlsruhe SC)	12
Matischak (Werder Bremen)	12
May (Borussia Neunkirchen)	12
Thielen (1.FC Cologne)	12
Ulsass (Eintracht Brunswick)	12

Bundesliga Promotion Playoffs

Qualifying Round: St Pauli v SSV Reutlingen (1-0, 1-4 aet); Reutlingen qualify for playoffs

Group 1	P	W	D	L	Goals	Pts
1. Borussia Mönchengladbach	6	4	1	1	17-7	9
2. SSV Reutlingen	6	2	2	2	8-11	6
3. Holstein Kiel	6	2	2	2	12-9	6
4. Wormatia Worms	6	1	1	4	7-17	3

Group 2	P	W	D	L	Goals	Pts
1. Bayern Munich	6	4	1	1	18-3	9
2. 1.FC Saarbrücken	6	3	0	3	12-13	6
3. Alemannia Aachen	6	2	2	2	11-12	6
4. Tennis Borussia Berlin	6	1	1	4	10-23	3

Regionalliga Berlin

Promotion Round	P	W	D	L	Goals	Pts
1. Tennis Borussia Berlin	26	17	8	1	67-23	42
2. SV Spandau	26	18	5	3	57-26	41
3. Tasmania 1900 Berlin	26	18	3	5	82-29	39
4. Wacker 04 Berlin	26	9	4	13	49-59	22
5. Berlin SV 92	26	8	4	14	28-61	20

Non-Promotion Round	P	W	D	L	Goals	Pts
1. BFC Südring	26	7	8	11	54-61	22
2. Blau-Weiss 90 Berlin	26	6	10	10	27-38	22
3. Hertha Zehlendorf	26	6	6	14	33-50	18
4. Viktoria 89 Berlin	26	7	3	16	47-69	17
5. Reinickendorf Füchse	26	6	5	15	28-56	17

No clubs were relegated this season
Top Scorer: Kraus (Tennis Borussia), 22 goals
Promoted: SC Gatow, VfB Hermsdorf, 1.FC Neukölln, SU Lichterfelde, SC Staaken, SC Tegel

Regionalliga Berlin Playoff
Reinickendorf Füchse v Rapide Wedding (4-1, 0-0); Füchse remain in Regionalliga

Regionalliga North

Club	P	W	D	L	Goals	Pts
1. Holstein Kiel	32	24	4	4	94-41	52
2. FC St Pauli	32	17	8	7	79-54	42
3. FC Altona 93	32	17	7	8	69-45	41
4. Arminia Hanover	32	17	6	9	76-49	40
5. Göttingen 05	32	17	3	12	62-40	37
6. VfL Wolfsburg	32	12	8	12	53-56	32
7. TuS Bremerhaven 93	32	11	9	12	46-55	31
8. ASV Bergedorf	32	14	2	16	61-62	30
9. Concordia Hamburg	32	13	4	15	44-57	30
10. VfL Osnabrück	32	12	5	15	71-65	29
11. VfB Lübeck	32	11	6	15	42-56	28
12. Victoria Hamburg	32	10	8	14	52-73	28
13. VfB Oldenburg	32	10	7	15	52-59	27
14. SV Friedrichsort	32	9	9	14	41-59	27
15. VfV Hildesheim	32	9	8	15	49-60	26
16. VfR Neumünster	32	11	4	17	52-71	26
17. Rasensport Harburg	32	6	6	20	39-89	18

Top Scorer: Saborowski (Holstein Kiel), 34 goals

Regionalliga North Promotion Playoffs

Group One	P	W	D	L	Goals	Pts
1. Itzehoe SV	6	4	1	1	11-8	9
2. TSV Uetersen	6	2	2	2	12-11	6
3. Olympia Wilhelmshaven	6	2	1	3	8-7	5
4. TuS Celle	6	2	0	4	13-18	4

1964-65

Group Two	P	W	D	L	Goals	Pts
1. Bremen SV	6	3	1	2	12-12	7
2. Union Salzgitter	6	2	2	2	12-11	6
3. Heide SV	6	2	2	2	14-15	6
4. Sperber Hamburg	6	2	1	3	13-13	5

Regionalliga South

Club	P	W	D	L	Goals	Pts
1. Bayern Munich	36	24	7	5	146-32	55
2. SSV Reutlingen	36	23	6	7	87-45	52
3. Kickers Offenbach	36	19	10	7	91-63	48
4. SV Waldhof	36	19	8	9	74-50	46
5. Hessen Kassel	36	17	6	13	74-52	40
6. VfR Mannheim	36	15	10	11	66-53	40
7. Kickers Stuttgart	36	15	10	11	69-59	40
8. SpVgg Fürth	36	16	7	13	72-62	39
9. Bayern Hof	36	16	4	16	65-58	36
10. FSV Frankfurt	36	15	6	15	52-59	36
11. FC Freiburg	36	11	13	12	60-68	35
12. ESV Ingolstadt	36	13	8	15	55-65	34
13. 1.FC Pforzheim	36	13	7	16	47-61	33
14. SV Darmstadt 98	36	11	11	14	49-66	33
15. Schweinfurt 05	36	14	4	18	49-55	32
16. Schwaben Augsburg	36	11	8	17	61-73	30
17. Wacker Munich	36	10	7	19	54-86	27
18. TSG Ulm 46	36	9	6	21	53-90	24
19. FC Emmendingen	36	1	2	33	41-158	4

Top Scorer: Ohlhauser (Bayern Munich), 42 goals

Regionalliga South Promotion Playoffs

Club	P	W	D	L	Goals	Pts
1. VfR Pforzheim	6	4	1	1	17-7	9
2. Sportfreunde Esslingen	6	3	2	1	13-10	8
3. SC Freiburg	6	1	3	2	7-14	5
4. FV Ebingen	6	0	2	4	10-16	2

Also Promoted: SpVgg Weiden, Opel Rüsselsheim

Regionalliga Southwest

Club	P	W	D	L	Goals	Pts
1. 1.FC Saarbrücken	34	27	4	3	92-33	58
2. Wormatia Worms	34	20	10	4	64-24	50
3. Eintracht Trier	34	21	6	7	67-27	48
4. Saar 05 Saarbrücken	34	20	6	8	69-33	46
5. Südwest Ludwigshafen	34	18	6	10	64-44	42
6. TuS Neuendorf	34	18	6	10	68-53	42
7. FK Pirmasens	34	19	3	12	76-44	41
8. SC Ludwigshafen	34	14	8	12	56-50	36
9. SV Weisenau	34	13	6	15	56-73	32
10. Phönix Bellheim	34	10	10	14	40-51	30
11. FSV Mainz 05	34	12	4	18	55-64	28
12. VfR Frankenthal	34	9	9	16	54-64	27
13. BSC Oppau	34	11	5	18	53-69	27
14. SV Völklingen	34	10	6	18	54-71	26
15. TSC Zweibrücken	34	10	3	21	53-82	23
16. Spfr Saarbrücken	34	8	5	21	36-72	21
17. VfR Kaiserslautern	34	6	6	22	32-79	18
18. Germania Metternich	34	4	9	21	26-82	17

SV Weisenau withdrew from the Regionalliga for the following season.

Top Scorer: Poklitar (1.FC Saarbrücken), 27 goals

Regionalliga Southwest Promotion Playoffs

Club	P	W	D	L	Goals	Pts
1. SV Alsenborn	4	2	2	0	12-4	6
2. SpVgg Bendorf	4	1	2	1	5-5	4
3. SV Ludweiler	4	1	0	3	3-11	2

Regionalliga West

Club	P	W	D	L	Goals	Pts
1. Borussia Mönchengladbach	34	23	6	5	92-39	52
2. Alemannia Aachen	34	21	7	6	69-23	49
3. Fortuna Düsseldorf	34	18	7	9	71-38	43
4. Rot-Weiss Oberhausen	34	17	8	9	55-35	42
5. Arminia Bielefeld	34	15	9	10	68-52	39
6. Wuppertal SV	34	14	8	12	54-52	36
7. Rot-Weiss Essen	34	14	6	14	56-53	34
8. Preussen Münster	34	13	7	14	50-48	33
9. Schwarz-Weiss Essen	34	10	13	11	58-59	33
10. Viktoria Cologne	34	14	5	15	41-48	33
11. Eintracht Duisburg	34	10	12	12	41-53	32
12. Westfalia Herne	34	13	5	16	45-56	31
13. Eintracht Gelsenkirchen	34	10	10	14	46-57	30
14. Spfr Hamborn	34	9	11	14	49-68	29
15. TSV Marl-Hüls	34	10	8	16	36-59	28
16. Bayer Leverkusen	34	8	10	16	48-55	26
17. STV Horst-Emscher	34	6	10	18	33-79	22
18. SV Homberg	34	6	8	20	24-62	20

Top Scorers: Meyer (Fortuna Düsseldorf) and Rupp (Borussia Mönchengladbach), 25 goals each

Promotion Playoff: VfL Bochum v SpVgg Erkenschwick (4-1, 2-3, 1-1 aet; Bochum won promotion on coin toss)

Also Promoted: VfB Bottrop

Third Division Champions

Baden (Nordbaden): Karlsruhe SC (Am.)
Baden (Südbaden): SC Freiburg
Bayern: SpVgg Weiden
Berlin: 1.FC Neukölln
Bremen: Bremen SV
Hamburg: Sperber Hamburg
Hessen: Opel Rüsselsheim
Mittelrhein: 1.FC Cologne (Am.)
Niederrhein: VfB Bottrop
Niedersachsen: Hanover 96 (Am.)

1964-65

Rheinland: SpVgg Bendorf
Saarland: SV Ludweiler
Schleswig-Holstein: Itzehoe SV
Südwest: SV Alsenborn
Westfalen: VfL Bochum
Württemberg: VfB Stuttgart (Am.)

West German Cup

First Round
1.FC Kaiserslautern 3, Karlsruhe SC 0
1.FC Nuremberg 2, 1.FC Cologne 0
Altona 93 0, Hanover 96 5
Eintracht Frankfurt 2, Borussia Neunkirchen 1
FSV Mainz 05 1, Werder Bremen 0
Hertha BSC Berlin 1, Eintracht Brunswick 5
Hessen Kassel 0, Hamburg SV 2
Kickers Offenbach 2, Wormatia Worms 4
Preussen Münster 0, Borussia Dortmund 1
Rot-Weiss Oberhausen 5, TSG Ulm 46 0
Schwaben Augsburg 5, FC Schalke 04 7 aet
SuS Northeim 0, SV Meiderich 1 aet
VfL Osnabrück 1, Alemannia Aachen 3
VfL Wolfsburg 3, TSV 1860 Munich 4
VfR Frankenthal 0, VfB Stuttgart 5
Westfalia Herne 3, Tennis Borussia Berlin 4 aet

Second Round
1.FC Kaiserslautern 1, Hanover 96 3
1.FC Nuremberg 3, Hamburg SV 1
Eintracht Frankfurt 1, FC Schalke 04 2
FSV Mainz 05 2, TSV 1860 Munich 2 aet (2-1)
Rot-Weiss Oberhausen 0, Alemannia Aachen 1
SV Meiderich 0, Eintracht Brunswick 1
Tennis Borussia Berlin 1, Borussia Dortmund 2
Wormatia Worms 0, VfB Stuttgart 2

Quarterfinals
Alemannia Aachen 2, Hanover 96 1
Eintracht Brunswick 0, Borussia Dortmund 2
FC Schalke 04 4, VfB Stuttgart 2
FSV Mainz 05 0, 1.FC Nuremberg 3

Semifinals
Alemannia Aachen 4, FC Schalke 04 3 aet
Borussia Dortmund 4, 1.FC Nuremberg 2

Final
in Hanover
Alemannia Aachen 0, Borussia Dortmund 2

West German Internationals
4/11/64 in Berlin 1-1 v Sweden (WCQ)
13/3/65 in Hamburg 1-1 v Italy
24/4/65 in Karlsruhe 5-0 v Cyprus (WCQ)
12/5/65 in Nuremberg 0-1 v England
26/5/65 in Basle 1-0 v Switzerland
6/6/65 in Rio de Janeiro 0-2 v Brazil

East German Oberliga

Club	P	W	D	L	Goals	Pts
1. ASK Vorwärts Berlin	26	17	3	6	51-24	37
2. SC Motor Jena	26	14	4	8	41-27	32
3. Chemie Leipzig	26	11	9	6	47-29	31
4. SC Leipzig	26	12	6	8	53-34	30
5. SC Empor Rostock	26	13	2	11	37-33	28
6. Lokomotive Stendal	26	9	8	9	47-42	26
7. SC Aufbau Magdeburg	26	9	7	10	35-35	25
8. Motor Zwickau	26	9	6	11	36-46	24
9. Wismut Aue	26	6	12	8	23-36	24
10. Dynamo Dresden	26	9	5	12	34-38	23
11. SC Karl-Marx Stadt	26	8	7	11	36-41	23
12. SC Dynamo Berlin	26	8	6	12	27-37	22
13. SC Neubrandenburg	26	7	6	13	34-58	20
14. Motor Steinach	26	8	3	15	28-49	19

Top Scorers
Bauchspiess (Chemie Leipzig) 14
Frenzel (SC Leipzig) 13
Backhaus (Lokomotive Stendal) 12
Steinmann (Karl-Marx-Stadt) 12
Trölitzsch (SC Leipzig) 12
H Müller (Motor Jena) 11
Rentzsch (Motor Zwickau) 11
P Ducke (Motor Jena) 10
Vogt (Vorwärts Berlin) 10
Güssau (Lokomotive Stendal) 9
Karow (Lokomotive Stendal) 9
Piepenburg (Vorwärts Berlin) 9
Walter (Aufbau Magdeburg) 9

Second Division (Staffel North)

Club	P	W	D	L	Goals	Pts
1. SC Chemie Halle	30	23	3	4	78-29	49
2. SC Cottbus	30	16	10	4	53-19	42
3. Vorwärts Rostock	30	16	4	10	51-32	36
4. Dynamo Schwerin	30	14	7	9	55-34	35
5. TSG Wismar	30	16	3	11	50-49	35
6. Stahl Eisenhüttenstadt	30	14	6	10	56-38	34
7. TSC Berlin	30	12	7	11	48-34	31
8. Motor Dessau	30	11	8	11	46-49	30
9. SC Potsdam	30	12	5	13	36-43	29
10. Vorwärts Neubrandenburg	30	8	12	10	46-47	28

11. Dynamo Hohenschönhausen	30	10	8	12	43-47	28
12. Vorwärts Cottbus	30	11	5	14	36-44	27
13. Einheit Greifswald	30	11	5	14	36-53	27
14. Empor Neustrelitz	30	10	4	16	44-57	24
15. Turbine Magdeburg	30	2	11	17	23-73	15
16. Aktivist Brieske-Ost	30	4	2	24	32-85	10

Promoted: Motor Babelsberg, Motor Hennigsdorf, Motor Köpenick

Second Division (Staffel South)

Club	P	W	D	L	Goals	Pts
1. SC Turbine Erfurt	30	17	8	5	53-26	42
2. Dynamo Eisleben	30	17	5	8	63-37	39
3. Vorwärts Leipzig	30	16	5	9	62-50	37
4. Chemie Zeitz	30	13	9	8	43-43	35
5. Aktivist K.M. Zwickau	30	14	5	11	59-40	33
6. Stahl Riesa	30	13	6	11	47-39	32
7. SC Einheit Dresden	30	11	10	9	42-38	32
8. Fortschritt Weissenfels	30	12	8	10	41-39	32
9. Motor Eisenach	30	12	6	12	40-42	30
10. Motor Weimar	30	11	8	11	43-49	30
11. Motor Wema Plauen	30	10	7	13	56-53	27
12. Wismut Gera	30	11	5	14	45-47	27
13. Motor Bautzen	30	9	9	12	44-46	27
14. Chemie Riesa	30	9	5	16	38-48	23
15. Motor West Karl-Marx-Stadt	30	8	2	20	22-53	18
16. Motor Rudisleben	30	4	8	18	30-78	16

Promoted: Chemie Buna Schkopau, Lokomotive Dresden, Motor Wama Görlitz, Vorwärts Meiningen

East German Cup Final
in Berlin
Aufbau Magdeburg 2, Motor Jena 1

East German Internationals
3/1/65 in Montevideo 2-0 v Uruguay
25/4/65 in Vienna 1-1 v Austria (WCQ)
23/5/65 in Leipzig (105,000) 1-1 v Hungary (WCQ)

European Cup
First Round
Partizan Tirana v 1.FC Cologne .... (0-0, 0-2)
Chemie Leipzig v ETO Vasas Gyor .... (0-2, 2-4)
Second Round
Panathinaikos v 1.FC Cologne .... (1-1, 1-2)
Quarterfinals
1.FC Cologne v Liverpool .... (0-0, 0-0, 2-2)
Liverpool won on coin toss

Cup-Winners' Cup
First Round
US Luxembourg v TSV 1860 Munich .... (0-4, 0-6)
Aufbau Magdeburg v Galatasaray .... (1-1, 1-1, 1-1)
Galatasaray won on coin toss
Second Round
Porto v TSV 1860 Munich .... (0-1, 1-1)
Quarterfinals
Legia Warsaw v TSV 1860 Munich .... (0-4, 0-0)
Semifinals
Torino v TSV 1860 Munich .... (2-0, 1-3, 0-2)
Final in London
West Ham United 2, TSV 1860 Munich 0

Fairs Cup
Group One
Eintracht Frankfurt v Kilmarnock .... (3-0, 1-5)
Group Two
Borussia Dortmund v Bordeaux .... (4-1, 0-2)
Manchester United v Borussia Dortmund .... (4-0, 6-1)
Group Five
SK Vienna v SC Leipzig .... (2-1, 1-0)
Group Nine
VfB Stuttgart v BK 1913 Odense .... (3-1, 1-0)
Dunfermline Athletic v VfB Stuttgart .... (1-0, 0-0)

1965-66

Munich's year

If any German team epitomises the ups and downs of football, it is *Turn und Sport Verein 1860 München*. Five years before the creation of the Bundesliga, 1860 had been relegated from the Oberliga South. Yet they bounced back to become one of the founder members of the Bundesliga. In the first season they finished seventh and won the West German Cup; the next year they came fourth and reached the final of the European Cup Winners' Cup. Now they joined 1.FC Cologne and Werder Bremen as the pundits' choice for the championship.

Before the season, TSV's *Trainer* Max Merkel bought striker Timo Konietzka from Dortmund and acquired the services of the Yugoslavian Zeljko Perusic. But the hearts of the fans had been won over by Perusic's compatriot Petar Radenkovic. Radenkovic, known to one and all as "Radi", had previously arrived in Germany with only two suitcases, no job and no accommodation, but with a determination to break into professional football. After one season with Wormatia Worms he was signed by TSV and he remained with them until 1970. As a goalkeeper he was safe and reliable, but it was his excursions outside the penalty area which captured the imagination. (That, and a record he cut, which reached number five in the German hit parade.)

By a strange quirk of the fixture list, TSV's first match of the season was against newly-promoted Bayern Munich, and a crowd of 44,000 saw Konietzka score on his debut before the match was a minute old. Bayern's Dieter Danzberg was sent off as 1860 held on to win the local derby 1-0. TSV played an exhilarating brand of attacking football based on a 4-2-4 system which was to bring them eighty goals, but their second match with Bayern was a 3-0 defeat which left them in third place, four points behind Borussia Dortmund. From that point on, 1860 showed far more consistency and were soon back in contention. With two matches still to play they were level on points with Dortmund. The match of the season brought the two top clubs together at Dortmund's "Rote Erde," where Borussia's unbeaten home record was shattered by goals from Rudi Brunnenmaier and skipper Peter Grosser which gave the visitors a 2-0 win.

But Dortmund's despair at being eliminated from the championship was tempered by the fact that three weeks earlier they had collected German football's first European trophy, the Cup-Winners' Cup. Borussia had survived a tricky second-round tie with Bulgaria's CSKA Sofia, winning 5-4 on aggregate, and beaten Atlético Madrid and West Ham United in succeeding rounds to reach the final against Liverpool in Glasgow. There, goals by Siegfried Held and Roger Hunt sent the game into extra time at 1-1, with Stan Libuda then getting the winner.

In the Fairs Cup, Germany's luck with the dreaded coin toss showed no signs of changing, as Hanover 96 went out to Barcelona after three competitive but inconclusive matches. 1860 reached the quarterfinals before going out to Chelsea.

As 1860 were clinching the championship, Bayern were finishing in a splendid third place with their young sweeper Franz Beckenbauer being voted Footballer of the Year. Bayern took part in an amazing match at Kaiserslautern on 23 April, when four players were sent off. Bayern came out ahead, 10-8 on players and 2-1 on goals. Meanwhile, Borussia Mönchengladbach's debut in the Bundesliga resulted in a less spectacular yet reasonably steady thirteenth place.

The other promoted team, Tasmania 1900 of Berlin, had a disastrous season—in fact, the most disastrous by far in the history of the Bundesliga. At season's end, Tasmania were fourteen points adrift of their closest foe, and had conceded almost seven times the number of goals they had scored. Things had started reasonably bright for the club when, with over 81,000 on hand for their league debut, they won 2-0 against Karlsruhe. Wulf-Ingo Usbeck scored both goals; the two others he would score that season made him the club's top scorer!

Tasmania managed just one more point—a draw against Kaiserslautern—before the half-way stage of the season. Their only other victory came in their home finale, against next-to-last Borussia Neunkirchen, by which time only a brave 2000 were scattered about the Olympiastadion. (Tasmania's home gate of 827 for the visit of Mönchengladbach remains the lowest ever in the Bundesliga.) As the season wore on, and gates slumped, Tasmania's debts mounted and eventually they sold Usbeck and a few other players to help make ends meet. But the club had very little talent to offer. None of the 24 players used had so much as a game's worth of prior Bundesliga experience, and afterward, only Usbeck played with a Bundesliga club again, appearing in nine matches for Nuremberg.

Tasmania may have been grilled in the Bundesliga, but deposed Hertha Berlin were doing most of the roasting in their Regionalliga. They won all but one of their 30 league matches, racking up 136 goals on the way to taking the title by seven points from Tennis Borussia. Hertha qualified for the promotion round, but it was Fortuna Düsseldorf and Rot-Weiss Essen from the Regionalliga West who finished atop the two playoff groups.

Borussia Neunkirchen, Schalke, and Kaiserslautern were the three clubs who looked most likely to join Tasmania in relegation from the Bundesliga. In the end, it was Neunkirchen who took the plunge, losing three of their last four matches. Karlsruhe wound up in sixteenth place, mainly as a result of their failing to win a match away from home all season. It was also the last appearance in the league table of Meiderich SV, as the club re-christened themselves MSV Duisburg.

Bayern rounded off an impressive inaugural season in the Bundesliga with an even more impressive campaign in the West German Cup, winning it for the second time in their history. A somewhat fortuitous quarterfinal triumph over Hamburg was followed by victory away to Nuremberg. Before 58,000, Hans Novak scored the winner in the eighth minute of extra time. Bayern faced Meiderich in the final and won comfortably, 4-2, with two goals from Dieter Brenninger and one each from Rainer Ohlhauser and Franz Beckenbauer.

Vorwärts Berlin repeated as East German champions, two points clear of Carl Zeiss Jena, who repeated as runners-up. Jena's home form was far and away the best in the league, but on their travels they lost seven of their thirteen matches, which proved costly. The cup final was played in the Stadion an der Müllerwiese in Bautzen, where 15,000 saw Hans-Bert Matoul score seventeen minutes from time to give Chemie Leipzig victory over Lokomotive Stendal.

The East German national side finished second behind Hungary in their World Cup qualifying group and did not reach the finals in England. But there was success for the West Germans, who made wholesale changes in personnel as they won their last two qualifying matches, 2-1 in Sweden and 6-0 in Cyprus. The game in Sweden marked the first international appearance of Franz Beckenbauer, and goalkeeper Josef "Sepp" Maier made his debut in a friendly against Ireland in Dublin. The Germans built an impressive ten-match unbeaten run stretching all the way to the World Cup Final. Beckenbauer would become a major part of West Germany's quest for the Jules Rimet trophy, but Maier's turn would have to wait: Hans Tilkowski was selected as the national team's goalkeeper.

In their first group match in England, West Germany thrashed Switzerland 5-0 in Sheffield, with Beckenbauer and Helmut Haller each scoring twice. They then played twice at Villa Park in Birmingham—0-0 against Argentina and 2-1 against Spain—to come top of the group and qualify for the quarterfinals. Uwe Seeler scored one of the goals, and the other was an amazing shot from a narrow angle by Lothar Emmerich.

Germany went back to Hillsborough for their quarterfinal tie with Uruguay. They won 4-0, with Haller again scoring twice—but the Uruguayans had two men sent off and it was only in the last twenty minutes that the Germans had made sure of the result. The semifinal was at Goodison Park in Liverpool, against the Soviet Union. It was a dour encounter, with both sides applying strong-arm tactics. West Germany won, 2-1, but nearly conceded an equaliser with seconds left to play.

And of course the final was against England at Wembley on July 30. Despite an early goal from Haller, Germany eventually fell behind and needed a late equaliser from Wolfgang Weber to take the game into extra time. The match was effectively decided by Soviet linesman Tofik Bakhramov who, in one of the most controversial incidents in footballing history, advised the Swiss referee that Geoff Hurst's shot against the crossbar had crossed the goal line. Hurst added a fourth—his third—in the dying moments, but the Germans had already resigned themselves to defeat.

Bundesliga

Club	P	W	D	L	Goals	Pts
1. TSV 1860 Munich	34	20	10	4	80-40	50
2. Borussia Dortmund	34	19	9	6	70-36	47
3. Bayern Munich	34	20	7	7	71-38	47
4. Werder Bremen	34	21	3	10	76-40	45
5. 1.FC Cologne	34	19	6	9	74-41	44
6. 1.FC Nuremberg	34	14	11	9	54-43	39
7. Eintracht Frankfurt	34	16	6	12	64-46	38
8. SV Meiderich	34	14	8	12	70-48	36
9. Hamburg SV	34	13	8	13	64-52	34
10. Eintracht Brunswick	34	11	12	11	49-49	34
11. VfB Stuttgart	34	13	6	15	42-48	32
12. Hanover 96	34	11	8	15	59-57	30
13. Borussia Mönchengladbach	34	9	11	14	57-68	29
14. FC Schalke 04	34	10	7	17	33-55	27
15. 1.FC Kaiserslautern	34	8	10	16	42-65	24
16. Karlsruhe SC	34	9	6	19	35-71	26
17. Borussia Neunkirchen	34	9	4	21	32-82	22
18. Tasmania 1900 Berlin	34	2	4	28	15-108	8

Top Scorers
Emmerich (Borussia Dortmund) 31
Konietzka (TSV 1860 Munich) 26
Schütz (Werder Bremen) 20
Grosser (TSV 1860 Munich) 18
Löhr (1.FC Cologne) 18
Pohlschmidt (Hamburg SV) 18
Huberts (Eintracht Frankfurt) 17
Ulsass (Eintracht Brunswick) 17
Rupp (Borussia Mönchengladbach) 16
Brunnenmeier (TSV 1860 Munich) 15
Siemensmeyer (Hanover 96) 15

Bundesliga Promotion Playoffs
Qualifying Round: 1.FC Saarbrücken v Göttingen 05 (4-0, 3-0); Saarbrücken qualify for playoff

Group 1	P	W	D	L	Goals	Pts
1. Fortuna Düsseldorf	6	4	0	2	17-8	8
2. FK Pirmasens	6	3	2	1	10-8	8
3. Hertha BSC Berlin	6	2	1	3	8-11	5
4. Kickers Offenbach	6	1	1	4	5-13	3

Group 2	P	W	D	L	Goals	Pts
1. Rot-Weiss Essen	6	4	0	2	10-6	8
2. FC St Pauli	6	4	0	2	10-8	8
3. 1.FC Saarbrücken	6	2	1	3	12-11	5
4. Schweinfurt 05	6	1	1	4	6-13	3

Regionalliga Berlin

Club	P	W	D	L	Goals	Pts
1. Hertha BSC Berlin	30	29	0	1	136-25	58
2. Tennis Borussia Berlin	30	21	2	7	108-50	44
3. SV Spandau	30	18	6	6	88-53	42
4. Wacker 04 Berlin	30	16	4	10	77-52	36
5. Hertha Zehlendorf	30	16	3	11	53-43	35
6. SC Staaken	30	14	6	10	54-47	34
7. BFC Südring	30	10	8	12	49-53	28
8. 1.FC Neukölln	30	11	6	13	54-47	28
9. SV 92 Berlin	30	13	1	16	49-53	27
10. Blau-Weiss 90 Berlin	30	10	5	15	50-58	25
11. Reinickendorf Füchse	30	10	5	15	50-70	25
12. VfB Hermsdorf	30	10	4	16	61-75	24
13. Lichterfeld SU	30	9	5	16	34-82	23
14. SC Tegel	30	8	6	16	34-76	22
15. SC Gatow	30	7	5	18	36-60	19
16. Viktoria 89 Berlin	30	3	4	23	34-93	10

Top Scorer: Tylinski (Tennis Borussia Berlin), 36 goals
Promoted: Kickers 1900 Berlin, Rapide Wedding

Regionalliga North

Club	P	W	D	L	Goals	Pts
1. FC St Pauli	32	20	4	8	84-39	44
2. Göttingen 05	32	20	3	9	65-32	43
3. Holstein Kiel	32	18	7	7	68-41	43
4. TuS Bremerhaven 93	32	15	8	9	61-47	38
5. VfB Lübeck	32	12	12	8	44-35	36
6. Arminia Hanover	32	15	5	12	67-49	35
7. VfL Osnabrück	32	14	4	14	56-55	32
8. VfL Wolfsburg	32	15	2	15	55-55	32
9. SC Concordia Hamburg	32	13	6	13	49-52	32
10. FC Altona 93	32	13	5	14	41-47	31
11. ASV Bergedorf 85	32	13	4	15	56-65	30
12. VfB Oldenburg	32	10	10	12	58-69	30
13. Bremen SV	32	13	2	17	58-68	28
14. Itzehoe SV	32	11	6	15	48-60	28
15. VfV Hildesheim	32	8	9	15	35-54	25
16. SV Friedrichsort	32	9	4	19	45-74	22
17. Victoria Hamburg	32	4	7	21	36-84	15

Top Scorer: Haecks (FC St Pauli), 26 goals

Regionalliga North Promotion Playoffs

Group One	P	W	D	L	Goals	Pts
1. SV Barmbek-Uhlenhorst	6	4	0	2	18-9	8
2. Eintracht Bremen	6	3	1	2	13-14	7
3. Leu Brunswick	6	2	1	3	10-13	5
4. Schleswig 06	6	2	0	4	6-11	4

Group Two	P	W	D	L	Goals	Pts
1. Sperber Hamburg	6	3	2	1	14-5	8
2. 1.FC Wolfsburg	6	3	2	1	10-6	8
3. Olympia Wilhelmshaven	6	2	1	3	6-9	5
4. VfR Neumünster	6	1	1	4	6-16	3

Playoff for first place: Sperber Hamburg 3, 1.FC Wolfsburg 2 aet; Sperber promoted to Regionalliga

Regionalliga South

Club	P	W	D	L	Goals	Pts
1. Schweinfurt 05	34	22	5	7	74-39	49
2. Kickers Offenbach	34	20	8	6	78-48	48
3. SV Waldhof	34	18	3	13	78-60	39
4. SpVgg Fürth	34	16	6	12	70-52	38
5. Kickers Stuttgart	34	14	9	11	65-52	37
6. Hessen Kassel	34	13	10	11	70-62	36
7. 1.FC Pforzheim	34	13	10	11	48-46	36
8. SSV Reutlingen	34	14	6	14	60-50	34
9. Bayern Hof	34	12	10	12	71-63	34
10. Opel Rüsselsheim	34	13	8	13	58-61	34
11. Schwaben Augsburg	34	13	7	14	66-62	33
12. VfR Mannheim	34	10	13	11	55-60	33
13. SV Darmstadt 98	34	14	5	15	54-71	33
14. FSV Frankfurt	34	14	4	16	61-76	32
15. FC Freiburg	34	11	7	16	55-59	29
16. ESV Ingolstadt	34	12	5	17	63-75	29
17. SpVgg Weiden	34	10	7	17	51-64	27
18. VfR Pforzheim	34	4	3	27	45-122	11

Top Scorer: Mikulasch (ESV Ingolstadt), 29 goals

Regionalliga South Promotion Playoffs

Club	P	W	D	L	Goals	Pts
1. FC Villingen 08	6	4	1	1	12-8	8
2. Germania Forst	6	4	0	2	14-10	8
3. Normania Gmünd	6	2	1	3	8-8	5
4. SV Oberkirch	6	1	0	5	7-15	2

Also Promoted: BC Augsburg, Germania Wiesbaden

Regionalliga Southwest

Club	P	W	D	L	Goals	Pts
1. FK Pirmasens	30	17	7	6	62-31	41
2. 1.FC Saarbrücken	30	18	4	8	89-40	40
3. FSV Mainz 05	30	16	6	8	66-39	38
4. TuS Neuendorf	30	18	2	10	81-62	38
5. Wormatia Worms	30	14	4	12	52-41	32
6. Saar 05 Saarbrücken	30	12	8	10	44-39	32
7. VfR Frankenthal	30	12	7	11	55-50	31
8. SV Völklingen	30	13	5	12	52-58	31
9. SV Alsenborn	30	11	8	11	57-55	30
10. SV Weisenau	30	13	2	15	61-66	28
11. Südwest Ludwigshafen	30	10	7	13	46-50	27
12. Phönix Bellheim	30	11	4	15	36-60	26
13. Eintracht Trier	30	9	7	14	44-49	25
14. SC Ludwigshafen	30	9	4	17	43-61	22
15. BSC Oppau	30	9	3	18	37-84	21
16. TSC Zweibrücken	30	7	4	19	41-81	18

Top Scorer: Poklitar (1.FC Saarbrücken), 30 goals

Regionalliga Southwest Promotion Playoffs

Club	P	W	D	L	Goals	Pts
1. Germania Metternich	4	2	1	1	7-5	5
2. FC 08 Homburg	4	1	2	1	6-7	4
3. VfR Kaiserslautern	4	1	1	2	6-7	3

Regionalliga West

Club	P	W	D	L	Goals	Pts
1. Fortuna Düsseldorf	34	26	6	2	79-22	58
2. Rot-Weiss Essen	34	23	7	4	74-31	53
3. Alemannia Aachen	34	24	3	7	97-40	51
4. Rot-Weiss Oberhausen	34	16	5	13	61-46	37
5. Wuppertal SV	34	13	11	10	49-43	37
6. Preussen Münster	34	13	8	13	55-47	34
7. Schwarz-Weiss Essen	34	13	8	13	47-47	34
8. Sportfreunde Hamborn 07	34	13	8	13	44-46	34
9. Viktoria Cologne	34	13	8	13	51-59	34
10. Arminia Bielefeld	34	13	6	15	60-58	32
11. Eintracht Duisburg	34	11	8	15	47-53	30
12. VfL Bochum	34	12	6	16	44-66	30
13. TSV Marl-Hüls	34	11	7	16	47-58	29
14. Bayer Leverkusen	34	9	8	17	49-75	26
15. Westfalia Herne	34	8	10	16	39-66	26
16. Eintracht Gelsenkirchen	34	7	12	15	36-67	26
17. VfB Bottrop	34	8	8	18	47-68	24
18. STV Horst-Emscher	34	6	5	23	42-78	17

Top Scorer: Glenski (Alemannia Aachen), 26 goals

Regionalliga West Promotion Playoffs

Club	P	W	D	L	Goals	Pts
1. VfR Neuss	6	4	2	0	12-2	10
2. SpVgg Hamm	6	3	0	3	13-13	6
3. SSV Hagen	6	2	2	2	9-9	6
4. SC Bonn	6	1	0	5	5-15	2

All four sides were promoted to the Regionalliga in the wake of Rot-Weiss Essen and Fortuna Düsseldorf's promotion to the Bundesliga.

Third Division Champions

Baden (Nordbaden): Germania Forst
Baden (Südbaden): SV Oberkirch
Bayern: BC Augsburg
Berlin: Rapide Wedding
Bremen: TuS Eintracht Bremen
Hamburg: Barmbek-Uhlenhorst
Hessen: Germania Wiesbaden
Mittelrhein: SG Düren 99

1965-66

Niederrhein: VfR Neuss
Niedersachsen: Hanover 96 (Am.)
Rheinland: Germania Metternich
Saarland: FC 08 Homburg
Schleswig-Holstein: VfR Neumünster
Südwest: VfR Kaiserslautern
Westfalen: SpVgg Hamm and SSV Hagen
Württemberg: Normannia Gmünd

West German Cup
First Round
1.FC Cologne 1, Tasmania 1900 Berlin 1 aet (2-0)
Bayern Munich 1, Eintracht Brunswick 0
Borussia Mönchengladbach 0, Borussia Neunkirchen 1 aet
Eintracht Frankfurt 2, SV Alsenborn 1
FC Freiburg 4, Alemannia Aachen 3
FC Schalke 04 3, Tennis Borussia Berlin 1 aet
FC St Pauli 4, 1.FC Saarbrücken 2
Fortuna Düsseldorf 1, Kickers Offenbach 2
Hanover 96 2, Hamburg SV 4
Holstein Kiel 3, Arminia Bielefeld 1
Karlsruhe SC 3, Preussen Münster 0
Schwaben Augsburg 0, 1.FC Nuremberg 1
SV Meiderich 2, VfB Stuttgart 0
SV Südwest Ludwigshafen 0, 1.FC Kaiserslautern 1
TuS Haste 1, SC Concordia Hamburg 2
Werder Bremen 4, TSV 1860 Munich 0

Second Round
1.FC Kaiserslautern 3, Holstein Kiel 0
1.FC Nuremberg 2, Eintracht Frankfurt 1
Bayern Munich 2, 1.FC Cologne 0
FC Freiburg 1, Karlsruhe SC 3
FC St Pauli 3, Kickers Offenbach 1
Hamburg SV 4, Borussia Neunkirchen 0
SV Meiderich 6, FC Schalke 04 0
Werder Bremen 2, SC Concordia Hamburg 0

Quarterfinals
FC St Pauli 0, 1.FC Nuremberg 1
1.FC Kaiserslautern 3, Werder Bremen 1
Hamburg SV 1, Bayern Munich 2
SV Meiderich 1, Karlsruhe SC 0

Semifinals
1.FC Nuremberg 1, Bayern Munich 2
SV Meiderich 4, 1.FC Kaiserslautern 3

Final
in Frankfurt
Bayern Munich 4, SV Meiderich 2

West German Internationals
26/9/65 in Stockholm 2-1 v Sweden (WCQ)
9/10/65 in Stuttgart 4-1 v Austria
14/11/65 in Nicosia 6-0 v Cyprus (WCQ)
23/2/66 in London 0-1 v England
23/3/66 in Rotterdam 4-2 v Holland
4/5/66 in Dublin 4-0 v Ireland
7/5/66 in Belfast 2-0 v Northern Ireland
1/6/66 in Ludwigshafen 1-0 v Rumania
23/6/66 in Hanover 2-0 v Yugoslavia
12/7/66 in Sheffield 5-0 v Switzerland (WC)
16/7/66 in Birmingham 0-0 v Argentina (WC)
20/7/66 in Birmingham 2-1 v Spain (WC)
23/7/66 in Sheffield 4-0 v Uruguay (WC)
25/7/66 in Liverpool 2-1 v Soviet Union (WC)
30/7/66 in London 2-4 v England aet (WC)

East German Oberliga

Club	P	W	D	L	Goals	Pts
1. Vorwärts Berlin	26	15	4	7	44-27	34
2. Carl Zeiss Jena	26	14	4	8	45-24	32
3. Lokomotive Leipzig	26	13	2	11	50-41	28
4. Hansa Rostock	26	11	6	9	41-34	28
5. Dynamo Dresden	26	11	6	9	34-31	28
6. Wismut Aue	26	11	6	9	33-33	28
7. FC Karl-Marx-Stadt	26	12	4	10	29-33	28
8. Chemie Leipzig	26	9	8	9	32-32	26
9. Dynamo Berlin	26	11	3	12	42-32	25
10. Motor Zwickau	26	9	6	11	28-35	24
11. Chemie Halle	26	7	9	10	26-33	23
12. Lokomotive Stendal	26	10	2	14	36-49	22
13. Rot-Weiss Erfurt	26	8	3	15	26-42	19
14. 1.FC Magdeburg	26	7	5	14	19-39	19

Top Scorers
Frenzel (Lokomotive Leipzig) 22
Begerad (Vorwärts Berlin) 13
Bauchspiess (Chemie Leipzig) 12
Backhaus (Lokomotive Stendal) 10
Mühlbächer (Dynamo Berlin) 9
Walter (Chemie Halle) 9
Engels (Dynamo Dresden) 8
V Franke (Lokomotive Leipzig) 8
Härtwig (Wismut Aue) 8
Henschel (Motor Zwickau) 8
Karow (Lokomotive Stendal) 8
Kochale (Dynamo Berlin) 8
Seifert (Rot-Weiss Erfurt) 8
W Wruck (Hansa Rostock) 8

Second Division (Staffel North)

Club	P	W	D	L	Goals	Pts
1. 1.FC Union Berlin	30	18	9	3	52-26	45
2. Post Neubrandenburg	30	16	7	7	42-36	39
3. Energie Cottbus	30	13	12	5	51-30	38
4. Vorwärts Cottbus	30	16	4	10	50-33	36
5. Stahl Eisenhüttenstadt	30	12	12	6	46-29	36
6. Vorwärts Rostock	30	12	9	9	53-39	33
7. Vorwärts Neubrandenburg	30	11	9	10	28-29	31
8. TSG Wismar	30	11	8	11	36-37	30
9. Motor Henningsdorf	30	10	8	12	50-39	28
10. Dynamo Schwerin	30	11	6	13	51-48	28
11. Motor Babelsberg	30	9	10	11	36-46	28
12. Motor Köpenick	30	8	10	12	30-37	26
13. Motor Dessau	30	8	10	12	41-54	26
14. Dynamo Hohenschönhausen	30	10	5	15	36-43	25
15. Aktivist Schwarze Pumpe	30	5	11	14	28-44	21
16. Einheit Greifswald	30	3	4	23	21-81	10

Promoted: Lokomotive Halberstadt, Lichtenberg 47, Motor Stralsund

Second Division (Staffel South)

Club	P	W	D	L	Goals	Pts
1. Wismut Gera	30	17	7	6	54-24	41
2. Motor Steinach	30	13	9	8	55-30	35
3. Motor Wema Plauen	30	13	8	9	56-40	34
4. Dynamo Eisleben	30	14	5	11	55-47	33
5. Vorwärts Leipzig	30	12	9	9	46-39	33
6. Aktivist K.M. Zwickau	30	14	5	11	41-37	33
7. Stahl Riesa	30	12	7	11	50-37	31
8. Chemie Zeitz	30	12	7	11	47-48	31
9. Vorwärts Meiningen	30	12	6	12	53-54	30
10. Motor Weimar	30	11	8	11	41-45	30
11. Motor Eisenach	30	10	9	11	45-50	29
12. Lokomotive Dresden	30	9	8	13	35-37	26
13. Motor Bautzen	30	11	4	15	39-64	26
14. Chemie Buna Schkopau	30	8	9	13	36-56	25
15. Motor Wama Görlitz	30	7	8	15	34-57	22
16. Fortschritt Weissenfels	30	7	7	16	36-58	21

Promoted: Aktivist Böhlen, Chemie Jena, Motor Nordhausen-West

East German Cup Final
in Bautzen
Chemie Leipzig 1, Lokomotive Stendal 0

East German Internationals
4/9/65 in Warna 2-3 v Bulgaria
9/10/65 in Budapest 2-3 v Hungary (WCQ)
31/10/65 in Leipzig 1-0 v Austria (WCQ)
27/4/66 in Leipzig 4-1 v Sweden
2/7/66 in Leipzig 5-2 v Chile

European Cup
First Round
Apoel Nicosia v Werder Bremen .... (0-5, 0-5)
Drumcondra v Vorwärts Berlin .... (1-0, 0-3)
Second Round
Partizan Belgrade v Werder Bremen .... (3-0, 0-1)
Vorwärts Berlin v Manchester United .... (0-2, 1-3)

Cup-Winners' Cup
First Round
Floriana v Borussia Dortmund .... (1-5, 0-8)
1.FC Magdeburg v Spora Luxembourg .... (1-0, 2-0)
Second Round
Borussia Dortmund v CSKA Sofia .... (3-0, 2-4)
1.FC Magdeburg v Sion .... (8-1, 2-2)
Quarterfinals
Atlético Madrid v Borussia Dortmund .... (1-1, 0-1)
West Ham United v 1.FC Magdeburg .... (1-0, 1-1)
Semifinals
West Ham United v Borussia Dortmund .... (1-2, 1-3)
Final in Glasgow
Borussia Dortmund 2, Liverpool 1 aet

Fairs Cup
First Round
1.FC Nuremberg v Everton .... (1-1, 0-1)
1.FC Cologne v Union Luxembourg .... (13-0, 4-0)
Malmö FF v TSV 1860 Munich .... (0-3, 0-4)
Second Round
Aris Saloniki v 1.FC Cologne .... (2-1, 0-2)
Goztepe Izmir v TSV 1860 Munich .... (2-1, 1-9)
Hanover 96 v FC Porto .... (5-0, 1-2)
Lokomotive Leipzig v Leeds United .... (1-2, 0-0)
Third Round
1.FC Cologne v Ujpest Dozsa .... (3-2, 0-4)
Servette v TSV 1860 Munich .... (1-1, 1-4)
Hanover 96 v Barcelona .... (2-1, 0-1, 1-1)
Barcelona won on coin toss
Quarterfinals
TSV 1860 Munich v Chelsea .... (2-2, 0-1)

1966-67

In Brunswick's defence

Whilst TSV 1860 Munich had been celebrating their championship win of 1966, humble Eintracht Brunswick had languished in tenth place. In the build-up to the Bundesliga's 1966-67 season, some pundits were tipping Brunswick for relegation. But *Trainer* Helmut Johannsen's emphasis on hard work and team spirit paid off in a big way, and to everyone's surprise Brunswick took the title. Goalkeeper Horst Wolter conceded only 27 goals all season and kept 17 clean sheets. But Eintracht's stuttering attack managed only 49 goals all season—the lowest total of any Bundesliga champion, and exactly the same as Werder Bremen, who finished in sixteenth place. Brunswick's title-winning points total of 43 is also the lowest in the history of the eighteen-club Bundesliga. But Brunswick were remarkably consistent: only once throughout the whole season did they go more than two consecutive matches without winning.

Eintracht's strategy for success was simple: take two points at home, and one point away. At home they won 13 of their 17 matches and conceded only eight goals, their highest score being an out-of-order 5-2 win over Bayern Munich. Their only defeat was in the local derby with Hanover 96, who took great pleasure in doing the double over their rivals from Niedersachsen. Even free-scoring attacking sides like Dortmund and Mönchengladbach, who each scored 70 goals during the season, only scored once in 180 minutes' play against Brunswick.

Eintracht were a team without stars and pretty much without charisma, even though their success brought them much greater media attention. Keeper Wolter was called up for international duty and he and Sepp Maier rivalled each other as successor to Hans Tilkowski. Klaus Gerwien and Lothar Ulsass also made international appearances, but Wolter's thirteen caps remains a record for a Brunswick player. Bigger crowds were obviously drawn to Hamburger Strasse as Brunswick topped the table, but their season average was still only around 25,000.

Brunswick effectively clinched the title with a week to spare by gaining a highly predictable 0-0 draw in Essen, thus consigning TSV Munich to runners-up spot barring any amazing results the week after. In their final home match Eintracht went a goal down to Borussia Mönchengladbach courtesy of Jupp Heynckes but scored twice in the last seven minutes through Ulsass and Erich Maas to keep the gap at two points.

Munich 1860 had spent a record DM175,000 fee on Friedel Lutz from Frankfurt, but their defence of the title had been ruined in the early part of the season with internal wrangling and a festering personality clash between *Trainer* Max Merkel and some of his senior players. At one point, 1860 found itself in seventeenth place. Merkel resigned at Christmas to take over at Nuremberg, who themselves were only one point off the bottom. Both teams then showed remarkable improvement and rapidly climbed the table. With three matches to go, TSV were even in with a fair chance of the championship until Merkel brought his Nuremberg team to Munich and gained a measure of revenge by winning 2-1. Nuremberg finished in tenth place.

This was to prove yet another disappointing season for the celebrated Gelsenkirchen side Schalke 04. Having dominated domestic football in the thirties and early forties, Schalke were one of the most famous clubs in all of Germany. But their last national championship had been in 1958, and since joining the Bundesliga they had been stuck in the wrong half of the table virtually every season. Crowds which had steadily grown each season had now begun to decline, and the club's fifteenth-place finish was a sad indication of how elusive success had become. Most humiliating of all, Schalke lost 11-0 at Mönchengladbach in January—the league's first double-digit defeat. *Trainer* Fritz Langer was replaced at the end of the season—and would go on to replace Günter Brocker at Werder Bremen.

The two clubs who had gained promotion the season before wound up being sent straight back down to the Regionalliga West. Rot-Weiss Essen and Fortuna Düsseldorf had been at the bottom of the Bundesliga for most of the season and when Karlsruhe began picking up points towards season's end there was no hope of safety for either of the new entrants. Both clubs wound up sacking their *Trainer*. Werder Bremen, champions two seasons earlier, suffered an alarming late-season loss of form and only just managed to avoid relegation.

For the first time—but certainly not for the last—there was no Bundesliga entry for the nation's largest city, Berlin. Tasmania recovered sufficiently from the agony of the previous season to finish fourth in the Berlin Regionalliga, but once again Hertha and Tennis Borussia were the dominant forces. Hertha dropped only three points all season, amassing a goal difference of +89 to finish seven points clear.

The promotion playoffs underwent a slight change, with the top two clubs from each Regionalliga now qualifying. Borussia Neunkirchen, champions of the Regionalliga Southwest, and Alemannia Aachen, winners of the Regionalliga West, finished atop their respective groups to gain entry into the Bundesliga.

Germania Metternich suffered through a horrendous season in the Regionalliga Southwest, failing to win a single match and scoring just nineteen goals in thirty matches. This would prove the only time in the Bundesliga era that a Regionalliga side would go through an entire season without a victory.

Interest in the West German Cup continued to heat up, and this season's competition broke all attendance records. The two finalists thoroughly deserved their place; Bayern Munich had scored at least three goals in every round leading up to the final, and Hamburg SV had outscored their opponents 13-1 over this same period. But the final proved to be horribly one-sided, as a crowd of 68,000 in Stuttgart saw Bayern retain the trophy with a crushing 4-0 victory. Two goals from 21-year-old Gerd Müller and one each from Rainer Ohlhauser and Dieter Brenninger did the damage.

The East German national team achieved a rare feat by going through their entire season of seven matches undefeated. Henning Frenzel scored a hat-trick in the 4-3 win over Holland in Leipzig but their very tight European Championship qualifying group was won by Hungary.

Karl-Marx-Stadt won the East German league rather comfortably, paced by their clever international left-half Dieter Erler, who was voted East German Footballer of the Year. The club were unbeaten at home and finished seven points clear of Lokomotive Leipzig. It would prove to be the only time Karl-Marx-Stadt would wear the champion's crown. The middle of the table was densely-packed, with no fewer than nine clubs—well over half the league—within a point of each other. At the bottom, Dynamo Berlin finished in thirteenth place and were relegated. The following season they would bounce back into the top flight, eventually to become the most successful club in East German footballing history.

There was an international debut for Gerd Müller in the West German side which played Turkey in Ankara. Müller, who shared Bundesliga goalscoring honours with the previous season's winner, Lothar Emmerich of Dortmund, did not feature in the following three matches, but made his home debut in the European Championship qualifying match against Albania in Dortmund. He scored four as Germany recorded a 6-0 win. There was also a debut for young Borussia Mönchengladbach defender Berti Vogts in the 1-0 away defeat to Yugoslavia, and although Germany later beat the same team 3-1 in Hamburg, a disappointing 0-0 draw in Albania allowed Yugoslavia to come top of the group and qualify for the finals.

Hot on the heels of Dortmund's success in the previous season's Cup-Winners' Cup came another European triumph for a Bundesliga side. It would prove to be the first of many for Bayern Munich, and it ensured the trophy Dortmund had captured remained on German soil. Bayern progressed steadily through the competition and beat Liege 5-1 in the semifinal to come up against Glasgow Rangers in the final. A crowd of 70,000 in Nuremberg saw Franz "Bulle" Roth score the only goal in extra time to give Bayern the trophy.

Bundesliga

Club	P	W	D	L	Goals	Pts
1. Eintracht Brunswick	34	17	9	8	49-27	43
2. TSV 1860 Munich	34	17	7	10	60-47	41
3. Borussia Dortmund	34	15	9	10	70-41	39
4. Eintracht Frankfurt	34	15	9	10	66-49	39
5. 1.FC Kaiserslautern	34	13	12	9	43-42	38
6. Bayern Munich	34	16	5	13	62-47	37
7. 1.FC Cologne	34	14	9	11	48-48	37
8. Borussia Mönchengladbach	34	12	10	12	70-49	34
9. Hanover 96	34	13	8	13	40-46	34
10. 1.FC Nuremberg	34	12	10	12	43-50	34
11. MSV Duisburg	34	10	13	11	40-42	33
12. VfB Stuttgart	34	10	13	11	48-54	33
13. Karlsruhe SC	34	11	9	14	54-62	31
14. Hamburg SV	34	10	10	14	37-53	30
15. FC Schalke 04	34	12	6	16	37-63	30
16. Werder Bremen	34	10	9	15	49-56	29
17. Fortuna Düsseldorf	34	9	7	18	44-66	25
18. Rot-Weiss Essen	34	6	13	15	35-53	25

Top Scorers

Emmerich (Borussia Dortmund)	28
G Müller (Bayern Munich)	28
Laumen (Borussia Mönchengladbach)	18
C Müller (Karlsruhe SC)	17
Heynckes (Borussia Mönchengladbach)	15
Rupp (Borussia Mönchengladbach)	15
Ulsass (Eintracht Brunswick)	15
Wosab (Borussia Dortmund)	15
Küppers (TSV 1860 Munich)	14
Löhr (1.FC Cologne)	13

Bundesliga Promotion Playoffs

Group 1

	P	W	D	L	Goals	Pts
1. Borussia Neunkirchen	8	5	1	2	17-12	11
2. Schwarz-Weiss Essen	8	4	2	2	13-9	10
3. Arminia Hanover	8	3	1	4	14-14	7
4. Bayern Hof	8	3	1	4	11-16	7
5. Hertha BSC Berlin	8	2	1	5	8-12	5

Group 2

	P	W	D	L	Goals	Pts
1. Alemannia Aachen	8	6	0	2	23-14	12
2. Kickers Offenbach	8	4	2	2	15-10	10
3. 1.FC Saarbrücken	8	2	4	2	14-15	8
4. Göttingen 05	8	1	4	3	9-13	6
5. Tennis Borussia Berlin	8	1	2	5	12-21	4

Regionalliga Berlin

Club	P	W	D	L	Goals	Pts
1. Hertha BSC Berlin	30	28	1	1	114-25	59
2. Tennis Borussia Berlin	30	22	6	2	101-30	50
3. SV Spandau	30	18	5	7	61-42	41
4. Tasmania 1900 Berlin	30	16	7	7	53-31	39
5. Hertha Zehlendorf	30	17	4	9	56-41	38
6. Wacker 04 Berlin	30	15	5	10	63-46	35
7. Rapide Wedding	30	10	6	14	42-58	26
8. VfB Hermsdorf	30	10	5	15	52-81	25
9. SV Berlin 92	30	9	6	15	37-49	24
10. 1.FC Neukölln	30	8	8	14	42-65	24
11. Blau-Weiss 90 Berlin	30	6	11	13	32-55	23
12. BFC Südring	30	6	10	14	44-59	22
13. Reinickendorf Füchse	30	7	8	15	39-57	22
14. Kickers 1900 Berlin	30	6	10	14	49-79	22
15. SC Staaken	30	6	8	16	36-53	20
16. SU Lichterfeld	30	4	4	22	42-92	12

Top Scorer: Krampitz (Hertha BSC Berlin), 25 goals
Promoted: Alemannia 90 Berlin, Sportfreunde Neukölln

Regionalliga North

Club	P	W	D	L	Goals	Pts
1. Arminia Hanover	32	21	5	6	78-28	47
2. Göttingen 05	32	18	9	5	65-24	45
3. Holstein Kiel	32	19	7	6	68-32	45
4. VfL Wolfsburg	32	19	2	11	57-33	40
5. FC St Pauli	32	16	7	9	71-44	39
6. Concordia Hamburg	32	16	4	12	50-40	36
7. VfL Osnabrück	32	11	10	11	61-50	32
8. FC Altona 93	32	10	11	11	43-46	31
9. VfB Oldenburg	32	13	4	15	49-73	30
10. VfB Lübeck	32	9	10	13	41-43	28
11. ASV Bergedorf 85	32	10	8	14	45-57	28
12. Itzehoe SV	32	13	2	17	56-74	28
13. Sperber Hamburg	32	9	8	15	42-54	25
14. SV Barmbek-Uhlenhorst	32	10	5	17	48-77	25
15. TuS Bremerhaven 93	32	7	10	15	34-57	24
16. VfV Hildesheim	32	8	6	18	25-57	23
17. Bremen SV	32	7	4	21	40-84	18

Top Scorer: Pröpper (VfL Osnabrück), 25 goals

Oberliga North Promotion Playoffs

Group One

	P	W	D	L	Goals	Pts
1. Phönix Lübeck	6	5	1	0	13-5	11
2. Leu Brunswick	6	2	1	3	6-8	5
3. 1.FC Wolfsburg	6	2	0	4	10-12	4
4. TSV Langenhorn	6	1	2	3	6-10	4

1966-67

Group Two	P	W	D	L	Goals	Pts
1. TuS Haste	6	3	2	1	12-8	8
2. Eintracht Bremen	6	3	1	2	10-11	7
3. Hamburg St Georg	6	2	2	2	10-10	6
4. VfL Bad Oldesloe	6	1	1	4	8-11	3

Regionalliga South

Club	P	W	D	L	Goals	Pts
1. Kickers Offenbach	34	20	10	4	65-33	50
2. Bayern Hof	34	21	8	5	81-44	50
3. SpVgg Fürth	34	20	8	6	80-36	48
4. Kickers Stuttgart	34	20	5	9	85-48	45
5. VfR Mannheim	34	15	12	7	61-43	42
6. SSV Reutlingen	34	16	8	10	59-44	40
7. FC Freiburg	34	15	7	12	62-50	37
8. Hessen Kassel	34	14	8	12	61-62	36
9. Schwaben Augsburg	34	13	8	13	64-63	34
10. Schweinfurt 05	34	16	2	16	43-47	34
11. SV Waldhof	34	12	9	13	50-57	33
12. Opel Rüsselsheim	34	12	4	18	51-60	28
13. FSV Frankfurt	34	12	4	18	37-58	28
14. SV Darmstadt 98	34	9	8	17	45-55	26
15. FC Villingen 08	34	10	6	18	47-76	26
16. BC Augsburg	34	10	5	19	49-73	25
17. Germania Wiesbaden	34	4	9	21	28-73	17
18. 1.FC Pforzheim	34	3	7	24	26-72	13

Top Scorer: Windhausen (SpVgg Fürth), 32 goals

Regionalliga South Promotion Playoffs

Club	P	W	D	L	Goals	Pts
1. TSV Backnang	6	4	0	2	13-11	8
2. FV Offenburg	6	4	0	2	14-6	8
3. ASV Feudenheim	6	3	1	2	13-8	7
4. FC Tuttlingen	6	0	1	5	5-20	1

Also Promoted: SSV Jahn Regensburg, SV Wiesbaden

Regionalliga Southwest

Club	P	W	D	L	Goals	Pts
1. Borussia Neunkirchen	30	20	6	4	73-27	46
2. 1.FC Saarbrücken	30	21	2	7	77-31	44
3. SV Weisenau	30	17	7	6	63-35	41
4. FSV Mainz 05	30	18	3	9	50-35	39
5. Eintracht Trier	30	15	8	7	67-48	38
6. FK Pirmasens	30	14	8	8	60-31	36
7. Südwest Ludwigshafen	30	13	10	7	49-34	36
8. SV Alsenborn	30	13	6	11	58-43	32
9. Röchling Völklingen	30	12	7	11	42-46	31
10. Saar 05 Saarbrücken	30	11	8	11	47-39	30
11. FC 08 Homburg	30	8	7	15	46-81	23
12. VfR Frankenthal	30	7	7	16	40-50	21
13. Wormatia Worms	30	5	11	14	31-48	21
14. TuS Neuendorf	30	8	5	17	35-64	21
15. Phönix Bellheim	30	6	6	18	40-71	18
16. Germania Metternich	30	0	3	27	19-114	3

SV Weisenau became SVW Mainz
Promoted: SC Friedrichsthal, SC Ludwigshafen, SSV Mülheim
Top Scorer: Brecht (SV Weisenau), 26 goals

Regionalliga West

Club	P	W	D	L	Goals	Pts
1. Alemannia Aachen	34	20	8	6	56-24	48
2. Schwarz-Weiss Essen	34	19	9	6	51-23	47
3. Arminia Bielefeld	34	17	11	6	72-39	45
4. VfL Bochum	34	18	9	7	67-42	45
5. Sportfreunde Hamborn 07	34	17	9	8	52-33	43
6. Rot-Weiss Oberhausen	34	13	14	7	67-52	40
7. Wuppertal SV	34	14	10	10	49-41	38
8. VfR Neuss	34	14	8	12	56-50	36
9. Preussen Münster	34	13	9	12	53-58	35
10. Bayer Leverkusen	34	12	8	14	57-62	32
11. Westfalia Herne	34	12	7	15	41-41	31
12. Eintracht Gelsenkirchen	34	10	10	14	48-53	30
13. Viktoria Cologne	34	10	9	15	36-39	29
14. TSV Marl-Hüls	34	7	12	15	38-49	26
15. SSV Hagen	34	8	8	18	35-69	24
16. SV Hamm	34	7	9	18	45-76	23
17. SC Bonn	34	6	10	18	27-48	22
18. Eintracht Duisburg	34	7	4	23	34-85	18

Top Scorer: Kuster (Arminia Bielefeld), 23 goals

Regionalliga West Promotion Playoffs

Club	P	W	D	L	Goals	Pts
1. SV Lüne	6	3	2	1	12-5	8
2. VfB Bottrop	6	3	2	1	7-4	8
3. Fortuna Cologne	6	2	1	3	6-12	5
4. SpVgg Erkenschwick	6	1	1	4	6-10	3

Third Division Champions

Baden (Nordbaden): ASV Feudenheim
Baden (Südbaden): FV Offenburg
Bayern: Jahn Regensburg
Berlin: Sportfreunde Neukölln
Bremen: Werder Bremen (Am.)
Hamburg: SV St. Georg Hamburg
Hessen: SV Wiesbaden
Mittelrhein: 1.FC Cologne (Am.)
Niederrhein: VfB Bottrop
Niedersachsen: Hanover 96 (Am.)
Rheinland: SSV Mülheim
Saarland: SC Friedrichsthal
Schleswig-Holstein: Phönix Lübeck

Südwest: SC Ludwigshafen
Westfalen: SpVgg Erkenschwick and Lünen SV
Württemberg: VfB Stuttgart (Am.)

West German Cup
First Round
1.FC Kaiserslautern 2, Hanover 96 1
1.FC Saarbrücken 2, VfB Stuttgart 4
Alemannia Aachen 1, FK Pirmasens 1 aet (1-0)
Arminia Hanover 1, TSV 1860 Munich 4
Borussia Dortmund 2, 1.FC Cologne 2 aet (0-1)
Eintracht Brunswick 2, MSV Duisburg 3 aet
FC Altona 93 0, Hamburg SV 6
FC Schalke 04 4, Borussia Mönchengladbach 2
FV 08 Duisburg 0, Schwarz-Weiss Essen 2
Hanover 96 (Am.) 2, Borussia Neunkirchen 2 aet (1-2 aet)
Hertha BSC Berlin 2, Bayern Munich 3 aet
Hessen Kassel 2, Werder Bremen 2 aet (1-2 aet)
Rot-Weiss Essen 1, Karlsruhe SC 2
SpVgg Erkenschwick 1, Kickers Stuttgart 0
VfB Lübeck 0, Kickers Offenbach 1 aet
Waldhof Mannheim 1, Fortuna Düsseldorf 3

Second Round
1.FC Cologne 0, Hamburg SV 0 aet (0-2)
1.FC Kaiserslautern 0, Kickers Offenbach 0 aet (0-1 aet)
Alemannia Aachen 4, Karlsruhe SC 2
Borussia Neunkirchen 1, Werder Bremen 1 aet (2-1)
Hamburg SV 2, 1.FC Cologne 0
Schwarz-Weiss Essen 1, Fortuna Düsseldorf 1 aet (0-1)
SpVgg Erkenschwick 1, Bayern Munich 3
TSV 1860 Munich 1, MSV Duisburg 0
VfB Stuttgart 0, FC Schalke 04 1

Quarterfinals
Alemannia Aachen 3, Borussia Neunkirchen 1
FC Schalke 04 2, Bayern Munich 3
Kickers Offenbach 0, Hamburg SV 0 aet (0-2)
TSV 1860 Munich 2, Fortuna Düsseldorf 0

Semifinals
Bayern Munich 3, TSV 1860 Munich 1
Hamburg SV 3, Alemannia Aachen 1

Final
in Stuttgart
Bayern Munich 4, Hamburg SV 0

West German Internationals
12/10/66 in Ankara 2-0 v Turkey
19/11/66 in Cologne 3-0 v Norway
22/2/67 in Karlsruhe 5-1 v Morocco
22/3/67 in Hanover 1-0 v Bulgaria
8/4/67 in Dortmund 6-0 v Albania
3/5/67 in Belgrade 0-1 v Yugoslavia (ECQ)

East German Oberliga

Club	P	W	D	L	Goals	Pts
1. FC Karl-Marx-Stadt	26	14	9	3	39-23	37
2. Lokomotive Leipzig	26	14	2	10	39-32	30
3. Motor Zwickau	26	9	9	8	41-26	27
4. Dynamo Dresden	26	11	5	10	35-31	27
5. Carl Zeiss Jena	26	11	5	10	31-29	27
6. 1.FC Union Berlin	26	9	9	8	33-35	27
7. Lokomotive Stendal	26	11	5	10	39-44	27
8. Vorwärts Berlin	26	10	6	10	43-34	26
9. Wismut Aue	26	11	4	11	45-43	26
10. Hansa Rostock	26	9	8	9	27-27	26
11. Chemie Halle	26	11	4	11	38-41	26
12. Chemie Leipzig	26	9	7	10	35-38	25
13. Dynamo Berlin	26	6	9	11	28-40	21
14. Wismut Gera	26	4	4	18	27-57	12

Motor Zwickau became Sachsenring Zwickau

Top Scorers
Rentzsch (Motor Zwickau) 17
Bauchspiess (Chemie Leipzig) 14
Einsiedel (Wismut Aue) 14
Backhaus (Lokomotive Stendal) 13
Frenzel (Lokomotive Leipzig) 13
Nöldner (Vorwärts Berlin) 10
Steinmann (Karl-Marx-Stadt) 10
Lehrmann (Chemie Halle) 9
Wruck (Vorwärts Berlin) 9
Güssau (Lokomotive Stendal) 8
Kreische (Dynamo Dresden) 8
Naumann (Lokomotive Leipzig) 8
Richter (Wismut Gera) 8
Stein (Carl Zeiss Jena) 8

Second Division (Staffel North)

Club	P	W	D	L	Goals	Pts
1. 1.FC Magdeburg	30	17	10	3	78-19	44
2. Post Neubrandenburg	30	18	7	5	61-26	43
3. Energie Cottbus	30	17	5	8	53-33	39
4. Stahl Eisenhüttenstadt	30	18	6	6	66-28	38
5. Vorwärts Cottbus	30	12	11	7	37-29	35
6. Vorwärts Neubrandenburg	30	11	11	8	41-36	33
7. TSG Wismar	30	11	9	10	52-45	31
8. Vorwärts Rostock	30	10	11	9	30-33	31

	P	W	D	L	Goals	Pts
9. Dynamo Schwerin	30	10	11	9	43-55	31
10. Motor Hennigsdorf	30	9	10	11	44-45	28
11. Lichtenberg 47	30	9	9	12	36-47	27
12. Motor Köpenick	30	7	11	12	29-38	25
13. Motor Babelsberg	30	8	8	14	32-55	24
14. Motor Dessau	30	6	10	14	28-48	22
15. Lokomotive Halberstadt	30	5	7	18	22-55	17
16. Motor Stralsund	30	1	6	23	22-80	8

Promoted: Aktivist Schwarze Pumpe, Chemie Premnitz, Motor Köpenick, Vorwärts Stralsund. Vorwärts Rostock were replaced by Hansa Rostock's second team.

Second Division (Staffel South)

Club	P	W	D	L	Goals	Pts
1. Rot-Weiss Erfurt	30	18	5	7	62-21	41
2. Stahl Riesa	30	18	5	7	54-27	41
3. Vorwärts Meiningen	30	15	5	10	53-36	35
4. Vorwärts Leipzig	30	12	9	9	38-25	33
5. Motor Wema Plauen	30	12	9	9	52-51	33
6. Motor Steinach	30	11	9	10	34-28	31
7. Aktivist K M Zwickau	30	12	7	11	43-39	31
8. Chemie Zeitz	30	11	8	11	43-34	30
9. Lokomotive Dresden	30	10	10	10	39-35	30
10. Motor Weimar	30	10	10	10	37-42	30
11. Motor Eisenach	30	10	10	10	41-45	28
12. Motor Bautzen	30	10	7	13	30-33	27
13. Dynamo Eisleben	30	11	7	12	35-47	27
14. Motor Nordhausen-West	30	9	9	12	28-41	27
15. Aktivist Böhlen	30	7	9	14	25-53	23
16. Chemie Jena	30	3	3	24	12-69	9

Promoted: Carl Zeiss Jena II, Fortschritt Weissenfels, Rot-Weiss Erfurt II

East German Cup Final
in Brandenburg
Motor Zwickau 3, Hansa Rostock 0

East German Internationals

4/9/66 in Karl-Marx-Stadt 6-0 v Egypt
11/9/66 in Erfurt 2-0 v Poland
21/9/66 in Gera 2-0 v Rumania
23/10/66 in Moscow 2-2 v USSR
5/4/67 in Leipzig 4-3 v Holland (ECQ)
17/5/67 in Helsingborg 1-0 v Sweden
4/6/67 in Copenhagen 1-1 v Denmark (ECQ)

European Cup
Preliminary Round
Waterford v Vorwärts Berlin .... (1-6, 0-6)
First Round
TSV 1860 Munich v Omonia Nicosia .... (8-0, 2-1)
Vorwärts Berlin v Gornik Zabrze .... (2-1, 1-2, 3-1)
Second Round
TSV 1860 Munich v Real Madrid .... (1-0, 1-3)

Cup-Winners' Cup
First Round
Tatran Presov v Bayern Munich .... (1-1, 2-3)
Chemie Leipzig v Legia Warsaw .... (3-0, 2-2)
Second Round
Shamrock Rovers v Bayern Munich .... (1-1, 2-3)
Chemie Leipzig v Standard Liege .... (2-1, 0-1)
Quarterfinals
Rapid Vienna v Bayern Munich .... (1-0, 0-2 aet)
Semifinals
Bayern Munich v Standard Liege .... (2-0, 3-1)
Final in Nuremberg
Bayern Munich 1, Glasgow Rangers 0 aet

Fairs Cup
First Round
Drumcondra v Eintracht Frankfurt .... (0-2, 1-6)
Djurgarden v Lokomotive Leipzig .... (1-3, 1-2)
1.FC Nuremberg v Valencia .... (1-2, 0-2)
VfB Stuttgart v Burnley .... (1-1, 0-2)
Second Round
Lokomotive Leipzig v FC Liege .... (0-0, 1-0)
Eintracht Frankfurt v Hvidovre .... (5-1, 2-2)
Third Round
Lokomotive Leipzig v Benfica .... (3-1, 1-2)
Eintracht Frankfurt v Ferencvaros .... (4-1, 1-2)
Quarterfinals
Eintracht Frankfurt v Burnley .... (1-1, 2-1)
Lokomotive Leipzig v Kilmarnock .... (1-0, 0-2)
Semifinals
Eintracht Frankfurt v Dinamo Zagreb .... (3-0, 0-4 aet)

1967-68

Der Club

In the 1920s, no team came close to rivalling 1.FC Nuremberg for supremacy in German football. National champions five times over the decade, they established a reputation so enviable that they came to be known simply as *Der Club*. (Except, that is, in East Germany, where 1.FC Magdeburg had also acquired that nickname.) Indeed, at one stage they played an amazing ninety consecutive matches without losing. Nuremberg went on to be crowned champions of Germany on three further occasions, the most recent being in 1961. Yet after joining the Bundesliga, the highest position they had finished in was sixth. The 1967-68 season was to see FCN finally add the title of Bundesliga champions to their impressive list of honours.

Four players from the 1961 side were still with the club—goalkeeper Roland Wabra, defenders Helmut Hilpert and Ferdinand Wenauer, and striker Heinz Strehl. But several other veterans had departed in Max Merkel's big clear-out at the end of the previous season, when *Der Club* finished a disappointing tenth. Not surprisingly, at the start of the season Nuremberg were not seen as one of the main contenders for what was regarded as a very open championship. No fewer than seven clubs were thought to have a genuine chance at the title: defending champions Brunswick, runners-up Munich 1860, Bayern, Cologne, Dortmund, Frankfurt, and Hanover.

The early leaders were Nuremberg and Mönchengladbach. Both took seven points from their first four games, and when they met each other in September a sellout crowd of 65,000 witnessed FCN's 1-0 home win. Nuremberg's away form was also sharp, and within one four-day period they came away with a 3-0 win at Brunswick and a 4-0 victory at Bremen. Not until the thirteenth game did they taste defeat, 2-0 at Duisburg. The high-point of the first half of the season—and one of the most famous matches in Nuremberg's history—was a 7-3 decapitation of rivals Bayern Munich, with a home crowd of 65,000 seeing Franz Brungs put five goals past Sepp Maier. At mid-season, Nuremberg had gained 27 points out of a possible

34 and were seven points ahead of their pursuers: Mönchengladbach, Munich 1860, MSV Duisburg and Bayern Munich.

Although the post-Christmas games saw a dip in form, Nuremberg gathered points steadily and clinched the title with one match to play by winning 2-0 at Bayern Munich, Strehl and Brungs getting the goals. With the league's best defensive record and a free-scoring attack, Nuremberg were hailed as worthy champions. They suffered few injuries and consequently used only fifteen different players all season. Normally, they were able to field the same settled team: Wabra; Fritz Popp and Horst Leupold; "Luggi" Müller, Wenauer and Karl-Heinz Ferschl; Zvezdan Cebinac, Strehl, Brungs, Heinz Müller and Georg Volkert. They rarely needed to make use of the new rule which permitted one substitute per team. In the final match of the season on May 25 against Brunswick, a crowd of 62,000 celebrated as Nuremberg overwhelmed the previous year's champions 4-1.

Under their new *Trainer* Fritz Langner Werder Bremen rebounded from the previous season's sixteenth place finish to take the runners-up spot, with Mönchengladbach having to settle for third. Favourites Dortmund and Munich 1860 played out undistinguished seasons and finished in the bottom half of the table. Dortmund proved to be the league's Jekyll-and-Hyde team, sporting one of the best home records in the country but failing to win a single match away. Hanover, having lured Jupp Heynckes away from Mönchengladbach in an effort to bolster their tepid attack, scored just nine times on their travels and could fare no better than tenth. Heynckes scored a disappointing ten goals and once again 96 were amongst the poorer-scoring teams in the league.

Borussia Neunkirchen, who had been relegated in 1966 and promoted in 1967, wilted after returning to the Bundesliga and finished in seventeenth place. Their away form was particularly catastrophic with only one point all season (a 0-0 draw at Hamburg) and an appalling 10-0 loss at Mönchengladbach. At home Neunkirchen were watched by average crowds of less than 10,000 and just over 2000 saw them suffer a 5-0 pasting at home to VfB Stuttgart in May. With four games still to go, Neunkirchen were relegated. They have not appeared in the Bundesliga since.

The club at the very bottom, to no one's great surprise, was Karlsruhe SC, who had failed to make any sort of impression in each of the first four seasons of the Bundesliga. This time around, they failed to pick up a single away win. Both Paul Frantz and Georg Gawliczek were released as KSC *Trainer* during the season, although Frantz managed to stay on as technical adviser.

Berlin finally regained a representative in the Bundesliga, as Hertha BSC put together another indomitable performance in their Regionalliga to finish five points in front of Tennis Borussia. This time in the promotion playoffs they held their nerve. Kickers Offenbach won the other promotion group after finishing second in the Regionalliga South. This meant that Arminia Hanover, who had won the Regionalliga North for the second straight year, once again failed to go up. Arminia would not come as close ever again.

SV Alsenborn finished comfortably in front in the Regionalliga Southwest. The battle for the second playoff spot was between TuS Neuendorf and FK Pirmasens. Pirmasens had accumulated more points than Neuendorf, but league officials had penalised bottom club SSV Mülheim three points for fielding an ineligible player.

Neuendorf were one of the clubs to have benefited from this breach and were officially put in second place, ahead of Pirmasens. Aware that Pirmasens would be losing out on a possible berth in the Bundesliga on a technicality, the league decided the two clubs should play a single match in Bad Kreuznach to determine who would advance to the promotion round. And Neuendorf won 3-2, after extra time.

The Cup holders nearly went out in sensational style in the first round. Jahn Regensburg held Bayern Munich to a 1-1 draw over 90 minutes, but put through their own net in the second period of extra time and wound up conceding two more goals to lose 4-1. Werder Bremen went out at the first hurdle, embarrassed 4-2 by SV Völklingen. Mönchengladbach nearly suffered a similar fate but a Herbert Laumen goal six minutes from time was enough to beat Bayern Hof on a snow-covered pitch.

Bayern Munich were eventually defeated by VfL Bochum of the Regionalliga West, who had beaten Karlsruhe, VfB Stuttgart, and Mönchengladbach on the way to the semifinal. Having lost their Cup-Winners' Cup semifinal with AC Milan earlier in the week, Bayern were perhaps not in the best frame of mind to deal with the Second Division side. Cologne, who had beaten Homburg, Eintracht Frankfurt, and Brunswick to reach the final—the latter two only after replays—were presented with an own-goal from Werner Jablonski after just 22 minutes and continued to ride their luck, eventually winning by a flattering 4-1.

Carl Zeiss Jena won the East German Oberliga by five clear points from Hansa Rostock. Jena had a 100% home record, scoring 29 goals and conceding only three in their thirteen matches at the Ernst Abbe Sportfeld. They also reached the East German Cup final in Halle, but allowed Union Berlin to come from a goal behind to win 2-1.

In Hanover, the West German national team played England for the first time since the 1966 World Cup Final. Franz Beckenbauer helped the Germans to a modest portion of revenge for the historic Wembley defeat. He scored the only goal of the match as the hosts won 1-0—the first time Germany had beaten England in a full international. There was also a rare victory over Brazil, 2-1 in Stuttgart.

For the third year in succession, there was a strong German showing in the Cup-Winners' Cup. Both defending champions Bayern and West German Cup winners Hamburg reached the semifinals, but only HSV managed to advance any further, beating Cardiff City 4-3 on aggregate to reach the final in Rotterdam. There, two first-half goals gave the trophy to AC Milan. Progress in the other competitions was poor, with Eintracht Brunswick narrowly losing out to Juventus in their quarterfinal European Cup tie.

Bundesliga

Club	P	W	D	L	Goals	Pts
1. 1.FC Nuremberg	34	19	9	6	71-37	47
2. Werder Bremen	34	18	8	8	68-51	44
3. Borussia Mönchengladbach	34	15	12	7	77-45	42
4. 1.FC Cologne	34	17	4	13	68-52	38
5. Bayern Munich	34	16	6	12	68-58	38
6. Eintracht Frankfurt	34	15	8	11	58-51	38
7. MSV Duisburg	34	13	10	11	69-58	36
8. VfB Stuttgart	34	14	7	13	65-54	35
9. Eintracht Brunswick	34	15	5	14	37-39	35
10. Hanover 96	34	12	10	12	48-52	34
11. Alemannia Aachen	34	13	8	13	52-66	34
12. TSV 1860 Munich	34	11	11	12	55-39	33
13. Hamburg SV	34	11	11	12	51-54	33
14. Borussia Dortmund	34	12	7	15	60-59	31
15. FC Schalke 04	34	11	8	15	42-48	30
16. 1.FC Kaiserslautern	34	8	12	14	39-67	28
17. Borussia Neunkirchen	34	7	5	22	33-93	19
18. Karlsruhe SC	34	6	5	23	32-70	17

Top Scorers
Löhr (1.FC Cologne) 27
Brungs (1.FC Nuremberg) 25
G Müller (Bayern Munich) 20
Laumen (Borussia Mönchengladbach) 19
Meyer (Borussia Mönchengladbach) 19
Ohlhauser (Bayern Munich) 19
Strehl (1.FC Nuremberg) 18
Emmerich (Borussia Dortmund) 18
Köppel (VfB Stuttgart) 17
Budde (MSV Duisburg) 16
Görts (Werder Bremen) 16

Bundesliga Promotion Playoffs

Group 1

	P	W	D	L	Goals	Pts
1. Kickers Offenbach	8	5	2	1	16-7	12
2. Bayer Leverkusen	8	3	5	0	17-10	10
3. Tennis Borussia Berlin	8	3	1	4	11-19	7
4. TuS Neuendorf	8	1	5	2	4-7	7
5. Arminia Hanover	8	1	2	5	6-11	4

Group 2

	P	W	D	L	Goals	Pts
1. Hertha BSC Berlin	8	4	3	1	12-7	11
2. Rot-Weiss Essen	8	3	3	2	9-9	9
3. SV Alsenborn	8	3	2	3	12-14	8
4. Göttingen 05	8	3	1	4	10-11	7
5. Bayern Hof	8	2	1	5	12-14	5

Regionalliga Berlin

Club	P	W	D	L	Goals	Pts
1. Hertha BSC Berlin	30	26	3	1	104-11	55
2. Tennis Borussia Berlin	30	23	4	3	108-29	50
3. Hertha Zehlendorf	30	18	5	7	69-45	41
4. Wacker 04 Berlin	30	17	6	7	90-58	40
5. Tasmania 1900 Berlin	30	12	11	7	57-32	35
6. BFC Südring	30	12	7	11	51-42	31
7. Spandau SV	30	12	6	12	62-53	30
8. Blau-Weiss 90 Berlin	30	12	6	12	43-47	30
9. SV Berlin 92	30	8	10	12	46-59	26
10. Alemannia 90 Berlin	30	8	9	13	44-58	25
11. Reinickendorf Füchse	30	9	6	15	51-68	24
12. 1.FC Neukölln	30	8	8	14	41-66	24
13. Rapide Wedding	30	7	7	16	51-72	21
14. Kickers 1900 Berlin	30	7	6	17	29-69	20
15. Sportfreunde Neukölln	30	6	3	21	32-111	15
16. VfB Hermsdorf	30	4	5	21	39-97	13

Top Scorer: Lunenburg (Tennis Borussia Berlin), 30 goals
Promoted: Meteor 06 Berlin, VfL Nord Berlin, SC Staaken

Regionalliga North

Club	P	W	D	L	Goals	Pts
1. Arminia Hanover	32	20	4	8	64-25	44
2. Göttingen 05	32	20	4	8	66-36	44
3. VfL Wolfsburg	32	17	9	6	61-34	43
4. FC St Pauli	32	17	7	8	60-30	41
5. TuS Bremerhaven 93	32	17	5	10	48-53	39
6. Phönix Lübeck	32	15	7	10	49-39	37
7. VfL Osnabrück	32	13	8	11	51-43	34
8. Holstein Kiel	32	14	5	13	47-37	33
9. VfB Lübeck	32	13	7	12	44-41	33
10. Sperber Hamburg	32	13	6	13	53-63	32
11. VfB Oldenburg	32	10	10	12	49-49	30
12. Itzehoe SV	32	10	7	15	50-64	27
13. Concordia Hamburg	32	10	3	19	42-52	23
14. SV Barmbek-Uhlenhorst	32	10	3	19	56-79	23
15. ASV Bergedorf	32	8	6	18	31-54	22
16. FC Altona 93	32	8	4	20	37-78	20
17. TuS Haste	32	8	3	21	40-71	19

Top Scorer: Kemmer (VfL Wolfsburg), 19 goals

Regionalliga North Promotion Playoffs

Group One

	P	W	D	L	Goals	Pts
1. Tus Celle	6	5	0	1	21-9	10
2. SV Friedrichsort	6	4	0	2	7-10	8
3. SV Meppen	6	2	0	4	7-10	4
4. Hamburg St Georg	6	1	0	5	7-13	2

Group Two	P	W	D	L	Goals	Pts
1. Heide SV	6	5	1	0	15-7	11
2. VfL Pinneberg	6	2	2	2	12-11	6
3. SV Woltmershauen	6	2	2	2	13-12	6
4. VfV Hildesheim	6	0	1	5	4-14	1

Regionalliga South

Club	P	W	D	L	Goals	Pts
1. Bayern Hof	34	23	8	3	85-36	54
2. Kickers Offenbach	34	21	11	2	75-27	53
3. SSV Reutlingen	34	22	1	11	77-39	45
4. Kickers Stuttgart	34	20	4	10	75-51	44
5. Schweinfurt 05	34	16	9	9	55-48	41
6. VfR Mannheim	34	15	8	11	75-55	38
7. SpVgg Fürth	34	17	4	13	48-39	38
8. Hessen Kassel	34	15	7	12	64-63	37
9. FC Freiburg	34	14	8	12	57-56	36
10. FC Villingen	34	12	11	11	41-43	35
11. Opel Rüsselsheim	34	12	7	15	59-60	31
12. SV Waldhof	34	12	6	16	55-62	30
13. Schwaben Augsburg	34	10	8	16	47-54	28
14. SV Darmstadt 98	34	8	8	18	45-71	24
15. Jahn Regensburg	34	8	6	20	37-77	22
16. FSV Frankfurt	34	5	10	19	37-61	20
17. TSG Backnang	34	4	10	20	45-94	18
18. SV Wiebaden	34	4	10	20	37-78	18

Top Scorer: Breuer (Bayern Hof) and Schäffner (VfR Mannheim), 27 goals each

Regionalliga South Promotion Playoffs

Club	P	W	D	L	Goals	Pts
1. VfL Neckarau	6	4	1	1	13-2	9
2. TSF Esslingen	6	4	0	2	12-11	8
3. SC Freiburg	6	1	2	3	5-13	4
4. FC Wangen	6	0	3	3	3-7	3

Also Promoted: ESV Ingolstadt, Rot-Weiss Frankfurt

Regionalliga Southwest

Club	P	W	D	L	Goals	Pts
1. SV Alsenborn	30	24	3	3	87-21	51
2. TuS Neuendorf	30	18	6	6	66-29	42
3. FK Pirmasens	30	18	5	7	57-31	41
4. FSV Mainz 05	30	15	8	7	57-32	38
5. 1.FC Saarbrücken	30	12	10	8	55-37	34
6. Südwest Ludwigshafen	30	13	7	10	45-32	33
7. Röchling Völklingen	30	12	9	9	53-47	33
8. Eintracht Trier	30	11	10	9	57-46	32
9. Saar 05 Saarbrücken	30	12	7	11	32-35	31
10. FC 08 Homburg	30	11	8	11	41-53	30
11. SVW Mainz	30	10	7	13	42-60	27
12. Wormatia Worms	30	8	9	13	34-40	25
13. VfR Frankenthal	30	9	7	14	35-63	25
14. SC Friedrichsthal	30	8	5	17	42-60	21
15. SC Ludwigshafen	30	3	4	23	27-90	10
16. SSV Mülheim	30	2	3	25	22-76	7

Top Scorer: Schieck (SV Alsenborn), 30 goals

Oberliga Südwest Promotion Playoffs

Club	P	W	D	L	Goals	Pts
1. FV Speyer	4	3	0	1	6-1	6
2. Teutonia Landsweiler-Reden	4	1	2	1	6-9	4
3. SpVgg Andernach	4	0	2	2	5-7	2

Regionalliga West

Club	P	W	D	L	Goals	Pts
1. Bayer Leverkusen	34	22	8	4	70-32	52
2. Rot-Weiss Essen	34	22	8	4	73-35	52
3. Rot-Weiss Oberhausen	34	23	5	6	77-32	51
4. Arminia Bielefeld	34	19	8	7	77-44	46
5. VfL Bochum	34	18	6	10	65-32	42
6. Fortuna Düsseldorf	34	11	13	10	65-49	35
7. Schwarz-Weiss Essen	34	12	11	11	56-46	35
8. Lünen SV	34	13	7	14	46-65	33
9. Sportfreunde Hamborn 07	34	11	9	14	60-61	31
10. Viktoria Cologne	34	12	7	15	48-51	31
11. TSV Marl-Hüls	34	12	7	15	49-56	31
12. VfR Neuss	34	12	7	15	51-61	31
13. Preussen Münster	34	10	9	15	45-50	29
14. Eintracht Gelsenkirchen	34	11	7	16	43-56	29
15. Wuppertal SV	34	10	8	16	31-51	28
16. Fortuna Cologne	34	7	9	18	45-81	23
17. Westfalia Herne	34	6	7	21	27-74	19
18. VfB Bottrop	34	3	8	23	20-72	14

Top Scorer: Kuster (Arminia Bielefeld), 28 goals

Regionalliga West Promotion Playoffs

Club	P	W	D	L	Goals	Pts
1. Eintracht Duisburg	6	4	1	1	10-5	9
2. SC Bonn	6	2	3	1	9-8	7
3. SSV Hagen	6	2	1	3	8-13	5
4. SpVgg Erkenschwick	6	1	1	4	10-11	3

Third Division Champions

Baden (Nordbaden): VfL Neckarau
Baden (Südbaden): SC Freiburg
Bayern: ESV Ingolstadt
Berlin: SC Staaken
Bremen: Werder Bremen (Am.)
Hamburg: VfL Pinneberg
Hessen: Rot-Weiss Frankfurt
Mittelrhein: SC Bonn
Niederrhein: Eintracht Duisburg

Niedersachsen: SV Meppen
Rheinland: SpVgg Andernach
Saarland: Teutonia Landsweiler-Reden
Schleswig-Holstein: SV Friedrichsort
Südwest: 1.FC Kaiserslautern (Am.)
Westfalen: SpVgg Erkenschwick
Württemberg: FC Wangen

West German Cup
First Round
Arminia Bielefeld 0, FC Schalke 04 1
Bayer Leverkusen 0, 1.FC Nuremberg 2
Bayern Hof 0, Borussia Mönchengladbach 1
Borussia Neunkirchen 2, Eintracht Brunswick 3
FC 08 Homburg 1, 1.FC Cologne 2
Hertha BSC Berlin 1, Hamburg SV 0 aet
Jahn Regensburg 1, Bayern Munich 4 aet
MSV Duisburg 4, Hanover 96 1
Preussen Münster 2, Alemannia Aachen 1
Röchling Völklingen 4, Werder Bremen 2
Schweinfurt 05 1, Eintracht Frankfurt 2 aet
SSV Reutlingen 7, Itzehoe SV 1
VfB Stuttgart 1, 1.FC Kaiserslautern 0
VfB Lübeck 0, TSV 1860 Munich 1
VfB Oldenburg 2, Borussia Dortmund 3
VfL Bochum 3, Karlsruhe SC 2

Second Round
1.FC Cologne 1, Eintracht Frankfurt 1 aet (1-0)
1.FC Nuremberg 4, Preussen Münster 0
Bayern Munich 3, MSV Duisburg 1
FC Schalke 04 2, Eintracht Brunswick 3
Hertha BSC Berlin 2, Röchling Völklingen 1
SSV Reutlingen 1, Borussia Dortmund 3
TSV 1860 Munich 2, Borussia Mönchengladbach 4
VfL Bochum 2, VfB Stuttgart 1

Quarterfinals
Bayern Munich 2, 1.FC Nuremberg 1
Borussia Dortmund 2, Hertha BSC Berlin 1
Eintracht Brunswick 1, 1.FC Cologne 1 aet (1-2)
VfL Bochum 2, Borussia Mönchengladbach 0

Semifinals
1.FC Cologne 3, Borussia Dortmund 0
VfL Bochum 2, Bayern Munich 1

Final
in Ludwigshafen
1.FC Cologne 4, VfL Bochum 1

West German Internationals
27/9/67 in Berlin 5-1 v France
7/10/67 in Hamburg 3-1 v Yugoslavia (ECQ)
22/11/67 in Bucharest 0-1 v Rumania
17/12/67 in Tirana 0-0 v Albania (ECQ)
6/3/68 in Brussels 3-1 v Belgium
17/4/68 in Basle 0-0 v Switzerland
8/5/68 in Cardiff 1-1 v Wales
1/6/68 in Hanover 1-0 v England
16/6/68 in Stuttgart 2-1 v Brazil

East German Oberliga

Club	P	W	D	L	Goals	Pts
1. Carl Zeiss Jena	26	17	5	4	51-19	39
2. Hansa Rostock	26	15	4	7	37-27	34
3. 1.FC Magdeburg	26	13	7	6	43-38	33
4. Vorwärts Berlin	26	9	10	7	34-29	26
5. Lokomotive Leipzig	26	9	7	10	39-35	25
6. FC Karl-Marx-Stadt	26	8	9	9	33-30	25
7. Sachsenring Zwickau	26	11	3	12	36-34	25
8. 1.FC Union Berlin	26	9	7	10	26-35	25
9. Rot-Weiss Erfurt	26	8	7	11	34-39	23
10. Chemie Halle	26	8	7	11	32-41	23
11. Wismut Aue	26	9	4	13	32-40	22
12. Chemie Leipzig	26	7	7	12	26-32	21
13. Dynamo Dresden	26	5	11	10	25-33	21
14. Lokomotive Stendal	26	7	6	13	26-42	20

Top Scorers
Kostmann (Hansa Rostock) 15
Löwe (Lokomotive Leipzig) 13
Vogel (Karl-Marx-Stadt) 12
Scheitler (Carl Zeiss Jena) 11
Stieler (Rot-Weiss Erfurt) 11
Uentz (1.FC Union Berlin) 11
Bauchspiess (Chemie Leipzig) 9
Sparwasser (1.FC Magdeburg) 9
Trölitzsch (Rot-Weiss Erfurt) 9
Begerad (Vorwärts Berlin) 8
Rentzsch (Sachsenring Zwickau) 8
Steinmann (Karl-Marx-Stadt) 8

Second Division (Staffel North)

Club	P	W	D	L	Goals	Pts
1. Dynamo Berlin	30	20	7	3	64-24	47
2. Energie Cottbus	30	20	4	6	52-22	44
3. Stahl Eisenhüttenstadt	30	14	9	7	54-33	37
4. Hansa Rostock II	30	14	7	9	46-33	35
5. Dynamo Schwerin	30	14	5	11	58-44	33
6. Post Neubrandenburg	30	12	7	11	55-43	31
7. Vorwärts Stralsund	30	9	11	10	33-36	29
8. Chemie Premnitz	30	9	11	10	36-45	29
9. Vorwärts Neubrandenburg	30	9	10	11	37-40	28

	P	W	D	L	Goals	Pts
10. TSG Wismar	30	9	10	11	31-46	28
11. Lichtenberg 47	30	8	11	11	27-37	27
12. Vorwärts Cottbus	30	8	10	12	36-40	26
13. Motor Hennigsdorf	30	9	8	13	55-63	26
14. Aktivist Schwarze Pumpe	30	8	7	15	29-43	23
15. Motor Köpenick	30	5	11	14	23-53	21
16. Motor Babelsberg	30	4	8	18	27-61	16

Promoted: Dynamo Berlin II, Chemie Wolfen, KKW Nord Greifswald

Second Division (Staffel South)

Club	P	W	D	L	Goals	Pts
1. Stahl Riesa	30	19	5	6	54-31	43
2. Wismut Gera	30	15	12	3	61-27	42
3. Vorwärts Meiningen	30	14	9	7	59-36	37
4. Motor Steinach	30	15	6	9	42-35	36
5. Vorwärts Leipzig	30	11	12	7	51-39	34
6. Carl Zeiss Jena II	30	11	11	8	41-31	33
7. Lokomotive Dresden	30	10	10	10	36-30	30
8. Aktivist K M Zwickau	30	10	8	12	40-44	28
9. Dynamo Eisleben	30	9	9	12	41-51	27
10. Motor Eisenach	30	11	5	14	43-65	27
11. Chemie Zeitz	30	8	10	12	40-41	26
12. Motor Wema Plauen	30	11	4	15	49-54	26
13. Rot-Weiss Erfurt II	30	9	7	14	48-47	25
14. Motor Bautzen	30	9	7	14	28-48	25
15. Motor Weimar	30	6	9	15	33-50	21
16. Fortschritt Weissenfels	30	6	8	16	28-65	20

Promoted: Aktivist Böhlen, Kali Werra Tiefenort, Chemie Riesa, Sachsenring Zwickau II

East German Cup Final
in Halle
1.FC Union Berlin 2, Carl Zeiss Jena 1

East German Internationals
13/9/67 in Amsterdam 0-1 v Holland (ECQ)
27/9/67 in Budapest 1-3 v Hungary (ECQ)
11/10/67 in Leipzig 3-2 v Denmark (ECQ)
29/10/67 in Leipzig 1-0 v Hungary (ECQ)
18/11/67 in Berlin 1-0 v Rumania (OGQ)
6/12/67 in Bucharest 1-0 v Rumania (OGQ)
2/2/68 in Santiago 2-2 v Chile

European Cup
First Round
Eintracht Brunswick walkover v Dinamo Tirana
Karl-Marx-Stadt v Anderlecht .... (1-3, 1-2)
Second Round
Rapid Vienna v Eintracht Brunswick .... (1-0, 0-2)
Quarterfinals
Eintracht Brunswick v Juventus .... (3-2, 0-1, 0-1)

Cup-Winners' Cup
First Round
Bayern Munich v Panathinaikos .... (5-0, 2-1)
Hamburg SV v Randers Freja .... (5-3, 2-0)
Moscow Torpedo v Motor Zwickau .... (0-0, 1-0)
Second Round
Bayern Munich v Vitoria Setubal .... (6-2, 1-1)
Wisla Krakow v Hamburg SV .... (0-1, 0-4)
Quarterfinals
Valencia v Bayern Munich .... (1-1, 0-1)
Hamburg SV v Olympique Lyon .... (2-0, 0-2, 2-0)
Semifinals
AC Milan v Bayern Munich .... (2-0, 0-0)
Hamburg SV v Cardiff City .... (1-1, 3-2)
Final in Rotterdam
AC Milan 2, Hamburg SV 0

Fairs Cup
First Round
Lokomotive Leipzig v Linfield .... (5-1, 0-1)
Eintracht Frankfurt v Nottingham Forest .... (0-1, 0-4)
Glasgow Rangers v Dynamo Dresden .... (2-1, 1-1)
Servette v TSV 1860 Munich .... (2-2, 0-4)
Napoli v Hanover 96 .... (4-0, 1-1)
1.FC Cologne v Slavia Prague .... (2-0, 2-2)
Second Round
Liverpool v TSV 1860 Munich .... (8-0, 1-2)
Glasgow Rangers v 1.FC Cologne .... (3-0, 1-3 aet)
Vojvodina v Lokmotive Leipzig .... (0-0, 2-0)

1968-69

First to worst

Defending champions they may have been, but 1.FC Nuremberg were in a financial mess. The sizeable profits from the previous season had been invested not in strengthening the team but in a sports complex—swimming pool, tennis courts, restaurants, and the like. Instead of players and *Trainer* being handsomely rewarded for the club's success, they suddenly found themselves being told to take a cut in their wages. Not surprisingly, two players—Karl-Heinz Ferschl and Franz Brungs—took the opportunity to move to Hertha Berlin.

Nuremberg kicked off the new season at home to Alemannia Aachen and lost 4-1. Another loss the following week in Offenbach and they were one off the bottom. But the season was still young, and few doubted that in spite of their financial problems *Der Club* would soon turn things around.

When play resumed after the winter break, Nuremberg lost to Aachen once more and found themselves in last place. It would be six more matches before they won again, by which time the club would find itself smack in the middle of a fiercely-contested relegation battle. As the end of the season approached, and each point became more and more critical, Merkel decided he had been through enough and left.

Interim boss Robert Körner and replacement Kuno Klötzer tried all they could just to keep the sinking ship afloat. But it also needed to be steered out of danger. With one match to play, FCN were left needing to win at Cologne to be sure of staying up. Cologne had not enjoyed the best of seasons—in fact, their thirteenth position was by far the worst they had suffered since the inception of the Bundesliga—but they won easily, 3-0. Unbelievably, the reigning champions had finished in seventeenth place and were relegated. Never before, and never again, has the Bundesliga witnessed such a spectacular decline.

Nuremberg's plight came as a great relief to Cologne, who would have gone down in their place had they lost their own season finalé. Kaiserslautern, Hertha

Berlin, and MSV Duisburg were also mopping the sweat from their collective brows. In any case, it was a record-breaking season for Duisburg, who managed to draw no fewer than sixteen of their 34 matches.

While these teams were struggling, Aachen, who had finished eleventh the previous season, were steadily inching their way up the table. Against all expectations, they finished as runners-up, albeit eight points distant. *Trainer* Michael Pfeiffer's side was not particularly strong; in fact, no team lost more matches at home than they did. Heinz-Gerd Klostermann's twelve goals put him amongst the top ten scorers, but he proved something of a one-season wonder and would only score four times the following year. Aachen would finish rock-bottom of the league in 1970 and depart from the Bundesliga, never to return.

Borussia Mönchengladbach had started the season with high hopes, having paid a record transfer fee of DM225,000 to VfB Stuttgart for striker Horst Köppel. But Köppel scored only five goals during the campaign and Borussia were unable to improve on the previous season's third-place finish. Eintracht Brunswick, champions two years earlier, were still finding it hard to score goals but kept out enough at the other end to finish a respectable fourth.

This season belonged entirely to Bayern Munich and marked the start of what would be a long line of championships unequalled in Bundesliga history. Having swapped one Yugoslavian *Trainer* ("Tschik" Cajkovski) for another Yugoslavian *Trainer* (Branko Zebec), Bayern became a more organised and better-disciplined team whilst still retaining the team spirit they had built up over the past three years. Since joining the Bundesliga, they had finished third, sixth, and fifth, and were widely recognised as championship contenders.

By the midpoint of the season, Bayern were well on top with 25 points and a goal difference of 35-13. The last match of the sequence was against Hanover 96, whom Cajkovski had joined as *Trainer*. It was an ill-tempered contest which Bayern lost 1-0, and Jupp Heynckes' dramatic fall after a confrontation with Gerd Müller earned the Bayern centre-forward a sending-off and a controversial eight-week ban. The bad winter weather softened the blow a little, as Bayern only played four matches in this period, losing to Kaiserslautern and Munich 1860, and drawing with Schalke and Hamburg. After watching his club go five matches without a victory, Müller returned from suspension and scored both goals in a 2-1 win over Hertha. Bayern came out of their slump and stayed well ahead of the pack, wrapping up the title four weeks before the end of the season despite losing that day's match 2-0 in Nuremberg.

Apart from Müller's absence, Bayern suffered very few illnesses or injuries and were able to retain a very settled side throughout the season. Although the headlines were usually grabbed by the likes of Müller, Franz Beckenbauer, Sepp Maier and Georg Schwarzenbeck, there were other major contributors to the team's success, such as Rainer Ohlhauser, Dieter Brenninger, Franz Roth, Werner Olk and Peter Pumm.

Bayern also became the first team to complete the "double" of cup and championship since Schalke 04 in 1937. The 1969 Cup Final was played before 64,000 fans in Frankfurt—ironically, against Schalke. Müller scored after thirteen minutes but Manfred Pohlschmidt equalised six minutes later. The winner came after 35 minutes when Müller appeared to have been fouled, but referee Helmut Fritz waved him on, and the Bayern striker proceeded to put the ball in the net with half the Schalke team thinking the play had been stopped.

Two Rot-Weiss clubs—Essen and Oberhausen—gained promotion from the Regionalliga West by winning their playoff groups. It was hard luck on third-placed VfL Bochum, who finished level on points with Essen and with a more impressive goal difference, but lost out on goal average. (Over the summer—and a season too late for Bochum—the DFB replaced goal average with goal difference.) VfL Osnabrück won the Regionalliga North at a canter, but looked less convincing after that. The cruellest defeat in German football that season, though, was inflicted on VfB Kiel, who finished top of the Oberliga Schleswig-Holstein along with SV Friedrichsort, but lost the championship on the drawing of lots.

Vorwärts Berlin captured their sixth—and last—East German league championship, dropping just two points at home all season. Runners-up Carl Zeiss Jena took all but three points at home, yet won only twice on their travels. Lokomotive Leipzig, who had finished fifth the season before, suffered an alarming loss of form and were relegated along with Union Berlin. In the cup final, 1.FC Magdeburg won 4-0 over Karl-Marx-Stadt, equalling the highest-ever score in the final. It was Magdeburg's third triumph in the competition in six years.

International politics led to the withdrawal of the East German teams from the European Cup and the Cup-Winners' Cup before a ball had been kicked. This stemmed from a first-round draw which pitted Glasgow Celtic against Ferencvaros of Hungary. The Scottish side expressed to UEFA their reluctance to fulfil the fixture because Hungarian troops—along with those of the Soviet Union and East Germany—had taken part in the suppression of the Czechoslovakian revolution earlier that year. UEFA assented to Western pressure and re-drew the entire first round—and the football associations of the Soviet Union, Hungary, Poland, and Bulgaria immediately withdrew their clubs from competition in counter-protest. Curiously, Hansa Rostock and Lokomotive Leipzig did not withdraw from the Fairs Cup, but both lost the first ties they played to keep their nation's participation to a minimum.

There was also a West German withdrawal from the competition. Hamburg SV pulled out of the quarterfinals of the Fairs Cup—because they couldn't find a suitable date to play. The harsh winter had created a considerable backlog of fixtures, and HSV found itself needing to play three Bundesliga matches in midweek. As they were also still in the West German Cup, and had to release fullback Willi Schulz for international duty, they suggested to their Turkish opponents, Göztepe Ismir, that the tie be decided on one match at a neutral site—but the Turks and UEFA declined.

The West German national team rounded off its season in style in Essen, with a 12-0 win over Cyprus in a World Cup qualifier, Müller scoring four and Wolfgang Overath three. This meant that Müller had scored in six consecutive internationals, and that West Germany were well-positioned to qualify for Mexico.

Bundesliga

Club	P	W	D	L	Goals	Pts
1. Bayern Munich	34	18	10	6	61-31	46
2. Alemannia Aachen	34	16	6	12	57-51	38
3. Borussia Mönchengladbach	34	13	11	10	61-46	37
4. Eintracht Brunswick	34	13	11	10	46-43	37
5. VfB Stuttgart	34	14	8	12	60-54	36
6. Hamburg SV	34	13	10	11	55-55	36
7. FC Schalke 04	34	14	7	13	45-40	35
8. Eintracht Frankfurt	34	13	8	13	46-43	34
9. Werder Bremen	34	14	6	14	59-59	34
10. TSV 1860 Munich	34	15	4	15	44-59	34
11. Hanover 96	34	9	14	11	47-45	32
12. MSV Duisburg	34	8	16	10	33-37	32
13. 1.FC Cologne	34	13	6	15	47-56	32
14. Hertha BSC Berlin	34	12	8	14	31-39	32
15. 1.FC Kaiserslautern	34	12	6	16	45-47	30
16. Borussia Dortmund	34	11	8	15	49-54	30
17. 1.FC Nuremberg	34	9	11	14	45-55	29
18. Kickers Offenbach	34	10	8	16	42-59	28

Top Scorers
G Müller (Bayern Munich) 30
Seeler (Hamburg SV) 23
Skoblar (Hanover 96) 17
Görts (Werder Bremen) 15
Laumen (Borussia Mönchengladbach) 15
Weiss (Eintracht Brunswick) 15
Rühl (1.FC Cologne) 14
Rupp (Werder Bremen) 13
Emmerich (Borussia Dortmund) 12
Hasebrink (Kaiserslautern) 12
Klostermann (Aachen) 12

Bundesliga Promotion Playoffs

Group 1	P	W	D	L	Goals	Pts
1. Rot-Weiss Oberhausen	8	5	1	2	17-9	11
2. FC Freiburg	8	5	1	2	16-10	11
3. SV Alsenborn	8	5	0	3	20-15	10
4. Hertha 03 Zehlendorf	8	3	1	4	15-16	7
5. VfB Lübeck	8	0	1	7	10-28	1

Group 2	P	W	D	L	Goals	Pts
1. Rot-Weiss Essen	8	6	2	0	28-9	14
2. VfL Osnabrück	8	4	3	1	13-8	11
3. Karlsruhe SC	8	3	2	3	14-15	8
4. Tasmania 1900 Berlin	8	2	0	6	5-17	4
5. TuS Neuendorf	8	1	1	6	8-19	3

Regionalliga Berlin

Club	P	W	D	L	Goals	Pts
1. Hertha Zehlendorf	30	23	5	2	84-32	51
2. Tasmania 1900 Berlin	30	21	8	1	75-26	50
3. Tennis Borussia Berlin	30	20	5	5	96-38	45
4. Wacker 04 Berlin	30	19	5	6	93-31	43
5. Spandau SV	30	19	4	7	73-42	42
6. 1.FC Neukölln	30	14	7	9	72-60	35
7. Rapide Wedding	30	10	8	12	52-49	28
8. Kickers 1900 Berlin	30	10	8	12	55-54	28
9. SV Berlin 92	30	9	9	12	58-63	27
10. Blau-Weiss 90 Berlin	30	8	8	14	41-53	24
11. SC Staaken	30	9	6	15	44-61	24
12. Meteor 06 Berlin	30	8	5	17	53-88	21
13. BFC Südring	30	8	4	18	38-62	20
14. Alemannia 90 Berlin	30	5	6	19	33-75	16
15. VfL Nord Berlin	30	5	5	20	50-107	15
16. Reinickendorf Füchse	30	2	7	21	26-102	11

Promoted: Sportfreunde Neukölln, TuS Wannsee
Top Scorer: Rendant (1.FC Neukölln), 25 goals

Regionalliga North

Club	P	W	D	L	Goals	Pts
1. VfL Osnabrück	32	24	5	3	94-27	53
2. VfB Lübeck	32	19	6	7	61-39	44
3. FC St Pauli	32	19	5	8	64-37	43
4. Göttingen 05	32	16	10	6	66-51	42
5. Arminia Hanover	32	15	8	9	51-35	38
6. Phönix Lübeck	32	15	8	9	55-41	38
7. VfL Wolfsburg	32	15	8	9	59-44	38
8. Holstein Kiel	32	12	8	12	47-51	32
9. TuS Bremerhaven 93	32	10	10	12	53-57	30
10. SV Barmbek-Uhlenhorst	32	11	5	16	48-57	27
11. ASV Bergedorf 85	32	11	4	17	56-67	26
12. Concordia Hamburg	32	7	12	13	41-64	26
13. VfB Oldenburg	32	9	7	16	47-59	25
14. Itzehoe SV	32	9	5	18	47-72	23
15. TuS Celle	32	6	8	18	48-71	20
16. SV Heide	32	7	6	19	46-79	20
17. Sperber Hamburg	32	6	7	19	39-71	19

Top Scorer: Kaniber (VfL Osnabrück), 30 goals

Regionalliga North Promotion Playoffs

Group One	P	W	D	L	Goals	Pts
1. Leu Brunswick	6	4	1	1	17-7	9
2. SV Friedrichsort	6	3	2	1	15-8	8
3. TSV Uertersen	6	1	2	3	13-17	4
4. Teutonia Uelzen	6	1	1	4	7-20	3

1968-69

Group Two
	P	W	D	L	Goals	Pts
1. Olympia Wilhelmshaven	6	4	0	2	10-4	8
2. VfB Kiel	6	4	0	2	9-7	8
3. SV Hemelingen	6	2	1	3	6-6	5
4. TSV Langenhorn	6	1	1	4	6-14	3

Regionalliga South
Club	P	W	D	L	Goals	Pts
1. Karlsruhe SC	34	18	7	9	73-43	43
2. FC Freiburg	34	18	7	9	67-42	43
3. Bayern Hof	34	17	8	9	53-30	42
4. Kickers Stuttgart	34	15	12	7	66-43	42
5. Jahn Regensburg	34	14	9	11	54-38	37
6. Schweinfurt 05	34	12	12	10	67-53	36
7. SpVgg Fürth	34	13	10	11	37-36	36
8. SV Darmstadt 98	34	13	9	12	50-45	35
9. SSV Reutlingen	34	12	11	11	49-58	35
10. Hessen Kassel	34	14	5	18	60-52	33
11. SV Waldhof	34	11	11	12	44-52	33
12. ESV Ingolstadt	34	12	9	13	50-60	33
13. FC 08 Villingen	34	12	8	14	45-54	32
14. VfR Mannheim	34	12	7	15	51-54	31
15. Opel Rüsselsheim	34	12	7	15	41-55	31
16. VfL Neckarau	34	7	12	15	34-65	26
17. Schwaben Augsburg	34	9	7	18	44-55	25
18. Rot-Weiss Frankfurt	34	7	5	22	36-86	19

Top Scorer: Klier (FC 08 Villingen), 23 goals

Regionalliga South Promotion Playoffs
Club	P	W	D	L	Goals	Pts
1. VfR Heilbronn	6	3	3	0	14-9	9
2. Germania Forst	6	2	3	1	9-8	7
3. VfB Freidrichsort	6	2	1	3	9-11	5
4. SV Waldkirch	6	1	1	4	8-12	3

Also Promoted: SpVgg Bayreuth, FSV Frankfurt

Regionalliga Southwest
Club	P	W	D	L	Goals	Pts
1. SV Alsenborn	30	18	8	4	69-25	44
2. TuS Neuendorf	30	17	10	3	56-23	44
3. 1.FC Saarbrücken	30	17	7	6	71-28	41
4. FK Pirmasens	30	16	8	6	65-36	40
5. Borussia Neunkirchen	30	16	5	9	54-34	37
6. Saar 05 Saarbrücken	30	13	8	9	51-36	34
7. Südwest Ludwigshafen	30	13	7	10	42-36	33
8. Wormatia Worms	30	12	6	12	49-53	30
9. FC 08 Homburg	30	11	7	12	40-49	29
10. Eintracht Trier	30	11	6	13	47-45	28
11. FV Speyer	30	9	6	15	40-59	24
12. Röchling Völklingen	30	8	8	14	41-64	24
13. FSV 05 Mainz	30	9	5	16	40-58	23
14. SVW Mainz	30	7	7	16	33-55	21
15. VfR Frankenthal	30	6	8	16	33-64	20
16. FC Landsweiler	30	3	2	25	33-99	8

Top Scorer: Weinkauff (FK Pirmasens), 26 goals

Regionalliga Southwest Promotion Playoffs
Club	P	W	D	L	Goals	Pts
1. ASV Landau	4	3	0	1	8-6	6
2. SC Friedrichsthal	4	2	1	1	10-5	5
3. SSV Mülheim	4	0	1	3	3-10	1

Regionalliga West
Club	P	W	D	L	Goals	Pts
1. Rot-Weiss Oberhausen	34	22	9	3	69-24	53
2. Rot-Weiss Essen	34	21	9	4	72-25	51
3. VfL Bochum	34	23	5	6	86-36	51
4. Fortuna Düsseldorf	34	18	9	7	64-35	45
5. Wuppertal SV	34	16	8	10	46-41	40
6. Schwarz-Weiss Essen	34	16	8	10	48-43	40
7. Arminia Bielefeld	34	14	10	10	63-47	38
8. Bayer Leverkusen	34	12	12	10	48-35	36
9. VfR Neuss	34	8	14	12	38-52	30
10. Lünen SV	34	8	12	14	39-47	28
11. Sportfreunde Hamborn 07	34	11	8	16	46-64	28
12. TSV Marl-Hüls	34	10	7	17	33-58	27
13. Fortuna Cologne	34	7	12	15	44-69	26
14. Preussen Münster	34	8	10	16	40-63	26
15. SC Bonn	34	10	5	19	45-70	25
16. Viktoria Cologne	34	5	13	16	33-53	23
17. Eintracht Duisburg	34	7	9	18	30-64	23
18. Eintracht Gelsenkirchen	34	8	6	20	47-65	22

Top Scorer: Kuster (Arminia Bielefeld) and Lippens (Rot-Weiss Essen), 23 each

Regionalliga West Promotion Playoffs
Club	P	W	D	L	Goals	Pts
1. Wattenscheid 09	6	4	1	1	12-4	9
2. SSVg Velbert	6	3	1	2	10-4	9
3. DJK Gütersloh	6	2	1	3	5-8	5
4. Borussia Brand	6	1	1	4	4-15	3

After these playoffs had commenced, six points were deducted from Eintracht Gelsenkirchen for fielding an ineligible player. Consequently, they were relegated. A special playoff was held to determine who would replace them:
SpVgg Erkenschwick 2, SSV Hagen 1 (Erkenschwick promoted to Regionalliga)

Third Division Champions
Baden (Nordbaden): Germania Forst
Baden (Südbaden): SV Waldkirch
Bayern: SpVgg Bayreuth
Berlin: TuS Wannsee
Bremen: TuS Bremerhaven
Hamburg: TSV Langenhorn

Hessen: FSV Frankfurt
Mittelrhein: SC Jülich 1910
Niederrhein: SSV Velbert
Niedersachsen: Leu Brunswick
Rheinland: SSV Mülheim
Saarland: SC Friedrichsthal
Schleswig-Holstein: SV Friedrichsort
Südwest: ASV Landau
Westfalen: DJK Gütersloh
Württemberg: VfR Heilbronn

West German Cup
First Round
Arminia Hanover 4, Schweinfurt 05 0
Bayern Munich 0, Kickers Offenbach 0 aet (1-0)
Borussia Mönchengladbach 5, Hertha BSC Berlin 2
Eintracht Brunswick 1, TSV 1860 Munich 0
Eintracht Frankfurt 6, Borussia Dortmund 2
Eintracht Trier 1, 1.FC Nuremberg 3
FC Freiburg 0, 1.FC Kaiserslautern 1
Jahn Regensburg 0, Alemannia Aachen 1
Rot-Weiss Essen 1, Werder Bremen 2
Rot-Weiss Oberhausen 2, FC Schalke 04 3 aet
SV Alsenborn 2, MSV Duisburg 1
TSV Langenhorn-Hamburg 1, Sperber Hamburg 2
VfB Stuttgart 1, 1.FC Cologne 0
VfL Wolfsburg 1, Hamburg SV 2
Wacker 04 Berlin 1, Hanover 96 4
Wormatia Worms 2, Preussen Münster 3

Second Round
1.FC Kaiserslautern 1, Eintracht Frankfurt 0
Alemannia Aachen 2, Preussen Münster 0
Bayern Munich 1, Hanover 96 0
FC Schalke 04 3, SV Alsenborn 1
Hamburg SV 2, Borussia Mönchengladbach 0 aet
Hanover 96 2, VfB Stuttgart 2 aet (1-0)
Sperber Hamburg 0, 1.FC Nuremberg 0 aet (0-7)
Werder Bremen 5, Eintracht Brunswick 0

Quarterfinals
1.FC Kaiserslautern 3, Werder Bremen 0
1.FC Nuremberg 1, Hanover 96 0
FC Schalke 04 2, Alemannia Aachen 0
Hamburg SV 0, Bayern Munich 2

Semifinals
1.FC Kaiserslautern 1, FC Schalke 04 1 aet (1-3)
Bayern Munich 2, 1.FC Nuremberg 0

Final
in Frankfurt
Bayern Munich 2, FC Schalke 04 1

West German Internationals
25/9/68 in Marseille 1-1 v France
13/10/68 in Vienna 2-0 v Austria (WCQ)
23/11/68 in Nicosia 1-1 v Cyprus (WCQ)
14/12/68 in Rio de Janiero 2-2 v Brazil
18/12/68 in Santiago 1-2 v Chile
22/12/68 in Mexico City 0-0 v Mexico
26/3/69 in Frankfurt 1-1 v Wales
16/4/69 in Glasgow 1-1 v Scotland (WCQ)
10/5/69 in Nuremberg 1-0 v Austria (WCQ)
21/5/69 in Essen 12-0 v Cyprus (WCQ)

East German Oberliga
Club	P	W	D	L	Goals	Pts
1. Vorwärts Berlin	26	15	4	7	47-28	34
2. FC Carl Zeiss Jena	26	13	6	7	43-22	32
3. 1.FC Magdeburg	26	13	5	8	43-41	31
4. Hansa Rostock	26	10	9	7	42-33	29
5. Sachsenring Zwickau	26	10	7	9	23-19	27
6. Chemie Leipzig	26	8	11	7	30-27	27
7. FC Karl-Marx-Stadt	26	10	6	10	35-36	26
8. Rot-Weiss Erfurt	26	10	5	11	32-27	25
9. Wismut Aue	26	9	7	10	33-31	25
10. Dynamo Berlin	26	10	5	11	25-36	25
11. Chemie Halle	26	6	10	10	32-35	22
12. Stahl Riesa	26	9	4	13	26-43	22
13. 1.FC Union Berlin	26	6	8	12	29-41	20
14. Lokomotive Leipzig	26	5	9	12	16-37	19

Top Scorers
Kostmann (Hansa Rostock) 18
Zink (Wismut Aue) 13
Piepenburg (Vorwärts Berlin) 12
P Ducke (Carl Zeiss Jena) 11
Sparwasser (1.FC Magdeburg) 11
Uentz (1.FC Union Berlin) 11
Vogel (Karl-Marx-Stadt) 11
Begerad (Vorwärts Berlin) 9
Boelssen (Chemie Halle) 8
Trölitzsch (Rot-Weiss Erfurt) 8
Walter (1.FC Magdeburg) 8

Second Division (Staffel North)
Club	P	W	D	L	Goals	Pts
1. Stahl Eisenhüttenstadt	30	21	5	4	64-28	47
2. Lokomotive Stendal	30	20	6	4	55-23	46
3. Hansa Rostock II	30	13	10	7	44-26	36
4. Dynamo Berlin II	30	16	4	10	55-43	36
5. Energie Cottbus	30	12	11	7	46-28	35
6. Vorwärts Stralsund	30	12	11	7	30-27	35
7. Vorwärts Cottbus	30	13	8	9	43-29	34
8. Post Neubrandenburg	30	12	9	9	48-35	33

	P	W	D	L	Goals	Pts
9. Chemie Wolfen	30	9	11	10	30-42	29
10. Vorwärts Neubrandenburg	30	10	8	12	36-35	28
11. Dynamo Schwerin	30	11	5	14	49-53	27
12. TSG Wismar	30	9	7	14	29-41	25
13. KKW Nord Greifswald	30	6	10	14	27-41	22
14. Motor Hennigsdorf	30	6	8	16	20-49	20
15. Lichtenberg 47	30	3	8	19	17-57	14
16. Chemie Premnitz	30	2	9	19	16-52	13

Promoted: Vorwärts Berlin II, 1.FC Magdeburg II, Stahl Eisenhüttenstadt II

Second Division (Staffel South)

Club	P	W	D	L	Goals	Pts
1. Dynamo Dresden	30	20	7	3	57-9	47
2. Vorwärts Meiningen	30	16	6	8	53-37	38
3. Motor Steinach	30	13	11	6	43-29	37
4. Wismut Gera	30	13	10	7	33-24	36
5. Carl Zeiss Jena II	30	10	10	10	36-37	30
6. Lokomotive Dresden	30	10	10	10	32-34	30
7. Aktivist Böhlen	30	10	10	10	33-38	28
8. Motor Eisenach	30	10	8	12	34-34	28
9. Vorwärts Leipzig	30	7	14	9	30-31	27
10. Dynamo Eisleben	30	10	7	13	26-36	26
11. Motor Wema Plauen	30	11	4	15	33-43	26
12. Sachsenring Zwickau II	30	9	8	13	31-50	25
13. Kali Werra Tiefenort	30	9	7	14	39-43	25
14. Chemie Zeitz	30	8	9	13	26-31	25
15. Chemie Riesa	30	8	8	14	32-40	24
16. Rot-Weiss Erfurt II	30	7	9	14	15-37	23

Promoted: Chemie Halle II, Motor Hermsdorf, Motor Nordhausen-West

East German Cup Final
in Dresden
1.FC Magdeburg 4, Karl-Marx-Stadt 0

East German Internationals
20/10/68 in Stargard 1-1 v Poland
23/3/69 in Berlin 2-2 v Italy
16/4/69 in Dresden 2-1 v Wales (WCQ)
22/6/69 in Magdeburg 0-1 v Chile
9/7/69 in Rostock 7-0 v Egypt
25/7/69 in Leipzig 2-2 v USSR

European Cup
First Round
1.FC Nuremberg v Ajax Amsterdam .... (1-1, 0-4)

Cup-Winners' Cup
First Round
Bordeaux v 1.FC Cologne .... (2-1, 0-3)
Second Round
ADO The Hague v 1.FC Cologne .... (0-1, 0-3)
Quarterfinals
1.FC Cologne v Randers Freja .... (2-1, 3-0)
Semifinals
1.FC Cologne v Barcelona .... (2-2, 1-4)

Fairs Cup
First Round
Hanover 96 v Odense .... (3-2, 1-0)
Metz v Hamburg SV .... (1-4, 2-3)
Wacker Innsbruck v Eintracht Frankfurt .... (2-2, 0-3)
Hansa Rostock v Nice .... (3-0, 1-2)
Legia Warsaw v TSV 1860 Munich .... (6-0, 3-2)
Lokomotive Leipzig walkover v KB Copenhagen
Second Round
AIK Stockholm v Hanover 96 .... (4-2, 2-5)
Hamburg SV v Slavia Prague .... (4-1, 1-3)
Juventus v Eintracht Frankfurt .... (0-0, 0-1 aet)
Hansa Rostock v Fiorentina .... (3-2, 1-0)
Hibernian v Lokomotive Leipzig .... (3-1, 1-0)
Third Round
Hamburg SV v Hibernian .... (1-0, 1-2)
Athletic Bilbao v Eintracht Frankfurt .... (1-0, 1-1)
Quarterfinals
Göztepe Ismir walkover v Hamburg SV

1969-70

Foals' gold

In their four seasons since being promoted to the Bundesliga, Borussia Mönchengladbach had displayed little difficulty in scoring goals. Totals of 57, 70, 77 and 61 meant that they had outscored every other side over this period. So *Trainer* Hennes Weisweiler finally concluded that he really ought to do something about his rather leaky defence.

On the final day of the previous season Weisweiler had missed Gladbach's match at Bremen in order to attend the relegation battle between Cologne and Nuremberg. It is widely reported that Weisweiler waited on the car park in order to intercept Nuremberg's Luggi Müller and that he signed him there and then. Shortly afterwards Weisweiler persuaded highly-experienced defender Klaus-Dieter Sieloff to leave VfB Stuttgart.

Mönchengladbach's season began with a 2-0 defeat at Schalke and a 2-1 home win over defending champions Bayern Munich. Another couple of victories brought fleeting fame to a youngster named Werner Kaiser, who scored three goals in three games. But Kaiser disappeared just as quickly and wound up playing for 1.FC Saarbrücken in the Regionalliga Southwest. With a couple of disappointing results leaving them in mid-table, *die Fohlen* (the Foals) embarked on an eleven-match unbeaten run culminating in a 6-1 romp over Oberhausen. The big match, however, was the fourteenth game of the season, where Borussia won 1-0 in Cologne before a crowd of 54,000 to take over leadership of the league.

From then on, Gladbach remained at the top. Much of the time they boasted a five-point lead over their pursuers, but the gap was whittled down alarmingly as the end of the season approached. Their final home match was against Hamburg SV, by which time Borussia were left needing a win to be assured of the title. The home team played superbly; fullback Berti Vogts scored with a long-range scorcher as Gladbach built up a comfortable 4-0 lead. But with one hand virtually on the championship plate, Borussia suddenly went to pieces and found themselves pegged back to 4-3. At this point the Gladbach players discovered *Trainer* Weisweiler on the field in the home penalty area, purple with rage and berating his defence before (not unexpectedly) being sent off by the referee. Gladbach managed to cling to the 4-3 scoreline and also won their final match in Oberhausen 4-3 to set a new Bundesliga record of 51 points. They finished four points above second-placed Bayern—whose 7-2 victory at home to Hanover on April 11 marked the start of a 73-match home unbeaten streak which would not end until over four years later. In March Bayern decided to replace their Yugoslavian *Trainer* Branko Zebec with an assistant to the West German national team named Udo Lattek. The little-known Lattek would spend the next five seasons at the helm, emerging as one of the most successful *Trainers* in German football history.

Hertha Berlin finished in third place, with an average home gate of over 41,000. Nearly 75,000 saw their opening-day win over MSV Duisburg, and in September 88,075 filled the Olympiastadion for their match with Cologne—a single-match attendance record which stands to this day. Wolfgang Gayer's second-half goal gave the hosts a 1-0 victory.

Alemannia Aachen, the surprise of the previous year, endured a dismal season, particularly away from home where they gained only one point and suffered heavy defeats at Bayern (6-0), Frankfurt (6-2), Hanover (5-0) and Stuttgart (5-0). At one stage Aachen went nineteen matches without a victory, scoring just eleven goals in the process. After a defeat at Brunswick (3-0) and a goalless draw at home to Bremen in December, *Trainer* Georg Stollenwerk was released, but replacement Willibert Weth would have to wait seventeen matches before Alemannia won again. And thus the previous season's runners-up were relegated.

Also relegated were the 1966 champions TSV 1860 Munich, who picked up just one victory away from home. It would be seven years until the Lions would regain their position in the top flight, by which time rivals Bayern would overtake them as the city's premier club. It also meant the last Bundesliga appearance for TSV's charismatic goalkeeper "Radi" Radenkovic.

Two years after threatening to take a Bundesliga scalp in the West German Cup, Jahn Regensburg created the shock of the season by knocking out Eintracht Brunswick in the first round. But they again stumbled against Bayern Munich. Bayern then lost to 1.FC Nuremberg—who were hammering away in the Regionalliga South after their relegation from the Bundesliga—before 70,000 in the Frankenstadion. But Offenbach, who had knocked out Munich 1860, Dortmund, and Frankfurt, won a thrilling extra-time encounter with Nuremberg in the following round. With just two minutes left to play, and the score at 2-2, Helmut Kremers scored for Offenbach. Helmut Nerlinger added a fourth to seal the victory.

The final was held in August as a curtain-raiser to the new season and provided a fascinating contrast between the all-out attacking style of Ernst Ocwirk's Cologne and the more measured, defensive approach of Aki Schmidt's Offenbach. Cologne were big favourites, but they were 2-0 down after twenty minutes, the first coming from Horst Gecks' magnificent 70-yard run. Cologne tried desperately to get themselves back into the match, but all they managed was a goal from Hannes Löhr and Offenbach went on to hoist their first—and to date only—major trophy.

For Kickers, who had finished bottom of the Bundesliga the previous year, it was a memorable season: they also finished a point in front of Karlsruhe to win the

Regionalliga South. They then put together a string of good results in the playoff to regain promotion to the top flight at the first attempt. Arminia Bielefeld, who had finished runners-up to VfL Bochum in the Regionalliga West, clinched the other promotion spot, conceding just three goals in their eight playoff matches.

It was also the start of a downward spiral for SV Alsenborn of the Regionalliga Southwest. For the third year in a row, Alsenborn had won their division, but each time in the promotion playoffs they had faltered. This season, they won both matches against VfL Osnabrück and Tennis Borussia Berlin but lost each of their games with Arminia Bielefeld and Karlsruhe SC. The third-place playoff finish kept them in the Regionalliga for yet another season. There, they would finish fifth, third, eighth, and tenth in the seasons to come and, somewhat controversially, failed to get into the Second Bundesliga in 1974 when 1.FC Saarbrücken were admitted in their place.

Carl Zeiss Jena were comfortable winners of the East German League, taking their second title in three years. Behind the sharp-shooting of Helmut Stein, Norbert Scheitler, and Peter Ducke, who together scored over half the club's goals, Jena finished seven points clear of runners-up Vorwärts Berlin and ended the season with an unbeaten home record. Vorwärts gained the other major domestic honour, winning the East German Cup Final over Lokomotive Leipzig.

East Germany lost 3-0 to Italy in Naples in the final match of their World Cup qualifying group and once again failed to qualify for the tournament. West Germany were strengthened by the decision of Uwe Seeler to stage a comeback at the age of 33. Despite having announced his retirement eighteen months earlier, and having missed the intervening thirteen games, Seeler was re-appointed captain and played a vital role in the West German World Cup campaign. The Germans, who had finished ahead of Scotland, Austria, and Cyprus in their qualifying group, began the tournament in Mexico against Morocco and were a goal down until the 56th minute. But Seeler equalised and Gerd Müller netted the winner. Müller ran riot against Bulgaria, scoring a hat-trick, and against Peru, scoring three times more. West Germany finished top of their group.

The ensuing quarterfinal was an epic tussle with England which went to extra-time. England had taken a commanding lead, but the Germans, inspired by winger Jürgen Grabowski's appearance as substitute, worked themselves back into the game. Uwe Seeler's back-headed equaliser was either one of the most brilliant goals in the history of the competition or a complete fluke, but Müller's close-range volley in extra time completed an amazing comeback.

After four matches in Leon, West Germany moved to Mexico City for the semifinal against Italy. This game was to mark the final international appearance of Hamburg's Willi Schulz, who had gained the first of his 66 caps back in 1959. Italy took a seventh-minute lead through Boninsegna, and the Germans had to wait until the 89th minute before levelling the score. Five goals were scored in extra time, three of them to Italy, with Beckenbauer's right shoulder heavily strapped to protect an injury. West Germany beat Uruguay 1-0 in the meaningless third place match, and Müller's ten goals made him the tournament's leading scorer.

Although Seeler was voted Germany's Footballer of the Year, Müller, whose 38 goals was far and away the best in the Bundesliga, upstaged him by being named European Footballer of the Year.

Bundesliga

Club	P	W	D	L	Goals	Pts
1. Borussia Mönchengladbach	34	23	5	6	71-29	51
2. Bayern Munich	34	21	5	8	88-37	47
3. Hertha BSC Berlin	34	20	5	9	67-41	45
4. 1.FC Cologne	34	20	3	11	83-38	43
5. Borussia Dortmund	34	14	8	12	60-67	36
6. Hamburg SV	34	12	11	11	57-54	35
7. VfB Stuttgart	34	14	7	13	59-62	35
8. Eintracht Frankfurt	34	12	10	12	54-54	34
9. FC Schalke 04	34	11	12	11	43-54	34
10. 1.FC Kaiserslautern	34	10	12	12	44-55	32
11. Werder Bremen	34	10	11	13	38-47	31
12. Rot-Weiss Essen	34	8	15	11	41-54	31
13. Hanover 96	34	11	8	15	49-61	30
14. Rot-Weiss Oberhausen	34	11	7	16	50-62	29
15. MSV Duisburg	34	9	11	14	35-48	29
16. Eintracht Brunswick	34	9	10	15	40-49	28
17. TSV 1860 Munich	34	9	7	18	41-56	25
18. Alemannia Aachen	34	5	7	22	31-83	17

Top Scorers
G Müller (Bayern Munich) 38
Weist (Borussia Dortmund) 20
Fischer (TSV 1860 Munich) 19
Laumen (Borussia Mönchengladbach) ... 19
Löhr (1.FC Cologne) 19
Seeler (Hamburg SV) 17
Rupp (1.FC Cologne) 16
Brungs (Hertha BSC Berlin) 15
Dausmann (Rot-Weiss Oberhausen) 15
Gayer (Hertha BSC Berlin) 13
Horr (Hertha BSC Berlin) 13

Bundesliga Promotion Playoffs

Group 1

	P	W	D	L	Goals	Pts
1. Arminia Bielefeld	8	5	2	1	13-3	12
2. Karlsruhe SC	8	5	1	2	16-8	11
3. SV Alsenborn	8	4	0	4	12-12	8
4. Tennis Borussia Berlin	8	1	3	4	7-13	5
5. VfL Osnabrück	8	1	2	8	6-18	4

Group 2

	P	W	D	L	Goals	Pts
1. Kickers Offenbach	8	5	2	1	17-8	12
2. VfL Bochum	8	4	1	3	14-7	9
3. Hertha 03 Zehlendorf	8	4	0	4	17-14	8
4. VfL Wolfsburg	8	2	2	4	13-21	6
5. FK Pirmasens	8	1	3	4	12-23	5

Regionalliga Berlin

Club	P	W	D	L	Goals	Pts
1. Hertha Zehlendorf	26	22	3	1	101-23	47
2. Tennis Borussia Berlin	26	18	3	5	70-23	39
3. Tasmania 1900 Berlin	26	16	7	3	64-23	39
4. Blau-Weiss 90 Berlin	26	13	8	5	63-33	34
5. Wacker 04 Berlin	26	13	8	5	58-36	34
6. SV Spandau	26	10	9	7	47-44	29
7. Rapide Wedding	26	9	8	9	46-51	26
8. 1.FC Neukölln	26	8	6	12	31-47	22
9. TuS Wannsee	26	7	7	12	32-36	21
10. SC Staaken	26	7	6	13	32-51	20
11. SV Berlin 92	26	4	11	11	34-50	19
12. Kickers 1900 Berlin	26	4	6	16	31-65	14
13. Meteor 06 Berlin	26	3	6	17	29-66	12
14. Sportfreunde Neukölln	26	2	4	20	15-105	8

Top Scorer: Faeder (Hertha Zehlendorf), 26 goals
Promoted: Alemannia 90 Berlin, VfL Nord Berlin

Regionalliga North

Club	P	W	D	L	Goals	Pts
1. VfL Osnabrück	32	21	5	6	75-38	47
2. VfL Wolfsburg	32	19	8	5	78-35	46
3. Holstein Kiel	32	17	10	5	64-37	44
4. FC St Pauli	32	18	6	8	56-33	42
5. Göttingen 05	32	18	5	9	65-42	41
6. TuS Bremerhaven 93	32	16	5	11	57-47	37
7. VfB Lübeck	32	14	8	10	46-41	36
8. Arminia Hanover	32	13	7	12	53-51	33
9. VfB Oldenburg	32	12	9	11	44-48	33
10. SV Barmbek-Uhlenhorst	32	10	10	12	42-45	30
11. TuS Celle	32	10	6	16	39-61	26
12. Itzehoe SV	32	10	4	18	57-71	24
13. Phönix Lübeck	32	8	8	16	41-61	24
14. Leu Brunswick	32	9	5	18	42-57	23
15. Olympia Wilhelmshaven	32	5	12	15	28-49	22
16. ASV Bergedorf 85	32	9	4	19	46-79	22
17. Concordia Hamburg	32	4	6	22	22-60	14

Top Scorer: Kemmer (VfL Wolfsburg), 25 goals

Regionalliga North Promotion Playoffs

Group One

	P	W	D	L	Goals	Pts
1. Sperber Hamburg	6	2	4	0	9-7	8
2. SV Meppen	6	2	3	1	15-12	7
3. Union Salzgitter	6	2	1	3	10-13	5
4. SV Friedrichsort	6	1	2	3	10-12	4

Group Two

	P	W	D	L	Goals	Pts
1. Heide SV	6	4	0	2	15-10	8
2. Polizei Bremen	6	2	2	2	11-11	6
3. TSV Langenhorn	6	2	2	2	6-9	6
4. OSV Hanover	6	1	2	3	12-14	4

The Regionalliga North was expanded from 17 to 18 clubs, so an additional playoff was held to determine the 18th club:

Club	P	W	D	L	Goals	Pts
1. SV Meppen	2	1	0	1	7-1	2
2. ASV Bergedorf 85	2	1	0	1	2-3	2
3. Polizei Bremen	2	1	0	1	3-6	2

Regionalliga South

Club	P	W	D	L	Goals	Pts
1. Kickers Offenbach	38	27	5	6	93-47	59
2. Karlsruhe SC	38	23	12	3	87-37	58
3. 1.FC Nuremberg	38	24	9	5	64-29	57
4. Bayern Hof	38	19	9	10	65-40	47
5. Schweinfurt 05	38	18	6	14	78-59	42
6. FC Freiburg	38	14	12	12	63-48	40
7. Hessen Kassel	38	15	10	13	54-50	40
8. SpVgg Fürth	38	14	10	14	49-50	38
9. FC Villingen 08	38	14	9	15	61-58	37
10. Jahn Regensburg	38	12	11	15	61-59	35
11. SSV Reutlingen	38	12	11	15	51-56	35
12. Kickers Stuttgart	38	13	7	18	61-57	33
13. Opel Rüsselsheim	38	12	9	17	50-50	33
14. VfR Heilbronn	38	11	11	16	50-57	33
15. VfR Mannheim	38	12	9	17	48-61	33
16. ESV Ingolstadt	38	10	10	18	55-77	30
17. SpVgg Bayreuth	38	9	12	17	58-80	30
18. SV Darmstadt 98	38	12	6	20	50-89	30
19. FSV Frankfurt	38	9	7	22	34-79	25
20. SV Waldhof	38	8	9	21	50-99	25

Top Scorer: Klier (FC 08 Villingen), 22 goals
Relegation playoff (in Fürth): ESV Ingolstadt 5, SpVgg Bayreuth 2; Bayreuth relegated

Regionalliga South Promotion Playoff

Club	P	W	D	L	Goals	Pts
1. SV Göppingen	6	3	3	0	12-6	9
2. FV 09 Weinheim	6	3	2	1	14-9	8
3. SV Tübingen	6	1	2	3	6-11	4
4. SV Waldkirch	6	0	3	3	6-12	3

Also Promoted: Viktoria Aschaffenburg, Wacker Munich

Regionalliga Southwest

Club	P	W	D	L	Goals	Pts
1. SV Alsenborn	30	20	7	3	69-23	47
2. FK Pirmasens	30	19	6	5	68-36	44
3. Südwest Ludwigshafen	30	16	7	7	45-30	39
4. Borussia Neunkirchen	30	15	7	8	63-40	37
5. FV Speyer	30	13	7	10	42-41	33
6. 1.FC Saarbrücken	30	12	8	10	47-31	32
7. ASV Landau	30	13	6	11	44-31	32
8. TuS Neuendorf	30	14	3	13	45-51	31
9. Saar 05 Saarbrücken	30	11	6	13	42-47	28
10. Eintracht Trier	30	12	4	14	36-48	28
11. Wormatia Worms	30	10	5	15	50-57	25
12. FSV 05 Mainz	30	10	5	15	37-58	25
13. Röchling Völklingen	30	8	7	15	34-41	23
14. FC 08 Homburg	30	8	4	18	41-54	20
15. SVW Mainz	30	7	6	17	38-76	20
16. SC Friedrichsthal	30	4	8	18	41-78	16

Top Scorer: Weinkauff (FK Pirmasens), 22 goals

Regionalliga Southwest Promotion Playoff

Club	P	W	D	L	Goals	Pts
1. VfR Frankenthal	4	3	1	0	12-5	7
2. VfB Theley	4	1	1	2	5-9	3
3. VfL Neuwied	4	0	2	2	5-8	2

Regionalliga West

Club	P	W	D	L	Goals	Pts
1. VfL Bochum	34	21	8	5	63-32	50
2. Arminia Bielefeld	34	20	8	6	61-30	48
3. Wuppertal SV	34	19	8	7	71-39	46
4. Fortuna Düsseldorf	34	18	8	8	65-33	44
5. Schwarz-Weiss Essen	34	18	6	10	60-41	42
6. Lünen SV	34	12	14	8	52-37	38
7. Preussen Münster	34	15	7	12	69-58	37
8. Wattenscheid 09	34	10	14	10	49-53	34
9. VfR Neuss	34	13	6	15	50-53	32
10. DJK Gütersloh	34	10	11	13	42-48	31
11. Bayer Leverkusen	34	10	11	13	48-65	31
12. Viktoria Cologne	34	11	8	15	53-57	30
13. SC Bonn	34	11	8	15	39-47	30
14. Fortuna Cologne	34	9	12	13	50-59	30
15. SpVgg Erkenschwick	34	10	7	17	38-53	27
16. Sportfreunde Hamborn 07	34	7	10	17	52-69	24
17. SSVg Velbert	34	6	10	18	37-73	22
18. TSV Marl-Hüls	34	4	8	22	29-81	16

Top Scorer: Walitza (VfL Bochum), 31 goals

Regionalliga West Promotion Playoffs

Club	P	W	D	L	Goals	Pts
1. Eintracht Gelsenkirchen	4	2	1	1	10-8	5
2. Westfalia Herne	4	1	2	1	5-7	4
3. SpVgg Sterkrade 06/07	4	1	1	2	6-6	3

Third Division Champions

Baden (Nordbaden): FV 09 Weinheim
Baden (Südbaden): SV Waldkirch
Bayern: Wacker Munich
Berlin: Alemannia 90 Berlin
Bremen: SV Polizei
Hamburg: TSV Langenhorn
Hessen: Eintracht Frankfurt (Am.)
Mittelrhein: SC Jülich 1910

1969-70 55

Niederrhein: SpVgg Sterkrade 06/07
Niedersachsen: Eintracht Brunswick (Am.)
Rheinland: VfL Neuwied
Saarland: VfB Theley
Schleswig-Holstein: SV Friedrichsort
Südwest: VfB Frankenthal
Westfalen: Eintracht Gelsenkirchen
Württemberg: SV Göppingen

West German Cup
First Round
1.FC Nuremberg 1, VfB Stuttgart 0
Arminia Hanover 0, Alemannia Aachen 3
Eintracht Gelsenkirchen 1, Borussia Mönchengladbach 3
FC 08 Villingen 1, Hamburg SV 3
FK Pirmasens 1, Hertha BSC Berlin 2
Göttingen 05 0, MSV Duisburg 1 aet
Hanover 96 3, Rot-Weiss Oberhausen 2
Jahn Regensburg 1, Eintracht Brunswick 0
Kickers Offenbach 4, TSV 1860 Munich 1
Rot-Weiss Essen 3, 1.FC Cologne 3 aet (1-5)
Schwarz-Weiss Essen 1, Borussia Dortmund 2
SV Alsenborn 1, FC Schalke 04 5
Tennis Borussia Berlin 0, Werder Bremen 2
VfL Osnabrück 1, Eintracht Frankfurt 2 aet
Wattenscheid 09 1, Bayern Munich 6
Wuppertal SV 1, 1.FC Kaiserslautern 0

Second Round
1.FC Cologne 6, MSV Duisburg 1
Alemannia Aachen 1, Werder Bremen 1 aet (1-1 aet; Aachen won on coin toss)
Bayern Munich 4, Jahn Regensburg 0
Eintracht Frankfurt 2, Hamburg SV 0
FC Schalke 04 0, Hertha BSC Berlin 0 aet (0-4)
Hanover 96 1, Borussia Mönchengladbach 3
Kickers Offenbach 2, Borussia Dortmund 1 aet
Wuppertal SV 0, 1.FC Nuremberg 3

Quarterfinals
1.FC Nuremberg 2, Bayern Munich 1
Alemannia Aachen 1, Hertha BSC Berlin 0
Borussia Mönchengladbach 2, 1.FC Cologne 3 aet
Eintracht Frankfurt 0, Kickers Offenbach 3

Semifinals
Alemannia Aachen 0, 1.FC Cologne 4
Kickers Offenbach 4, 1.FC Nuremberg 2 aet

Final
in Hanover
Kickers Offenbach 2, 1.FC Cologne 1

West German Internationals
21/9/69 in Vienna 1-1 v Austria
24/9/69 in Sofia 1-0 v Bulgaria
22/10/69 in Hamburg 3-2 v Scotland (WCQ)
11/2/70 in Seville 0-2 v Spain
8/4/70 in Stuttgart 1-1 v Rumania
9/5/70 in Berlin 2-1 v Ireland
13/5/70 in Hanover 1-0 v Yugoslavia
3/6/70 in Leon 2-1 v Morocco (WC)
7/6/70 in Leon 5-2 v Bulgaria (WC)
10/6/70 in Leon 3-1 v Peru (WC)
14/6/70 in Leon 3-2 v England aet (WC)
17/6/70 in Mexico City 3-4 v Italy aet (WC)
20/6/70 in Mexico City 1-0 v Uruguay (WC)

East German Oberliga

Club	P	W	D	L	Goals	Pts
1. Carl Zeiss Jena	26	16	7	3	50-16	39
2. Vorwärts Berlin	26	12	8	6	43-34	32
3. Dynamo Dresden	26	13	5	8	36-26	31
4. Chemie Leipzig	26	11	8	7	33-27	30
5. Sachsenring Zwickau	26	9	10	7	25-26	28
6. Dynamo Berlin	26	10	8	8	29-32	28
7. Wismut Aue	26	10	7	9	31-34	27
8. 1.FC Magdeburg	26	10	4	12	37-37	24
9. Rot-Weiss Erfurt	26	8	8	10	32-40	24
10. Chemie Halle	26	8	6	12	35-34	22
11. Stahl Riesa	26	9	4	13	31-35	22
12. Hansa Rostock	26	7	7	12	22-33	21
13. FC Karl-Marx-Stadt	26	7	5	14	27-42	19
14. Stahl Eisenhüttenstadt	26	5	7	14	21-36	17

Top Scorers
Skrowny (Chemie Leipzig) 12
Begerad (Vorwärts Leipzig) 11
Nowotny (Chemie Halle) 10
Lehmann (Stahl Riesa) 9
Scheitler (Carl Zeiss Jena) 9
Sparwasser (1.FC Magdeburg) 9
Stein (Carl Zeiss Jena) 9
Albrecht (Rot-Weiss Erfurt) 8
P Ducke (Carl Zeiss Jena) 8
Freyer (Stahl Riesa) 8
Piepenburg (Vorwärts Berlin) 8
Vogel (Karl-Marx-Stadt) 8

Second Division (Staffel North)

Club	P	W	D	L	Goals	Pts
1. 1.FC Union Berlin	30	19	5	6	58-17	43
2. Lokomotive Stendal	30	18	6	6	62-25	42
3. Dynamo Berlin II	30	14	11	5	43-29	39
4. Energie Cottbus	30	14	10	6	45-30	38

1969-70

		P	W	D	L	Goals	Pts
5.	Post Neubrandenburg	30	14	5	11	41-40	33
6.	KKW Nord Greifswald	30	11	10	9	40-41	32
7.	Hansa Rostock II	30	12	7	11	40-36	31
8.	Vorwärts Stralsund	30	10	10	10	28-34	30
9.	Stahl Eisenhüttenstadt II	30	8	11	11	30-33	27
10.	Chemie Wolfen	30	8	11	11	32-37	27
11.	Vorwärts Cottbus	30	7	13	10	31-46	27
12.	TSG Wismar	30	10	6	4	33-43	26
13.	Vorwärts Berlin II	30	9	7	14	45-43	25
14.	Dynamo Schwerin	30	9	6	15	39-46	24
15.	Vorwärts Neubrandenburg	30	6	9	15	22-47	21
16.	1.FC Magdeburg II	30	4	7	19	30-72	15

Promoted: Stahl Brandenburg, Motor WW Warnemünde. Stahl Eisenhüttenstadt II did not participate at this level in the following season.

Second Division (Staffel South)

Club	P	W	D	L	Goals	Pts
1. Lokomotive Leipzig	30	22	4	4	83-23	48
2. Wismut Gera	30	21	5	4	47-16	47
3. Sachsenring Zwickau II	30	15	4	11	52-46	34
4. Kali Werra Tiefenort	30	13	8	9	32-37	34
5. Chemie Böhlen	30	10	11	9	33-38	31
6. Chemie Halle II	30	11	9	10	33-42	31
7. Dynamo Eisleben	30	8	14	8	36-31	30
8. Carl Zeiss Jena II	30	12	5	13	39-36	29
9. Vorwärts Meiningen	30	10	8	12	51-38	28
10. Motor Wema Plauen	30	6	16	8	39-42	28
11. Motor Nordhausen-West	30	9	9	12	27-40	27
12. Lokomotive Dresden	30	8	10	12	38-41	26
13. Motor Steinach	30	10	5	15	39-44	25
14. Motor Eisenach	30	8	9	13	28-45	25
15. Motor Hermsdorf	30	5	12	13	31-58	22
16. Vorwärts Leipzig	30	2	11	17	21-52	15

Promoted: Chemie Glauchau, Chemie Leipzig II, Dynamo Dresden II

East German Cup Final
in Dresden
Vorwärts Berlin 4, Lokomotive Leipzig 2

East German Internationals
22/10/69 in Cardiff 3-1 v Wales (WCQ)
22/11/69 in Naples 0-3 v Italy (WCQ)
8/12/69 in Baghdad 1-1 v Iraq
19/12/69 in Cairo 3-1 v Egypt
16/5/70 in Krakow 1-1 v Poland
26/7/70 in Jena 5-0 v Iraq

European Cup
First Round
Bayern Munich v St. Etienne .... (2-0, 0-3)
Vorwärts Berlin v Panathinaikos .... (2-0, 1-1)
Second Round
Vorwärts Berlin v Red Star Belgrade .... (2-1, 2-3)
Quarterfinals
Vorwärts Berlin v Feyenoord .... (1-0, 0-2)

Cup-Winners' Cup
First Round
Shamrock Rovers v FC Schalke 04 .... (2-1, 0-3)
1.FC Magdeburg v MTK Budapest .... (1-0, 1-1 aet)
Second Round
IFK Norrköping v FC Schalke 04 .... (0-0, 0-1)
1.FC Magdeburg v Academica Coimbra .... (1-0, 0-2)
Quarterfinals
Dynamo Zagreb v FC Schalke 04 .... (1-3, 0-1)
Semifinals
FC Schalke 04 v Manchester City .... (1-0, 1-5)

Fairs Cup
First Round
VfB Stuttgart v Malmö FF .... (3-0, 1-1)
Union Las Palmas v Hertha BSC Berlin .... (0-0, 0-1)
TSV 1860 Munich v Skeid Oslo .... (2-2, 1-2)
Hanover 96 v Ajax Amsterdam .... (2-1, 0-3)
Carl Zeiss Jena v Altay Izmir .... (1-0, 0-0)
Hansa Rostock v Panionios Athens .... (3-0, 0-2)
Second Round
Hertha BSC Berlin v Juventus .... (3-1, 0-0)
VfB Stuttgart v Napoli .... (0-0, 0-1)
Carl Zeiss Jena v Cagliari .... (2-0, 1-0)
Hansa Rostock v Inter Milan .... (2-1, 0-3)
Third Round
Vitoria Setubal v Hertha BSC Berlin .... (1-1, 0-1)
Carl Zeiss Jena v Ujpest Dozsa .... (1-0, 3-0)
Quarterfinals
Hertha BSC Berlin v Inter Milan .... (1-0, 0-2)
Carl Zeiss Jena v Ajax Amsterdam .... (3-1, 1-5)

1970-71

The darkest hours

Borussia Mönchengladbach, strengthened by the return of Jupp Heynckes from Hanover 96, were determined to become the first team to retain the Bundesliga championship. Although their 0-0 home stalemate against Hanover was the first time they had failed to score at home for nearly two years, they established a new Bundesliga record by going the first thirteen matches of the season undefeated, albeit with six wins and seven draws. The next game was a 4-2 defeat against their bogey team, Hertha BSC, and despite winning the following three matches Gladbach arrived at the halfway stage one point adrift of Bayern Munich at the top.

The mid-season revelation that Herbert Laumen and Peter Dietrich were to be allowed to go to Werder Bremen in the summer was something of a surprise, as were two successive defeats, 2-0 at home to lowly Arminia Bielefeld and 3-2 in the local derby at Cologne. But Gladbach were not to be beaten again, as they finished the season with just three defeats—even though the league table shows four matches lost.

Why the discrepancy? It came about during the home fixture with Werder Bremen on April 3. The score was level at 1-1 with only two minutes left to play, when Gladbach hoisted a hopeful high ball into the Bremen six-yard box. Under challenge from Laumen, Werder keeper Günter Bernard pushed the ball over the bar. But the two players collided and ended up in the back of the net. The left goalpost snapped off at ground level and the goal collapsed. Now what? The referee was quite happy to allow the groundsmen as much time as they required to repair the structure, but the Gladbach players wouldn't co-operate and decided they wanted the match abandoned—in the hope of gaining full points from a subsequent replay. On the day they appeared to have got their way, but a quickly-convened DFB hearing awarded the match 2-0 to Bremen.

The championship race grew hotter and hotter. With two matches left, Gladbach were leading Bayern on goal difference. Gladbach won 4-3 at home to bottom side Rot-Weiss Essen, nearly throwing the match away after having gone 4-1 up with half an hour to play. Meanwhile Bayern were beating Eintracht Brunswick 4-1 at home. So with one match left, Bayern had taken over the lead by one goal.

On the last day of the season, June 5, Bayern were away to MSV Duisburg and Gladbach were away to Eintracht Frankfurt. At half time, there was no score in Duisburg and Frankfurt were drawing 1-1 with Borussia. The outcome of the championship came down to the last 45 minutes of the season. Heynckes scored twice in the last twelve minutes as Borussia cantered to a 4-1 win. But two goals from Rainer Budde sank Bayern's title aspirations, as Duisburg won 2-0. Gladbach wound up being champions by two clear points.

Things were equally as exciting at the bottom end of the table—and considerably more controversial. Although Rot-Weiss Essen were already doomed to relegation, going into the last match there were still six clubs scrambling to avoid the other spot. Seventeenth-placed Arminia Bielefeld went to third-placed Hertha BSC Berlin and pulled off an astonishing 1-0 victory to make a last-gasp escape, leaving Kickers Offenbach, who had lost 4-2 in Cologne, to take the drop. A mightily-relieved Rot-Weiss Oberhausen clung to Bundesliga status on goal difference, just one goal better off than Offenbach. But huge sections of the 37,000 crowd in the Berlin Olympiastadion had spent a great deal of the afternoon chanting "Fix! Fix!"

The following day was the 50th birthday of Horst-Gregario Canellas, the President of Kickers Offenbach. At a party in his honour, at exactly twelve o'clock, he produced a tape recorder and asked everyone to gather round. He pressed the play button—and German football entered its darkest hours. As the reels went round, the shocked listeners heard proof of bribery and corruption in the Bundesliga almost beyond belief.

It transpired that—just as the crowd in the Olympiastadion had suspected—the Hertha players had accepted large sums of money from Bielefeld to let Arminia win. The DFB started an urgent enquiry, and soon discovered that this was only the tip of the iceberg. As far back as April 17, Schalke 04 had accepted bribes to lose their match in Bielefeld, and Offenbach had also tried to buy a few favourable results. More and more offences came to light, and many other manipulations were suspected but never proven. After lengthy legal processes stretching well into next season and in some cases going on for almost six years, no fewer than 52 players were fined or banned.

Fifteen Hertha players were found to have received bribes and were banned. Eintracht Brunswick's entire playing squad of sixteen was suspended—for accepting bribes to *win* what for them was a meaningless match. Thirteen Schalke players were banned, including Klaus Fischer, Stan Libuda, Rolf Russmann, Dieter Burdenski, Jürgen Wittkamp, Jürgen Sobieray and Klaus Fichtel—all household names playing for one of Germany's biggest clubs. The *Trainers* of Oberhausen and Bielefeld were banned, along with various chairmen and directors. The whole sordid affair rumbled on for years to come.

The scandal was to have a profound impact at the turnstiles. Over the next two seasons, gates would fall by over two million, from a per-match average of 20,064 in 1971 to just 16,372 in 1973—which remains the lowest in Bundesliga history. Fortunately, the arrival of the 1974 World Cup would regenerate interest.

It was also an unforgettable season for Rudi Gutendorf, who became the first Bundesliga *Trainer* to be sacked twice in the same season, by Schalke in September and by Offenbach in February. Offenbach managed another "first" by getting through three different *Trainers*, having used Aki Schmidt for a couple of months, then Gutendorf, and finally giving Kuno Klötzer a whole four months—but all in vain; Kickers were relegated.

The West German Cup continued to prove a happy hunting ground for Bayern, who won their fourth *Pokal* in the last six years. For the first time, penalty kicks were used to decide matches still drawn after extra time of a replay, and it was VfL Wolfsburg who created history by becoming the first side ever to lose in this manner, going out to Schalke 3-1 in *Elfmeterschiessen* after 2-2 and 1-1 draws. Tasmania Berlin, a name nearly forgotten in top-level football, but easy winners of the Regionalliga Berlin, made headlines of a sort for their first-round victory over Eintracht Brunswick.

Cologne again played the role of beaten finalists as young Edgar Schneider thumped a shot from the left wing into the far corner of the net with two minutes of extra time to play, giving Bayern the win. Oddly, Gerd Müller, who had scored ten times in the three rounds leading up to the final, failed to get himself on the scoresheet in the 2-1 victory. There had been further frustration for Cologne several weeks earlier: a semifinal defeat against Juventus in the Fairs Cup which yet again prevented them from appearing in the final of a major European competition.

Two clubs who would go on to enjoy lengthy spells in the first division gained promotion from the Regionalliga West in this season. VfL Bochum won seven and Fortuna Düsseldorf six of their eight playoff matches, and both finished comfortably atop their respective promotion groups. Bochum would spend the next 21 seasons in the top flight, during which time they would never finish any higher than eighth.

Dynamo Dresden won the East German Oberliga for the first time since 1953, dropping only one point at home in the process. They won six of their away matches, with no other side, not even second-placed Carl Zeiss Jena, able to win more than twice on the road. Dresden also won the cup, becoming the first East German side ever to do the double. Klaus Sammer scored both their goals in the 2-1 cup final victory over Dynamo Berlin in Leipzig.

The top team in the East German Second Division was unquestionably Karl-Marx-Stadt, who knocked in 72 goals on the way to winning the southern section by twelve points. Vorwärts Stralsund were promoted from the northern group to spend their first-ever season in Division One. There was to be a new look to the East German Second Division after this season, with the two-division concept being expanded to five, thus giving a golden opportunity for clubs like Wismut Pirna-Copitz and Einheit Grevesmühlen. The five-Staffel league would continue for twelve more years before being reduced to two in 1984.

In September, an enormous crowd gathered in Nuremberg for a friendly between West Germany and Hungary, to pay tribute to Uwe Seeler as he made a second (and final) farewell international appearance for his country. The Germans won 3-1. Seeler had made his debut in the national side in 1954, and had scored 43 times in his 72 matches, 40 of which had been as captain. Another player ending his international career this season was the robust fullback Karl-Heinz Schnellinger, with 47 caps.

Bundesliga

Club	P	W	D	L	Goals	Pts
1. Borussia Mönchengladbach	34	20	10	4	77-35	50
2. Bayern Munich	34	19	10	5	74-36	48
3. Hertha BSC Berlin	34	16	9	9	61-43	41
4. Eintracht Brunswick	34	16	7	11	52-40	39
5. Hamburg SV	34	13	11	10	54-63	37
6. FC Schalke 04	34	15	6	13	44-40	36
7. MSV Duisburg	34	12	11	11	43-47	35
8. 1.FC Kaiserslautern	34	15	4	15	54-57	34
9. Hanover 96	34	12	9	13	53-49	33
10. Werder Bremen	34	11	11	12	41-40	33
11. 1.FC Cologne	34	11	11	12	46-56	33
12. VfB Stuttgart	34	11	8	15	49-49	30
13. Borussia Dortmund	34	10	9	15	54-60	29
14. Arminia Bielefeld	34	12	5	17	34-53	29
15. Eintracht Frankfurt	34	11	6	17	39-56	28
16. Rot-Weiss Oberhausen	34	9	9	16	54-69	27
17. Kickers Offenbach	34	9	9	16	49-65	27
18. Rot-Weiss Essen	34	7	9	18	48-68	23

Top Scorers
- Kobluhn (Rot-Weiss Oberhausen) 24
- Müller (Bayern Munich) 22
- Vogt (1.FC Kaiserslautern) 22
- Horr (Hertha BSC Berlin) 20
- Laumen (Borussia Mönchengladbach) 20
- Heynckes (Borussia Mönchengladbach) 19
- Keller (Hanover 96) 19
- Lippens (Rot-Weiss Essen) 19
- Ulsass (Eintracht Brunswick) 18
- Fischer (Schalke 04) 15
- Weiss (VfB Stuttgart) 15

Bundesliga Promotion Playoffs

Group 1

	P	W	D	L	Goals	Pts
1. VfL Bochum	8	7	0	1	23-11	14
2. VfL Osnabrück	8	3	1	4	11-13	7
3. FK Pirmasens	8	3	1	4	11-14	7
4. Karlsruhe SC	8	3	1	4	9-12	7
5. Tasmania 1900 Berlin	8	2	1	5	13-17	5

Group 2

	P	W	D	L	Goals	Pts
1. Fortuna Düsseldorf	8	6	2	0	19-7	14
2. Borussia Neunkirchen	8	4	1	3	11-9	9
3. FC St Pauli	8	3	2	3	10-15	8
4. 1.FC Nuremberg	8	3	1	4	15-10	7
5. Wacker 04 Berlin	8	1	0	7	6-20	2

Regionalliga Berlin

Club	P	W	D	L	Goals	Pts
1. Tasmania 1900 Berlin	33	29	3	1	110-20	61
2. Wacker 04 Berlin	33	24	3	6	75-34	51
3. Blau-Weiss 90 Berlin	33	24	2	7	95-38	50
4. Tennis Borussia Berlin	33	20	4	9	68-39	44
5. Hertha Zehlendorf	33	14	6	13	75-63	34
6. Spandau SV	33	13	7	13	59-70	33
7. TuS Wannsee	33	10	6	17	48-84	26
8. Alemannia 90 Berlin	33	8	8	17	41-61	24
9. Rapide Wedding	33	6	11	16	46-66	23
10. 1.FC Neukölln	33	7	7	19	53-78	21
11. SC Staaken	33	7	7	19	35-76	21
12. VfL Nord Berlin	33	2	4	27	31-107	8

Top Scorer: Kipp (Wacker 04 Berlin), 38 goals
Promoted: SV 92 Berlin, Meteor 06

Regionalliga North

Club	P	W	D	L	Goals	Pts
1. VfL Osnabrück	34	16	12	6	70-39	44
2. FC St Pauli	34	17	9	8	53-31	43
3. VfB Lübeck	34	16	10	8	63-45	42
4. Holstein Kiel	34	17	8	9	66-50	42
5. SV Barmbek-Uhlenhorst	34	15	11	8	63-39	41
6. Olympia Wilhelmshaven	34	14	13	7	37-27	41
7. Göttingen 05	34	13	12	9	63-42	38
8. TuS Bremerhaven 93	34	15	7	12	54-48	37
9. VfL Wolfsburg	34	12	12	10	56-48	36
10. TuS Celle	34	12	9	13	52-55	33
11. Leu Brunswick	34	12	6	16	59-55	30
12. Itzehoe SV	34	11	8	15	49-65	30
13. Phönix Lübeck	34	9	11	14	38-58	29
14. Arminia Hanover	34	10	8	16	46-61	28
15. Sperber Hamburg	34	8	12	14	34-51	28
16. SV Heide	34	8	11	15	38-56	27
17. VfB Oldenburg	34	9	8	17	40-57	26
18. SV Meppen	34	5	7	22	43-97	17

Top Scorer: Schulz (Holstein Kiel), 21 goals

Regionalliga North Promotion Playoffs

Group One

	P	W	D	L	Goals	Pts
1. Polizei Bremen	6	5	0	1	19-12	10
2. Union Salzgitter	6	4	0	2	15-8	8
3. VfL Pinneberg	6	2	0	4	7-10	4
4. TSV Westerland	6	1	0	5	8-19	2

Group Two

	P	W	D	L	Goals	Pts
1. OSV Hannover	6	5	1	0	13-5	11
2. TSV Rendsburg	6	3	0	3	8-6	6
3. Eintracht Nordhorn	6	2	1	3	9-12	5
4. SpVgg Blankenese	6	0	2	4	7-14	2

Regionalliga South

Club	P	W	D	L	Goals	Pts
1. 1.FC Nuremberg	36	23	9	4	81-39	55
2. Karlsruhe SC	36	19	7	10	59-40	45
3. Hessen Kassel	36	17	9	10	71-45	43
4. TSV 1860 Munich	36	16	9	11	59-40	41
5. Jahn Regensburg	36	17	7	12	65-64	41
6. Schweinfurt 05	36	15	10	11	73-58	40
7. SpVgg Fürth	36	14	11	11	55-38	39
8. VFR Heilbronn	36	14	11	11	61-50	39
9. FC Freiburg	36	14	9	13	60-55	37
10. Kickers Stuttgart	36	15	7	14	59-63	37
11. ESV Ingolstadt	36	13	10	13	54-56	36
12. FV Villingen 08	36	13	9	14	43-50	35
13. Bayern Hof	36	13	8	15	52-52	34
14. Opel Rüsselsheim	36	11	11	14	41-49	33
15. SSV Reutlingen	36	12	8	16	53-59	32
16. VfR Mannheim	36	9	13	14	50-68	31
17. SV Göppingen	36	7	14	15	47-67	28
18. Viktoria Aschaffenburg	36	6	8	22	42-83	20
19. Wacker Munich	36	4	10	22	39-88	18

Top Scorer: Bründl (Kickers Stuttgart), 21 goals

Regionalliga South Promotion Playoffs

Club	P	W	D	L	Goals	Pts
1. SpVgg Ludwigsburg	6	4	0	2	9-9	8
2. Waldhof Mannheim	6	4	0	2	19-6	8
3. FC Singen 04	6	4	0	2	12-10	8
4. FC Emmendingen	6	0	0	6	3-18	0

Because the top three sides finished level on points, an additional round was played to determine who would be promoted:
First Phase: SpVgg Ludwigsburg - bye; Waldhof Mannheim 2, FC Singen 04 2 (aet; Mannheim won on penalties)
Second Phase: Waldhof Mannheim 2, SpVgg Ludwigsburg 1. (Mannheim promoted to Regionalliga)
Also Promoted: SpVgg Bayreuth, SV Darmstaft 98

Regionalliga Southwest

Club	P	W	D	L	Goals	Pts
1. Borussia Neunkirchen	30	18	8	4	82-26	44
2. FK Pirmasens	30	19	6	5	69-29	44
3. Südwest Ludwigshafen	30	18	7	5	56-22	43
4. 1.FC Saarbrücken	30	16	7	7	61-39	39
5. SV Alsenborn	30	16	6	8	77-49	38
6. TuS Neuendorf	30	16	6	8	51-29	38
7. FSV Mainz 05	30	15	5	10	57-49	35
8. FC 08 Homburg	30	12	6	12	46-50	30
9. ASV Landau	30	10	9	11	36-43	29
10. Röchling Völklingen	30	11	5	14	43-50	27
11. Eintracht Trier	30	7	10	13	53-68	24
12. Wormatia Worms	30	9	5	16	44-58	23
13. VfR Frankenthal	30	6	10	14	33-53	22
14. FV Speyer	30	7	7	16	46-66	21
15. Saar 05 Saarbrücken	30	2	8	20	26-85	12
16. VfB Theley	30	5	1	24	32-96	11

Top Scorer: Lenz (SV Alsenborn), 25 goals

Regionalliga Southwest Promotion Playoffs

Club	P	W	D	L	Goals	Pts
1. Phönix Bellheim	4	2	1	1	8-4	5
2. SpVgg Andernach	4	1	2	1	6-6	4
3. SV Fraulautern	4	1	1	2	7-11	3

Regionalliga West

Club	P	W	D	L	Goals	Pts
1. VfL Bochum	34	26	4	4	81-27	56
2. Fortuna Düsseldorf	34	25	6	3	70-26	56
3. Wuppertal SV	34	24	7	3	81-27	55
4. Fortuna Cologne	34	16	7	11	71-46	39
5. Eintracht Gelsenkirchen	34	17	5	12	62-54	39
6. Alemannia Aachen	34	15	4	15	59-58	34
7. Bayer Leverkusen	34	13	7	14	64-62	33
8. DJK Gütersloh	34	14	5	15	49-58	33
9. Preussen Münster	34	13	5	16	62-57	31
10. Viktoria Cologne	34	10	11	13	36-46	31
11. Schwarz-Weiss Essen	34	10	9	15	56-63	29
12. Westfalia Herne	34	11	7	16	45-72	29
13. Wattenscheid 09	34	9	10	15	45-52	28
14. Lünen SV	34	10	7	17	53-59	27
15. SpVgg Erkenschwick	34	11	4	19	37-62	26
16. VfR Neuss	34	8	8	18	48-68	24
17. SC Bonn	34	9	6	19	37-66	24
18. Sportfreunde Hamborn 07	34	6	6	22	36-89	18

Top Scorer: Walitza (VfL Bochum), 28 goals

Regionalliga West Promotion Playoffs

Club	P	W	D	L	Goals	Pts
1. Arminia Gütersloh	4	2	2	0	5-2	6
2. VfL Klafeld-Geisweid	4	1	2	1	5-6	4
3. Bayer Uerdingen	4	0	2	2	4-6	2

All three clubs were promoted because VfL Bochum and Fortuna Düsseldorf were promoted to the Bundesliga

Third Division Champions

Baden (Nordbaden): SV Waldhof Mannheim
Baden (Südbaden): FC Emmendingen
Bayern: SpVgg Bayreuth
Berlin: BSV 92 Berlin
Bremen: Polizei Bremen
Hamburg: VfL Pinneberg
Hessen: SV Darmstadt 98
Mittelrhein: SC Jülich 1910
Niederrhein: Bayer Uerdingen

1970-71

Niedersachsen: OSV Hanover
Rheinland: SpVgg Andernach
Saarland: SV Fraulautern
Schleswig-Holstein: TSV Rendsburg
Südwest: Phönix Bellheim
Westfalen: Arminia Gütersloh
Württemberg: VfB Stuttgart (Am.)

West German Cup
First Round
Borussia Neunkirchen 0, 1.FC Kaiserslautern 1
FC 08 Homburg 1, MSV Duisburg 1 aet (0-4)
FC St Pauli 2, Eintracht Frankfurt 3 aet
Fortuna Düsseldorf 3, Werder Bremen 1 aet
Hanover 96 2, Hamburg SV 3 aet
Hessen Kassel 2, Bayern Munich 2 (0-3)
Holstein Kiel 2, VfB Stuttgart 1
Rot-Weiss Oberhausen 4, Rot-Weiss Essen 3
SSV Reutlingen 2, 1.FC Cologne 5
SV Alsenborn 1, Borussia Mönchengladbach 1 aet (1-3)
Tasmania 1900 Berlin 1, Eintracht Brunswick 0
TSV Westerland 0, Borussia Dortmund 4
VfB Heilbronn 2, Kickers Offenbach 0
VfL Wolfsburg 2, FC Schalke 04 2 aet (1-1 aet; Schalke won on penalties)
Wattenscheid 09 1, Hertha BSC Berlin 2
Wuppertal SV 5, Arminia Bielefeld 0

Second Round
1.FC Kaiserslautern 1, Bayern Munich 1 aet (0-5)
Eintracht Frankfurt 1, 1.FC Cologne 4
FC Schalke 04 4, VfR Heilbronn 0
Fortuna Düsseldorf 4, Wuppertal SV 0
Hamburg SV 3, Borussia Dortmund 1 aet
Hertha BSC Berlin 1, Borussia Mönchengladbach 3
Holstein Kiel 2, Rot-Weiss Oberhausen 5 aet
MSV Duisburg 2, Tasmania 1900 Berlin 0

Quarterfinals
1.FC Cologne 2, Hamburg SV 0
Bayern Munich 4, MSV Duisburg 0
FC Schalke 04 1, Rot-Weiss Oberhausen 0
Fortuna Düsseldorf 3, Borussia Mönchengladbach 1

Semifinals
FC Schalke 04 2, 1.FC Cologne 3
Fortuna Düsseldorf 0, Bayern Munich 1

Final
in Stuttgart
Bayern Munich 2, 1.FC Cologne 1 aet

West German Internationals
9/9/70 in Nuremberg 3-1 v Hungary
17/10/70 in Cologne 1-1 v Turkey (ECQ)
18/11/70 in Zagreb 0-2 v Yugoslavia
22/11/70 in Athens 3-1 v Greece
17/2/71 in Tirana 1-0 v Albania (ECQ)
25/4/71 in Istanbul 3-0 v Turkey (ECQ)
12/6/71 in Karlsruhe 2-0 v Albania (ECQ)
22/6/71 in Oslo 7-1 v Norway
27/6/71 in Gothenburg 0-1 v Sweden
30/6/71 in Copenhagen 3-1 v Denmark

East German Oberliga

Club	P	W	D	L	Goals	Pts
1. Dynamo Dresden	26	18	3	5	56-29	39
2. Carl Zeiss Jena	26	14	5	7	58-29	33
3. Chemie Halle	26	10	10	6	35-29	30
4. 1.FC Magdeburg	26	10	7	9	37-38	27
5. 1.FC Union Berlin	26	8	11	7	27-33	27
6. Sachsenring Zwickau	26	11	4	11	40-42	26
7. Vorwärts Berlin	26	10	6	10	38-44	26
8. Hansa Rostock	26	10	5	11	31-25	25
9. Dynamo Berlin	26	10	5	11	31-29	25
10. Lokomotive Leipzig	26	9	6	11	42-46	24
11. Wismut Aue	26	8	5	13	30-36	21
12. Stahl Riesa	26	6	9	11	28-41	21
13. Rot-Weiss Erfurt	26	6	9	11	28-44	21
14. Chemie Leipzig	26	5	9	12	27-43	19

Top Scorers
Kreische (Dynamo Dresden) 17
Rentzsch (Sachsenring Zwickau) 15
P Ducke (Carl Zeiss Jena) 14
Sparwasser (1.FC Magdeburg) 14
Lischke (Stahl Riesa) 13
Vogel (Carl Zeiss Jena) 11
Geisler (Lokomotive Leipzig) 9
Hahn (Hansa Rostock) 9
Löwe (Lokomotive Leipzig) 9
Piepenburg (Vorwärts Berlin) 9
Stein (Carl Zeiss Jena) 9

Second Division (Staffel North)

Club	P	W	D	L	Goals	Pts
1. Vorwärts Stralsund	26	15	8	3	44-15	38
2. TSG Wismar	26	14	7	5	39-23	35
3. Chemie Wolfen	26	12	10	4	32-23	34
4. Energie Cottbus	26	11	11	4	41-27	33
5. Dynamo Berlin II	26	11	8	7	46-38	30
6. Dynamo Schwerin	26	12	5	9	44-38	29
7. Vorwärts Berlin II	26	10	8	8	43-32	28
8. Stahl Brandenburg	26	12	3	11	42-40	27

9. Lokomotive Stendal 26 9 8 9 31-30 26
10. KKW Nord Greifswald 26 9 7 10 32-35 25
11. Vorwärts Cottbus 26 7 5 14 33-41 19
12. Hansa Rostock II 26 6 6 14 28-44 18
13. Post Neubrandenburg 26 6 4 16 22-36 16
14. Motor WW Warnemünde 26 1 4 21 12-67 6
No formal relegation

Second Division (Staffel South)

Club	P	W	D	L	Goals	Pts
1. Karl-Marx-Stadt	30	23	4	3	72-16	50
2. Vorwärts Meiningen	30	13	12	5	53-29	38
3. Motor Nordhausen-West	30	14	10	6	52-36	38
4. Motor Wema Plauen	30	17	4	9	46-35	38
5. Wismut Gera	30	12	11	7	39-29	35
6. Chemie Halle II	30	13	9	8	45-39	35
7. Lokomotive Dresden	30	11	10	9	37-32	32
8. Carl Zeiss Jena II	30	10	9	11	39-40	29
9. Chemie Böhlen	30	11	7	12	40-44	29
10. Kali Werra Tiefenort	30	8	10	12	32-47	26
11. Dynamo Eisleben	30	8	9	13	38-45	25
12. Dynamo Dresden II	30	7	10	13	36-40	24
13. Chemie Leipzig II	30	8	7	15	37-58	23
14. Sachsenring Zwickau II	30	8	6	16	37-62	22
15. Motor Steinach	30	8	5	17	31-42	21
16. Chemie Glauchau	30	2	11	17	22-62	15

No formal relegation. Chemie Leipzig II did not participate at this level for the following season.

East German Cup Final
in Halle
Dynamo Dresden 2, Dynamo Berlin 1 aet

East German Internationals
6/9/70 in Rostock 5-0 v Poland
11/11/70 in Dresden 1-0 v Holland (ECQ)
15/11/70 in Luxembourg 5-0 v Luxembourg (ECQ)
25/11/70 in London 1-3 v England
2/2/71 in Santiago 1-0 v Chile
8/2/71 in Montevideo 3-0 v Uruguay
10/2/71 in Montevideo 1-1 v Uruguay
24/4/71 in Gera 2-1 v Luxembourg (ECQ)
9/5/71 in Leipzig 1-2 v Yugoslavia (ECQ)
16/8/71 in Guadalajara 1-0 v Mexico

European Cup
First Round
Borussia Mönchengladbach v EPA Larnaca .... (6-0, 10-0)
Fenerbahce v Carl Zeiss Jena .... (0-4, 0-1)
Second Round
Borussia Mönchengladbach v Everton .... (1-1, 1-1)
Everton won on penalties
Carl Zeiss Jena v Sporting Lisbon .... (2-1, 2-1)
Quarterfinals
Carl Zeiss Jena v Red Star Belgrade .... (3-2, 0-4)

Cup-Winners' Cup
First Round
Kickers Offenbach v FC Bruges .... (2-1, 0-2)
Vorwärts Berlin v Bologna .... (0-0, 1-1 aet)
Second Round
Benfica v Vorwärts Berlin .... (2-0, 0-2 aet)
Vorwärts Berlin won on penalties
Quarterfinals
PSV Eindhoven v Vorwärts Berlin .... (2-0, 0-1)

Fairs Cup
First Round
La Gantoise v Hamburg SV .... (0-1, 1-7)
1.FC Cologne v Sedan .... (5-1, 0-1)
Bayern Munich v Glasgow Rangers .... (1-0, 1-1)
Nykoping v Hertha BSC Berlin .... (2-4, 1-4)
Partizan Belgrade v Dynamo Dresden .... (0-0, 0-6)
Second Round
Leeds United v Dynamo Dresden .... (1-0, 1-2)
Dinamo Zagreb v Hamburg SV .... (4-0, 0-1)
Fiorentina v 1.FC Cologne .... (1-2, 0-1)
Bayern Munich v Coventry City .... (6-1, 1-2)
Hertha BSC Berlin v Spartak Trnava .... (1-0, 1-3)
Third Round
Spartak Trnava v 1.FC Cologne .... (0-1, 0-3)
Bayern Munich v Sparta Rotterdam .... (2-1, 3-1)
Quarterfinals
Arsenal v 1.FC Cologne .... (2-1, 0-1)
Liverpool v Bayern Munich .... (3-0, 1-1)
Semifinals
1.FC Cologne v Juventus .... (1-1, 0-2)

1971-72

Bomber der Nation

The Bundesliga's ninth season was overshadowed by the effects of the bribery scandal, with some clubs in imminent danger of having to find entirely new playing squads. As was to be expected, the legal processes took a long time to complete, and it was not until 15 April 1972—Round 28 of the season—that the verdict on Arminia Bielefeld was reached. Arminia were to be permitted to fulfil their remaining six fixtures, but were to be placed at the bottom of the league table with all their figures replaced with a row of noughts. In other words, they were relegated.

Kickers Offenbach were also found guilty of illegal conduct, but, having been relegated the previous season, were deemed to have been punished sufficiently. Ironically, they won the Regionalliga South and their promotion playoff group to gain promotion back into the Bundesliga—and replace Bielefeld. With all this going on, disillusioned spectators deserted the Bundesliga in droves. Crowds fell by 800,000 on the previous year and were to drop even further in 1973.

On the field, Mönchengladbach's championship challenge faded because of a poor away record, and consequently the only team to seriously challenge Bayern Munich was Schalke 04—before all their players were banned. Bayern, their squad unaffected by the scandal, scored a record 69 goals in their home matches, winning 6-2 against Bremen, 6-3 against Frankfurt, 7-0 against Oberhausen and 11-1 against relegated Dortmund. They dropped points in only three home matches: against Cologne, Stuttgart, and, surprisingly, Bielefeld. Bayern's total of 101 goals scored this season remains a Bundesliga record. Gerd Müller, the *Bomber der Nation,* scored forty of them—again an all-time high, and not bad for a player once labelled "short and fat" by the previous Bayern *Trainer,* Zlatko Cajkovski.

Bayern Munich players accounted for over half of the German national team—goalkeeper Sepp Maier, sweeper and skipper Franz Beckenbauer, defenders Georg "Katsche" Schwarzenbeck and Paul Breitner, midfielder Uli Hoeness, and Müller up front. A few years earlier, Breitner and Hoeness had been brought to the club as nineteen-year-olds by *Trainer* Udo Lattek. As early as the fifth match of the season Bayern played host to Mönchengladbach and beat them 2-0. Later in the season they drew 2-2 and finished twelve points ahead of the defending champions.

The season developed into a two-horse race, and it was Schalke who led by three points at mid-season. But as the final day dawned, Bayern were still one point ahead—with the two due to close out their seasons against each other in the new Munich Olympiastadion. The match in fact marked the official opening of the stadium, and 80,000 saw an emphatic 5-1 home win.

Joining Offenbach in gaining promotion to the Bundesliga were Wuppertal SV, who had scored 111 goals in their 34 Regionalliga West matches. Almost of half of them were scored by Günter Pröpper, whose incredible 52-goal output put even Müller's tally in the shade. Wuppertal scored 26 more times in their eight playoff matches, where they didn't drop a point. But second-place Rot-Weiss Essen, who popped in 113 goals, were pipped for promotion in their group on goal difference.

Beginning with this season, the DFB decided to make the West German Cup a two-legged affair, and consequently there were few shocks. Hertha Berlin were given the rudest one after the second leg of their first-round tie with Schalke, which they had won 3-0. They had, however, fielded an ineligible player, and the DFB decided to award the match to Schalke 2-0—with the result that Schalke had won 5-1 on aggregate instead of losing 4-3. Holders Bayern went out in the quarterfinals, losing the second leg in Cologne 5-1 without Sepp Maier, who was injured—but not seriously enough to end his string of consecutive Bundesliga appearances, which would eventually run to 442.

Cologne faced Schalke in one of the semifinals, the second leg of which proved to be one of the most dramatic in the history of the competition. Cologne had won the first leg convincingly, 4-1, but found themselves 3-0 down after 41 minutes of the second. Hannes Löhr then scored for Cologne, and in the 59th minute referee Dieter Heckeroth awarded Cologne a controversial penalty for an alleged hand-ball. Löhr converted and Cologne had restored their aggregate advantage to 6-4. Backed by a boisterous crowd of 35,000, Schalke pressed for an equaliser and were mystifyingly awarded a penalty ten minutes from time, but Klaus Beverungen failed to convert it. Three minutes later, a third penalty was awarded, this time for a foul on Schalke's Erwin Kremers by Cologne's Jupp Kapellmann. Erwin's twin brother Helmut made no mistake to bring the aggregate score to 6-5. Cologne, now hanging on for dear life, tried to waste as much time as they could, but Heckeroth saw fit to add five minutes for stoppages and squeezed in another penalty in the dying seconds of play for Kapellmann's challenge on Rolf Rüssmann. Helmut Kremers made good with his second spot kick. Extra time was required, which led to a sixth penalty, to Cologne, but Schalke goalkeeper Norbert Nigbur saved Werner Biskup's effort and eventually the outcome of the match was decided—fittingly, on penalties. Schalke won the shoot-out 6-5.

Kaiserslautern were Schalke's opponents in the final. They had twice beaten Werder Bremen 2-1 in their semifinal, but were no match for the *Königsblauen* (Royal Blues) in Hanover. The 5-0 pasting handed to them was the most lopsided final result in the history of the competition, as Schalke dominated virtually from start to finish. Helmut Kremers opened and closed the scoring, with Klaus Scheer, Herbert Lütkebohmert, and Klaus Fischer netting in between.

Hamburg stalwart Uwe Seeler announced his retirement from the game. He had made his debut for HSV as a 17-year-old in 1953, and was top goalscorer in top-level German league football in 1956, 1959, 1960 and 1961. In ten seasons with Hamburg in the Oberliga North he averaged nearly thirty goals a season, and in the nine years following the creation of the Bundesliga he scored 137 goals in his 239 appearances. His 74 international caps between 1954 and 1970 had produced 43 goals and he had been named German Footballer of the Year three times.

In the European Cup, Dynamo Dresden went out in the first round to eventual winners Ajax Amsterdam, but Mönchengladbach eased into the second round, where they annihilated Inter Milan 7-1 in the home leg at the Bökelberg. However, a beer can had been thrown from the crowd onto the pitch, and a Milan player claimed to have been hit by it. UEFA annulled the result and ordered a re-match to be played in Berlin. By this time, Gladbach had travelled to Milan and, up against an overtly physical Inter side and a weak referee, had lost 4-2, so the subsequent 0-0 draw in Berlin was a bitter disappointment. In addition, Gladbach's "Luggi" Müller broke his leg in the match and missed the rest of the season.

In the Cup-Winners' Cup, both German entrants made it to the last four. Bayern Munich then lost to Glasgow Rangers, and Dynamo Berlin lost on penalties to Dynamo Moscow. In the newly-named UEFA Cup, Brunswick and Carl Zeiss Jena reached the last sixteen where they suffered emphatic second-leg defeats.

East Germany's participation in the UEFA Cup was marred by tragedy. On the eve of Chemie Halle's first round, second-leg match with PSV Eindhoven, Wolfgang Hoffman, a 21-year-old reserve player, died in a fire at the Het Silveren Seepaerd Hotel in Den Bosch, where the team was staying. The fire had broken out on the ground floor and spread upwards quickly. Several Halle players and other guests had to escape by jumping from windows; Hoffmann's room was on the third floor. Teammate Klaus Urbanczyk was seriously injured helping to save others from the blaze. The second leg was never played; Halle withdrew from the competition.

Meanwhile the army-sponsored team of Vorwärts Berlin had been delegated lock, stock, and barrel to the border town of Frankfurt-an-der-Oder, and the new Vorwärts Frankfurt finished in a reasonable fifth place. But 1.FC Magdeburg, sporting a 100% home record, deservedly won the Oberliga.

The West German amateur team played in the Olympics and came up against the East German Olympic team, which had become virtually their full national side. In a portent of things to come, the East Germans won the match 3-2. East Germany reached the playoff for the bronze medal, and 80,000 in the Munich Olympiastadion saw them draw 2-2 with the U.S.S.R. after extra time, with goals from Hans-Jürgen Kreische and Eberhard Vogel. Both teams were awarded bronze medals.

East Germany's European Championship qualifying group was headed by Yugoslavia, but the full West German national side came safely through their group. The competition had been revamped and, with it taking place over a much shorter period of time, attracted considerably more interest. In the two-leg quarterfinal, West Germany beat England 3-1 at Wembley. The two teams then played out a 0-0 draw in Berlinensuring the Germans of passage to the semifinals in Belgium. There, Germany played some magnificent football to beat the Belgians 2-1 on the strength of two Müller goals and the Soviet Union 3-0, again with two strikes from Müller, to become European champions.

Bundesliga

Club	P	W	D	L	Goals	Pts
1. Bayern Munich	34	24	7	3	101-38	55
2. FC Schalke 04	34	24	4	6	76-35	52
3. Borussia Mönchengladbach	34	18	7	9	82-40	43
4. 1.FC Cologne	34	15	13	6	64-44	43
5. Eintracht Frankfurt	34	16	7	11	71-61	39
6. Hertha BSC Berlin	34	14	9	11	46-55	37
7. 1.FC Kaiserslautern	34	14	7	13	59-53	35
8. VfB Stuttgart	34	13	9	12	52-56	35
9. VfL Bochum	34	14	6	14	59-69	34
10. Hamburg SV	34	13	7	14	52-52	33
11. Werder Bremen	34	11	9	14	63-58	31
12. Eintracht Brunswick	34	8	15	11	43-48	31
13. Fortuna Düsseldorf	34	10	10	14	40-53	30
14. MSV Duisburg	34	10	7	17	36-51	27
15. Rot-Weiss Oberhausen	34	7	11	16	33-66	25
16. Hanover 96	34	10	3	21	54-69	23
17. Borussia Dortmund	34	6	8	20	34-83	20
18. Arminia Bielefeld	34	6	7	21	41-75	0

Arminia Bielefeld were awarded no points this season for their part in the bribery scandal.

Top Scorers

G Müller (Bayern Munich)	40
Fischer (FC Schalke 04)	22
Walitza (VfL Bochum)	22
Keller (Hanover 96)	20
Heynckes (Borussia Mönchengladbach)	19
Schneer (FC Schalke 04)	18
Netzer (Borussia Mönchengladbach)	17
Rupp (1.FC Köln)	16
U Hoeness (Bayern Munich)	13
Hosic (1.FC Kaiserslautern)	13
Nickel (Eintracht Frankfurt)	13
Weist (Werder Bremen)	13

Bundesliga Promotion Playoffs

Group 1

	P	W	D	L	Goals	Pts
1. Wuppertal SV	8	8	0	0	26-5	16
2. VfL Osnabrück	8	3	2	3	8-15	8
3. Borussia Neunkirchen	8	3	0	5	20-16	6
4. Bayern Hof	8	2	1	5	17-16	5
5. Tasmania 1900 Berlin	8	2	1	5	8-27	5

Group 2

	P	W	D	L	Goals	Pts
1. Kickers Offenbach	8	5	3	0	29-7	13
2. Rot-Weiss Essen	8	5	3	0	22-6	13
3. FC St Pauli	8	2	3	3	7-17	7
4. Wacker 04 Berlin	8	2	1	5	8-29	5
5. Röchling Völklingen	8	1	0	6	14-22	2

Regionalliga Berlin

Club	P	W	D	L	Goals	Pts
1. Wacker 04 Berlin	33	24	5	4	85-28	53
2. Tasmania 1900 Berlin	33	24	4	5	83-23	52
3. Blau-Weiss 90 Berlin	33	22	7	4	102-37	51
4. Tennis Borussia Berlin	33	22	6	5	82-26	50
5. Spandau SV	33	14	6	13	51-60	34
6. Hertha Zehlendorf	33	10	8	15	56-66	28
7. 1.FC Neukölln	33	11	5	17	45-66	27
8. Alemannia 90 Berlin	33	9	7	17	37-55	25
9. SV Berlin 92	33	7	8	18	27-63	22
10. Rapide Wedding	33	9	4	20	42-83	22
11. TuS Wannsee	33	7	4	22	27-79	18
12. Meteor 06 Berlin	33	4	6	23	40-91	14

Top Scorer: John (Blau Weiss 90 Berlin), 39 goals
Promoted: Preussen Berlin, Rot-Weiss Neukölln

Regionalliga North

Club	P	W	D	L	Goals	Pts
1. FC St Pauli	34	24	6	4	86-37	54
2. VfL Osnabrück	34	21	7	6	62-20	49
3. VfL Wolfsburg	34	20	5	9	63-38	45
4. SV Barmbek-Uhlenhorst	34	19	7	8	53-33	45
5. Göttingen 05	34	20	4	10	67-48	44
6. VfB Lübeck	34	14	11	9	50-41	39
7. Leu Brunswick	34	13	12	9	60-47	38
8. Olympia Wilhelmshaven	34	13	7	14	36-33	33
9. SV Heide	34	11	10	13	50-50	32
10. TuS Celle	34	12	7	15	52-64	31
11. Holstein Kiel	34	12	6	16	48-56	30
12. Phönix Lübeck	34	8	14	12	43-59	30
13. OSV Hanover	34	12	6	16	47-69	30
14. Arminia Hanover	34	10	8	16	43-51	28
15. TuS Bremerhaven 93	34	8	9	17	42-60	25
16. Itzehoe SV	34	8	5	21	36-60	21
17. Sperber Hamburg	34	6	7	21	34-69	19
18. Polizei Bremen	34	6	7	21	31-68	19

Top Scorer: Hussner (FC St Pauli), 23 goals

Regionalliga North Promotion Playoffs

Group One

	P	W	D	L	Goals	Pts
1. VfB Oldenburg	6	3	2	1	20-13	8
2. Concordia Hamburg	6	3	2	1	7-4	8
3. Preussen 07 Hamelin	6	3	2	1	8-9	8
4. TSV Rendsburg	6	0	0	6	6-15	0

Group Two

	P	W	D	L	Goals	Pts
1. SV Meppen	6	4	0	2	12-8	8
2. ASV Bergedorf 85	6	3	1	2	9-7	7
3. SV Blumenthal	6	2	2	2	7-7	6
4. Schleswig 06	6	1	1	4	8-14	3

Regionalliga South

Club	P	W	D	L	Goals	Pts
1. Kickers Offenbach	36	21	15	0	99-33	57
2. Bayern Hof	36	22	8	6	88-42	52
3. TSV 1860 Munich	36	18	10	8	62-34	46
4. Hessen Kassel	36	13	14	9	57-47	40
5. Karlsruhe SC	36	15	7	14	52-44	37
6. FC Freiburg	36	13	11	12	47-57	37
7. SV Darmstadt 98	36	14	8	14	49-44	36
8. VfR Heilbronn	36	14	8	14	55-59	36
9. 1.FC Nuremberg	36	12	10	14	49-62	34
10. SSV Reutlingen	36	11	11	14	48-60	33
11. Kickers Stuttgart	36	12	9	15	55-71	33
12. Schweinfurt 05	36	12	8	16	56-62	32
13. SpVgg Bayreuth	36	10	12	14	40-52	32
14. SpVgg Fürth	36	10	11	15	37-48	31
15. SpVgg Ludwigsburg	36	9	13	14	42-56	31
16. Jahn Regensburg	36	10	11	15	47-63	31
17. Opel Rüsselsheim	36	9	12	15	44-66	30
18. FV Villingen 08	36	8	12	16	43-53	28
19. ESV Ingolstadt	36	10	8	18	46-63	28

Top Scorer: Kostedde (Kickers Offenbach), 27 goals

Regionalliga South Promotion Playoffs

Club	P	W	D	L	Goals	Pts
1. SV Waldhof	6	4	1	1	18-6	9
2. FC Singen 04	6	4	1	1	8-4	9
3. SSV 1846 Ulm	6	1	2	3	7-13	4
4. FC Rastatt 04	6	0	2	4	5-15	2

Because the top two clubs finished level on points, a deciding match was played to determine who would be promoted: SV Waldhof 1, FC Singen 04 0 (Mannheim promoted to Regionalliga)
Also Promoted: VfR Bürstadt, Wacker Munich

Regionalliga Southwest

Club	P	W	D	L	Goals	Pts
1. Borussia Neunkirchen	30	19	10	1	77-22	48
2. Röchling Völklingen	30	18	5	7	55-34	41
3. SV Alsenborn	30	17	4	9	63-38	38
4. FSV Mainz 05	30	15	7	8	57-41	37
5. TuS Neuendorf	30	13	7	10	54-34	33
6. FK Pirmasens	30	12	8	10	56-49	32
7. Wormatia Worms	30	13	6	11	63-63	32
8. ASV Landau	30	11	8	11	41-44	30
9. FC 08 Homburg	30	11	7	12	38-30	29
10. Südwest Ludwigshafen	30	11	7	12	41-39	29
11. FV Speyer	30	9	10	11	37-57	28
12. 1.FC Saarbrücken	30	10	6	14	34-42	26
13. Eintracht Trier	30	6	12	12	51-71	24
14. Phönix Bellheim	30	9	5	16	44-67	23
15. VfR Frankenthal	30	6	9	15	34-50	21
16. SV Andernach	30	2	5	23	29-93	9

Top Scorer: Lenz (SV Alsenborn), 28 goals

Regionalliga Southwest Promotion Playoffs

Club	P	W	D	L	Goals	Pts
1. Sportfreunde Eisbachtal	4	2	1	1	5-3	5
2. VfB Theley	4	1	2	1	5-5	4
3. Eintracht Bad Kreuznach	4	1	1	2	4-6	3

Regionalliga West

Club	P	W	D	L	Goals	Pts
1. Wuppertal SV	34	28	4	2	111-23	60
2. Rot-Weiss Essen	34	24	6	4	113-37	54
3. Fortuna Cologne	34	21	6	7	76-41	48
4. Alemannia Aachen	34	14	14	6	51-38	42
5. Schwarz-Weiss Essen	34	15	9	10	57-48	39
6. SpVgg Erkenschwick	34	13	10	11	41-52	36
7. Bayer Uerdingen	34	13	9	12	49-51	35
8. Bayer Leverkusen	34	15	5	14	41-49	35
9. Arminia Gütersloh	34	12	7	15	48-56	31
10. Eintracht Gelsenkirchen	34	11	9	14	50-60	31
11. Preussen Münster	34	12	7	15	43-57	31
12. Wattenscheid 09	34	9	12	13	43-49	30
13. DJK Gütersloh	34	12	5	17	44-75	29
14. Westfalia Herne	34	9	10	15	39-52	28
15. Lünen SV	34	10	7	17	34-50	27
16. VfR Neuss	34	8	5	21	42-69	21
17. Viktoria Cologne	34	6	9	19	34-62	21
18. VfL Klafeld-Geisweid	34	5	4	25	24-71	14

Top Scorer: Pröpper (Wuppertal SV), 52 goals
1.FC Styrum became 1.FC Mülheim-Styrum

Regionalliga West Promotion Playoffs

Club	P	W	D	L	Goals	Pts
1. Sportfreunde Siegen	6	5	0	1	13-6	10
2. 1.FC Styrum	6	3	2	1	9-5	8
3. SC Bonn	6	1	3	2	7-9	5
4. STV Horst-Emscher	6	0	1	5	4-13	1

Third Division Champions

Baden (Nordbaden): SV Waldhof
Baden (Südbaden): FC Rastatt 04
Bayern: Wacker Munich
Berlin: BFC Preussen Berlin
Bremen: SV Blumenthal
Hamburg: ASV Bergedorf 85
Hessen: VfR Bürstadt
Mittelrhein: SC Bonn
Niederrhein: 1.FC Styrum

1971-72

Niedersachsen: VfB Oldenburg
Rheinland: Sportfreunde Eisbachtal
Saarland: VfB Theley
Schleswig-Holstein: TSV Rendsburg
Südwest: Eintracht Bad Kreuznach
Westfalen: Sportfreunde Siegen
Württemberg: SSV 1846 Ulm

West German Cup

First Round
Arminia Bielefeld 1, MSV Duisburg 1 (1-3)
Bayer Leverkusen 0, Borussia Mönchengladbach 3 (2-4)
Borussia Neunkirchen 2, Eintracht Brunswick 4 (0-0)
FC Freiburg 1, Hamburg SV 2 (2-2)
FC Schalke 04 3, Hertha BSC Berlin 1 (0-3); second leg later awarded to Schalke 2-0 for Hertha having fielded an ineligible player
FC St Pauli 1, Rot-Weiss Oberhausen 1 (1-2)
Fortuna Cologne 2, Bayern Munich 1 (0-6)
FV 1912 Essen 1, 1.FC Cologne 9 (0-5)
Holstein Kiel 5, Hanover 96 4 (1-7)
Kickers Offenbach 1, Borussia Dortmund 1 (3-0)
Schweinfurt 05 1, Eintracht Frankfurt 0 (1-6)
SpVgg Bad Pyrmont 1, Werder Bremen 4 (0-6)
SV Alsenborn 0, Fortuna Düsseldorf 0 (0-3)
Tasmania 1900 Berlin 2, VfL Bochum 2 (0-2)
VfR Heilbronn 1, VfB Stuttgart 1 (0-4)
Wuppertal SV 2, 1.FC Kaiserslautern 1 (2-3 aet; Kaiserslautern won on penalties)

Second Round
Borussia Mönchengladbach 4, Eintracht Frankfurt 2 (2-3)
Eintracht Brunswick 0, Bayern Munich 0 (1-3 aet)
Fortuna Düsseldorf 1, FC Schalke 04 1 (1-2)
Hanover 96 0, VfL Bochum 0 (4-2)
Kickers Offenbach 3, 1.FC Cologne 1 (0-4)
MSV Duisburg 2, Rot-Weiss Oberhausen 2 (0-1)
VfB Stuttgart 4, 1.FC Kaiserslautern 3 (1-3)
Werder Bremen 4, Hamburg SV 2 (0-1)

Quarterfinals
Bayern Munich 3, 1.FC Cologne 0 (1-5)
Borussia Mönchengladbach 2, FC Schalke 04 2 (0-1)
Hanover 96 0, Werder Bremen 2 (1-2)
Rot-Weiss Oberhausen 3, 1.FC Kaiserslautern 1 (0-5 aet)

Semifinals
1.FC Cologne 4, FC Schalke 04 1 (2-5 aet; Schalke won on penalties)
1.FC Kaiserslautern 2, Werder Bremen 1 (2-1)

Final
in Hanover
FC Schalke 04 5, 1.FC Kaiserslautern 0

West German Internationals
8/9/71 in Hanover 5-0 v Mexico
10/10/71 in Warsaw 3-1 v Poland (ECQ)
17/11/71 in Hamburg 0-0 v Poland (ECQ)
29/3/72 in Budapest 2-0 v Hungary
29/4/72 in London 3-1 v England (EC)
13/5/72 in Berlin 0-0 v England (EC)
26/5/72 in Munich 4-1 v Soviet Union
14/6/72 in Antwerp 2-1 v Belgium (EC)
18/6/72 in Brussels 3-0 v Soviet Union (EC)

East German Oberliga

Club	P	W	D	L	Goals	Pts
1. 1.FC Magdeburg	26	17	4	5	48-23	38
2. Dynamo Berlin	26	13	9	4	45-40	35
3. Dynamo Dresden	26	12	9	5	59-30	33
4. Carl Zeiss Jena	26	12	7	7	42-34	31
5. Vorwärts Frankfurt/Oder	26	9	9	8	33-36	27
6. Chemie Halle	26	10	7	9	40-44	27
7. Sachsenring Zwickau	26	7	11	8	26-25	25
8. Lokomotive Leipzig	26	9	7	10	30-31	25
9. Hansa Rostock	26	8	8	10	27-24	24
10. Wismut Aue	26	7	9	10	34-46	23
11. 1.FC Union Berlin	26	5	11	10	21-32	21
12. FC Karl-Marx-Stadt	26	7	5	14	34-48	19
13. Stahl Riesa	26	5	8	13	23-41	18
14. Vorwärts Stralsund	26	6	6	14	20-48	18

Top Scorers
Kreische (Dynamo Dresden) 14
Abraham (1.FC Magdeburg) 13
Streich (Hansa Rostock) 12
Sachse (Dynamo Dresden) 11
Johannsen (Dynamo Berlin) 10
Rentzsch (Sachsenring Zwickau) 10
P. Ducke (Carl Zeiss Jena) 8
Scheitler (Carl Zeiss Jena) 8
Terletzki (Dynamo Berlin) 8

Oberliga Promotion Playoffs

Club	P	W	D	L	Goals	Pts
1. Rot-Weiss Erfurt	8	6	2	0	32-5	14
2. Chemie Leipzig	8	3	4	1	11-5	10
3. Stahl Eisenhüttenstadt	8	3	3	2	10-11	9
4. TSG Wismar	8	3	0	5	11-19	6
5. Motor Werdau	8	0	1	7	7-31	1

Second Division (Staffel A)

Club	P	W	D	L	Goals	Pts
1. TSG Wismar	22	14	6	2	47-21	34
2. Hansa Rostock II	22	11	9	2	42-22	31
3. Dynamo Schwerin	22	13	4	5	46-20	30
4. Vorwärts Neubrandenburg	22	9	11	2	51-21	29
5. KKW Nord Greifswald	22	11	4	7	31-22	26
6. Veritas Wittenberge	22	10	4	8	41-41	24
7. Post Neubrandenburg	22	7	7	8	27-28	21
8. Motor WW Warnemünde	22	8	5	9	30-32	21
9. Nord Togelow	22	6	4	12	24-49	16
10. Lokomotive Bergen	22	5	4	13	37-53	14
11. Einheit Grevesmühlen	22	4	5	13	20-43	13
12. Aufbau Boizenburg	22	2	1	19	20-64	5

Promoted: Schiffahrt/Hafen Rostock, Motor Schwerin, VB Waren

Second Division (Staffel B)

Club	P	W	D	L	Goals	Pts
1. Dynamo Berlin II	22	15	4	3	45-17	34
2. Stahl Eisenhüttenstadt	22	13	5	4	37-19	31
3. Energie Cottbus	22	10	7	5	29-25	27
4. Vorwärts Frankfurt/Oder II	22	10	6	6	39-32	26
5. Aktivist Schwarze Pumpe	22	7	11	4	24-22	25
6. Dynamo Fürstenwalde	22	10	3	9	43-38	23
7. EAB Lichtenburg 47	22	6	8	8	27-28	20
8. Stahl Hennigsdorf	22	8	4	10	31-35	20
9. Vorwärts Cottbus	22	7	5	10	22-29	19
10. Motor Babelsberg	22	6	5	11	34-37	17
11. Aktivist Brieske-Senftenberg	22	4	7	11	34-42	15
12. Einheit Pankow	22	2	3	17	12-53	7

Aktivist Schwarze Pumpe did not participate at this level in the following season

Promoted: Motor Eberswalde, Motor Hennigsdorf, Aufbau Grossräschen, Motor Köpenick

Second Division (Staffel C)

Club	P	W	D	L	Goals	Pts
1. Chemie Leipzig	20	13	6	1	35-7	32
2. Lokomotive Stendal	20	11	7	2	34-16	29
3. Vorwärts Leipzig	20	10	5	5	35-21	25
4. Chemie Halle II	20	8	5	7	35-33	21
5. Chemie Böhlen	20	7	7	6	28-29	21
6. Lok/Vorwärts Halberstadt	20	6	8	6	18-19	20
7. Stahl Brandenburg	20	7	5	8	30-26	19
8. 1.FC Magdeburg II	20	7	3	10	25-30	17
9. Dynamo Eisleben	20	4	9	17	21-30	17
10. Lokomotive Ost Leipzig	20	4	2	14	19-51	10
11. Chemie Buna Schkopau	20	3	3	14	15-33	9

Promoted: Lokomotive Leipzig II, Motor/Vorwärts Oschersleben, Veritas Wittenberge, Chemie Wolfen

Second Division (Staffel D)

Club	P	W	D	L	Goals	Pts
1. Motor Werdau	20	12	5	3	39-33	29
2. Lokomotive Dresden	20	11	6	3	42-20	28
3. Dynamo Dresden II	20	10	4	8	37-24	24
4. Wismut Aue II	20	11	2	7	32-26	24
5. Vorwärts Löbau	20	9	4	7	32-29	22
6. Motor Wema Plauen	20	8	3	9	42-37	19
7. Wismut Pirna-Copitz	20	7	5	8	21-33	19
8. Sachsenring Zwickau II	20	7	4	9	38-37	18
9. Chemie Zeitz	20	7	3	10	32-29	17
10. Fortschritt Greiz	20	5	3	12	26-54	13
11. Chemie Glauchau	20	3	1	16	23-52	7

Promoted: Aktivist Schwarze Pumpe, Karl-Marx-Stadt II, TSG Gröditz

Second Division (Staffel E)

Club	P	W	D	L	Goals	Pts
1. Rot-Weiss Erfurt	22	19	2	1	87-14	40
2. Vorwärts Meiningen	22	14	5	3	55-20	33
3. Carl Zeiss Jena II	22	15	2	5	50-21	32
4. Wismut Gera	22	11	8	3	44-25	30
5. Motor Nordhausen-West	22	11	3	8	45-34	25
6. Zentronik Sömmerda	22	8	5	9	31-29	21
7. Motor Hermsdorf	22	9	2	11	41-37	20
8. Kali Werra Tiefenort	22	8	3	11	31-42	19
9. Motor Steinach	22	7	3	12	28-49	17
10. Motor Weimar	22	6	1	15	25-47	13
11. Motor Suhl	22	5	2	15	24-56	12
12. Lokomotive Meiningen	22	1	0	21	10-97	2

Promoted: Rot-Weiss Erfurt II, Chemie Glas Ilmenau, Stahl Maxhütte

East German Cup Final
in Leipzig
Carl Zeiss Jena 2, Dynamo Dresden 1

East German Internationals
18/9/71 in Leipzig 1-1 v Mexico
25/9/71 in Berlin 1-1 v Czechoslovakia
10/11/71 in Rotterdam 2-3 v Holland (ECQ)
16/11/71 in Belgrade 0-0 v Yugoslavia (ECQ)
27/5/72 in Leipzig 1-0 v Uruguay
31/5/72 in Rostock 0-0 v Uruguay

European Cup
First Round
Cork Hibs v Borussia Mönchengladbach .... (0-5, 1-2)
Ajax Amsterdam v Dynamo Dresden .... (2-0, 0-0)
Second Round
Inter Milan v Borussia Mönchengladbach .... (4-2, 0-0)

Cup-Winners' Cup
First Round
Skoda Pilsen v Bayern Munich .... (0-1, 1-6)
Dynamo Berlin v Cardiff City .... (1-1, 1-1 aet)
Dynamo Berlin won on penalties
Second Round
Liverpool v Bayern Munich .... (0-0, 1-3)
AC Beerschot v Dynamo Berlin .... (1-3, 1-3)
Quarterfinals
Steaua Bucharest v Bayern Munich .... (1-1, 0-0)
Atvidaberg v Dynamo Berlin .... (0-2, 2-2)
Semifinals
Bayern Munich v Glasgow Rangers .... (1-1, 0-2)
Dynamo Berlin v Dynamo Moscow .... (1-1, 1-1 aet)
Dynamo Moscow won on penalties

UEFA Cup
First Round
Hertha BSC Berlin v Elfsborg .... (3-1, 4-1)
Hamburg SV v St. Johnstone .... (2-1, 0-3)
St. Etienne v 1.FC Cologne .... (1-1, 1-2)
Glentoran v Eintracht Brunswick .... (0-1, 1-6)
Carl Zeiss Jena v Lokomotive Plovdiv .... (3-0, 1-3)
PSV Eindhoven walkover v Chemie Halle
Second Round
1.FC Cologne v Dundee .... (2-1, 2-4)
Eintracht Brunswick v Athletic Bilbao .... (2-1, 2-2)
AC Milan v Hertha BSC Berlin .... (4-2, 1-2)
OFK Belgrade v Carl Zeiss Jena .... (1-1, 0-4)
Third Round
Eintracht Brunswick v Ferencvaros .... (1-1, 2-5)
Carl Zeiss Jena v Wolverhampton Wanderers .... (0-1, 0-3)

1972-73

From start to finish

For the first time in the history of the Bundesliga, one club topped the table from the first game to the last: Bayern Munich. This was hardly surprising, given that their line-up contained six international stars fresh from West Germany's triumph in the European Championships in Brussels.

Over the summer, Bayern had decided that in future, their home matches would no longer be played in TSV 1860 Munich's Grünwalder Strasse Stadion but in the city's brand-new 78,000-capacity Olympiastadion. The Bayern players had mixed feelings about this move, preferring to stay at the old stadium for all but the big games, but the DFB vetoed this proposal. Still, Bayern gained extra income from the larger crowds, in turn attracting new players by offering larger salaries. Their average attendance in this season wound up being nearly 31,000—well above anything they had ever known.

Bayern were admired and envied throughout Germany, but for all their success they never achieved the popularity of their arch-rivals Borussia Mönchengladbach. Bayern goalkeeper Sepp Maier once admitted that this used to really annoy the Bayern players. Maier always felt that his side were the more attractive and more professional team and pointed out that they won most of their matches against Gladbach. But if Bayern were starting to look practically invincible, two events early in 1973 brought them back down to earth. First, their undefeated sequence at home, which now stretched to 67 games in all competitions and had spanned more than three years, was shattered by Kickers Offenbach with a 4-2 defeat in the West German Cup. Then, Bayern suffered a 4-0 trouncing in their European Cup quarterfinal at Ajax Amsterdam. After this match, an angry Maier picked up all his goalkeeping equipment and threw it out of his hotel window. He believed that the type of footballs used by the Dutch were particularly smooth and slippery and had therefore spent ages gluing foam onto the palms of his gloves. Not that it had the slightest effect, as it rained all evening.

In the league, Bayern pressed steadily on towards the title, which they clinched with four matches still to play. Their eventual eleven-point margin over Cologne remains a Bundesliga record. But in general, the Bundesliga's tenth season was rather uninspiring. Average attendance slumped to a record low of 16,372 per game, with most clubs hit hard at the turnstiles. Hertha Berlin saw their average gates tumble from nearly 44,000 to under 24,000 in one season. The repercussions of the bribery scandal still rumbled on, with a strange consequence on 27 April 1973—the match between Schalke and Cologne had to be called off at short notice, as some of the Schalke players banned by the DFB had applied to the criminal courts to have the bans lifted.

Günter Netzer's eighth and last season in the Bundesliga was also rather pedestrian, both personally and for his club, Mönchengladbach. After success with the national team in the European Championships, he spent most of this season struggling against injuries and was only able to make eighteen league appearances. Gladbach finished fifth, one place below the surprise of the season, newly-promoted Wuppertal SV. But on their occasional good days, Gladbach's refreshing attack-minded team produced victories by scores of 6-0, 6-1, 6-2, 5-0, 5-2 and 4-3. Netzer and his *Trainer* Hennes Weisweiler were the lynch-pins of Borussia's "good mood football". When Weisweiler had arrived at the Bökelberg in 1964 he had shown great perception in giving each player his most suitable role. Netzer for example used to play up front, but the *Trainer*'s masterstroke was to move him into midfield and use him as a playmaker. But relationships between *Trainer* and star player had soured, and during this season they reached an all-time low. On occasions Weisweiler and Netzer wouldn't even talk to each other, and Berti Vogts used to have to act as intermediary, passing messages between the two.

An alleged lack of fitness was the reason Netzer was omitted from Gladbach's starting line-up for the West German Cup Final against Cologne. Netzer had responded by trying to walk out on the team at their training camp, but teammates persuaded him to stay. Netzer later admitted that the decision to leave him out was quite correct as he wasn't match-fit, his mother had died shortly before, and his transfer to Real Madrid for one million marks had just been made public.

The rest of the story has become part of German footballing folklore. When summoned to go onto the field as a substitute at half-time, with the score 1-1, Netzer refused. With no further goals before the end of ninety minutes, the game went into extra time and Gladbach chose to make a substitution. Whether Weisweiler intended to put in Netzer is moot; some maintain Netzer simply took the field before Weisweiler had the chance to send in anyone else. But with virtually his first touch of the ball, Netzer took a pass from Rainer Bonhof and beat Cologne keeper Gerhard Welz with a first-time effort which proved to be the matchwinner. And so the "king" took his leave of the Bundesliga.

Fortuna Düsseldorf finished third, a tremendous improvement on the previous season's thirteenth place. *Trainer* Heinz Lucas had made two shrewd acquisitions which helped to turn the club around: midfielder Gerd Zewe from Borussia Neunkirchen over the summer and Dieter Brei from Arminia Bielefeld in mid-season. Fortuna's gates jumped from an average of 14,700 the season before to over 25,700 in the newly-refurbished Rheinstadion.

There were just two changes of *Trainer* during the season, fewer than any other in the league's history. Hans Hipp was one of the casualties, dismissed by Hanover 96 in March, a week after his team had lost 2-0 to relegation-threatened Hamburg. Hannes Baldauf took over but with one match left to play, Hanover were in seventeenth place needing both a win and an Eintracht Brunswick loss to be sure of staying up. Eintracht duly lost at home to Düsseldorf and Hanover won 4-0 at Wuppertal to keep Baldauf in his job—at least until March of the following season. The other casualty was Kaiserslautern's Dietrich Wiese.

Meanwhile, the two-legged format of the West German Cup had become something of a laughingstock. The total number of fans watching the competition was less than two seasons ago, when there had been half as many ties. Most matches struggled to attract five-figure crowds and even third-round matches like Gladbach v Kaiserslautern could only draw 12,000. The DFB sheepishly decided to revert to the single-match tie for the following season.

Indeed, cup football had reached its saturation point in West Germany, for this was the one and only season when the DFB also organised a League Cup. The initial stages consisted of eight groups of four teams, with the eight group winners then playing two-legged matches in a straight knockout competition. The final was played on 6 June 1973 in Hamburg's Volksparkstadion, in front of 30,000. Hamburg SV strolled to a 4-0 win through goals from Caspar Memering, Peter Nogly, Franz-Josef Hönig, and Peter Hidien. But, like a two-legged West German Cup, the concept seemed a bit half-baked and few people mourned the decision to scrap the *Liga-Pokal* after just one season.

For the fourth time since the Bundesliga began—and for the second year in a row—St. Pauli took the Regionalliga North title. But yet again the Hamburg club failed to gain promotion to the first division, finishing second in their playoff group behind Fortuna Cologne. Rot-Weiss Essen, who finished ahead of Fortuna in the Regionalliga West, took the other spot with an unbeaten record in the playoffs.

The Regionalliga Berlin was split into a promotion and relegation group, with Blau-Weiss 90 Berlin edging out Wacker 04 for the championship. But Blau-Weiss could only manage two out of a possible sixteen points in the playoff round, the lone victory being a 3-2 win over FSV 05 Mainz. Meanwhile seven years after their disastrous season in Bundesliga, beleaguered Tasmania 1900 found themselves insolvent and disbanded. A new Tasmania, Tasmania 73 Berlin, would replace them.

The East German champions were Dynamo Dresden, who thumped in 61 goals, the highest total of any team since 1962. Hans-Jürgen Kreische scored 26 of them, becoming the league's leading scorer for the third consecutive year. The season also saw the final appearance in the Oberliga of 39-year-old Alois Glaubitz of Sachsenring Zwickau, after a 17-year career which spanned 428 league games.

Mönchengladbach reached the final of the UEFA Cup for the season's best German performance in Europe. They had been banned from playing at home in the first two rounds, owing to the beer can incident against Inter Milan the season before, but still managed to come away with aggregate wins over Aberdeen and Hvidovre. On being allowed to return to the Bökelberg they thumped Cologne, Kaiserslautern, and Twente Enschede to reach the final against Liverpool. But they were unable to come back from a 3-0 first-leg defeat at Anfield. It would not be the last time the two clubs would meet in a European final.

Bundesliga

Club	P	W	D	L	Goals	Pts
1. Bayern Munich	34	25	4	5	93-29	54
2. 1.FC Cologne	34	16	11	7	66-51	43
3. Fortuna Düsseldorf	34	15	12	7	62-45	42
4. Wuppertal SV	34	15	10	9	62-49	40
5. Borussia Mönchengladbach	34	17	5	12	82-61	39
6. VfB Stuttgart	34	17	3	14	71-65	37
7. Kickers Offenbach	34	14	7	13	61-60	35
8. Eintracht Frankfurt	34	15	4	15	58-54	34
9. 1.FC Kaiserslautern	34	12	10	12	58-68	34
10. MSV Duisburg	34	12	9	13	53-54	33
11. Werder Bremen	34	12	7	15	50-52	31
12. VfL Bochum	34	11	9	14	50-68	31
13. Hertha BSC Berlin	34	11	8	15	53-64	30
14. Hamburg SV	34	10	8	16	53-59	28
15. FC Schalke 04	34	10	8	16	46-61	28
16. Hanover 96	34	9	8	17	49-65	26
17. Eintracht Brunswick	34	9	7	18	33-56	25
18. Rot-Weiss Oberhausen	34	9	4	21	45-84	22

Top Scorers
G Müller (Bayern Munich) 36
Heynckes (Borussia Mönchengladbach) 28
Pröpper (Wuppertal SV) 21
Kostedde (Kickers Offenbach) 19
Wlitza (VfL Bochum) 18
U Hoeness (Bayern Munich) 17
Wunder (MSV Duisburg) 17
Geye (Fortuna Düsseldorf) 16
Budde (Fortuna Düsseldorf) 14
Reimann (Hanover 96) 14

Bundesliga Promotion Playoffs

Group 1

	P	W	D	L	Goals	Pts
1. Fortuna Cologne	8	6	1	1	25-5	13
2. FC St Pauli	8	4	2	2	23-18	10
3. FSV 05 Mainz	8	3	3	2	17-11	9
4. Karlsruhe SC	8	2	2	4	17-23	6
5. Blau-Weiss 90 Berlin	8	1	0	7	10-35	2

Group 2

	P	W	D	L	Goals	Pts
1. Rot-Weiss Essen	8	6	2	0	23-8	14
2. SV Darmstadt 98	8	2	4	2	18-14	8
3. Röchling Völklingen	8	3	1	4	10-17	7
4. VfL Osnabrück	8	3	0	5	12-17	6
5. Wacker 04 Berlin	8	1	3	4	9-16	5

Regionalliga Berlin

Top Half

	P	W	D	L	Goals	Pts
1. Blau-Weiss 90 Berlin	32	21	6	5	78-32	48
2. Wacker 04 Berlin	32	23	1	9	87-42	47
3. Tennis Borussia Berlin	32	18	7	7	73-29	43
4. Tasmania 1900 Berlin	32	18	7	7	62-39	43
5. Hertha Zehlendorf	32	13	5	14	78-79	31
6. SV Berlin 92	32	10	6	16	39-52	26

Bottom Half

	P	W	D	L	Goals	Pts
1. SV Spandau	32	13	4	15	53-55	30
2. Rapide Wedding	32	12	4	16	43-55	28
3. Preussen Berlin	32	11	4	17	48-58	26
4. 1.FC Neukölln	32	10	4	18	42-74	24
5. Alemannia 90 Berlin	32	7	7	18	30-70	21
6. Rot-Weiss Neukölln	32	6	5	21	27-75	17

Top Scorer: Stolzenburg (Hertha Zehlendorf), 33 goals
Promoted: BC Südost Berlin, Westend 01 Berlin

Regionalliga North

Club	P	W	D	L	Goals	Pts
1. FC St Pauli	34	26	4	4	94-33	56
2. VfL Osnabrück	34	24	3	7	75-41	51
3. VfL Wolfsburg	34	19	8	7	71-35	48
4. Göttingen 05	34	18	7	9	60-36	43
5. SV Barmbek-Uhlenhorst	34	12	16	6	47-35	40
6. VfB Lübeck	34	15	10	9	48-42	40
7. Holstein Kiel	34	12	13	9	63-47	37
8. Phönix Lübeck	34	15	7	12	55-58	37
9. Arminia Hanover	34	11	12	11	48-41	34
10. SV Meppen	34	9	12	13	51-62	30
11. VfB Oldenburg	34	12	4	18	54-73	28
12. Olympia Wilhelmshaven	34	8	11	15	47-55	27
13. SV Heide	34	8	9	17	44-54	25
14. TuS Bremerhaven 93	34	6	13	15	40-60	25
15. OSV Hanover	34	10	5	19	51-74	25
16. Itzehoe SV	34	8	9	17	27-58	25
17. TuS Celle	34	6	10	18	40-70	22
18. Leu Brunswick	34	6	9	19	37-78	21

Top Scorer: Segler (VfL Osnabrück), 24 goals

Regionalliga North Promotion Playoffs

Group One

	P	W	D	L	Goals	Pts
1. Concordia Hamburg	6	3	3	0	15-7	9
2. Union Salzgitter	6	2	3	1	10-12	7
3. Flensburg 08	6	2	2	2	7-7	6
4. VfB Peine	6	1	0	5	9-15	2

Group Two

	P	W	D	L	Goals	Pts
1. VfL Pinneberg	6	4	1	1	15-9	9
2. Blumenthal SV	6	3	1	2	12-12	7
3. BSC Brunsbüttel	6	1	2	3	11-14	4
4. Preussen 07 Hamelin	6	1	2	3	11-14	4

Regionalliga South

Club	P	W	D	L	Goals	Pts
1. SV Darmstadt 98	34	20	6	8	72-37	46
2. Karlsruhe SC	34	19	7	8	72-48	45
3. TSV 1860 Munich	34	17	8	9	79-50	42
4. SpVgg Bayreuth	34	19	4	11	51-38	42
5. 1.FC Nuremberg	34	17	7	10	61-52	41
6. VfR Heilbronn	34	18	4	12	64-48	40
7. SV Chio Waldhof	34	16	7	11	60-44	39
8. Kickers Stuttgart	34	15	5	14	60-51	35
9. SpVgg Fürth	34	14	7	13	48-50	35
10. Hessen Kassel	34	13	7	14	59-58	33
11. Jahn Regensburg	34	14	5	15	53-53	33
12. Bayern Hof	34	12	7	15	67-60	31
13. VfR Bürstadt	34	12	7	15	54-62	31
14. Schweinfurt 05	34	11	9	14	54-72	31
15. FC Freiburg	34	11	7	16	48-73	29
16. SpVgg Ludwigsburg	34	10	8	16	53-62	28
17. SSV Reutlingen	34	7	6	21	41-84	20
18. Wacker Munich	34	4	3	27	37-91	11

Top Scorer: Keller (TSV 1860 Munich), 26 goals

Regionalliga South Promotion Playoffs

Club	P	W	D	L	Goals	Pts
1. VfR Mannheim	6	3	2	1	13-6	8
2. FC Villingen 08	6	3	1	2	14-8	7
3. SSV 1846 Ulm	6	2	2	2	8-11	6
4. SC Baden-Baden	6	0	3	3	5-15	3

Also Promoted: FC Augsburg, FSV Frankfurt

Regionalliga Southwest

Club	P	W	D	L	Goals	Pts
1. FSV 05 Mainz	30	18	8	4	80-41	44
2. Röchling Völklingen	30	17	10	3	53-19	44
3. FK Pirmasens	30	17	7	6	73-40	41
4. Wormatia Worms	30	14	11	5	70-39	39
5. Borussia Neunkirchen	30	16	6	8	59-35	38
6. ASV Landau	30	14	7	9	51-32	35
7. FC 08 Homburg	30	14	6	10	72-52	34
8. SV Alsenborn	30	11	9	10	52-47	31
9. Südwest Ludwigshafen	30	8	14	8	37-37	30
10. VfB Theley	30	9	9	12	39-53	27
11. TuS Neuendorf	30	7	12	11	37-50	26
12. FV Speyer	30	9	7	14	34-46	25
13. 1.FC Saarbrücken	30	7	10	13	37-49	24
14. Sportfreunde Eisbachtal	30	5	10	15	43-83	20
15. Eintracht Trier	30	5	2	23	34-83	12
16. Phönix Bellheim	30	2	6	22	35-100	10

Top Scorer: Dier (Wormatia Worms), Klier (FSV Mainz 05), and Ludwig (SV Alsenborn), 19 goals each

Regionalliga Southwest Promotion Playoffs

Club	P	W	D	L	Goals	Pts
1. Eintracht Bad Kreuznach	4	3	1	0	9-4	7
2. FC Ensdorf	4	2	1	1	6-4	5
3. SpVgg Andernach	4	0	0	4	4-11	0

Regionalliga West

Club	P	W	D	L	Goals	Pts
1. Rot-Weiss Essen	34	26	3	5	104-40	55
2. Fortuna Cologne	34	21	8	5	85-29	50
3. Bayer Uerdingen	34	16	11	7	73-50	43
4. Borussia Dortmund	34	16	9	9	77-45	41
5. Wattenscheid 09	34	16	8	10	70-60	40
6. Alemannia Aachen	34	15	9	10	66-50	39
7. Sportfreunde Siegen	34	14	11	9	55-53	39
8. 1.FC Mülheim-Styrum	34	13	12	9	46-56	38
9. DJK Gütersloh	34	14	9	11	51-56	37
10. SpVgg Erkenschwick	34	16	4	14	73-60	36
11. Arminia Bielefeld	34	9	12	13	46-66	30
12. Schwarz-Weiss Essen	34	11	7	16	41-58	29
13. Preussen Münster	34	11	7	16	47-66	29
14. Eintracht Gelsenkirchen	34	10	6	18	44-65	26
15. Westfalia Herne	34	7	10	17	34-52	24
16. Arminia Gütersloh	34	7	10	17	44-68	24
17. Bayer Leverkusen	34	6	7	21	38-76	19
18. Lünen SV	34	1	11	22	43-87	13

Top Scorer: Burgsmüller (Bayer Uerdingen), 29 goals

Regionalliga West Promotion Playoffs

Club	P	W	D	L	Goals	Pts
1. Rot-Weiss Lüdenscheid	6	3	2	1	17-13	8
2. Viktoria Cologne	6	3	2	1	10-9	8
3. Union Ohligs	6	2	2	2	11-11	6
4. VfB Bielefeld	6	1	0	5	8-13	2

Union Ohligs became OSC Solingen

Third Division Champions

Baden (Nordbaden): VfR Mannheim
Baden (Südbaden): SC Baden-Baden
Bayern: FC Augsburg
Berlin: BBC Südost
Bremen: SV Blumenthal
Hamburg: VfL Pinneberg
Hessen: FSV Frankfurt
Mittelrhein: SpVgg Frechen 20
Niederrhein: Union Ohligs
Niedersachsen: Union Salzgitter
Rheinland: SpVgg Andernach
Saarland: FC Ensdorf
Schleswig-Holstein: Flensburg 08
Südwest: Eintracht Bad Kreuznach
Westfalen: VfB Bielefeld
Württemberg: SSV 1846 Ulm

West German Cup
First Round
FC Freiburg 3, Borussia Mönchengladbach 1 (1-7)
FC St Pauli 3, Kickers Offenbach 1 (0-3)
FK Pirmasens 4, Rot-Weiss Oberhausen 1 (0-4)
Fortuna Cologne 2, 1.FC Cologne 1 (0-4 aet)
Hanover 96 1, Eintracht Frankfurt 0 (2-4)
Kickers Stuttgart 1, Eintracht Brunswick 1 (1-5)
OSV Hanover 0, Hertha BSC Berlin 6 (0-3)
Preussen Münster 2, MSV Duisburg 1 (0-3)
Rot-Weiss Essen 5, Hamburg SV 3 (0-5 aet)
SpVgg Bayreuth 4, 1.FC Kaiserslautern 2 (0-4)
Südwest Ludwigshafen 1, FC Schalke 04 3 (1-3)
SV Barmbek-Uhlenhorst 1, Bayern Munich 4 (0-7)
VfL Wolfsburg 2, VfB Stuttgart 2 (2-3)
Wacker 04 Berlin 1, Werder Bremen 5 (0-4)
Wormatia Worms 4, VfL Bochum 4 (1-3)
Wuppertal SV 3, Fortuna Düsseldorf 0 (0-2)

Second Round
Eintracht Brunswick 1, Eintracht Frankfurt 0 (2-2)
FC Schalke 04 0, Borussia Mönchengladbach 2 (1-1)
Hamburg SV 2, 1.FC Cologne 2 (1-4)
MSV Duisburg 1, Hertha BSC Berlin 2 (2-4)
Rot-Weiss Oberhausen 1, Bayern Munich 2 (1-3)
VfB Stuttgart 2, 1.FC Kaiserslautern 1 (0-2 aet)
VfL Bochum 4, Werder Bremen 4 (1-2)
Wuppertal SV 3, Kickers Offenbach 2 (0-3)

Quarterfinals
Borussia Mönchengladbach 2, 1.FC Kaiserslautern 1 (3-1)
Eintracht Brunswick 0, 1.FC Cologne 5 (2-3)
Kickers Offenbach 2, Bayern Munich 2 (4-2)
Werder Bremen 2, Hertha BSC Berlin 0 (2-2)

Semifinals
1.FC Cologne 5, Kickers Offenbach 0 (1-1)
Werder Bremen 1, Borussia Mönchengladbach 3 (2-4)

Final
in Düsseldorf
Borussia Mönchengladbach 2, 1.FC Cologne 1 aet

West German League Cup
Quarterfinals
Arminia Bielefeld 0, Borussia Mönchengladbach 3 (3-9)
Bayern Hof 1, Schalke 04 1 (2-7)
Eintracht Brunswick 2, Hamburg SV 1 (0-2)
Fortuna Cologne 2, Eintracht Frankfurt 3 (3-3)

Semifinals
Borussia Mönchengladbach 3, Eintracht Frankfurt 1 (0-1)
Schalke 04 1, Hamburg SV 0 (1-4 aet)

Final
in Hamburg
Hamburg SV 4, Borussia Mönchengladbach 0

West German Internationals
15/11/72 in Düsseldorf 5-1 v Switzerland
14/2/73 in Munich 2-3 v Argentina
28/3/73 in Düsseldorf 3-0 v Czechoslovakia
9/5/73 in Munich 0-1 v Yugoslavia
12/5/73 in Hamburg 3-0 v Bulgaria
16/6/73 in Berlin 0-1 v Brazil

East German Oberliga

Club	P	W	D	L	Goals	Pts
1. Dynamo Dresden	26	18	6	2	61-30	42
2. Carl Zeiss Jena	26	15	9	2	46-21	39
3. 1.FC Magdeburg	26	14	6	6	50-28	34
4. Lokomotive Leipzig	26	12	6	8	57-41	30
5. FC Karl-Marx-Stadt	26	11	8	7	33-32	30
6. Dynamo Berlin	26	9	8	9	41-42	26
7. Vorwärts Frankfurt/Oder	26	10	5	11	54-46	25
8. Sachsenring Zwickau	26	8	8	10	37-43	24
9. Chemie Leipzig	26	5	11	10	21-26	21
10. Hansa Rostock	26	6	8	12	36-44	20
11. Wismut Aue	26	7	6	13	27-46	20
12. Rot-Weiss Erfurt	26	8	3	15	37-56	19
13. 1.FC Union Berlin	26	7	4	15	22-45	18
14. Chemie Halle	26	4	8	14	35-57	16

Top Scorers
Kreische (Dynamo Dresden) ... 26
Vogel (Carl Zeiss Jena) ... 17
Matoul (Lokomotive Leipzig) ... 14
Streich (Hansa Rostock) ... 13
Löwe (Lokomotive Leipzig) ... 12
Dietzsch (Sachsenring Zwickau) ... 11
Johannsen (Dynamo Berlin) ... 11
Frenzel (Lokomotive Leipzig) ... 10
Lauck (1.FC Union Berlin) ... 10
Paschek (Vorwärts Frankfurt/Oder) ... 10
Lenz (Hansa Rostock) ... 9
Pommerenke (1.FC Magdeburg) ... 9
Schnuphase (Rot-Weiss Erfurt) ... 9
H Weisshaupt (Rot-Weiss Erfurt) ... 9

Oberliga Promotion Playoff

Club	P	W	D	L	Goals	Pts
1. Stahl Riesa	8	5	2	1	21-7	12
2. Energie Cottbus	8	4	2	2	10-14	10
3. Vorwärts Stralsund	8	2	4	2	9-8	8
4. Chemie Zeitz	8	2	2	4	12-17	6
5. Vorwärts Leipzig	8	1	2	5	8-14	4

Second Division (Staffel A)

Club	P	W	D	L	Goals	Pts
1. Vorwärts Stralsund	22	15	6	1	52-16	36
2. TSG Wismar	22	14	3	5	39-27	31
3. Dynamo Schwerin	22	13	4	5	62-32	30
4. Vorwärts Neubrandenburg	22	13	3	6	44-23	29
5. Hansa Rostock II	22	9	8	5	42-28	26
6. KKW Nord Greifswald	22	11	2	9	44-23	24
7. Schiffahrt/Hafen Rostock	22	7	6	9	32-38	20
8. Motor Schwerin	22	7	4	11	28-44	18
9. Post Neubrandenburg	22	6	4	12	27-35	16
10. Nord Torgelow	22	4	7	11	21-48	15
11. Motor WW Warnemünde	22	2	7	13	17-48	11
12. VB Waren	22	1	6	15	10-56	8

Promoted: Demminer VB, Einheit Güstrow, TSG Bau Rostock

Second Division (Staffel B)

Club	P	W	D	L	Goals	Pts
1. Dynamo Berlin II	22	13	6	3	35-14	32
2. Energie Cottbus	22	14	3	5	41-17	31
3. Vorwärts Frankfurt/Oder II	22	10	8	4	39-25	28
4. Stahl Eisenhüttenstadt	22	9	9	4	29-21	27
5. Dynamo Fürstenwalde	22	11	3	8	46-37	25
6. Vorwärts Cottbus	22	7	9	6	32-30	23
7. Stahl Hennigsdorf	22	7	8	7	35-28	22
8. Motor Eberswalde	22	7	7	8	31-27	21
9. Lichtenberg 47	22	6	6	10	34-35	18
10. Motor Hennigsdorf	22	6	6	10	26-32	18
11. Motor Köpenick	22	4	5	13	17-36	13
12. Aufbau Grossräschen	22	2	2	18	8-71	6

In the Dynamo Berlin II v Motor Köpenick match, two points were awarded to Dynamo with a scoreline of 0-0.

Promoted: Motor Babelsburg, 1.FC Union Berlin, Einheit Pankow, Aufbau Schwedt

Second Division (Staffel C)

Club	P	W	D	L	Goals	Pts
1. Vorwärts Leipzig	22	13	5	4	47-24	31
2. Stahl Brandenburg	22	12	4	6	34-21	28
3. Chemie Halle II	22	9	8	5	48-34	26
4. Lok/Vorwärts Halberstadt	22	9	8	5	31-25	26
5. Lokomotive Stendal	22	10	4	8	36-40	24
6. Chemie Böhlen	22	7	7	8	30-32	21
7. 1.FC Lokomotive Leipzig II	22	8	5	9	26-28	21
8. 1.FC Magdeburg II	22	7	6	9	28-34	20
9. Veritas Wittenberge	22	6	7	9	47-66	19
10. Chemie Wolfen	22	6	6	10	29-35	18
11. Dynamo Eisleben	22	7	3	12	42-39	17
12. Motor/Vorwärts Oschersleben	22	4	5	13	23-43	13

Chemie Böhlen did not participate at this level in the following season.

Promoted: Chemie Buna Schkopau, Rotation Leipzig, Motor Schönebeck.

Second Division (Staffel D)

Club	P	W	D	L	Goals	Pts
1. Dynamo Dresden II	22	14	6	2	60-24	34
2. Stahl Riesa	22	12	8	2	40-14	32
3. Aktivist Schwarze Pumpe	22	10	4	8	26-28	24
4. Lokomotive Dresden	22	7	9	6	29-27	23
5. Sachsenring Zwickau II	22	8	6	8	33-30	22
6. TSG Gröditz	22	6	9	7	26-28	21
7. Vorwärts Löbau	22	7	7	8	21-28	21
8. Karl-Marx-Stadt II	22	8	4	10	35-36	20
9. Motor Werdau	22	8	4	10	38-46	20
10. Motor Wema Plauen	22	7	5	10	26-34	19
11. Wismut Aue II	22	5	6	11	21-33	16
12. Wismut Pirna-Copitz	22	2	8	12	21-48	12

Promoted: Aktivist Brieske-Senftenburg, Motor Germania Karl-Marx-Stadt, Stahl Riesa II

Second Division (Staffel E)

Club	P	W	D	L	Goals	Pts
1. Chemie Zeitz	22	11	8	3	42-19	30
2. Wismut Gera	22	13	3	6	44-26	29
3. Carl Zeiss Jena II	22	9	9	4	30-14	27
4. Vorwärts Meiningen	22	9	9	4	32-18	27
5. Rot-Weiss Erfurt II	22	9	6	7	29-23	24
6. Stahl Maxhütte	22	10	4	8	24-38	24
7. Zentronik Sömmerda	22	6	7	9	20-21	19
8. Motor Steinach	22	5	9	8	28-30	19
9. Motor Nordhausen-West	22	8	3	11	28-34	19
10. Motor Hermsdorf	22	5	9	8	20-29	19
11. Kali Werra Tiefenort	22	5	6	11	21-35	16
12. Chemie Glas Ilmenau	22	3	5	14	10-41	11

Promoted: Motor Eisenach, Chemie Schwarza, Motor Suhl

East German Cup Final
in Dessau
1.FC Magdeburg 3, Lokomotive Leipzig 2

1972-73

East German Internationals
28/8/72 in Munich 4-0 v Ghana (OG)
1/9/72 in Nuremberg 1-2 v Poland (OG)
3/9/72 in Passau 0-2 v Hungary (OG)
10/9/72 in Munich 2-2 v USSR (OG)
The other four matches East Germany played in the 1972 Olympic Games are not recognised as full internationals.
7/10/72 in Dresden 5-0 v Finland (WCQ)
1/11/72 in Bratislava 3-1 v Czechoslovakia
15/2/72 in Bogota 2-0 v Colombia
18/2/73 in Quito 1-1 v Ecuador
7/4/73 in Magdeburg 2-0 v Albania (WCQ)
18/4/73 in Antwerp 0-3 v Belgium
16/5/73 in Karl-Marx-Stadt 2-1 v Hungary
27/5/73 in Bucharest 0-1 v Rumania (WCQ)
6/6/73 in Tampere 5-1 v Finland (WCQ)
17/7/73 in Reykjavik 2-1 v Iceland
19/7/73 in Reykjavik 2-0 v Iceland

European Cup
First Round
Galatasaray v Bayern Munich .... (1-1, 0-6)
1.FC Magdeburg v Turku Palloseura .... (6-0, 3-1)
Second Round
Omonia Nicosia v Bayern Munich .... (0-9, 0-4)
Juventus v 1.FC Magdeburg .... (1-0, 1-0)
Quarterfinals
Ajax Amsterdam v Bayern Munich .... (4-0, 1-2)

Cup-Winners' Cup
First Round
FC Schalke 04 v Slavia Sofia .... (2-1, 3-1)
Carl Zeiss Jena v Mikkeli .... (6-1, 2-3)
Second Round
Cork Hibs v FC Schalke 04 .... (0-0, 0-3)
Carl Zeiss Jena v Leeds United .... (0-0, 0-2)
Quarterfinals
FC Schalke 04 v Sparta Prague .... (2-1, 0-3)

UEFA Cup
First Round
Aberdeen v Borussia Mönchengladbach .... (2-3, 3-6)
1.FC Cologne v Bohemians Dublin .... (2-1, 3-0)
Stoke City v 1.FC Kaiserslautern .... (3-1, 0-4)
Liverpool v Eintracht Frankfurt .... (2-0, 0-0)
Dynamo Dresden v VÖEST Linz .... (2-0, 2-2)
SC Angers v Dynamo Berlin .... (1-1, 1-2)
Second Round
Borussia Mönchengladbach v Hvidovre .... (3-0, 3-1)
Viking Stavanger v 1.FC Cologne .... (1-0, 1-9)
CUF Barreirense v 1.FC Kaiserslautern .... (1-3, 1-0)
Dynamo Berlin v Levsky Spartak .... (3-0, 0-2)
Ruch Chorzow v Dynamo Dresden .... (0-1, 0-3)
Third Round
1.FC Cologne v Borussia Mönchengladbach .... (0-0, 0-5)
Ararat Yerevan v 1.FC Kaiserslautern .... (2-0, 0-2 aet)
Kaiserslautern won on penalties
FC Porto v Dynamo Dresden .... (1-2, 0-1)
Dynamo Berlin v Liverpool .... (0-0, 1-3)
Quarterfinals
1.FC Kaiserslautern v Borussia Mönchengladbach ... (1-2, 1-7)
Liverpool v Dynamo Dresden .... (2-0, 1-0)
Semifinals
Borussia Mönchengladbach v Twente Enschede ...... (3-0, 2-1)
Final
Liverpool v Borussia Mönchengladbach .... (3-0, 0-2)

1973-74

Champions of everything

To win the Bundesliga championship, the European Cup and the World Cup in the same season has to be the ultimate achievement for a German footballer. So 1973-74 had to be the best year in the footballing career of many Bayern Munich stars: Sepp Maier, Franz Beckenbauer, Gerd Müller, Georg Schwarzenbeck—and Uli Hoeness, whose playing record eventually encompassed 250 Bundesliga games and 35 international appearances.

Perhaps this was the very season which cemented Germany's footballing image of efficiency and professionalism. And if the epitome of this approach was Bayern Munich, then one vital component was surely Hoeness and his single-minded determination to succeed. Hoeness had worked his way up through the German schoolboy, youth and amateur teams to become a regular member of the national team at the age of twenty-one. He was also not afraid to voice his opinions, even if they clashed with those of the established stars like Maier and Beckenbauer.

Before the season, Bayern showed their determination to hang on to the championship by paying a record transfer fee to Cologne for wing-half Jupp Kapellmann. They also managed to persuade Gerd Müller to reject several lucrative offers from Spanish clubs. And, in the first season where jersey advertising was permitted, they extracted a healthy sum from their new sponsors, Adidas.

The first part of their season, though, was not without its problems—among them, a near-catastrophe in the European Cup. Swedish champions Atvidaberg pulled back a two-goal first-leg deficit to lead 3-2. But Hoeness then levelled the aggregate scores and later converted the decisive penalty after extra-time had failed to resolve the deadlock. Bayern's confidence was also called into question during an amazing match at the Betzenberg in October. With half an hour left to play, they were cruising to an emphatic victory, leading Kaiserslautern 4-1. But inexplicably they then went to pieces. Lautern scored six without reply to win 7-4 before 34,000 incredulous supporters. The result certainly shook Bayern, and skipper Beckenbauer decided it was time to assert his authority over young stars like Hoeness and Paul Breitner, who appeared to be playing for themselves rather than for the team. Bayern's performances grew stronger and stronger. Four days after the Kaiserslautern debacle, Bayern came from behind to beat Dynamo Dresden 4-3 in their European Cup tie, and in the away leg Hoeness showed his mastery of the quick counter-attack to score twice in a 3-3 draw.

At the halfway stage Bayern were on top on goal average, and after Christmas they put together a 15-match unbeaten run to stake their claim for the title. But there were other pressing matters. After knocking out Dresden, Bayern took care of the Bulgarian and Hungarian champions to reach the final of the European Cup. There, they looked to be in danger of losing to Atlético Madrid after Luis scored in extra time. But a last-gasp goal from Schwarzenbeck earned a replay two days later, when two Hoeness goals helped demolish the Spanish champions 4-0.

By this time Bayern had already been confirmed as Bundesliga champions. They had beaten Kickers Offenbach the previous Saturday, so their final game of the season at second-placed Mönchengladbach was virtually meaningless—which was just as well, as it took place the day after the replay against Madrid. The 5-0 thumping delivered by Gladbach didn't seriously dampen Bayern's celebration of a hat-trick of three consecutive titles, the first team to achieve this feat since organised football began in Germany.

Hoeness would later declare that, since it was obvious that this sort of achievement simply couldn't be repeated, the only way to go was down. Perhaps sharing the same sentiments—or resenting Beckenbauer's authority—Breitner left the club and joined Real Madrid. But even so, it was hard to believe that it would take six years before Bayern were to win the championship again.

Mönchengladbach finished runners-up to Bayern, the two clubs having stayed in the same position from Round 21 onward. Fortuna Düsseldorf again came third, the last time the club would reach such heights. But the previous season's fourth-placed team, Wuppertal SV, skidded to sixteenth, their confidence shattered by a 7-1 defeat at Gladbach and a 4-1 home loss to Bayern in consecutive games early in the new year.

Not many were terribly surprised by Fortuna Cologne and Hanover 96 occupying the bottom two spots at the end of the season. Hanover had finished just one place away from relegation in each of the previous two seasons and had gone through ten *Trainers* in their ten Bundesliga seasons; Fortuna were a small club with average gates of only 11,500, and had occupied one of the relegation spots almost the entire season. When Wuppertal drew at Stuttgart on the last day, Fortuna's loss to Kickers Offenbach sent them back down after just one season in the top flight.

In the regional leagues, some 83 teams had been battling to gain sufficient qualifying points to be included in the new Second Bundesliga. Based on performances over the past five seasons, the top qualifiers were Eintracht Brunswick (Regionalliga North), Rot-Weiss Oberhausen (West), Wacker 04 (Berlin), Borussia Neunkirchen (Southwest) and TSV 1860 Munich (South). Helmut Haller had returned to his hometown club FC Augsburg after 11 years in Italy with Bologna and Juventus, and he inspired his club to honours in the Regionalliga South. The previous year, Augsburg had earned promotion by winning the Bavarian Amateurliga and they now stormed to the championship of the Regionalliga South to claim their place in the new league. Augsburg's away match at Munich 1860, played in the Olympiastadion, attracted a crowd of over 80,000.

The end of the season also saw a reorganisation of amateur football in north Germany, with the formation of the Oberliga North from the top clubs of the amateur leagues of Niedersachsen, Bremen, Hamburg, and Schleswig-Holstein.

Eintracht Frankfurt won the West German Cup, played just before the start of the following season, 3-1 over Hamburg after extra time. Frankfurt had beaten Bayern in the semifinal, 3-2, thanks to a fortunate 90th minute penalty converted by Jürgen Kalb. Though not quite matching the excitement of the previous season's final, both teams attacked from the opening kickoff, and extra-time goals from Bernd Hölzenbein and Bernd Nickel gave Eintracht their first-ever cup triumph.

This season was unquestionably the most productive in East German football history. For the only time in their history, the national team actually managed to qualify for the World Cup. And, also for the only time in history, an East German club lifted one of the three major European club trophies. 1.FC Magdeburg won the Oberliga by finishing three points clear of Carl Zeiss Jena, but their real triumph came in the European Cup-Winners' Cup. They disposed of Dutch, Czechoslovakian, and Bulgarian opposition to face Sporting Lisbon in the semifinal. There, they held the Portugese to a draw in the first leg and won at home, setting up an encounter with AC Milan—conquerors of Mönchengladbach in the other semifinal—in Rotterdam. Just 5,000 were on hand in the Feyenoord Stadium to witness one of the rare moments of East German footballing glory, as Milan gave away an own goal and Paule Seguin scored for Magdeburg in a 2-0 victory.

The East German nationals completed a marvellous run of twelve consecutive wins before being held to a 1-1 draw by England in a friendly in front of 100,000 in Leipzig. By that time, East Germans had already been celebrating finishing top of their World Cup qualifying group. And they wound up being drawn in the same initial group as West Germany—whom they had never played in a full international.

The two German national sides had both avoided defeat against Australia and Chile before they met each other in Hamburg. A packed Volksparkstadion saw Jürgen Sparwasser score the only goal in the 78th minute to give the East Germans a 1-0 win, arguably their most famous in international competition. Nevertheless, both Germanys managed to qualify for the next round. In the second phase, East Germany's sixteen-match unbeaten run came to an end when Rivelino's goal gave Brazil a 1-0 win in Hanover. A subsequent 2-0 defeat by Holland then signalled the East Germans' exit from the tournament.

Meanwhile, West Germany enjoyed unconvincing victories over Yugoslavia and Sweden to set up a vital clash with Poland, which took place on a Frankfurt pitch ankle-deep in water in places following torrential rain. A single goal from Müller put Germany at the top of the group and into the final.

Despite the shock of conceding a first-minute penalty to Neeskens—for a foul which may have been committed outside the penalty area—the Germans came back and took the game to the over-confident Dutch. Berti Vogts effectively man-marked Johann Cruyff out of the game as the hosts equalised through a Breitner penalty and then took the lead with an opportunist strike from Müller to clinch the match. West Germany had won its first World Cup in twenty years—and only once in the next sixteen years would they *not* appear in the final.

Bundesliga

Club	P	W	D	L	Goals	Pts
1. Bayern Munich	34	20	9	5	95-53	49
2. Borussia Mönchengladbach	34	21	6	7	93-52	48
3. Fortuna Düsseldorf	34	16	9	9	61-47	41
4. Eintracht Frankfurt	34	15	11	8	63-50	41
5. 1.FC Cologne	34	16	7	11	69-56	39
6. 1.FC Kaiserslautern	34	15	8	11	80-69	38
7. FC Schalke 04	34	16	5	13	72-68	37
8. Hertha BSC Berlin	34	11	11	12	56-60	33
9. VfB Stuttgart	34	12	7	15	58-57	31
10. Kickers Offenbach	34	11	9	14	56-62	31
11. Werder Bremen	34	9	13	12	48-56	31
12. Hamburg SV	34	13	5	16	53-62	31
13. Rot-Weiss Essen	34	10	11	13	56-70	31
14. VfL Bochum	34	9	12	13	45-57	30
15. MSV Duisburg	34	11	7	16	42-56	29
16. Wuppertal SV	34	8	9	17	42-65	25
17. Fortuna Cologne	34	8	9	17	46-79	25
18. Hanover 96	34	6	10	18	50-66	22

Top Scorers

G Müller (Bayern Munich)	30
Heynckes (Borussia Mönchengladbach)	30
Toppmöller (1.FC Kaiserslautern)	21
Fischer (FC Schalke 04)	21
Sandberg (1.FC Kaiserslautern)	19
U Hoeness (Bayern Munich)	18
D Müller (1.FC Cologne)	17
Ohlicher (VfB Stuttgart)	17
Geye (Fortuna Düsseldorf)	16
Löhr (1.FC Cologne)	16
Pröpper (Wuppertal SV)	16

Bundesliga Promotion Playoffs

Group 1

	P	W	D	L	Goals	Pts
1. Eintracht Brunswick	8	5	1	2	13-6	11
2. 1.FC Nuremberg	8	5	1	2	18-12	11
3. Wattenscheid 09	8	3	2	3	11-11	8
4. Wacker 04 Berlin	8	3	1	4	13-18	7
5. 1.FC Saarbrücken	8	1	1	6	6-14	3

Group 2

	P	W	D	L	Goals	Pts
1. Tennis Borussia Berlin	8	3	4	1	13-11	10
2. FC Augsburg	8	2	5	1	18-17	9
3. Rot-Weiss Oberhausen	8	4	1	3	15-12	9
4. Borussia Neunkirchen	8	2	3	3	8-11	7
5. FC St Pauli	8	2	1	5	15-18	5

Regionalliga Berlin

Club	P	W	D	L	Goals	Pts
1. Tennis Borussia Berlin	33	31	1	1	103-19	63
2. Wacker 04 Berlin*	33	25	3	5	118-33	53
3. Blau-Weiss 90 Berlin	33	16	4	13	78-48	36
4. Hertha Zehlendorf	33	13	9	11	51-44	35
5. SC Westend 01 Berlin	33	14	6	13	60-62	34
6. Rapide Wedding	33	13	5	15	50-66	31
7. 1.FC Neukölln	33	11	8	14	65-75	30
8. SV Berlin 92	33	14	2	17	46-68	30
9. BC Südost Berlin	33	12	5	16	53-66	29
10. SV Spandau	33	12	5	16	49-62	29
11. Preussen Berlin	33	8	7	18	41-64	23
12. Alemannia 90 Berlin	33	1	1	31	15-122	3

* qualified for Second Division

Top Scorer: Stolzenburg (Tennis Borussia Berlin), 33 goals

Regionalliga North

Club	P	W	D	L	Goals	Pts
1. Eintracht Brunswick	36	30	3	3	125-23	63
2. FC St Pauli*	36	26	4	6	113-48	56
3. VfL Osnabrück*	36	18	14	4	84-43	50
4. VfL Wolfsburg*	36	19	8	9	77-51	46
5. SV Barmbek-Uhlenhorst*	36	15	13	8	48-38	43
6. VfB Oldenburg	36	18	6	12	71-55	42
7. Olympia Wilhelmshaven*	36	16	7	13	74-57	39
8. SV Meppen	36	13	12	11	55-54	38
9. Arminia Hanover	36	11	16	9	57-59	38
10. Concordia Hamburg	36	15	6	15	44-56	36
11. OSV Hanover	36	11	13	12	70-67	35
12. Göttingen 05*	36	12	9	15	55-46	33
13. Holstein Kiel	36	11	9	16	54-73	31
14. TuS Bremerhaven 93	36	11	9	16	35-61	31
15. SV Heide	36	8	7	21	48-76	23
16. VfB Lübeck	36	8	6	22	34-80	22
17. Itzehoe SV	36	7	7	22	48-107	21
18. VfL Pinneberg	36	5	10	21	43-76	20
19. Phönix Lübeck	36	6	5	25	40-105	17

* qualified for Second Division

Top Scorer: Gersdorff (Eintracht Brunswick), 35 goals

Regionalliga South

Club	P	W	D	L	Goals	Pts
1. FC Augsburg*	34	20	8	6	79-47	48
2. 1.FC Nuremberg*	34	18	8	8	63-42	44
3. TSV 1860 Munich*	34	19	5	10	74-35	43
4. SV Darmstadt 98*	34	20	2	12	64-38	42
5. SpVgg Bayreuth*	34	14	9	11	65-55	37
6. Kickers Stuttgart*	34	13	10	11	60-50	36
7. SV Chio Waldhof*	34	16	4	14	62-60	36
8. Karlsruhe SC*	34	14	8	12	50-48	36
9. Bayern Hof*	34	16	2	16	73-65	34
10. SpVgg Fürth*	34	14	6	14	48-45	34
11. FSV Frankfurt	34	14	6	14	54-54	34
12. VfR Heilbronn*	34	12	10	12	69-74	34
13. VfR Mannheim*	34	12	7	15	53-75	31
14. VfR Oli Bürstadt	34	10	9	15	44-57	29
15. Schweinfurt 05*	34	13	3	18	39-54	29
16. Hessen Kassel	34	10	8	16	47-57	28
17. FC Freiburg	34	6	8	20	31-81	20
18. Jahn Regensburg	34	4	9	21	39-77	17

* qualified for Second Division
Top Scorer: Obermeier (FC Augsburg), 25 goals

Regionalliga Southwest

Club	P	W	D	L	Goals	Pts
1. Borussia Neunkirchen*	30	20	5	5	64-29	45
2. 1.FC Saarbrücken*	30	19	5	6	59-27	43
3. FC 08 Homburg*	30	18	5	7	65-35	41
4. Röchling Völklingen*	30	16	7	7	62-28	39
5. FSV Mainz 05*	30	17	4	9	88-49	38
6. Wormatia Worms*	30	15	8	7	58-42	38
7. Eintracht Bad Kreuznach	30	13	7	10	55-36	33
8. FK Pirmasens*	30	11	10	9	63-47	32
9. ASV Landau	30	12	7	11	46-41	31
10. SV Alsenborn	30	10	7	13	41-48	27
11. Südwest Ludwigshafen	30	8	10	12	44-48	26
12. TuS Neuendorf	30	10	4	16	37-58	24
13. VfB Theley	30	10	3	17	37-60	23
14. Sportfreunde Eisbachtal	30	7	5	18	48-87	19
15. FV Speyer	30	3	7	20	31-84	13
16. FC Ensdorf	30	1	6	23	18-86	8

* qualified for Second Division
Top Scorer: Klier (FSV Mainz 05), 28 goals

Regionalliga West

Club	P	W	D	L	Goals	Pts
1. Wattenscheid 09*	34	25	5	4	102-39	55
2. Rot-Weiss Oberhausen*	34	25	4	5	85-43	54
3. Bayer Uerdingen*	34	22	7	5	82-40	51
4. 1.FC Mülheim-Styrum*	34	20	4	10	76-49	44
5. Preussen Münster*	34	15	8	11	57-49	38
6. Borussia Dortmund*	34	15	7	12	63-50	37
7. Alemannia Aachen*	34	15	7	12	57-55	37
8. Schwarz-Weiss Essen*	34	12	10	12	57-53	34
9. DJK Gütersloh*	34	10	12	12	54-55	32
10. Rot-Weiss Lüdenscheid	34	12	8	14	47-58	32
11. SpVgg Erkenschwick*	34	8	14	12	54-69	30
12. Sportfreunde Siegen	34	9	10	15	59-76	28
13. Arminia Gütersloh	34	9	10	15	47-66	28
14. Arminia Bielefeld*	34	9	9	16	41-52	27
15. OSC Solingen	34	7	11	16	46-68	25
16. Eintracht Gelsenkirchen	34	7	8	19	42-73	22
17. Westfalia Herne	34	7	5	22	44-78	19
18. Viktoria Cologne	34	3	13	18	42-82	19

* qualified for Second Division
Top Scorer: Burgsmüller (Bayer Uerdingen), 29 goals

Third Division Champions

Baden (Nordbaden): FV Karlsruhe
Baden (Südbaden): FV Offenburg
Bayern: ASV Herzogenaurach
Berlin: SC Staaken
Bremen: SV Blumenthal
Hamburg: Victoria Hamburg
Hessen: Viktoria Aschaffenburg
Mittelrhein: Bayer Leverkusen
Niederrhein: VfB Marathon Remscheid
Niedersachsen: Preussen 07 Hamelin
Rheinland: SV Leiwen
Saarland: SV St. Ingbert
Schleswig-Holstein: Flensburg 08
Südwest: FK Clausen
Westfalen: TuS Neuenrade
Württemberg: VfR Aalen and FC Villingen 08

West German Cup
First Round
1.FC Cologne 2, Eintracht Brunswick 0
1.FC Kaiserslautern 5, Rot-Weiss Essen 3 aet
1.FC Nuremberg 4, FSV Mainz 05 1
Arminia Bielefeld 2, Alemannia Aachen 1
Bayern Munich 3, MSV Duisburg 1
Borussia Dortmund 1, Hanover 96 4
FC Schalke 04 1, Wattenscheid 09 2
Fortuna Cologne 3, VfB Stuttgart 2 aet
Hamburg SV 3, SV Darmstadt 98 1
Hertha BSC Berlin 2, Fortuna Düsseldorf 2 aet (1-1 aet; Hertha won on penalties)
Hessen Kassel 2, Barmbek-Uhlenhorst 1
Kickers Offenbach 2, VfR Heilbronn 2 aet (3-2 aet)
Tennis Borussia Berlin 1, Eintracht Frankfurt 8
TuS Neuendorf 0, Wuppertal SV 2
VfB Oldenburg 0, Borussia Mönchengladbach 6
VfL Bochum 2, Werder Bremen 2 aet (1-2)

Second Round
1.FC Cologne 1, Wuppertal SV 0
Arminia Bielefeld 1, 1.FC Kaiserslautern 1 aet (0-3)
Borussia Mönchengladbach 2, Hamburg SV 2 aet (1-1 aet; Hamburg won on penalties)
Fortuna Cologne 0, Hanover 96 0 aet (0-2)
Hessen Kassel 2, Eintracht Frankfurt 3
Kickers Offenbach 3, 1.FC Nuremberg 2
Wattenscheid 09 0, Hertha BSC Berlin 0
Werder Bremen 1, Bayern Munich 2

Quarterfinals
Bayern Munich 3, Hanover 96 2
Eintracht Frankfurt 4, 1.FC Cologne 3 aet
Kickers Offenbach 2, 1.FC Kaiserslautern 2 aet (3-2 aet)
Wattenscheid 09 0, Hamburg SV 1 aet

Semifinals
Eintracht Frankfurt 3, Bayern Munich 2
Hamburg SV 1, Kickers Offenbach 0

Final
in Düsseldorf
Eintracht Frankfurt 3, Hamburg SV 1 aet

West German Internationals
5/9/73 in Moscow 1-0 v Soviet Union
10/10/73 in Hanover 4-0 v Austria
13/10/73 in Gelsenkirchen 2-1 v France
14/11/73 in Glasgow 1-1 v Scotland
24/11/73 in Stuttgart 2-1 v Spain
23/2/74 in Barcelona 0-1 v Spain
26/2/74 in Rome 0-0 v Italy
27/3/74 in Frankfurt 2-1 v Scotland
17/4/74 in Dortmund 5-0 v Hungary
1/5/74 in Hamburg 2-0 v Sweden
14/6/74 in Berlin 1-0 v Chile (WC)
18/6/74 in Hamburg 3-0 v Australia (WC)
22/6/74 in Hamburg 0-1 v East Germany (WC)
26/6/74 in Düsseldorf 2-0 v Yugoslavia (WC)
30/6/74 in Düsseldorf 4-2 v Sweden (WC)
3/7/74 in Frankfurt 1-0 v Poland (WC)
7/7/74 in Munich 2-1 v Holland (WC)

East German Oberliga

Club	P	W	D	L	Goals	Pts
1. 1.FC Magdeburg	26	16	7	3	50-27	39
2. Carl Zeiss Jena	26	16	4	6	55-26	36
3. Dynamo Dresden	26	15	5	6	55-40	35
4. Vorwärts Frankfurt/Oder	26	13	8	5	48-27	34
5. Lokomotive Leipzig	26	11	8	7	49-35	30
6. Dynamo Berlin	26	12	3	11	42-41	27
7. Hansa Rostock	26	10	5	11	37-35	25
8. Sachsenring Zwickau	26	10	5	11	37-41	25
9. FC Karl-Marx-Stadt	26	7	10	9	42-46	24
10. Wismut Aue	26	7	8	11	29-38	22
11. Stahl Riesa	26	7	9	10	25-42	21
12. Rot-Weiss Erfurt	26	5	9	12	27-39	19
13. Chemie Leipzig	26	3	9	14	22-39	15
14. Energie Cottbus	26	1	8	17	16-58	10

Top Scorers
Matoul (Lokomotive Leipzig) 20
Streich (Hansa Rostock) 14
Kotte (Dynamo Dresden) 12
Sparwasser (1.FC Magdeburg) 12
Dietzsch (Sachsenring Zwickau) 11
Schumann (Carl Zeiss Jena) 10
Wolf (Karl-Marx-Stadt) 10
Zierau (Vorwärts Frankfurt/Oder) 10
Andrich (Vorwärts Frankfurt/Oder) 9
P Ducke (Carl Zeiss Jena) 9
Hoffmann (1.FC Magdeburg) 9
Vogel (Carl Zeiss Jena) 9

Oberliga Promotion Playoff

Club	P	W	D	L	Goals	Pts
1. Chemie Halle	8	6	1	1	12-5	13
2. Vorwärts Stralsund	8	3	4	1	12-6	10
3. 1.FC Union Berlin	8	4	2	2	11-6	10
4. Chemie Böhlen	8	2	2	4	6-10	6
5. Wismut Gera	8	0	1	7	3-17	1

Second Division (Staffel A)

Club	P	W	D	L	Goals	Pts
1. Vorwärts Stralsund	22	18	3	1	51-13	39
2. Post Neubrandenburg	22	11	8	3	43-22	30
3. Dynamo Schwerin	22	11	5	6	35-19	27
4. Vorwärts Neubrandenburg	22	10	6	6	40-17	26
5. TSG Wismar	22	10	4	8	38-31	24
6. KKW Nord Greifswald	22	9	5	8	36-30	23
7. Hansa Rostock II	22	9	4	9	31-26	22
8. Schiffahrt/Hafen Rostock	22	8	3	11	33-40	19
9. TSG Bau Rostock	22	4	8	10	16-31	16
10. Einheit Güstrow	22	6	4	12	26-47	16
11. Demminer VB	22	4	4	14	19-63	12
12. Motor Schwerin	22	2	6	14	12-41	10

Hansa Rostock II - two points deducted
Promoted: Lokomotive Bergen, Aufbau Boizenburg, VB Waren, Veritas Wittenberge

Second Division (Staffel B)

Club	P	W	D	L	Goals	Pts
1. 1.FC Union Berlin	22	15	4	3	48-13	34
2. Stahl Eisenhüttenstadt	22	11	7	4	46-28	29
3. Dynamo Berlin II	22	9	7	6	41-26	25
4. Lichtenberg 47	22	9	7	6	25-21	25
5. Stahl Hennigsdorf	22	7	7	8	39-38	21
6. Vorwärts Frankfurt/Oder II	22	8	5	9	33-36	21
7. Aufbau Schwedt	22	7	7	8	24-29	21
8. Dynamo Fürstenwalde	22	8	4	10	40-55	20
9. Motor Babelsberg	22	7	5	10	36-36	19
10. Vorwärts Cottbus	22	9	1	12	34-41	19
11. Motor Eberswalde	22	6	7	9	24-31	19
12. Einheit Pankow	22	3	5	14	24-60	11

Promoted: NARVA Berlin, Stahl Finow, Motor Ludwigsfelde, Aufbau Schwedt

Second Division (Staffel C)

Club	P	W	D	L	Goals	Pts
1. Chemie Halle	22	19	3	0	75-17	41
2. 1.FC Magdeburg II	22	12	7	3	36-23	31
3. Lok/Vorwärts Halberstadt	22	13	2	7	35-29	28
4. Lokomotive Stendal	22	10	6	6	53-20	26
5. Vorwärts Leipzig	22	10	5	7	28-21	25
6. Stahl Brandenburg	22	9	5	8	43-35	23
7. Lokomotive Leipzig II	22	10	3	9	37-31	23
8. Veritas Wittenberge	22	8	5	9	36-47	21
9. Chemie Buna Schkopau	22	6	7	9	27-27	19
10. Rotation 1950 Leipzig	22	3	4	15	20-50	10
11. Chemie Wolfen	22	3	3	16	15-41	9
12. Motor Schönebeck	22	3	2	17	18-62	8

Promoted: Vorwärts Dessau, Dynamo Eisleben, Lokomotive Ost Leipzig

Second Division (Staffel D)

Club	P	W	D	L	Goals	Pts
1. Chemie Böhlen	22	13	6	3	36-24	32
2. Aktivist Brieske-Senftenberg	22	9	8	5	29-30	26
3. Sachsenring Zwickau II	22	8	8	6	34-29	24
4. Aktivist Schwarze Pumpe	22	9	6	7	32-27	24
5. Motor Werdau	22	9	5	8	31-27	23
6. Dynamo Dresden II	22	7	8	7	37-26	22
7. TSG Gröditz	22	8	6	8	24-23	22
8. Lokomotive Dresden	22	7	7	8	34-33	21
9. Motor Germania K-M-S	22	7	5	10	33-44	19
10. Stahl Riesa II	22	8	2	12	35-36	18
11. Vorwärts Löbau	22	6	5	11	33-45	17
12. Karl-Marx-Stadt II	22	5	6	11	23-37	16

Both points in the Dynamo Dresden II v Aktivist Brieske-Senftenberg match were awarded to Aktivist, with a scoreline of 0-0.

Chemie Böhlen were placed in Staffel C for the following season

Promoted: Wismut Aue II, Motor Bautzen, Lokomotive Cottbus

Second Division (Staffel E)

Club	P	W	D	L	Goals	Pts
1. Wismut Gera	22	16	5	1	44-12	37
2. Carl Zeiss Jena II	22	12	7	3	50-16	31
3. Motor Suhl	22	11	6	5	40-28	28
4. Chemie Zeitz	22	8	8	6	35-25	24
5. Motor Nordhausen-West	22	8	8	6	32-29	24
6. Motor Steinach	22	7	8	7	22-28	22
7. Zentronik Sömmerda	22	7	8	7	32-27	22
8. Vorwärts Meiningen	22	7	8	7	32-27	22
9. Rot-Weiss Erfurt II	22	6	6	10	25-32	18
10. Chemie Schwarza	22	2	11	9	14-32	15
11. Motor Eisenach	22	3	7	12	28-50	13
12. Stahl Maxhütte	22	3	3	16	20-63	9

Both points in the Stahl Maxhütte v Zentronik Sömmerda match were awarded to Sömmerda, with a scoreline of 0-0.

Vorwärts Meiningen did not participate at this level in the following season.

Promoted: Motor Hermsdorf, Vorwärts Plauen, TSG Ruhla, Kali Werra Tiefenort

East German Cup Final
in Leipzig
Carl Zeiss Jena 3, Dynamo Dresden 1 aet

1973-74

East German Internationals
26/9/73 in Leipzig 2-0 v Rumania (WCQ)
17/10/73 in Leipzig 1-0 v USSR
3/11/73 in Tirana 4-1 v Albania (WCQ)
21/11/73 in Budapest 1-0 v Hungary
26/2/74 in Tunis 4-0 v Tunisia
28/2/74 in Algiers 3-1 v Algeria
13/3/74 in Berlin 1-0 v Belgium
27/3/74 in Dresden 1-0 v Czechoslovakia
23/5/74 in Rostock 1-0 v Norway
29/5/74 in Leipzig 1-1 v England
14/6/74 in Hamburg 2-0 v Australia (WC)
18/6/74 in Berlin 1-1 v Chile (WC)
2/6/74 in Hamburg 1-0 v West Germany (WC)
26/6/74 in Hanover 0-1 v Brazil (WC)
30/6/74 in Gelsenkirchen 0-2 v Holland (WC)
3/7/74 in Gelsenkirchen 1-1 v Argentina (WC)

European Cup
First Round
Bayern Munich v Atvidaberg .... (3-1, 1-3 aet)
Bayern won on penalties
Dynamo Dresden v Juventus .... (2-0, 2-3)
Second Round
Bayern Munich v Dynamo Dresden .... (4-3, 3-3)
Quarterfinals
Bayern Munich v CSKA Sofia .... (4-1, 1-2)
Semifinals
Ujpest Dozsa v Bayern Munich .... (1-1, 0-3)
Final in Brussels
Bayern Munich 1, Atlético Madrid 1 aet (4-0)

Cup-Winners' Cup
First Round
Vestmannajar v Borussia Mönchengladbach .... (0-7, 1-9)
Breda NAC v 1.FC Magdeburg .... (0-0, 0-2)
Second Round
Borussia Mönchengladbach v Glasgow Rangers ..... (3-0, 2-3)
Banik Ostrava v 1.FC Magdeburg .... (2-0, 0-3 aet)
Quarterfinals
Glentoran v Borussia Mönchengladbach .... (0-2, 0-5)
1.FC Magdeburg v Beroe Stara .... (2-0, 1-1)
Semifinals
AC Milan v Borussia Mönchengladbach .... (2-0, 0-1)
Sporting Lisbon v 1.FC Magdeburg .... (1-1, 1-2)
Final in Rotterdam
1.FC Magdeburg 2, AC Milan 0

UEFA Cup
First Round
VfB Stuttgart v Olympiakos Nicosia .... (9-0, 4-0)
Fortuna Düsseldorf v Naestved IF .... (1-0, 2-2)
Eskisehirspor v 1.FC Cologne .... (0-0, 0-2)
Ruch Chorzow v Wuppertal SV .... (4-1, 4-5)
Torino v Lokomotive Leipzig .... (1-2, 1-2)
Carl Zeiss Jena v Mikkeli MP .... (3-0, 3-0)
Second Round
Olympique Marseilles v 1.FC Cologne .... (2-0, 0-6)
VfB Stuttgart v Tatran Presov .... (3-1, 5-3)
Admira Vienna v Fortuna Düsseldorf .... (2-1, 0-3)
Lokomotive Leipzig v Wolverhampton Wanderers .... (3-0, 1-4)
Ruch Chorzow v Carl Zeiss Jena .... (3-0, 0-1)
Third Round
Fortuna Düsseldorf v Lokomotive Leipzig .... (2-1, 0-3)
Nice v 1.FC Cologne .... (1-0, 0-4)
Dynamo Kiev v VfB Stuttgart .... (2-0, 0-3)
Quarterfinals
VfB Stuttgart v Vitoria Setubal .... (1-0, 2-2)
1.FC Cologne v Tottenham Hotspur .... (1-2, 0-3)
Ipswich Town v Lokomotive Leipzig .... (1-0, 0-1 aet)
Leipzig won on penalties
Semifinals
Feyenoord v VfB Stuttgart .... (2-1, 2-2)
Lokomotive Leipzig v Tottenham Hotspur .... (1-2, 0-2)

1974-75

A second Bundesliga

After three successive championships, Bayern once again began the season as odds-on favourites. Only Mönchengladbach seemed to possess the necessary self-confidence to do anything about it. In fact they were determined to finish ahead of their arch-rivals. *Trainer* Hennes Weisweiler drummed it into his players that they were just as good as Bayern. He also stressed to his team how important it was to start the season with a win.

But things didn't quite go according to plan. On the opening day Borussia lost 3-1 at home to Hamburg SV. Bayern, though, were inexplicably hammered 6-0 at Kickers Offenbach. And while Gladbach soon got themselves together, taking eleven points from their next seven games, Bayern never managed to find their form and wound up finishing a surprisingly distant tenth.

Bayern's infallibility had crumbled. They had been undefeated at home in the league for four and a half years—an incredible run of 73 matches, 62 of which were wins—until Schalke went to the Olympiastadion at the end of September and took both points with a 2-0 victory. Soon *Trainer* Udo Lattek found himself out of a job, and was replaced by Dettmar Cramer, who may or may not have been under contract to manage the U.S. national team. It was a move the club's management came to regret, as Bayern continued to falter. General Manager Robert Schwan would later confess that appointing Cramer was the biggest mistake of his life.

Gladbach's form stuttered up to Christmas, but they then put together a 17-match unbeaten sequence to open up a gap between themselves and their nearest challengers: Hertha, Frankfurt and Hamburg. Eventually, everything clicked into place: an admirable team spirit, outstanding coaching, fanatical support, and a squad of exceptionally talented, well-motivated players, including Rainer Bonhof, Wolfgang Kleff, Jupp Heynckes, Herbert Wimmer, Hans-Jürgen Wittkamp, Uli Stielike, Henning Jensen, Alan Simonsen, Horst Köppel, and Berti Vogts. Gladbach's formidable attack registered 86 goals, and their forwards were said to be so greedy they'd even steal the ball off each other on the opponents' goal line.

Borussia's celebrations following their amazing 5-1 away win in the final of the UEFA Cup against Twente Enschede were muted in the wake of Weisweiler's declaration that he was leaving the club to become manager of Barcelona. After more than ten years as *Trainer* at the Bökelberg, amassing a remarkable record of 169 wins, 85 draws and 86 defeats, his departure marked the end of an era.

Hertha Berlin finished as Bundesliga runners-up, though they and the rest of the Bundesliga never looked capable of catching Mönchengladbach. *Trainer* Georg Kessler was not blessed with an abundance of goalscoring talent—only the reliable Erich Beer managed to find the target with any regularity—but he had few injury problems, enabling him to use just fifteen players all season.

Bayern's league form may have been disappointing, but they made up for it with a second straight appearance in the European Cup Final. The Bavarians and 1.FC Magdeburg were given a bye into the second round, where they were drawn to play against each other. Bayern won 3-2 in Munich and 2-1 in Magdeburg, and then beat Ararat Yerevan and St. Etienne to reach the final. Their 2-0 win over Leeds in Paris was plagued with curious decisions from referee Kitabjian, who was subsequently struck off the UEFA list. English fans will remember this as a match they deserved to win; for the Germans the goals from Roth and Müller in the last twenty minutes were seen as poetic justice in light of Terry Yorath's fourth-minute tackle on Björn Andersson, which ended the Swede's career. Ten days after lifting the European Cup, Müller scored all five goals for his club in a league match against Düsseldorf—but Bayern lost 6-5.

Gladbach, too, walked off with a European trophy, thanks to a memorable performance in the second leg of the UEFA Cup Final against Twente Enschede which ensured a 5-1 win. A Jupp Heynckes hat-trick and two goals from Alan Simonsen were just the tonic for an overly cautious, goalless first leg. An earlier brace of goals from Simonsen, the wily Danish international, helped Borussia put out Bundesliga rivals Cologne in the semifinals. (Cologne, whose Müngersdorf Stadion was undergoing a major renovation, were forced to play their home matches in the Müngersdorf Velodrome.)

As from this season, the bottom three teams in the league—not just two—were to be relegated. This meant VfB Stuttgart's continuous membership of the Bundesliga came to an end. In spite of the fact that fifteenth-placed Werder Bremen failed to win any of their last five matches, VfB still wound up behind them. Less surprising was the relegation of Wuppertal and Tennis Borussia Berlin, both of whom looked doomed from early on. Wuppertal *Trainer* Horst Buhtz was sacked in October, but Tennis Borussia persisted with Georg Gawliczek all season. His goalkeeper Hubert Birkenmeier would spend two more seasons with the club before moving to FC Freiburg and on to New York, where he became a highly-respected goalkeeper in the North American Soccer League.

This was also the first season of the new German Second Bundesliga, which was divided into North and South sections culled from the old *Regionalligen*. The champions of each of the Second Divisions led the way from very early on. Hanover topped the *Zweite Liga Nord* from the thirteenth match of the season, whilst Karlsruhe led the *Zweite Liga Süd* from the fifth match on. The third team to be promoted to the Bundesliga was decided by a playoff between the divisional runners-up: Bayer Uerdingen from the North and FK Pirmasens from the South. Pirmasens had qualified for the playoff by the skin of their teeth: rivals Bayern Hof needed only to complete their regular season with a win over Darmstadt to pip them. But Darmstadt's Hans Lindemann scored with seven minutes left to play to defeat Hof 2-1 before a stunned 17,500. In the playoff, Peter Falter scored a hat-trick for Uerdingen in an easy second-leg win for a comprehensive aggregate victory and a place in Division One for the first time in their history.

The new Second Bundesliga South provided contrasting fortunes for the two rivals from Mannheim. VfR Mannheim wound up relegated, never to return. But SV Chio Waldhof established themselves and were able to progress into the unified Second Division in 1981 and the Bundesliga itself in 1983. Waldhof had acquired their strange middle name in 1972, in a sponsorship deal with Chio, a manufacturer of snacks, before dropping it in 1978. Several other minor clubs included their sponsor's name at this time, possibly the strangest-sounding being Gummi-Meyer Landau of the Amateurliga Südwest. Today, apart from the curious exception of the two Bayer works teams, this practice is prohibited by the DFB.

There was also a reorganisation of the West German Cup this season, with the first round involving a staggering 128 clubs instead of 32. Teams entered in the first round now had to win six matches rather than four to reach the final. The first round therefore had a rather strange look, with ties like FC Rodalben v TSV Taunusstein-Bleidenstadt vying for attention with Bayern Munich v VfB Stuttgart. As expected, there were a number of lopsided contests in the early rounds, but six amateur-division clubs managed to reach the last sixteen, including VfB Eppingen. They created the shock of the competition when, before a home crowd of over 15,000, they put out the previous season's beaten finalists, Hamburg SV, 2-1. Eppingen then came away with a fortunate win at Sandhausen before their Cup march ended at home to Bremen, where 25,000 saw them lose to Werder.

Second Division Borussia Dortmund reached the semifinals, but lost in extra time to a Bernard Dietz goal at Duisburg. In the other semifinal, Rot-Weiss Essen's Manfred Burgsmüller scored in the 85th minute to force extra time, but then Eintracht Frankfurt's Klaus Beverungen and Bernd Lorenz each notched a goal to give Frankfurt a 3-1 victory, putting them into the final for the second straight year. The final was played in a downpour in Hanover where, from a 57th minute Eintracht corner, Karl-Heinz Körbel scored from six yards for the only goal. Duisburg hit the post two minutes later, but Eintracht were worthy winners and retained the cup.

The East German Cup Final between Sachsenring Zwickau and Dynamo Dresden was drawn 2-2 after extra time and was the first ever to be decided on penalties. Hans-Jürgen Dörner missed one of Dresden's, and the winner for Zwickau was scored by their goalkeeper, Jürgen Croy. This was the first cup final to be held in East Berlin since 1965—and a record crowd of 55,000 turned out for the occasion. Not surprisingly, the East German F.A. decided to make the Berlin cup final an annual event. Magdeburg, with East German Footballer of the Year Jürgen Pommerenke running the midfield, won their second consecutive league championship. But after the relative success of the previous season, the East German nationals had a very poor year, culminating in a feeble display in their European Championship qualifying tie with Iceland, which they lost 2-1.

Bundesliga

Club	P	W	D	L	Goals	Pts
1. Borussia Mönchengladbach	34	21	8	5	86-40	50
2. Hertha BSC Berlin	34	19	6	9	61-43	44
3. Eintracht Frankfurt	34	18	7	9	89-49	43
4. Hamburg SV	34	18	7	9	55-38	43
5. 1.FC Cologne	34	17	7	10	77-51	41
6. Fortuna Düsseldorf	34	16	9	9	66-55	41
7. FC Schalke 04	34	16	7	11	52-37	39
8. Kickers Offenbach	34	17	4	13	72-62	38
9. Eintracht Brunswick	34	14	8	12	52-42	36
10. Bayern Munich	34	14	6	14	57-63	34
11. VfL Bochum	34	14	5	15	53-53	33
12. Rot-Weiss Essen	34	10	12	12	56-68	32
13. 1.FC Kaiserslautern	34	13	5	16	56-55	31
14. MSV Duisburg	34	12	6	16	59-77	30
15. Werder Bremen	34	9	7	18	45-69	25
16. VfB Stuttgart	34	8	8	18	50-79	24
17. Tennis Borussia Berlin	34	5	6	23	38-89	16
18. Wuppertal SV	34	2	8	24	32-86	12

Top Scorers
Heynckes (Borussia Mönchengladbach) 27
D Müller (1.FC Cologne) 24
G Müller (Bayern Munich) 23
Sandberg (1.FC Kaiserslautern) 20
Burgsmüller (Rot-Weiss Essen) 18
Kostedde (Kickers Offenbach) 18
Simonsen (Borussia Mönchengladbach) 18
Fischer (FC Schalke 04) 17
Ohlicher (VfB Stuttgart) 17
Hölzenbein (Eintracht Frankfurt) 16

Promotion Playoff
FK Pirmasens v Bayer Uerdingen (4-4, 0-6); Uerdingen promoted to Bundesliga

Second Division North

Club	P	W	D	L	Goals	Pts
1. Hanover 96	38	25	4	9	93-39	54
2. Bayer Uerdingen	38	20	11	7	66-38	51
3. FC St Pauli	38	22	6	10	77-48	50
4. Arminia Bielefeld	38	18	4	6	68-47	50
5. Fortuna Cologne	38	21	4	13	69-43	46
6. Borussia Dortmund	38	17	12	9	65-44	46
7. Wattenscheid 09	38	18	10	10	72-53	46
8. VfL Osnabrück	38	16	10	12	81-62	42
9. Preussen Münster	38	17	8	13	74-63	42
10. Göttingen 05	38	15	9	14	60-66	39
11. 1.FC Mülheim-Styrum	38	12	12	14	47-65	36
12. Schwarz-Weiss Essen	38	13	8	17	55-69	36
13. Wacker 04 Berlin	38	13	7	18	54-68	33
14. DJK Gütersloh	38	11	10	17	57-63	32
15. Alemannia Aachen	38	11	8	19	57-71	30
16. SpVgg Erkenschwick	38	9	11	18	49-70	29
17. Olympia Wilhelmshaven	38	10	7	21	54-81	27
18. Rot-Weiss Oberhausen	38	6	15	17	38-66	27
19. VfL Wolfsburg	38	10	6	22	61-89	26
20. Barmbek-Uhlenhorst	38	6	8	24	34-86	20

Promoted: Bayer Leverkusen, SV Spandau, Westfalia Herne, Union Solingen.

Top Scorers
Graul (Arminia Bielefeld) 29
Schock (VfL Osnabrück) 26
Wenzel (FC St Pauli) 24
Dahl (Hanover 96) 23
Kasperski (Hanover 96) 20
Kucharski (Hanover 96) 20
John (Wacker 04 Berlin) 19
Krause (VfL Wolfsburg) 19
Stegmayer (Hanover 96) 19
Fritsche (Schwarz-Weiss Essen) 18

Second Division South

Club	P	W	D	L	Goals	Pts
1. Karlsruhe SC	38	22	6	10	76-50	50
2. FK Pirmasens	38	19	10	9	75-62	48
3. Schweinfurt 05	38	19	10	9	65-59	48
4. Bayern Hof	38	18	10	10	65-46	46
5. TSV 1860 Munich	38	20	5	13	64-45	45
6. 1.FC Nuremberg	38	17	8	13	70-52	42
7. 1.FC Saarbrücken	38	15	11	12	72-52	41
8. SV Chio Waldhof	38	16	8	14	52-42	40
9. SpVgg Bayreuth	38	15	10	13	53-50	40
10. SV Darmstadt 98	38	16	7	15	68-62	39
11. FSV Mainz 05	38	14	10	14	63-60	38
12. FC Augsburg	38	12	13	13	61-63	37
13. Röchling Völklingen	38	11	12	15	56-54	34
14. FC 08 Homburg	38	13	8	17	71-74	34
15. SpVgg Fürth	38	12	10	16	40-48	34
16. Kickers Stuttgart	38	13	7	18	52-61	33
17. VfR Heilbronn	38	10	10	18	51-78	30
18. Borussia Neunkirchen	38	11	6	21	49-73	28
19. Wormatia Worms	38	9	9	20	36-66	27
20. VfR Mannheim	38	8	10	20	43-85	26

Promoted: FSV Frankfurt, Eintracht Bad Kreuznach, Jahn Regensburg, SSV Reutlingen

Top Scorers
Hoffmann (Karlsruhe SC) 25
Keller (TSV 1860 Munich) 23
Ludwig (FC 08 Homburg) 21
Walitza (1.FC Nuremberg) 21
Dussier (Röchling Völklingen) 17

Emmerich (Schweinfurt 05) 16
Seubert (Schweinfurt 05) 16
Werner (Bayern Hof) 16
Aumeier (Schweinfurt 05) 15
Erhardt (FK Pirmasens) 15
Pankotsch (FC 08 Homburg) 15
Warken (Röchling Völklingen) 15
Weinkauff (FK Pirmasens) 15

Third Division Champions
Baden (Nordbaden): VfB Eppingen
Baden (Südbaden): FV Offenburg
Bayern: Jahn Regensburg
Berlin: SV Spandau
Hessen: FSV Frankfurt
Mittelrhein: Bayer Leverkusen
Niederrhein: Union Solingen
Nord: VfB Oldenburg
Rheinland: Eintracht Trier
Saarland: ASC Dudweiler
Südwest: Eintracht Bad Kreuznach
Westfalen: Westfalia Herne
Württemberg: SSV Reutlingen

West German Cup
First Round
1.FC Nuremberg 2, Wacker Munich 2 aet (5-2)
Alemannia Aachen 1, SpVgg Erkenschwick 0
Arminia Bielefeld 1, Eintracht Frankfurt 3
ASC Dudweiler 0, FC Emmendingen 1
Barmbek-Uhlenhorst 1, Sportfreunde Siegen 2
Bayern Munich 3, VfB Stuttgart 2
Borussia Dortmund 3, VfR Heilbronn 0
Bremerhaven 93 1, VfL Wolfsburg 2
Eintracht Brunswick 4, Hertha BSC Berlin 1 (aet)
Eintracht Bad Kreuznach (I) 2, Westfalia Herne 0
Eintracht Bad Kreuznach (II) 1, Bayer Leverkusen 3
Eintracht Nordhorn 5, Westend 01 Berlin 1
FC 08 Homburg 3, TuS Schwachhausen 0
FC Rodalben 0, TSV Taunusstein-Bleidenstadt 1 aet
FC Augsburg 2, 1.FC Saarbrücken 1
FC St Pauli 3, SC Neunenahr 0
FK Pirmasens 7, VfR Neumünster 1
Fortuna Düsseldorf 6, ASV Neumarkt 0
FV Baden 1, Arminia Hanover 3
FV Eppelborn 4, Sportfreunde Eisbachtal 2
FV Lörrach 1, ASV Gummi-Meyer Landau 2
FV Weinheim 1, Bayer Uerdingen 4 aet
Göttingen 05 3, Hanover 96 2
Holstein Kiel 6, Rot-Weiss Frankfurt 1
Karlsruhe SC 0, Bayern Hof 1

Olympia Wilhelmshafen 4, Eintracht Trier 1
OSV Hanover 2, Rot-Weiss Essen 5
Preussen Münster 0, Hamburg SV 4
Rapide Wedding Berlin 3, TuS Mayen 0
Rot-Weiss Oberhausen 4, TuS Langerwehe 2 aet
SB Heidenheim 2, Hertha 03 Zehlendorf 2 aet (0-5)
SC Herford 0, VfL Bochum 3
SC Jülich 1910 2, SV Göppingen 1
Schwarz-Weiss Essen 3, Wattenscheid 09 0
Schweinfurt 05 3, 1.FC Kaiserslautern 4
Sportfreunde Hamborn 07 1, Fortuna Cologne 3
SpVgg Ludwigsburg 2, 1.FC Mülheim-Styrum 2 aet (1-3)
SpVgg Bayreuth 1, FC Schalke 04 2
SV Blumenthal 1, MSV Duisburg 3
SV Chio Waldhof 4, SV Heide 0
SV Darmstadt 98 2, Wuppertal SV 1
SV Leiwen 2, 1.FC Pforzheim 2 aet (0-0 aet; Pforzheim won on penalties)
SV Rheydt 1, Tennis Borussia Berlin 2
SV Sandhausen 3, FC Wunstorf 1
SV Spandau 2, Hamburg SV (Am.) 0
TSG Usingen 3, FSV Teutonia Obernau 2
TSV 1860 Munich 3, Wormatia Worms 2 aet
TSV Ersen 0, VfB Dillingen 1 aet
TSV Giessen-Kleinlinden 1, Rot-Weiss Lüdenscheid 2
TSV Weissenburg 0, SpVgg Fürth 5
TuS Ahlen 1, VfB Theley 2
TV Gültstein 0, Borussia Mönchengladbach 5
Union Solingen 2, Kickers Offenbach 1
VfB Eppingen 2, Röchling Völklingen 1
VfB Homberg 1, DJK Gütersloh 3
VfB Lübeck 3, Bayern Munich (Am.) 1
VfB Mannheim 8, Sperber Hamburg 0
VfB Oldenburg 2, 1.FC Cologne 6
VfB Stuttgart (Am.) 8, FC 08 Villingen 4 aet
VfL Osnabrück 0, Borussia Neunkirchen 2
Viktoria Cologne 4, Kickers Stuttgart 0
Victoria Hamburg 1, FC Altona 93 2 aet
Wacker 04 Berlin 0, FSV Frankfurt 1 aet
Werder Bremen 11, BSC Grünhöfe 1

Second Round
1.FC Kaiserslautern 7, SV Spandau 1
1.FC Mülheim-Styrum 2, VfR Mannheim 0
Alemannia Aachen 2, Borussia Neunkirchen 1
Armina Hanover 6, ASC Dudweiler 0
ASV Gummi-Mayer Landau 0, FC Augsburg 1
Bayer Leverkusen 2, Eintracht Nordhorn 0
Bayern Hof 2, VfL Bochum 2 aet (0-5)
Bayern Munich 2, Rot-Weiss Oberhausen 0
Borussia Mönchengladbach 3, 1.FC Cologne 5
Eintracht Bad Kreuznach 2, TSV 1860 Munich 4

FC Schalke 04 6, Hertha 03 Zehlendorf 0
FC St Pauli 8, FSV Mainz 05 3
FK Pirmasens 6, VfB Lübeck 0
Fortuna Cologne 7, Olympia Wilhelmshaven 2
Fortuna Düsseldorf 4, FV Eppelborn 1
Holstein Kiel 0, Bayer Uerdingen 1
MSV Duisburg 3, 1.FC Nuremberg 0
Rot-Weiss Essen 6, DJK Gütersloh 2
Rot-Weiss Lüdenscheid 3, Eintracht Brunswick 5
Schwarz-Weiss Essen 2, SV Darmstadt 98 0
Sportfreunde Siegen 1, Göttingen 05 0
SpVgg Fürth 1, Borussia Dortmund 1 aet (0-1)
SV Chio Waldhof 0, SV Sandhausen 1
Tennis Borussia Berlin 4, Rapide Wedding Berlin 0
TSV Tanusstein-Bleidenstadt 0, FC 08 Homburg 0 aet (0-0 aet; Tanusstein-Bleidenstadt won on penalties)
Union Solingen 1, Eintracht Frankfurt 2 aet
VfB Dillingen 2, SC Jülich 1910 2 aet (0-4)
VfB Eppingen 2, Hamburg SV 1
VfB Stuttgart (Am.) 2, 1.FC Pforzheim 0
VfB Theley 2, FC Altona 93 4 aet
VfL Wolfsburg 1, Werder Bremen 4
Viktoria Cologne 6, TSG Usingen 1 aet

Third Round
1.FC Cologne 4, FC St Pauli 1
1.FC Mülheim-Styrum 0, Eintracht Frankfurt 3
Bayer Uerdingen 0, VfL Bochum 2
Bayern Munich 2, MSV Duisburg 3
Borussia Dortmund 2, Sportfreunde Siegen 1
Eintracht Brunswick 1, Viktoria Cologne 2
FC Altona 93 2, Arminia Hanover 0
FK Pirmasens 4, TSV 1860 Munich 2
Fortuna Cologne 2, FC Schalke 04 0
Fortuna Düsseldorf 3, 1.FC Kaiserslautern 2
SC Jülich 1910 4, TSV Taunusstein-Bleidenstadt 2
Schwarz-Weiss Essen 1, Rot-Weiss Essen 2
SV Sandhausen 1, VfB Eppingen 2
Tennis Borussia Berlin 1, Alemannia Aachen 0
VfB Stuttgart (Am.) 2, Bayer Leverkusen 0
Werder Bremen 2, FC Augsburg 2 aet (2-1)

Fourth Round
Eintracht Frankfurt 1, VfL Bochum 0
Fortuna Cologne 0, SC Jülich 1910 0 aet (1-0)
Fortuna Düsseldorf 5, 1.FC Cologne 2
MSV Duisburg 7, FC Altona 93 0
Rot-Weiss Essen 6, FK Pirmasens 0
VfB Eppingen 0, Werder Bremen 2
VfB Stuttgart (Am.) 2, Tennis Borussia Berlin 1
Viktoria Cologne 0, Borussia Dortmund 0 aet (0-3)

Quarterfinals
Eintracht Frankfurt 4, Fortuna Cologne 2
Rot-Weiss Essen 1, Fortuna Düsseldorf 0
VfB Stuttgart (Am.) 0, Borussia Dortmund 4
Werder Bremen 0, MSV Duisburg 2

Semifinals
Eintracht Frankfurt 3, Rot-Weiss Essen 1 aet
MSV Duisburg 2, Borussia Dortmund 1 aet

Final
in Hanover
Eintracht Frankfurt 1, MSV Duisburg 0

West German Internationals
4/9/74 in Basle 2-1 v Switzerland
20/11/74 in Piraeus 2-2 v Greece (ECQ)
22/12/74 in Valetta 1-0 v Malta (ECQ)
12/3/75 in London 0-2 v England
27/4/75 in Sofia 1-1 v Bulgaria (ECQ)
17/5/75 in Frankfurt 1-1 v Holland

East German Oberliga

Club	P	W	D	L	Goals	Pts
1. 1.FC Magdeburg	26	17	7	2	57-28	41
2. Carl Zeiss Jena	26	17	4	5	42-23	38
3. Dynamo Dresden	26	12	8	6	42-30	32
4. Dynamo Berlin	26	10	10	6	47-29	30
5. Vorwärts Frankfurt/Oder	26	8	10	8	37-31	26
6. Stahl Riesa	26	11	4	11	34-42	26
7. Sachsenring Zwickau	26	9	7	10	42-39	25
8. Lokomotive Leipzig	26	9	6	11	37-39	24
9. Rot-Weiss Erfurt	26	9	5	12	37-42	23
10. FC Karl-Marx-Stadt	26	7	8	11	28-38	22
11. Chemie Halle	26	5	11	10	37-49	21
12. Wismut Aue	26	7	7	12	24-43	21
13. Hansa Rostock	26	7	6	13	29-35	20
14. Vorwärts Stralsund	26	4	7	15	21-46	15

Top Scorers
Vogel (Chemie Halle) 17
Pommerenke (1.FC Magdeburg) 15
Vogel (Carl Zeiss Jena) 14
Andrich (Vorwärts Frankfurt/Oder) 13
Peter (Chemie Halle) 13
H Weisshaupt (Rot-Weiss Erfurt) 13
Hoffmann (1.FC Magdeburg) 11
Johannsen (Dynamo Berlin) 11
J Schykowski (Sachsenring Zwickau) 11
Frenzel (Lokomotive Leipzig) 10

Oberliga Promotion Playoff

Club	P	W	D	L	Goals	Pts
1. Chemie Leipzig	8	5	2	1	12-5	12
2. Energie Cottbus	8	4	1	3	15-10	9
3. Wismut Gera	8	3	2	3	12-10	8
4. Dynamo Schwerin	8	3	1	4	8-15	7
5. 1.FC Union Berlin	8	1	2	5	10-17	4

Second Division (Staffel A)

Club	P	W	D	L	Goals	Pts
1. Dynamo Schwerin	22	15	3	4	54-27	33
2. KKW North Greifswald	22	12	5	5	45-31	29
3. Vorwärts Neubrandenburg	22	10	8	4	47-24	28
4. Veritas Wittenberge	22	10	8	4	50-34	28
5. Post Neubrandenburg	22	11	6	5	41-28	28
6. Hansa Rostock II	22	9	5	8	39-26	23
7. TSG Wismar	22	8	5	9	43-39	21
8. TSG Bau Rostock	22	6	7	9	28-31	19
9. Schiffahrt/Hafen Rostock	22	6	7	9	31-46	19
10. Lokomotive Bergen	22	4	8	10	27-38	16
11. Aufbau Boizenburg	22	5	2	15	25-74	12
12. VB Waren	22	2	4	16	20-52	8

Both points in the Vorwärts Neubrandenburg v Hansa Rostock II match were awarded to Vorwärts, with a scoreline of 0-0.
Promoted: Einheit Grevesmühlen, Einheit Güstrow, Nord Torgelow. Vorwärts Neubrandenburg were placed in Staffel B and Veritas Wittenberge were placed in Staffel C for the following season. Hansa Rostock II did not participate at this level in the following season.

Second Division (Staffel B)

Club	P	W	D	L	Goals	Pts
1. 1.FC Union Berlin	22	15	5	2	54-20	35
2. Dynamo Berlin II	22	11	7	4	38-22	29
3. Stahl Eisenhüttenstadt	22	12	5	5	44-30	29
4. Stahl Hennigsdorf	22	9	4	9	40-39	22
5. Vorwärts Frankfurt/Oder II	22	7	7	8	39-32	21
6. Stahl Finow	22	7	7	8	33-32	21
7. Dynamo Fürstenwalde	22	7	7	8	34-38	21
8. Lichtenburg 47	22	6	7	9	17-25	19
9. Motor Babelsburg	22	8	3	11	30-45	19
10. Motor Ludwigsfelde	22	7	3	12	32-45	17
11. NARVA Berlin	22	6	5	11	18-35	17
12. Aufbau Schwedt	22	5	4	13	24-40	14

Promoted: Motor Eberswalde, Einheit Pankow.

Second Division (Staffel C)

Club	P	W	D	L	Goals	Pts
1. Chemie Leipzig	22	17	3	2	57-16	37
2. Dynamo Eisleben	22	9	10	3	45-31	28
3. Chemie Buna Schkopau	22	11	3	8	39-30	25
4. Vorwärts Dessau	22	8	9	5	32-29	25
5. Chemie Böhlen	22	10	4	8	42-33	24
6. 1.FC Magdeburg II	22	9	5	8	35-29	23
7. Lokomotive Stendal	22	10	3	9	27-30	23
8. Stahl Brandenburg	22	10	2	10	35-25	22
9. Stahl Blankenburg	22	9	4	9	25-27	22
10. Lokomotive Leipzig II	22	7	6	9	32-37	20
11. Lok/Vorwärts Halberstadt	22	2	4	16	19-49	8
12. Lokomotive Ost Leipzig	22	2	3	17	17-69	7

Promoted: Aktivist Espenhain, Chemie Halle II, Chemie Premnitz, Einheit Wernigerode. Chemie Böhlen were placed in Staffel D for the following season.

Second Division (Staffel D)

Club	P	W	D	L	Goals	Pts
1. Energie Cottbus	22	13	8	1	50-21	34
2. Lokomotive Dresden	22	13	4	5	38-25	30
3. Dynamo Dresden II	22	12	4	6	39-25	28
4. Sachsenring Zwickau II	22	10	7	5	32-30	27
5. Motor Werdau	22	10	4	8	47-40	24
6. Aktivist Schwarze Pumpe	22	6	10	6	30-27	22
7. TSG Gröditz	22	8	5	9	37-28	21
8. Wismut Aue II	22	7	7	8	36-27	21
9. Motor Bautzen	22	6	8	8	21-28	20
10. Aktivist Brieske-Senftenburg	22	7	5	10	26-24	19
11. Lokomotive Cottbus	22	3	5	14	23-52	11
12. Motor Germania K-M-S	22	2	3	17	13-65	7

Promoted: Energie Cottbus II, Stahl Riesa II. Sachsenring Zwickau were placed in Staffel E for the following season.

Second Division (Staffel E)

Club	P	W	D	L	Goals	Pts
1. Wismut Gera	22	16	4	2	57-20	36
2. Motor Suhl	22	10	6	6	53-25	26
3. Vorwärts Plauen	22	11	4	7	48-32	26
4. Carl Zeiss Jena II	22	9	8	5	36-27	26
5. Motor Nordhausen-West	22	9	5	8	34-38	23
6. Zentronik Sömmerda	22	6	9	7	28-27	21
7. Chemie Zeitz	22	6	9	7	30-34	21
8. Motor Hermsdorf	22	8	5	9	39-45	21
9. Kali Werra Tiefenort	22	8	4	10	32-36	20
10. Rot-Weiss Erfurt II	22	8	4	10	29-34	20
11. Motor Steinach	22	4	5	13	29-68	13
12. TSG Ruhla	22	3	5	14	20-49	11

Promoted: Karl-Marx-Stadt II, Chemie Schwarza, Motor Veilsdorf, Motor Weimar.

1974-75

East German Cup Final
in Berlin
Sachsenring Zwickau 2, Dynamo Dresden 2 aet (Zwickau won on penalties)

East German Internationals
4/9/74 in Warsaw 3-1 v Poland
25/9/74 in Prague 1-3 v Czechoslovakia
9/10/74 in Frankfurt/Oder 2-0 v Canada
12/10/74 in Magdeburg 1-1 v Iceland (ECQ)
30/10/74 in Glasgow 0-3 v Scotland
16/11/74 in Paris 2-2 v France (ECQ)
7/12/74 in Leipzig 0-0 v Belgium (ECQ)
25/3/75 in Berlin 0-0 v Bulgaria
28/5/75 in Halle 1-2 v Poland
5/6/75 in Reykjavik 1-2 v Iceland (ECQ)
29/7/75 in Toronto 3-0 v Canada
31/7/75 in Ottawa 7-1 v Canada

European Cup
First Round
Bayern Munich and 1.FC Magdeburg received byes
Second Round
Bayern Munich v 1.FC Magdeburg .... (3-2, 2-1)
Quarterfinals
Bayern Munich v Ararat Erevan .... (2-0, 0-1)
Semifinals
St. Etienne v Bayern Munich .... (0-0, 0-2)
Final in Brussels
Bayern Munich 2, Leeds United 0

Cup-Winners' Cup
First Round
Eintracht Frankfurt v Monaco .... (3-0, 2-2)
Slavia Prague v Carl Zeiss Jena .... (1-0, 0-1 aet)
Slavia won on penalties
Second Round
Eintracht Frankfurt v Dynamo Kiev .... (2-3, 1-2)
Carl Zeiss Jena v Benfica .... (1-1, 0-0)

UEFA Cup
First Round
1.FC Cologne v Kokkolan PV .... (5-1, 4-1)
Hamburg SV v Bohemians Dublin .... (3-0, 1-0)
Wacker Innsbruck v Borussia Mönchengladbach ..... (2-1, 0-3)
Torino v Fortuna Düsseldorf .... (1-1, 1-3)
Freja Randers v Dynamo Dresden .... (1-1, 0-0)
Vorwärts Frankfurt/Oder v Juventus .... (2-1, 0-3)
Second Round
Borussia Mönchengladbach v Lyon .... (1-0, 5-2)
Hamburg SV v Steagul Rosu Brasov .... (8-0, 2-1)
Dinamo Bucharest v 1.FC Cologne .... (1-1, 2-3)
ETO Raba Györ v Fortuna Düsseldorf .... (2-0, 0-3)
Dynamo Dresden v Dynamo Moscow .... (1-0, 0-1 aet)
Dresden won on penalties
Third Round
Hamburg SV v Dynamo Dresden .... (4-1, 2-2)
Borussia Mönchengladbach v Real Zaragoza .... (5-0, 4-2)
Partizan Belgrade v 1.FC Cologne .... (1-0, 1-5)
FC Amsterdam v Fortuna Düsseldorf .... (3-0, 2-1)
Quarterfinals
Banik Ostrava v Borussia Mönchengladbach .... (0-1, 1-3)
1.FC Cologne v FC Amsterdam .... (5-1, 3-2)
Juventus v Hamburg SV .... (2-0, 0-0)
Semifinal
1.FC Cologne v Borussia Mönchengladbach .... (1-3, 0-1)
Final
Borussia Mönchengladbach v Twente Enschede ...... (0-0, 5-1)

1975-76

Udo's new champion

With Udo Lattek having taken over from Hennes Weisweiler as *Trainer,* Borussia Mönchengladbach adopted a totally different style of play. Instead of basing their game around their attack, they—like an increasing number of clubs around the world—adopted a safety-first approach. The two *Trainers* were also totally different characters. Weisweiler lived for football, day and night, while Lattek displayed a much more detached attitude. And having previously been in charge at Bayern Munich, Lattek did not find it easy to gain acceptance from the Gladbach players.

Despite the change of tactics, Mönchengladbach remained a mighty team. There was a hierarchy of established senior players like Berti Vogts, Jupp Heynckes, Uli Stielike, Herbert Wimmer and Rainer Bonhof who set the tone; everyone else played a supporting role. Any disagreements were always sorted out internally, with nothing ever reaching the press. Borussia always exuded peace and calm.

Gladbach pulled away from their rivals in the early part of the season and by Christmas topped the league with 25 points from 17 games. They kept their nerve as other teams lost theirs and held on to their lead right through the season, finishing four points clear of second-placed Hamburg. A highlight of the season was doing the double over 1.FC Cologne, 2-1 at home and 4-0 away. Their worst defeat was 4-0 at Bayern Munich in March—before 75,000 in the Olympiastadion—but Gladbach had easily won the home clash 4-1 earlier on.

Borussia's more defensive attitude meant that they scored twenty goals fewer than the previous season. Eintracht Frankfurt emerged as the league's top marksmen, Bernd Hölzenbein, Bernd Nickel, Rüdiger Wenzel, Jürgen Grabowski and Charly Körbel each scoring in double figures, but could only finish in mid-table. Schalke's Klaus Fischer led the league with 29—or one more than the entire Bayer Uerdingen squad could produce. Bayer's 28-goal attack was the worst since Tasmania Berlin's infamous 1965-66 campaign.

Bayern recovered from the shock of the previous season to finish third behind Gladbach and Hamburg, who under Kuno Klötzer were turning into a formidable team. Never before had HSV finished as high as second, and with just six points dropped at home and the league's stingiest defence, Hamburg served notice that they were on their way to greater things. Hertha Berlin, though, had fallen from second to eleventh place, unable to attack or defend with any conviction. They lost 7-4 to Bayern Munich on the last day of the season, with Gerd Müller helping himself to five.

This was also the season when Hermann Neuberger took over as President of the DFB. But perhaps the biggest celebrations—apart from those in Mönchengladbach—were in Cologne on November 12, when the completely renovated Müngersdorf Stadion was re-opened with a friendly between 1.FC Cologne and their local rivals from a couple of miles south, Fortuna.

No fewer than eight clubs changed *Trainers* this season—a record at the time. The first to go was Otto Rehhagel at Kickers Offenbach, followed by Tschik Cajkovski (Cologne), Helmut Kronsbein (Hanover), Herbert Burdenski (Bremen), Max Merkel (Schalke), Willibert Kremer (Duisburg), Sepp Piontek (Düsseldorf), and Dietrich Wiese, who left Frankfurt of his own accord and took over at Düsseldorf the following season.

Life in the fledgling Second Bundesliga was tough on Berlin side Spandau SV, who started the season by giving up nineteen goals in their first three games and finished with one of the worst-ever records in the division. In the south, tiny FC Homburg were proving more successful at making the adjustment. They finished in third place, eleven places better than the season before, but still somewhat adrift of the promotion race. Likewise, Röchling Völklingen enjoyed a considerable degree of success, paced by the league's top marksman, Karl-Heinz Granitza, who went on to brief fame in the North American Soccer League with the Chicago Sting.

1.FC Saarbrücken and 1.FC Nuremberg contested the leadership of the Second Division South for most of the season, while in the North, Borussia Dortmund and Tennis Borussia Berlin battled for supremacy. "TeBe" won 4-1 against the division's third Berlin club, Wacker 04, before 25,000 to assure themselves of first place. This meant Dortmund and Nuremberg had to be content with playing off against each other for promotion, and their two matches drew over 106,000 fans. Dortmund won them both to return to the top flight after a four-year absence.

Attendance at the West German Cup topped the one million mark, but average crowds of 8500 were nothing to shout about; with 128 clubs involved in the first round, there were simply a lot more ties to be played. Völklingen pushed Hertha Berlin hard in the quarterfinals and were unlucky to go out 2-1 at home in a replay. Holders Eintracht Frankfurt had lost to Hertha in the previous round thanks to Lorenz Horr's goal ten minutes into extra time.

One of the semifinals pitted Hamburg against Bayern Munich. Peter Nogly earned HSV a replay with a goal five minutes from the end of extra time before 52,000 at the Volksparkstadion. In Munich four weeks later, conditions had reduced the game to a farce, the pitch littered with puddles. Gerd Müller's 53rd minute penalty was saved by HSV keeper Rudi Kargus and just as the 55,000 soggy spectators were preparing for a further half-hour's drenching, Georg Volkert's cross was headed in by Kurt Eigl on the stroke of full time to put the visitors in the final.

There, HSV duly defeated an injury-depleted Kaiserslautern side 2-0 on the strength of goals from Nogly and Ole Björnmose.

Two Bundesliga clubs competed in the European Cup: Bayern as holders and Gladbach as champions. Gladbach went out somewhat unluckily to Real Madrid at the Bernabeu in the quarter final following some questionable decisions by the Dutch referee. Bayern, though, knocked out Real in the semis to make it to the final again, where Franz Beckenbauer inspired his teammates to victory over St. Etienne in Glasgow. Franz Roth belted a 25-yard free kick midway through the second half for the game's only goal. Beckenbauer's performance in the final undoubtedly helped him to become German Footballer and European Footballer of the Year, each for the second time.

Two German teams reached the semifinals of the Cup-Winners' Cup this season, but Eintracht Frankfurt lost to West Ham United and Sachsenring Zwickau went out to a formidable Anderlecht side featuring the likes of Van der Elst, Haan, and Rensenbrink. In the UEFA Cup, Dynamo Dresden reached the last eight before losing 1-2 to eventual winners Liverpool, and Hamburg lost 1-2 in the semifinal to FC Bruges because of an own-goal.

When the West German national side lined up to play a friendly against Austria in Vienna, there was a debut in the number two shirt for Manfred Kaltz—the first of what would be 69 caps. Substitute Erich Beer came on to replace injured skipper Beckenbauer and scored both goals in a 2-0 win. The following match, a European Championship qualifier against Greece in Düsseldorf, was a disappointing 1-1 draw and proved to be the last of Günter Netzer's 37 international appearances. However, wins against Malta and Bulgaria put the German side at the top of their qualifying group, and they went on to beat Spain 3-1 on aggregate to reach the last four.

The final phase of the tournament took place in Yugoslavia, and Germany knocked out the host nation 4-2 after extra time, with all four German goals scored by the substitutes, Dieter Müller (a hat-trick) and Heinz Flohe. The final against Czechoslovakia was unresolved at 2-2 after extra time, with Müller and Bernd Hölzenbein having scored the German goals. This meant it was time for West Germany's first taste of the penalty shoot-out, and they lost the championship when Uli Hoeness blasted his kick over the crossbar.

In the East German league, 575 goals were scored—or an average of 3.16, the highest since 1960. It was perhaps appropriate that Dynamo Dresden, the league's top scorers, won the championship, a comfortable six points clear of second-placed Dynamo Berlin. Dresden lost only one match at home all season (4-2 to Chemie Halle) and just one on their travels (1-0 to Rot-Weiss Erfurt). But Lokomotive Leipzig won the cup, defeating Vorwärts Frankfurt 3-0 on the strength of Henning Frenzel's goals on either side of halftime.

The East German national team didn't lose a match this season, but it was not quite enough to atone for the previous season's embarrassment against Iceland. Belgium headed the qualifying group with eight points, leaving the Germans on seven. But East Germany sent its full national side to the Olympic Games in Montreal, and came back with the gold medal. They beat Poland in the final before 72,000 in Montreal, Hartmut Schade, Martin Hoffmann and Reinhard Häfner scoring the goals.

Bundesliga

Club	P	W	D	L	Goals	Pts
1. Borussia Mönchengladbach	34	16	13	5	66-37	45
2. Hamburg SV	34	17	7	10	59-32	41
3. Bayern Munich	34	15	10	9	72-50	40
4. 1.FC Cologne	34	14	11	9	62-45	39
5. Eintracht Brunswick	34	14	11	9	52-48	39
6. FC Schalke 04	34	13	11	10	76-55	37
7. 1.FC Kaiserslautern	34	15	7	12	66-60	37
8. Rot-Weiss Essen	34	13	11	10	61-67	37
9. Eintracht Frankfurt	34	13	10	11	79-58	36
10. MSV Duisburg	34	13	7	14	55-62	33
11. Hertha BSC Berlin	34	11	10	13	59-61	32
12. Fortuna Düsseldorf	34	10	10	14	47-57	30
13. Werder Bremen	34	11	8	15	44-55	30
14. VfL Bochum	34	12	6	16	49-62	30
15. Karlsruhe SC	34	12	6	16	46-59	30
16. Hanover 96	34	9	9	16	48-60	27
17. Kickers Offenbach	34	9	9	16	40-72	27
18. Bayer Uerdingen	34	6	10	18	28-69	22

Top Scorers
Fischer (FC Schalke 04) 29
Beer (Hertha BSC Berlin) 23
G Müller (Bayern Munich) 23
Toppmöller (1.FC Kaiserslautern) 22
Hrubesch (Rot-Weiss Essen) 18
Sandberg (1.FC Kaiserslautern) 17
Frank (Eintracht Brunswick) 16
Hölzenbein (Eintracht Frankfurt) 16
Simonsen (Borussia Mönchengladbach) 16
Löhr (1.FC Cologne) 15
Nickel (Eintracht Frankfurt) 15

Promotion Playoff
1.FC Nuremberg v Borussia Dortmund (0-1, 2-3); Dortmund promoted to Bundesliga

Second Division North

Club	P	W	D	L	Goals	Pts
1. Tennis Borussia Berlin	38	25	4	9	86-43	54
2. Borussia Dortmund	38	22	8	8	93-37	52
3. Preussen Münster	38	20	9	9	65-42	49
4. Fortuna Cologne	38	19	7	12	74-49	45
5. Wuppertal SV	38	18	9	11	76-53	45
6. VfL Osnabrück	38	19	7	12	61-47	45
7. Schwarz-Weiss Essen	38	19	6	13	63-52	44
8. Wattenscheid 09	38	17	9	12	71-58	43
9. Arminia Bielefeld	38	14	14	10	49-46	42
10. Westfalia Herne	38	16	8	14	60-57	40
11. Göttingen 05	38	15	7	16	63-54	37
12. Alemannia Aachen	38	12	12	14	45-53	36
13. Union Solingen	38	11	14	13	45-56	36
14. FC St Pauli	38	13	8	17	70-82	34
15. Bayer Leverkusen	38	12	8	18	46-61	32
16. Wacker 04 Berlin	38	11	9	18	51-82	31
17. 1.FC Mülheim	38	10	10	18	54-76	30
18. SpVgg Erkenschwick	38	10	19	9	45-69	29
19. DJK Gütersloh	38	12	4	22	52-70	28
20. SV Spandau	38	2	4	32	33-115	8

Promoted: SC Bonn, Arminia Hanover, SC Herford, VfL Wolfsburg

Top Scorers
Stolzenburg (Tennis Borussia Berlin) 27
Fritsche (Schwarz-Weiss Essen) 22
Gerber (Wuppertal SV) 19
Hartl (Borussia Dortmund) 18
Mühlenberg (VfL Osnabrück) 18
Abel (Westfalia Herne) 17
Ludwig (Fortuna Cologne) 17
John (St Pauli/Wacker Berlin) 15
Kasperski (Borussia Dortmund) 15
Neumann (FC St Pauli) 15

Second Division South

Club	P	W	D	L	Goals	Pts
1. 1.FC Saarbrücken	38	23	11	4	66-28	57
2. 1.FC Nuremberg	38	24	6	8	78-42	54
3. FC 08 Homburg	38	19	13	6	72-41	51
4. TSV 1860 Munich	38	19	9	10	78-55	47
5. SpVgg Bayreuth	38	18	11	9	71-55	47
6. Röchling Völklingen	38	18	9	11	72-65	45
7. SV Darmstadt 98	38	19	5	14	76-64	43
8. SV Chio Waldhof	38	16	10	12	64-55	42
9. Bayern Hof	38	18	5	15	60-56	41
10. SpVgg Fürth	38	17	3	18	64-52	37
11. VfB Stuttgart	38	16	4	18	67-60	36
12. FSV Mainz 05	38	12	12	14	81-92	36
13. FSV Frankfurt	38	15	5	18	49-63	35
14. FK Pirmasens	38	13	7	18	66-78	33
15. FC Augsburg	38	12	8	18	57-56	32
16. Kickers Stuttgart	38	13	6	19	57-70	32
17. Jahn Regensburg	38	8	14	16	48-74	30
18. Schweinfurt 05	38	9	8	21	50-72	26
19. Eintracht Bad Kreuznach	38	8	7	23	49-83	23
20. SSV Reutlingen	38	5	3	30	35-99	13

Promoted: KSV Baunatal, BSV Schwenningen, Eintracht Trier, FV Würzburg 04. FSV Mainz 05 were relegated after their professional licence was revoked

100   **1975-76**

Top Scorers
Granitza (Röchling Völklingen) 29
Hofmann (SpVgg Fürth) 23
Keller (TSV 1860 Munich) 23
Emmerich (Schweinfurt 05) 21
Nüssing (1.FC Nuremberg) 21
Walitza (1.FC Nuremberg) 21
Werner (FC Bayern Hof) 20
Lenz (FC 08 Homburg) 19
Diener (FC 08 Homburg) 18
Sebert (SV Chio Waldhof) 18

Third Division Champions
Baden (Nordbaden): VfR Mannheim
Baden (Südbaden): FC Villingen 08
Bayern: Wacker Munich
Berlin: Union 06 Berlin
Hessen: KSV Baunatal
Mittelrhein: SC Bonn
Niederrhein: 1.FC Bocholt
Nord: Arminia Hanover
Rheinland: Eintracht Trier
Saarland: Borussia Neunkirchen
Südwest: Wormatia Worms
Westfalen: SC Herford
Württemberg: SpVgg Ludwigsburg 07

West German Cup
First Round
1.FC Cologne 2, Olympia Wilhelmshaven 0
1.FC Kaiserslautern 2, VfR Mannheim 0
1.FC Mülheim 4, SpVgg 06/07 Sterkrade 2
1.FC Nuremberg 2, Rot-Weiss Essen 1
Arminia Bielefeld 4, SV St. Georg Hamburg 0
ASV Gummi-Mayer Landau 1, Hanover 96 7
ASV Idar-Oberstein 3, SG Frankfurt Hoechst 2
Bayern Munich 3, 1.FC Saarbrücken 1
Borussia Neunkirchen 2, Kickers Offenbach 0
Eintracht Frankfurt 6, Viktoria Cologne 0
Eintracht Höhr-Grenzhausen 4, SV Spielberg 3
FC 08 Homburg 4, Union Solingen 0
FC Augsburg 0, Fortuna Düsseldorf 1
FC St Pauli 1, FK Pirmasens 1 aet (2-5)
FK Clausen 0, Wormatia Worms 2
Fortuna Cologne 6, ASV 85 Bergedorf 1
FSV Frankfurt 1, SpVgg Fürth 1 aet (0-1)
FSV Mainz 05 7, TSV Osterholz-Tenever 2
FV 09 Weinheim 1, Hertha BSC Berlin 7
FV Offenburg 2, FSV Cappel 0
Hamburg SV 4, 1.FC Cologne (Am.) 0
Hassia Bingen 7, Frisia Husum 0
Hertha 03 Zehlendorf 0, SV Blumenthal 1 aet
Hessen Kassel 1, Alemannia Aachen 0
Karlsruhe SC 4, SpVgg Bayreuth 2
Kickers Stuttgart 1, Holstein Kiel 1 aet (2-1)
MTV Fürth 2, MSV Duisburg 10
Preussen Münster 7, Siemensstadt Berlin 1
Rapide Wedding Berlin 2, VfB Stuttgart 9
Röchling Völklingen 5, Wacker 04 Berlin 1
SC Herford 3, SC Friedrichsthal 1
SC Jülich 1910 3, Wacker 04 Berlin 0
SC Freiburg 2, Victoria Hamburg 1
Schwarz-Weiss Essen 2, Bayer Uerdingen 1 aet
SGO Bremen 5, FC Herzogenaurach 1
Sportfreunde Schwäbisch-Hall 5, TuS Mayen 1
Sportfreunde Siegen 4, ATS Kulmbach 2
Sportfreunde Salzgitter 0, SV Weiskirchen 1
SpVgg Erkenschwick 2, VfL Bochum 3
SpVgg 07 Ludwigsburg 0, Borussia Dortmund 6
SpVgg Andernach 0, DJK Gütersloh 2
SpVgg Freudenschadt 0, Eintracht Brunswick 7
SpVgg Lindau 0, Itzehoe SV 0
SV 06/07 Bünde 2, VfR Pforzheim 2 aet (2-1)
SV Auersmacher 6, VfB Gaggenau 0
SV Chio Waldhof 2, SV Cuxhaven 1
SV Darmstadt 98 4, VfB Eppingen 1
SV Hasborn 3, VfL Neuwied 1
SV Spandau 2, Rot-Weiss Oberhausen 1
Tennis Borussia Berlin 2, Schweinfurt 05 0
TSG Thannhausen 0, Bayer Leverkusen 6
TSV 1860 Munich 2, Göttingen 05 1
TuS Xanten 0, SV Woltmershausen 2
Union Salzgitter 5, TSV Abbehausen 0
VfB Oldenburg 0, FC Schalke 04 6
VfB Stuttgart (Am.) 1, SV Barmbek-Ulhenhorst 3
VfL Osnabrück 3, VfL Wolfsburg 2
VfL Trier 3, TSV Kücknitz 6 aet
VfR Heilbronn 3, Rot-Weiss Lüdenscheid 2 aet
VfR Oli Bürstadt 1, Bayern Hof 2
Wattenscheid 09 4, SC Concordia Hamburg 0
Werder Bremen 0, Borussia Mönchengladbach 3
Westfalia Herne 3, FC Freiburg 1
Wuppertal SV 3, Schwarz-Weiss Essen (Am.) 0

Second Round
1.FC Cologne 8, SC Freiburg 2
1.FC Mülheim 1, Bayern Hof 3 aet
1.FC Nuremberg 1, Fortuna Cologne 0 aet
Arminia Bielefeld 5, Eintracht Höhr-Grenzhausen 1
Bayer Leverkusen 0, VfL Bochum 2
Borussia Mönchengladbach 3, SV Hasborn 0
FC Schalke 04 2, Borussia Dortmund 1
FK Pirmasens 7, SV Spandau 1

FSV Mainz 05 1, Röchling Völklingen 2
FV Offenburg 1, Eintracht Frankfurt 5
Hamburg SV 4, Union Salzgitter 0
Hanover 96 1, FC 08 Homburg 2
Hertha BSC Berlin 4, VfB Stuttgart 2
Hessen Kassel 2, Fortuna Düsseldorf 3
MSV Duisburg 4, Karlsruhe SC 0
Preussen Münster 1, Wuppertal SV 0
SC Jülich 1910 5, SpVgg Lindau 1
Schwarz-Weiss Essen 3, SGO Bremen 0
Sportfreunde Schwäbisch-Hall 0, Kickers Stuttgart 5
Sportfreunde Siegen 1, Tennis Borussia Berlin 2
SpVgg Fürth 7, SV Woltmershausen 1
SV 06/07 Bünde 0, Bayern Munich 3
SV Barmbek-Uhlenhorst 2, Hassia Bingen 3 aet
SV Blumenthal 1, 1.FC Kaiserslautern 5
SV Chio Waldhof 4, TSV 1860 Munich 1
SV Darmstadt 98 4, VfR Heilbronn 0
SV Weiskirchen 4, SV Auersmacher 1
TSV Kücknitz 0, DJK Gütersloh 1
VfL Osnabrück 3, Borussia Neunkirchen 2
Wattenscheid 09 4, SC Herford 0
Westfalia Herne 4, ASV Idar-Oberstein 0
Wormatia Worms 0, Eintracht Brunswick 3

Third Round
1.FC Cologne 2, SpVgg Fürth 1
Arminia Bielefeld 3, DJK Gütersloh 2
Bayern Munich 3, Tennis Borussia Berlin 0
Eintracht Frankfurt 3, VfL Osnabrück 0
FC 08 Homburg 1, SV Chio Waldhof 0
FC Schalke 04 1, Eintracht Brunswick 2
Fortuna Düsseldorf 4, VfL Bochum 4 aet (3-1 aet)
Hamburg SV 4, SC Jülich 1910 0
Kickers Stuttgart 1, Hertha BSC Berlin 3
MSV Duisburg 0, Borussia Mönchengladbach 1
Preussen Münster 2, Schwarz-Weiss Essen 2 aet (2-3)
Röchling Völklingen 4, Hassia Bingen 1
SV Darmstadt 98 3, 1.FC Nuremberg 1 aet
SV Weiskirchen 0, FK Pirmasens 1
Wattenscheid 09 2, Bayern Hof 3
Westfalia Herne 1, 1.FC Kaiserslautern 3

Fourth Round
1.FC Kaiserslautern 2, Eintracht Brunswick 0
Bayern Hof 0, Hamburg SV 2
FC 08 Homburg 3, SV Darmstadt 98 0
FK Pirmasens 0, Bayern Munich 2
Fortuna Düsseldorf 3, Borussia Mönchengladbach 2
Hertha BSC Berlin 1, Eintracht Frankfurt 0 aet
Röchling Völklingen 1, Arminia Bielefeld 0
Schwarz-Weiss Essen 1, 1.FC Cologne 1 aet (0-1 aet)

Quarterfinals
1.FC Cologne 2, Bayern Munich 5
1.FC Kaiserslautern 3, Fortuna Düsseldorf 0
FC 08 Homburg 1, Hamburg SV 2
Hertha BSC Berlin 1, Röchling Völklingen 1 aet (2-1)

Semifinals
1.FC Kaiserslautern 4, Hertha BSC Berlin 2
Hamburg SV 2, Bayern Munich 2 aet (1-0)

Final
in Frankfurt
Hamburg SV 2, 1.FC Kaiserslautern 0

West German Internationals
3/9/75 in Vienna 2-0 v Austria
11/10/75 in Düsseldorf 1-1 v Greece (ECQ)
19/11/75 in Stuttgart 1-0 v Bulgaria (ECQ)
20/12/75 in Istanbul 5-0 v Turkey
28/2/76 in Dortmund 8-0 v Malta (ECQ)
24/4/76 in Madrid 1-1 v Spain (EC)
22/5/76 in Munich 2-0 v Spain (EC)
17/6/76 in Belgrade 4-2 v Yugoslavia aet (EC)
20/6/76 in Belgrade 2-2 v Czechoslovakia aet (EC); Czechoslovakia won on penalties

East German Oberliga

Club	P	W	D	L	Goals	Pts
1. Dynamo Dresden	26	19	5	2	70-23	43
2. Dynamo Berlin	26	17	3	6	67-24	37
3. 1.FC Magdeburg	26	15	6	5	59-33	36
4. Lokomotive Leipzig	26	12	7	7	40-34	31
5. Carl Zeiss Jena	26	11	7	8	50-43	29
6. Wismut Aue	26	9	9	8	30-35	27
7. Rot-Weiss Erfurt	26	8	10	8	44-36	26
8. Chemie Halle	26	9	7	10	37-35	25
9. Sachsenring Zwickau	26	7	8	11	29-43	22
10. Stahl Riesa	26	7	7	12	35-46	21
11. FC Karl-Marx-Stadt	26	7	7	12	25-41	21
12. Vorwärts Frankfurt/Oder	26	8	4	14	41-57	20
13. Chemie Leipzig	26	3	8	15	25-62	14
14. Energie Cottbus	26	3	6	17	23-63	12

Top Scorers
Kreische (Dynamo Dresden) 24
Vogel (Carl Zeiss Jena) 19
Riediger (Dynamo Berlin) 18
Sparwasser (1.FC Magdeburg) 13
Streich (1.FC Magdeburg) 13
Hoffmann (1.FC Magdeburg) 12
Netz (Dynamo Berlin) 12
Runge (Stahl Riesa) 12

Erler (Wismut Aue) 11
Peter (Chemie Halle) 10
Terletzki (Dynamo Berlin) 10
H Weisshaupt (Rot-Weiss Erfurt) 10

Oberliga Promotion Playoff
Club	P	W	D	L	Goals	Pts
1. Hansa Rostock	8	5	3	0	20-8	13
2. 1.FC Union Berlin	8	5	2	1	13-8	12
3. Motor Werdau	8	3	1	4	14-13	7
4. Motor Suhl	8	2	1	5	12-21	5
5. Vorwärts Dessau	8	1	1	6	9-18	3

Second Division (Staffel A)
Club	P	W	D	L	Goals	Pts
1. Hansa Rostock	22	17	5	0	65-17	39
2. Vorwärts Stralsund	22	16	3	3	58-21	35
3. Post Neubrandenburg	22	15	4	3	59-21	34
4. TSG Wismar	22	15	2	5	48-27	32
5. Dynamo Schwerin	22	11	4	7	49-30	26
6. KKW Greifswald	22	7	7	8	32-29	21
7. Schiffahrt/Hafen Rostock	22	5	9	8	27-40	19
8. TSG Bau Rostock	22	7	5	10	31-48	19
9. Einheit Güstrow	22	4	8	10	27-47	16
10. Einheit Grevesmühlen	22	4	1	17	19-50	9
11. Nord Togelow	22	3	3	16	21-67	9
12. Lokomotive Bergen	22	1	3	18	19-58	5

Promoted: Motor Schwerin, RB Trinwillershagen

Second Division (Staffel B)
Club	P	W	D	L	Goals	Pts
1. 1.FC Union Berlin	22	13	5	4	41-20	31
2. Stahl Eisenhüttenstadt	22	12	5	5	47-26	29
3. Dynamo Berlin II	22	12	3	7	35-24	27
4. Vorwärts Neubrandenburg	22	11	5	6	39-32	27
5. Motor Eberswalde	22	10	4	8	33-34	24
6. Stahl Hennigsdorf	22	10	3	9	48-35	23
7. Vorwärts Frankfurt/Oder II	22	8	5	9	38-32	21
8. Dynamo Fürstenwalde	22	8	5	9	37-39	21
9. Motor Babelsberg	22	7	6	9	29-30	20
10. Stahl Finow	22	7	5	10	22-37	19
11. Lichtenburg 47	22	5	3	14	24-55	13
12. Einheit Pankow	22	3	3	16	18-47	9

Promoted: Rotation Berlin, Motor Hennigsdorf, TSG Neustrelitz

Second Division (Staffel C)
Club	P	W	D	L	Goals	Pts
1. Chemie Halle II	22	13	5	4	44-24	31
2. 1.FC Magdeburg II	22	9	7	9	37-29	25
3. Vorwärts Dessau	22	8	9	5	24-22	25
4. Dynamo Eisleben	22	10	4	8	43-30	24
5. Lokomotive Stendal	22	6	11	5	33-24	23
6. Einheit Wernigerode	22	10	3	9	40-38	23
7. Chemie Buna Schkopau	22	8	6	8	42-39	22
8. Stahl Brandenburg	22	6	10	6	34-34	22
9. Stahl Blankenburg	22	8	6	8	24-26	22
10. Vertias Wittenberge	22	7	6	9	32-43	20
11. Aktivist Espenhain	22	4	6	12	23-45	14
12. Chemie Premnitz	22	3	7	12	23-45	13

Promoted: Lokomotive Halberstadt, Stahl Thale

Second Division (Staffel D)
Club	P	W	D	L	Goals	Pts
1. Motor Werdau	22	15	5	2	50-17	35
2. Wismut Gera	22	12	6	4	36-19	30
3. Chemie Böhlen	22	11	6	5	51-24	28
4. Dynamo Dresden II	22	9	7	6	47-29	25
5. Wismut Aue II	22	9	6	7	29-27	24
6. Stahl Riesa II	22	9	4	9	39-41	22
7. Lokomotive Dresden	22	8	5	9	32-41	21
8. Vorwärts Plauen	22	7	5	10	34-38	19
9. TSG Gröditz	22	7	5	10	30-38	19
10. Aktivist Schwarze Pumpe	22	8	3	11	25-38	19
11. Energie Cottbus II	22	6	6	10	24-26	18
12. Motor Bautzen	22	0	4	18	11-70	4

Promoted: Motor Altenburg, Fortschritt Bischofswerda, Aktivist Brieske-Senftenburg, Fortschritt Krumhermersdorf. Wismut Gera were placed in Staffel E for the following season

Second Division (Staffel E)
Club	P	W	D	L	Goals	Pts
1. Carl Zeiss Jena II	22	13	5	4	43-19	31
2. Motor Suhl	22	11	8	3	49-29	30
3. Chemie Zeitz	22	10	7	5	34-17	27
4. Zentronik Sömmerda	22	10	4	8	39-36	24
5. Motor Nordhausen	22	7	9	6	30-27	23
6. Karl-Marx-Stadt II	22	8	6	8	31-27	22
7. Sachsenring Zwickau II	22	9	3	10	28-37	21
8. Motor Weimar	22	7	6	9	21-21	20
9. Motor Hermsdorf	22	6	6	10	26-40	18
10. Kali Werra Tiefenort	22	4	9	9	25-33	17
11. Motor Vellsdorf	22	5	6	11	24-52	16
12. Chemie Schwarza	22	5	5	12	19-31	15

Promoted: Umformtechnik Erfurt, Chemie IW Ilmenau, Fortschritt Weida

East German Cup Final
in Berlin
Lokomotive Leipzig 3, Vorwärts Frankfurt/Oder 0

1975-76

East German Internationals
3/9/75 in Moscow 0-0 v USSR
27/9/75 in Brussels 2-1 v Belgium (ECQ)
12/10/75 in Leipzig 2-1 v France (ECQ)
19/11/75 in Brno 1-1 v Czechoslovakia (OGQ)
7/4/76 in Leipzig 0-0 v Czechoslovakia (OGQ)
21/4/76 in Cottbus 5-0 v Algeria
27/7/76 in Montreal 2-1 v USSR (OG)
31/7/76 in Montroal 3 1 v Poland (OG)
Note: The other three games played by East Germany at the 1976 Olympic Games are not recognised as full internationals.

European Cup
First Round
Jeunesse D'Esch v Bayern Munich .... (0-5, 1-3)
Borussia Mönchengladbach v Wacker Innsbruck ..... (1-1, 6-1)
Malmö FF v 1.FC Magdeburg .... (2-1, 1-2 aet)
Malmö won on penalties
Second Round
Malmö FF v Bayern Munich .... (1-0, 0-2)
Borussia Mönchengladbach v Juventus .... (2-0, 2-2)
Quarterfinals
Bayern Munich v Benfica .... (0-0, 1-5)
Borussia Mönchengladbach v Real Madrid .... (2-2, 1-1)
Semifinals
Real Madrid v Bayern Munich .... (1-1, 0-2)
Final in Glasgow
Bayern Munich 1, St. Etienne 0

Cup-Winners' Cup
First Round
Eintracht Frankfurt v Coleraine .... (5-1, 6-2)
Panathinaikos v Sachsenring Zwickau .... (0-0, 0-2)
Second Round
Atlético Madrid v Eintracht Frankfurt .... (1-2, 0-1)
Fiorentina v Sachsenring Zwickau .... (1-0, 0-1 aet)
Zwickau won on penalties
Quarterfinals
Sturm Graz v Eintracht Frankfurt .... (0-2, 0-1)
Glasgow Celtic v Sachsenring Zwickau .... (1-1, 0-1)
Semifinals
Eintracht Frankfurt v West Ham United .... (2-1, 1-3)
Sachsenring Zwickau v Anderlecht .... (0-3, 0-2)

UEFA Cup
First Round
MSV Duisburg v Paralimni .... (7-1, 3-2)
Hertha BSC Berlin v HJK Helsinki .... (4-1, 2-1)
1.FC Cologne v B 1903 Copenhagen .... (2-0, 3-2 aet)
Young Boys Berne v Hamburg SV .... (0-0, 2-4)
Carl Zeiss Jena v Marseilles .... (3-0, 1-0)
ASA Tirgu Mures v Dynamo Dresden .... (2-2, 1-4)
Second Round
MSV Duisburg v Levsky Spartak Sofia .... (3-2, 1-2)
Hertha BSC Berlin v Ajax Amsterdam .... (1-0, 1-4)
Red Star Belgrade v Hamburg SV .... (1-1, 0-4)
Spartak Moscow v 1.FC Cologne .... (2-0, 1-0)
Carl Zeiss Jena v Stal Mielec .... (1-0, 0-1 aet)
Mielec won on penalties
Honved v Dynamo Dresden .... (2-2, 0-1)
Third Round
Hamburg SV v FC Porto .... (2-0, 1-2)
Dynamo Dresden v Torpedo Moscow .... (3-0, 1-3)
Quarterfinals
Hamburg SV v Stal Mielec .... (1-1, 1-0)
Dynamo Dresden v Liverpool .... (0-0, 1-2)
Semifinals
Hamburg SV v FC Bruges .... (1-1, 0-1)

1976-77

One more time

1.FC Cologne were expecting great things this season, with Hennes Weisweiler—who had lost a power struggle to Johann Cruyff at Barcelona—returning to the Bundesliga as their *Trainer*. Cologne had also paid the Bundesliga's first-ever million-mark transfer fee for the Belgian Roger van Gool from FC Bruges. The President of local rivals Fortuna was reported to have said "For that sort of money, I'd have bought a van Gogh, not a van Gool."

Some Cologne players appreciated Weisweiler's arrival rather less than others. Club captain Wolfgang Overath, in his fourteenth season with the club and a veteran of 81 international appearances, did not see eye-to-eye with the new *Trainer* and found himself on the substitutes' bench quite frequently, particularly for away matches when his absence was not as conspicuous. The disagreements reached a climax in January at an away fixture in Kaiserslautern, when during the second half Overath signalled that he wanted to come off but Weisweiler refused to substitute him.

Nevertheless, with Heinz Flohe in superb form and Dieter Müller hitting the net with consistency, it was only a leaky defence which prevented Cologne finishing higher than fifth. They won the West German Cup by overcoming Hertha Berlin in the last-ever occasion when the final was allowed to go to a replay (it's penalties after extra time nowadays). Having experienced such wretched luck in the competition in seasons past, Cologne were worthy winners: they scored 33 goals in their eight matches, and fourteen of those came from Müller.

By the time of Cologne's victory, Overath had announced his retirement—and Weisweiler promptly left him out of the side for the replay. Overath's final game for his club was a testimonial against the German World Cup-winning side of 1974. Overath later admitted that in a way he was glad he felt obliged to leave at this time, otherwise he could perhaps have carried on playing for too long and missed the chance to go out whilst still at the top.

Also leaving the Bundesliga at the end of the season—albeit temporarily—was Franz Beckenbauer, lured over the Atlantic to join Pele and company in New York with the Cosmos. Bayern had another disappointing season, particularly away from home: November saw the start of a run of 28 consecutive away matches without a win. Gerd Müller kept on scoring, though, and in the 9-0 win against bottom team Tennis Borussia he once again netted five times—for the fifth time as a professional. Müller also scored twice in the most remarkable match of the season as Bayern came back from 4-0 down to beat VfL Bochum 6-5. But the club were unable to perform a similar feat of extrication in the European Cup. They went out to Dynamo Kiev in the quarterfinals, failing to make it four in a row as *Europameister*.

Eintracht Frankfurt could well have claimed the title if they hadn't started the season so badly, for they went 22 games undefeated, dropping only seven points out of a possible 44 from November until the end of the season. But it was Mönchengladbach who came out on top, having yet again opened up a gap early in the season. With 27 points at the half-way stage Gladbach got by with just 17 points after that, and still managed to clinch the title by gaining a 2-2 draw in Munich in their final game. Had they lost that match, Schalke 04 in all probability would have taken the championship.

But in their ever-growing catalogue of Bundesliga championships this was not a particularly memorable season for Gladbach, although today many would claim with some justification that this was their *last* memorable season. Some of their star players were no longer able to perform to the level of previous years, some had left the club to play abroad, and some were plagued by injuries, including Jupp Heynckes and Berti Vogts. Gladbach's defence may have remained reasonably solid, but their attack wasn't firing on all cylinders, and the club's goals total was the lowest since their debut season in the Bundesliga. They did manage to reach the European Cup Final but, up against an inspired Liverpool side, Alan Simonsen's goal was not enough to counter those of Terry McDermott, Tommy Smith and Phil Neal. The talented Simonsen gained some consolation by being voted European Footballer of the Year. At the end of the season, the tenacious Uli Stielike left Gladbach for Real Madrid, where he was to spend eight successful years.

There was a European trophy for the Bundesliga courtesy of Hamburg SV, who benefited from a relatively easy draw and scored in each match. They impressively retrieved a 3-1 first-leg deficit against Atlético Madrid with a solid 2-0 win in the Volksparkstadion to reach the final. There, in front of 65,000 in Amsterdam, they overcame Anderlecht on the strength of Georg Volkert's penalty and a goal from Felix Magath. It was HSV's first European success, having lost in the final of the same competition eight years earlier.

The Second Division North was won by FC St. Pauli, who had sat atop the table from the 24th round onward and were paced by 27 goals from Franz Gerber, the division's top scorer. In the south, the race was between TSV 1860 Munich and VfB Stuttgart. In April, a crowd of over 77,000 saw a goalless draw between the two clubs at the Olympiastadion; earlier in the season, 50,000 had seen Stuttgart beat TSV at the Neckarstadion. Meanwhile FK Pirmasens, who had so nearly gained promotion to the top flight two seasons before, only narrowly avoided relegation. It was just a temporary stay of execution, though—the club would finish bottom the following season, never to return.

The West German Cup produced a number of memorable matches this season and a number of terribly one-sided results. VfL Osnabrück recorded their biggest-ever victory: 12-1 over Union 06 Berlin, with Reinhold Nordmann scoring four. Erwin Kostedde scored six in Borussia Dortmund's 10-0 pasting of Concordia Haaren, and Bernd Dürnberger's hat-trick led Bayern to a 10-0 win over Hanover 96's amateur team.

In the second round, Bayern gained a measure of revenge for the previous season's semifinal loss to Hamburg, winning 5-1 before 26,000 at the Olympiastadion. There was an even more impressive win for Eintracht Frankfurt: 10-2 over Hertha Zehlendorf. Karlsruhe found themselves having to replay their match with Homburg—which they had won 2-0—when it was revealed they had fielded an ineligible player. Homburg, rewarded with a home tie, duly won, 1-0.

The third round saw Munich 1860 bounced out of the competition by Second Division FC Augsburg, with over 25,000 witnessing the 2-1 home victory. The round also produced the unusual pairing of VfB Stuttgart's amateurs against Bayern Munich's amateurs, Bayern winning 2-1. Meanwhile their more famous colleagues were pummelling TV Unterboihingen 10-1, with Gerd Müller claiming five. The draw for the fourth round produced the rare pairing of Bayern's professional side against Bayern's amateur side in the most local of local derbies, but only 6,500 saw big Bayern beat little Bayern, 5-3.

The most thrilling contest of the competition was Bayer Uerdingen's quarterfinal home tie with Frankfurt. Eintracht took a 3-1 lead into the last six minutes. Then Friedhelm Funkel scored for Uerdingen and, with virtually the last kick of the match, Jan Mattsson scrambled an equaliser. Uerdingen poached three further goals in extra time to win 6-3 before an amazed 20,000. Meanwhile Rot-Weiss Essen reached the semifinals by winning 2-1 at Bayreuth—despite conceding sixteen corners and earning just two.

In the qualifying competition for the 1978 Under-21 European Championship, East Germany gained one point in a 1-1 draw in Turkey, but lost two players. Norbert Nachtweih and Jürgen Pahl, both of Halle, left the team's hotel and headed for the West German embassy seeking political asylum. They wound up joining Eintracht Frankfurt. In East German domestic competition, Dynamo Dresden did the double for the second time. They finished four points clear of Magdeburg in the league and scored twice in the last five minutes to beat Lokomotive Leipzig 3-2 in the cup final. Oberliga gates were on the way up, with crowds averaging 13,827—the highest figure since 1955. There was even plenty of interest in the national team: 95,000 turned up in Leipzig to see East Germany beat the Soviet Union 2-1, with goals from Reinhard Häfner and Jürgen Sparwasser.

The West German national side visited Cardiff and recorded a 2-0 win over Wales, providing Karl-Heinz Rummenigge with the first of his 95 caps. Franz Beckenbauer also played in Cardiff and in two further internationals to accumulate a record number of 103 caps before finishing his international career with a 1-0 defeat in Paris by France. Beckenbauer had captained the German team in the last 47 consecutive matches and had scored 14 times.

Bundesliga

Club	P	W	D	L	Goals	Pts
1. Borussia Mönchengladbach	34	17	10	7	58-34	44
2. FC Schalke 04	34	17	9	8	77-52	43
3. Eintracht Brunswick	34	15	13	6	56-38	43
4. Eintracht Frankfurt	34	17	8	9	86-57	42
5. 1.FC Cologne	34	17	6	11	83-61	40
6. Hamburg SV	34	14	10	10	67-56	38
7. Bayern Munich	34	14	9	11	74-65	37
8. Borussia Dortmund	34	12	10	12	73-64	34
9. MSV Duisburg	34	11	12	11	60-51	34
10. Hertha BSC Berlin	34	13	8	13	55-54	34
11. Werder Bremen	34	13	7	14	51-59	33
12. Fortuna Düsseldorf	34	11	9	14	52-54	31
13. 1.FC Kaiserslautern	34	12	5	17	53-59	29
14. 1.FC Saarbrücken	34	9	11	14	43-55	29
15. VfL Bochum	34	11	7	16	47-62	29
16. Karlsruhe SC	34	9	10	15	53-75	28
17. Tennis Borussia Berlin	34	6	10	18	47-85	22
18. Rot-Weiss Essen	34	7	8	19	49-103	22

Top Scorers
D Müller (1.FC Cologne) 34
G Müller (Bayern Munich) 28
Hölzenbein (Eintracht Frankfurt) 26
Fischer (FC Schalke 04) 24
Frank (Eintracht Brunswick) 24
Kaczor (VfL Bochum) 21
Hrubesch (Rot-Weiss Essen) 20
Wendt (Tennis Borussia Berlin) 20
Wenzel (Eintracht Frankfurt) 20
Toppmöller (1.FC Kaiserslautern) 19

Promotion Playoff
TSV 1860 Munich v Arminia Bielefeld (4-0, 0-4, 2-0); TSV 1860 Munich promoted to Bundesliga

Second Division North

Club	P	W	D	L	Goals	Pts
1. FC St Pauli	38	19	6	3	69-36	54
2. Arminia Bielefeld	38	19	12	7	50-26	50
3. Wuppertal SV	38	18	11	9	81-55	47
4. Bayer Uerdingen	38	16	11	11	78-52	43
5. Hanover 96	38	18	7	13	73-48	43
6. Preussen Münster	38	15	13	10	73-52	43
7. Alemannia Aachen	38	16	11	11	69-56	43
8. Schwarz-Weiss Essen	38	16	11	11	63-55	43
9. VfL Osnabrück	38	18	7	13	84-77	43
10. Bayer Leverkusen	38	14	12	12	59-58	40
11. Westfalia Herne	38	15	9	14	77-73	39
12. Fortuna Cologne	38	14	10	14	67-62	38
13. Arminia Hanover	38	15	8	15	64-62	38
14. SC Herford	38	12	12	14	62-63	36
15. Wattenscheid 09	38	12	9	17	65-80	33
16. SC Bonn	38	14	5	19	53-72	33
17. Göttingen 05	38	11	9	18	57-67	31
18. Wacker 04 Berlin	38	9	9	20	43-79	27
19. Union Solingen	38	6	8	24	46-96	20
20. VfL Wolfsburg	38	5	6	27	46-119	16

SC Bonn were relegated after their professional licence was revoked. Union Solingen were thus reinstated.
Promoted: 1.FC Bocholt, OSC Bremerhaven, Rot-Weiss Lüdenscheid.

Top Scorers
Gerber (FC St Pauli) 27
Kehr (Alemannia Aachen) 23
Schock (VfL Osnabrück) 23
Budde (Wuppertal SV) 22
Hammes (Wattenscheid 09) 21
Wunder (Hanover 96) 21
Mrosko (Arminia Hanover) 19
Klinge (Göttingen 05) 18
Wolf (Preussen Münster) 18
Funkel (Bayer Uerdingen) 17
Milewski (Hanover 96) 17
Schonert (Bayer Leverkusen) 17
Wallek (VfL Wolfsburg) 17

Second Division South

Club	P	W	D	L	Goals	Pts
1. VfB Stuttgart	38	24	9	5	100-36	57
2. TSV 1860 Munich	38	24	8	6	78-29	56
3. Kickers Offenbach	38	22	9	7	86-52	53
4. FC 08 Homburg	38	23	3	12	84-56	49
5. 1.FC Nuremberg	38	18	13	7	77-51	49
6. SV Darmstadt 98	38	18	10	10	68-48	46
7. FSV Frankfurt	38	14	12	12	65-58	40
8. SpVgg Fürth	38	13	14	11	55-51	40
9. FC Augsburg	38	17	6	15	72-73	40
10. Kickers Stuttgart	38	16	7	15	59-53	39
11. SV Chio Waldhof	38	16	5	17	70-57	37
12. Bayern Hof	38	12	13	13	61-53	37
13. FV 04 Würzburg	38	14	9	15	49-81	37
14. SpVgg Bayreuth	38	12	10	16	60-64	34
15. KSV Baunatal	38	11	11	16	64-82	33
16. Röchling Völklingen	38	13	6	19	47-71	32
17. Eintracht Trier	38	12	4	22	46-68	28
18. FK Pirmasens	38	5	9	24	43-85	19
19. Jahn Regensburg	38	7	5	26	42-87	19
20. BSV Schwenningen	38	4	7	27	31-102	15

Röchling Völklingen withdrew from the Second Division for the following season
Promoted: FC Freiburg, VfR Oli Bürstadt, Wormatia Worms

Top Scorers
Emmerich (Wacker 04 Berlin) 24
Heck (SV Chio Waldhof) 23
Lenz (FC 08 Homburg) 23
Hitzfeld (VfB Stuttgart) 22
Hofman (FSV Frankfurt) 21
Walitza (1.FC Nuremberg) 21
Diener (FC 08 Homburg) 20
Rausch (Kickers Offenbach) 18
Falter (TSV 1860 Munich) 17
Hofeditz (KSV Baunatal) 17

Third Division Champions
Baden (Nordbaden): SV Neckargerach
Baden (Südbaden): FC Freiburg
Bayern: Kickers Würzburg
Berlin: BFC Preussen Berlin
Hessen: VfR Bürstadt
Mittelrhein: 1.FC Cologne (Am.)
Niederrhein: Fortuna Düsseldorf (Am.)
Nord: TuS Bremerhaven 93
Rheinland: TuS Neuendorf-Koblenz
Saarland: Borussia Neunkirchen
Südwest: Wormatia Worms
Westfalen: Rot-Weiss Lüdenscheid
Württemberg: SSV Reutlingen

West German Cup
First Round
1.FC Cologne (Am.) 1, Röchling Völklingen 2
1.FC Kaiserslautern 1, VfR Mannheim 0
1.FC Mülheim 0, SG Egelsbach 3
Arminia Bielefeld 6, FC Passau 2 aet
Arminia Gütersloh 4, SV Darmstadt 98 3 aet
Bayer Leverkusen 4, IF Tönning 0
Bayer Uerdingen 6, VfB Weidenau 0
Bayern Hof 3, VfB Oldenburg 2
Borussia Dortmund 10, Concordia Haaren 0
Borussia Mönchengladbach 0, Eintracht Brunswick 2
Bremerhaven 93 3, VfR Neuss 0
FC 08 Homburg 2, SpVgg Erkenschwick 1
FC Konstanz 0, Alemannia Aachen 2
FC Niederembt 1, SV Spandau 3
FK Pirmasens 5, Preussen Münster 1
Fortuna Cologne 4, Westfalia Herne 1
Fortuna Düsseldorf 3, Eintracht Trier 1
FSV Frankfurt 5, SpVgg Freudenstadt 0
FV Faurndau 1, FC Hanau 93 4
Hamburg SV 4, Schwarz-Weiss Essen 1
Hanover 96 (Am.) 0, Bayern Munich 10
Hanover 96 0, MSV Duisburg 1
Hertha 03 Zehlendorf 1, TuS Mayen 0
Hertha BSC Berlin (Am.) 0, DJK Gütersloh 2
Hertha BSC Berlin 7, TuS Langerwehe 3
Itzehoe SV 0, 1.FC Cologne 7
Jahn Regensburg 3, VfR Heilbronn 1
Karlsruhe SC 2, 1.FC Bocholt 0
Kickers Offenbach 4, SpVgg Bayreuth 4 aet (1-4)
Phönix Lübeck 0, Eintracht Bad Kreuznach 2
Preussen 07 Hamelin 0, 1.FC Saarbrücken 5
Saar 05 Saarbrücken 1, Eintracht Frankfurt 6
SC Freiburg 1, Kickers Stuttgart 6
SC Lüne 0, SG Ellingen/Bonefeld 1 aet
SC Urania Hamburg 1, FC St Pauli 6
Schweinfurt 05 2, Hassia Bingen 3
Sportfreunde Eisbachtal 1, TSG Leihgestern 1 aet (2-0)
Sportfreunde Salzgitter 2, SC Hülse 1920 1
SpVgg Andernach 1, FSV Mainz 05 1 aet (0-3)
SpVgg Steinhagen 0, VfL Bochum 3
SSV Dillenburg 1, Bayern Munich (Am.) 3
SV Chio Waldhof 6, Bremen SV 0
SV Meppen 2, Rot-Weiss Essen 3 aet
SV Neckargerach 3, SSV 1846 Ulm 1
SV Wiesbaden 1, FC Schalke 04 3
SVO Germaringen 9, VfR Laboe 0
Tennis Borussia Berlin 5, Sparta Bremerhaven 0
TSV 1860 Munich 1, Wuppertal SV 0 aet
TSV Güntersleben 1, SSV Reutlingen 2 aet
TuS Feuchtwangen 4, SV Weiskirchen 3 aet
TV Unterboihingen 8, SG Dielheim 2
Union Solingen 1, VfR Pegulan Frankenthal 1 aet (1-0)
VfB Stuttgart 3, SpVgg Fürth 0
VfB Theley 2, BFC Preussen Berlin 0
VfL Osnabrück 12, Union 06 Berlin 1
VfL Pinneberg 0, FC Augsburg 4
VfR Achern 2, BV Bad Lippspringe 0
VfR Pforzheim 2, Olympia Bocholt 3
Victoria Hamburg 1, FC Ensdorf 0
Wacker 04 Berlin 1, FC 08 Villingen 0
Wattenscheid 09 5, TuRa Harksheide 1
Werder Bremen (Am.) 0, 1.FC Nuremberg 3
Werder Bremen 4, Südwest Ludwigshafen 0
Wormatia Worms 2, Göttingen 05 1

Second Round
1.FC Saarbrücken 0, Rot-Weiss Essen 3
Alemannia Aachen 0, Borussia Dortmund 0 aet (0-2)
Arminia Bielefeld 6, SVO Germaringen 0
Bayer Leverkusen 3, FC St Pauli 1 aet
Bayer Uerdingen 3, FSV Mainz 05 0
Bayern Munich 5, Hamburg SV 1
Bremerhaven 93 1, VfL Bochum 3
Eintracht Frankfurt 10, Hertha 03 Zehlendorf 2

FC 08 Homburg 1, Karlsruhe SC 0 (originally 0-2; match void)
FC Hanau 93 1, TSV 1860 Munich 6
FC Schalke 04 6, SG Ellingen/Bonefeld 1
Fortuna Düsseldorf 2, 1.FC Cologne 4 aet
FSV Frankfurt 2, Eintracht Bad Kreuznach 1 aet
Hertha BSC Berlin 3, Bayern Hof 1
Jahn Regensburg 1, Fortuna Cologne 2 aet
Kickers Stuttgart 1, 1.FC Kaiserslautern 1 aet (1-3)
Röchling Völklingen 2, Eintracht Brunswick 1
SG Egelsbach 0, VfL Osnabrück 2
Sportfreunde Eisbachtal 0, Hassia Bingen 4
Sportfreunde Salzgitter 1, Bayern Munich (Am.) 2
SpVgg Bayreuth 2, SSV Reutlingen 1
SV Neckargerach 2, FK Pirmasens 3
SV Spandau 2, SV Darmstadt 98 3
Tennis Borussia Berlin 4, Olympia Bocholt 4 aet (1-1 aet; Tennis Borussia won on penalties)
TuS Feuchtwangen 2, DJK Gütersloh 3 aet
VfB Stuttgart 2, Union Solingen 0
VfB Theley 0, MSV Duisburg 4
VfR Achern 1, TV Unterboihingen 2
Victoria Hamburg 2, SV Chio Waldhof 5
Wacker 04 Berlin 0, 1.FC Nuremberg 5
Werder Bremen 4, Wattenscheid 09 1
Wormatia Worms 1, FC Augsburg 2

Third Round
1.FC Cologne 5, Tennis Borussia Berlin 1
1.FC Nuremberg 3, SV Chio Waldhof 2
Bayer Uerdingen 3, 1.FC Kaiserslautern 1
Bayern Munich (Am.) 2, VfB Stuttgart 1
Bayern Munich 10, TV Unterboihingen 1
DJK Gütersloh 0, FC 08 Homburg 6
FC Augsburg 2, TSV 1860 Munich 1
FC Schalke 04 1, FSV Frankfurt 0
FK Pirmasens 3, Arminia Bielefeld 4
MSV Duisburg 4, Fortuna Cologne 0
Röchling Völklingen 2, Eintracht Frankfurt 3
Rot-Weiss Essen 5, VfL Bochum 1
SpVgg Bayreuth 2, Hassia Bingen 1
SV Darmstadt 98 0, Hertha BSC Berlin 1 aet
VfL Osnabrück 3, Borussia Dortmund 1 aet
Werder Bremen 3, Bayer Leverkusen 0

Fourth Round
1.FC Cologne 7, FC 08 Homburg 2
1.FC Nuremberg 1, VfL Osnabrück 0
Bayer Uerdingen 2, Werder Bremen 0
Bayern Munich 5, Bayern Munich (Am.) 3
FC Schalke 04 2, Eintracht Frankfurt 2 aet (3-4)
MSV Duisburg 1, Hertha BSC Berlin 2
Rot-Weiss Essen 2, Arminia Bielefeld 0

SpVgg Bayreuth 2, FC Augsburg 0

Quarterfinals
1.FC Cologne 4, 1.FC Nuremberg 2
Bayer Uerdingen 6, Eintracht Frankfurt 3 aet
Hertha BSC Berlin 4, Bayern Munich 2 aet
SpVgg Bayreuth 1, Rot-Weiss Essen 2

Semifinals
1.FC Cologne 4, Rot-Weiss Essen 0
Bayer Uerdingen 0, Hertha BSC Berlin 1

Final
in Hanover
1.FC Cologne 1, Hertha BSC Berlin 1 aet (replay: 1-0)

West German Internationals
6/10/76 in Cardiff 2-0 v Wales
17/11/76 in Hanover 2-0 v Czechoslovakia
23/2/77 in Paris 0-1 v France
27/4/77 in Cologne 5-0 v Northern Ireland
30/4/77 in Belgrade 2-1 v Yugoslavia
5/6/77 in Buenos Aires 3-1 v Argentina
8/6/77 in Montevideo 2-0 v Uruguay
12/6/77 in Rio de Janeiro 1-1 v Brazil
14/6/77 in Mexico City 2-2 v Mexico

East German Oberliga

Club	P	W	D	L	Goals	Pts
1. Dynamo Dresden	26	16	6	4	66-27	38
2. 1.FC Magdeburg	26	14	6	6	47-28	34
3. Carl Zeiss Jena	26	14	5	7	45-31	33
4. Dynamo Berlin	26	14	4	8	43-27	32
5. Lokomotive Leipzig	26	10	9	7	40-29	29
6. Rot-Weiss Erfurt	26	8	9	9	27-35	25
7. Chemie Halle	26	7	10	9	34-39	24
8. Sachsenring Zwickau	26	7	8	11	32-34	22
9. FC Karl-Marx-Stadt	26	10	2	14	35-39	22
10. Wismut Aue	26	6	10	10	27-45	22
11. 1.FC Union Berlin	26	7	7	12	30-42	21
12. Vorwärts Frankfurt/Oder	26	9	3	14	23-36	21
13. Stahl Riesa	26	8	5	13	28-47	21
14. Hansa Rostock	26	6	8	12	23-41	20

Top Scorers
Streich (1.FC Magdeburg) 17
Kreische (Dynamo Dresden) 13
Sachse (Dynamo Dresden) 12
Vogel (Chemie Halle) 12
Schnuphase (Carl Zeiss Jena) 10
Sparwasser (1.FC Magdeburg) 10
Heidler (Dynamo Dresden) 8

Frenzel (Lokomotive Leipzig) 7
Kotte (Dynamo Dresden) 7
Netz (Dynamo Berlin) 7
Terletzki (Dynamo Berlin) 7
Vogel (Carl Zeiss Jena) 7

Oberliga Promotion Playoff

Club	P	W	D	L	Goals	Pts
1. Chemie Böhlen	8	5	2	1	17-11	12
2. Wismut Gera	8	3	4	1	14-10	10
3. Chemie Leipzig	8	3	3	2	11-10	9
4. Vorwärts Stralsund	8	3	1	4	10-8	7
5. Stahl Hennigsdorf	8	0	2	6	8-21	2

Second Division (Staffel A)

Club	P	W	D	L	Goals	Pts
1. Vorwärts Stralsund	22	15	6	1	67-14	36
2. Dynamo Schwerin	22	15	4	3	54-20	34
3. Post Neubrandenburg	22	13	6	3	65-19	32
4. TSG Bau Rostock	22	13	4	5	44-28	30
5. TSG Wismar	22	10	7	5	50-36	27
6. KKW Greifswald	22	9	8	5	45-29	26
7. Schiffahrt/Hafen Rostock	22	8	6	8	39-34	22
8. Einheit Güstrow	22	8	3	11	27-54	19
9. RB Trinwillershagen	22	7	0	15	31-66	14
10. Motor Schwerin	22	2	7	13	28-63	11
11. Einheit Gravesmühlen	22	3	4	15	25-59	10
12. Nord Torgelow	22	1	1	20	24-77	3

Promoted: Demminer VB, ISG Schwerin, Motor Wolgast. Post Neubrandenburg were placed in Staffel B for the following season

Second Division (Staffel B)

Club	P	W	D	L	Goals	Pts
1. Stahl Hennigsdorf	22	15	2	5	52-21	32
2. Stahl Eisenhüttenstadt	22	14	3	5	46-12	31
3. Vorwärts Neubrandenburg	22	13	4	5	41-22	30
4. Motor Eberswalde	22	11	4	7	36-24	26
5. Motor Babelsberg	22	9	6	7	39-31	24
6. Rotation Berlin	22	9	5	8	29-28	23
7. Aufbau Schwedt	22	9	3	10	31-39	21
8. Motor Hennigsdorf	22	7	5	10	26-36	19
9. Dynamo Fürstenwalde	22	7	4	11	35-39	18
10. TSG Neustrelitz	22	7	3	12	23-42	17
11. Stahl Finow	22	4	5	13	23-46	13
12. Lichtenberg 47	22	5	0	17	19-60	10

Promoted: Bergmann Borsig Berlin, Traktor Gross-Lindow

Second Division (Staffel C)

Club	P	W	D	L	Goals	Pts
1. Chemie Leipzig	22	14	5	3	46-22	33
2. Stahl Blankenburg	22	11	5	6	41-22	27
3. Einheit Wernigerode	22	11	4	7	50-34	26
4. Chemie Buna Schkopau	22	10	6	6	30-22	26
5. Dynamo Eisleben	22	10	6	6	26-21	26
6. Aktivist Espenhain	22	9	5	8	27-27	23
7. Vorwärts Dessau	22	7	7	8	30-34	21
8. Stahl Brandenburg	22	6	7	9	21-27	19
9. Stahl Thale	22	5	8	9	23-31	18
10. Vertias Wittenberge	22	7	3	12	22-48	17
11. Lokomotive Stendal	22	4	8	10	27-30	16
12. Lokomotive Halberstadt	22	4	4	14	18-43	12

Promoted: Chemie Premnitz, TSG Schkeuditz, Chemie Schönebeck, Chemie Wolfen. Aktivist Espenhain were placed in Staffel D for the following season

Second Division (Staffel D)

Club	P	W	D	L	Goals	Pts
1. Chemie Böhlen	20	14	3	3	49-21	31
2. Lokomotive Dresden	20	11	5	4	36-18	27
3. Vorwärts Plauen	20	9	4	7	39-30	22
4. Aktivist Brieske-Senftenberg	20	7	8	5	23-22	22
5. Energie Cottbus	20	7	6	7	45-23	20
6. TSG Gröditz	20	7	6	7	30-33	20
7. Motor Werdau	20	7	5	8	28-37	19
8. Aktivist Schwarze Pumpe	20	4	9	7	23-28	17
9. Fortschritt Bischofswerda	20	5	6	9	32-40	16
10. Motor Altenburg	20	4	5	11	25-43	13
11. Fortschritt Krumhermersdorf	20	5	3	12	23-58	13

Promoted: Motor WAMA Görlitz, Motor Ascota Karl-Marx-Stadt, Dynamo Lübben

Second Division (Staffel E)

Club	P	W	D	L	Goals	Pts
1. Wismut Gera	22	15	5	2	64-19	35
2. Motor Suhl	22	14	3	5	48-28	31
3. Kali Werra Tiefenort	22	13	5	4	36-18	31
4. Motor Nordhausen	22	6	11	5	26-27	23
5. Fortschritt Weida	22	8	7	7	34-37	23
6. Zentronik Sömmerda	22	8	6	8	36-29	22
7. Chemie Zeitz	22	8	6	8	29-25	22
8. Motor Hermsdorf	22	8	4	10	27-43	20
9. Motor Weimar	22	8	3	11	36-39	19
10. Chemie IW Ilmenau	22	6	2	14	24-43	14
11. Umformtechnik Erfurt	22	4	5	13	24-37	13
12. Motor Veilsdorf	22	2	7	13	18-57	11

Promoted: Dynamo Gera, Landbau Bad Langensalza, Motor Steinach

East German Cup Final
in Berlin
Dynamo Dresden 3, Lokomotive Leipzig 2

East German Internationals
22/9/76 in Berlin 1-1 v Hungary
27/10/76 in Sliven 4-0 v Bulgaria
17/11/76 in Dresden 1-1 v Turkey (WCQ)
2/4/77 in Valetta 1-0 v Malta (WCQ)
27/4/77 in Bucharest 1-1 v Rumania
12/7/77 in Buenos Aires 0-2 v Argentina
28/7/77 in Leipzig 2-1 v USSR

European Cup
First Round
Koge v Bayern Munich .... (0-5, 1-2)
Austria Vienna v Borussia Mönchengladbach .... (1-0, 0-3)
Dynamo Dresden v Benfica .... (2-0, 0-0)
Second Round
Torino v Borussia Mönchengladbach .... (1-2, 0-0)
Banik Ostrava v Bayern Munich .... (2-1, 0-5)
Ferencvaros v Dynamo Dresden .... (1-0, 0-4)
Quarterfinals
Borussia Mönchengladbach v FC Brugge .... (2-2, 1-0)
Bayern Munich v Dynamo Kiev .... (1-0, 0-2)
FC Zurich v Dynamo Dresden .... (2-1, 2-3)
Semifinals
Dynamo Kiev v Borussia Mönchengladbach .... (1-0, 0-2)
Final in Rome
Liverpool 3, Borussia Mönchengladbach 1

Cup-Winners' Cup
First Round
Hamburg SV v Keflavik .... (3-0, 1-1)
Lokomotive Leipzig v Heart of Midlothian .... (2-0, 1-5)
Second Round
Hamburg SV v Heart of Midlothian .... (4-2, 4-1)
Quarterfinals
MTK Budapest v Hamburg SV .... (1-1, 1-4)
Semifinals
Atlético Madrid v Hamburg SV .... (3-1, 0-3)
Final in Amsterdam
Hamburg SV 2, Anderlecht 0

UEFA Cup
First Round
FC Porto v FC Schalke 04 .... (2-2, 2-3)
1.FC Cologne v GKS Tychy .... (2-0, 1-1)
Paralimni v 1.FC Kaiserslautern .... (1-3, 0-8)
Eintracht Brunswick v Holbaek IF .... (7-0, 0-1)
Schachtjor Donetsk v Dynamo Berlin .... (3-0, 1-1)
1.FC Magdeburg v Cesena .... (3-0, 1-3)
Second Round
1.FC Cologne v Grasshoppers Zurich .... (2-0, 3-2)
1.FC Kaiserslautern v Feyenoord .... (2-2, 0-5)
Eintracht Brunswick v Español .... (2-1, 0-2)
Sportul Studentesc Budapest v FC Schalke 04 ..... (0-1, 0-4)
1.FC Magdeburg v Dinamo Zagreb .... (2-0, 2-2)
Third Round
RWD Molenbeek v FC Schalke 04 .... (1-0, 1-1)
Queen's Park Rangers v 1.FC Cologne .... (3-0, 1-4)
1.FC Magdeburg v Videoton .... (5-0, 0-1)
Quarterfinals
1.FC Magdeburg v Juventus .... (1-3, 0-1)

1977-78

Twelve is not enough

After nine years' domination by Bayern Munich and Borussia Mönchengladbach, the Bundesliga enjoyed an open and competitive season. Regarded by many as the world's premier football league, it attracted unprecedented levels of attention. New players arrived from far and wide: Hamburg imported Kevin Keegan from Liverpool and Ivan Buljan from Hajduk Split, 1.FC Cologne signed Japanese international Yasuhiko Okudera, and Eintracht Brunswick even managed to lure Paul Breitner back from Spain.

Crowds were at an all time high—a total of over 8,300,000, or an average of 27,158 a game. Hertha Berlin enjoyed a temporary return to the good old days, attracting over 79,400 to the Olympiastadion for the visit of Cologne. And it was Cologne who went on to become champions for the first time since the inaugural Bundesliga season. Few might have expected it after a 5-1 defeat at the hands of Fortuna Düsseldorf on opening day, but Cologne topped the table by their fifth game, thanks in no small part to a 7-2 whipping of Werder Bremen in round three. In that match, Cologne's prolific marksman Dieter Müller scored six goals—a record unequalled to this day. Skipper Heinz Flohe had a memorable season for club and country. He attributed his team's success to *Trainer* Hennes Weisweiler's "iron discipline" and the immense talents of Müller, Okudera, Herbert Zimmermann, Harald Konopka, Herbert Neumann, and Harald "Toni" Schumacher.

Newly-promoted VfB Stuttgart were packing them in at the Neckarstadion, where they attracted an average gate of 53,186—a league record no club has come close to beating. Not surprisingly, Stuttgart finished with the league's best home record, an early-season 2-1 loss to Hamburg their only defeat. A surprisingly strong fourth-place finish assured Jürgen Sundermann's team of a spot in the UEFA Cup.

It was not nearly as happy a tale for FC St. Pauli, another of the newly-promoted clubs. This was their first season in the top flight, after many years of formidable performances in the old Regionalliga North, and more recently in the

Second Division North. St. Pauli spent virtually all season at the wrong end of the table, unable to patch the gaping holes in their defence which saw them concede more goals than anyone else. The fate of the third newly-promoted club, TSV 1860 Munich, was more or less sealed after they failed to win any of their first fourteen matches. Eventually they climbed off the bottom, but the hole they had dug for themselves was just too deep.

Not that their city rivals fared much better. This was Bayern Munich's weakest season since joining the Bundesliga, failing to win away from home and conceding more goals than they scored. They even suffered an embarrassing 6-3 defeat at MSV Duisburg in November, with four of the goals coming from Bernhard Dietz—not bad for a fullback! Few were surprised when *Trainer* Dettmar Cramer was shown the door before the season was half over. What was surprising, and indeed somewhat bizarre, was how his replacement was arranged. Cramer simply exchanged jobs with Gyula Lorant, the *Trainer* of Eintracht Frankfurt.

The local derby between Bochum and Schalke at the Ruhrstadion in March produced one of football's most peculiar refereeing decisions. Schalke were leading 1-0 when Bochum's Dieter Bast was sent off in the 53rd minute. Teammate Hans-Joachim Abel protested furiously to referee Udo Zuchantke about the decision, but to no avail. Abel decided to take the law into his own hands when play resumed, repeatedly kicking Schalke players who were nowhere near the ball until Zuchantke had no option but to produce the red card. But Abel refused to go—and sympathetic Bochum fans invaded the pitch. Abel was still on the field when play was eventually resumed, but instead of summoning the police, Zuchantke decided to forget about the red card and now showed Abel a yellow one. The reprieved striker scored an equaliser in the 54th minute—and Bochum drew 1-1. Not surprisingly, this turned out to be the last Bundesliga match Zuchantke officated.

One of Cologne's finest performances was a 5-2 away win over Mönchengladbach at the Bökelberg, but as the season neared its end the table-toppers lost their way whilst Gladbach chalked up a series of wins to narrow the gap. With one match remaining, the two clubs' points totals were level, and both were well ahead of third-placed Hertha. Cologne's fans had cause for celebration, however, as their goal-difference was a mighty +40, well ahead of Gladbach's +30, and their final match was away to St. Pauli. As long as Cologne won, even 1-0, then Gladbach could only overtake them by beating their opponents Borussia Dortmund by at least twelve goals.

Of course, football is nothing if not a funny game. And so, on the final day of the season Mönchengladbach beat Dortmund 12-0. Dortmund, who were in a safe mid-table position, had mysteriously fielded an under-strength team and played in something of a funk. The subsequent furore led to the Dortmund board requesting the immediate departure of reserve keeper Peter Endrulat and *Trainer* Otto Rehhagel. But justice had been done. Cologne won 5-0 at St. Pauli and clinched the championship with three goals to spare.

Not content with just their first league title in fourteen years, Cologne also walked off with the West German Cup. Having scored 26 goals in their seven ties and conceded only one, they were worthy winners. In the final, they faced Fortuna Düsseldorf, who had looked mighty impressive in their semifinal dismantling of Duisburg. But Fortuna wasted chance upon chance and eventually fell behind when an unmarked Bernd Cullmann scored from Harald Konopka's cross. With Toni Schumacher having a solid game in goal, there was no way back for Düsseldorf, and a late strike from Roger van Gool sealed the double for Cologne.

Two Westfalian rivals, Arminia Bielefeld and Preussen Münster, dominated the Second Division North for much of the season. Münster, however, faded away toward season's end and it was Rot-Weiss Essen who stormed their way to second place behind Bielefeld on the strength of five straight wins to close out the season. The key to Essen's success was their imposing centre-forward, Horst Hrubesch, who scored an amazing 42 goals in 35 matches.

The race in the South was less clear-cut, with SpVgg Bayreuth, 1.FC Nuremberg, and SV Darmstadt 98 all challenging for the top spot. In the end it was Darmstadt who finished the strongest and came away from the pack, whilst Bayreuth faded to fourth. Homburg enjoyed another successful season, although they were rarely able to attract more than a few thousand fans to their Waldstadion. A similar problem was also affecting proud Nuremberg. Despite finishing in the playoff spot, the one-time champions attracted just 6,000 for their crucial end-of-season contest with Mannheim and rarely drew crowds in excess of 10,000.

At the end of the season, there was a reorganisation of top-level German amateur football, with the creation of eight *Oberligen,* or third divisions. The champions of each of these leagues would be automatically promoted to the Second Bundesliga in the respective North or South division—except the winners in Berlin, who would play off against the Oberliga North runners-up.

Karlheinz Förster of VfB Stuttgart was called up into the national team this year, making his debut as a substitute in the friendly against Brazil in Hamburg. West Germany then headed for World Cup '78 in Argentina—without Förster—and gave an impressive display in a 6-0 demolition of Mexico. Despite 0-0 draws with Poland and Tunisia, the Germans qualified for the next stage, but further draws with Italy and Holland were followed by a bitterly disappointing 3-2 loss to Austria and West Germany's tournament was over. It was also over for Berti Vogts, whose international career ended with 96 caps, the last nineteen as captain.

Having shown such world-class form all season, Flohe sustained a bad injury in his 39th international appearance against Italy in the World Cup, which was to be followed by a very poor season and rows with Weisweiler, eventually leading to his transfer to Munich 1860. After only three months down south, Flohe broke his leg badly after an illegal tackle and never played football again. He had made 343 Bundesliga appearances, scoring 81 goals.

The East German national side enjoyed their highest-ever home win with a 9-0 defeat of Malta in a World Cup qualifying match, with three goals each for Joachim Streich and Martin Hoffmann. But they came second to Austria in their group and didn't go to Argentina. Dynamo Dresden boasted a 100% home record and became the first club to win the Oberliga for three consecutive years. Henning Frenzel of Lokomotive Leipzig retired after a nineteen-year career of 420 league appearances and 152 goals, and 56 caps and 19 goals for East Germany.

Mönchengladbach were the most successful German team in Europe. Their semifinal tie with Liverpool was a re-match of the previous season's final. Goals from Hannes and Bonhof gave Borussia a 2-1 first leg lead, but the return leg at Anfield proved too intimidating and the English side won easily, 3-0.

Bundesliga

Club	P	W	D	L	Goals	Pts
1. 1.FC Cologne	34	22	4	8	86-41	48
2. Borussia Mönchengladbach	34	20	8	6	86-44	48
3. Hertha BSC Berlin	34	15	10	9	59-48	40
4. VfB Stuttgart	34	17	5	12	58-40	39
5. Fortuna Düsseldorf	34	15	9	10	49-36	39
6. MSV Duisburg	34	15	7	12	62-59	37
7. Eintracht Frankfurt	34	16	4	14	59-52	36
8. 1.FC Kaiserslautern	34	16	4	14	64-63	36
9. FC Schalke 04	34	14	6	14	47-52	34
10. Hamburg SV	34	14	6	14	61-67	34
11. Borussia Dortmund	34	14	5	15	57-71	33
12. Bayern Munich	34	11	10	13	62-64	32
13. Eintracht Brunswick	34	14	4	16	43-55	32
14. VfL Bochum	34	11	9	14	49-51	31
15. Werder Bremen	34	13	5	16	48-57	31
16. TSV 1860 Munich	34	7	8	19	41-60	22
17. 1.FC Saarbrücken	34	6	10	18	39-70	22
18. FC St Pauli	34	6	6	22	44-86	18

Top Scorers
D Müller (1.FC Cologne) ... 24
G Müller (Bayern Munich) ... 24
Toppmöller (Kaiserslautern) ... 21
Burgsmüller (Borussia Dortmund) ... 20
Fischer (FC Schalke 04) ... 20
Heynckes (Borussia Mönchengladbach) ... 18
Granitza (Hertha BSC Berlin) ... 17
Simonsen (Borussia Mönchengladbach) ... 17
Gerber (FC St Pauli) ... 16
Seliger (MSV Duisburg) ... 16

Bundesliga Promotion Playoff
1.FC Nuremberg v Rot-Weiss Essen (1-0, 2-2); Nuremberg promoted to Bundesliga

Second Division North

Club	P	W	D	L	Goals	Pts
1. Arminia Bielefeld	38	23	5	10	74-40	51
2. Rot-Weiss Essen	38	21	8	9	82-49	50
3. Preussen Münster	38	18	13	7	65-47	49
4. Fortuna Cologne	38	19	10	9	79-62	48
5. Hanover 96	38	19	5	14	68-57	43
6. Wattenscheid 09	38	16	9	13	76-65	41
7. Bayer Uerdingen	38	15	11	12	75-64	41
8. Bayer Leverkusen	38	16	7	15	58-51	39
9. Union Solingen	38	13	13	12	60-60	39
10. Tennis Borussia Berlin	38	12	12	14	58-57	36
11. Wuppertal SV	38	12	12	14	56-59	36
12. Westfalia Herne	38	12	11	15	53-59	35
13. Rot-Weiss Lüdenscheid	38	12	11	15	59-75	35
14. Alemannia Aachen	38	10	14	14	51-62	34
15. Arminia Hanover	38	12	10	16	63-78	34
16. VfL Osnabrück	38	9	15	14	56-62	33
17. SC Herford	38	12	9	17	51-58	33
18. 1.FC Bocholt	38	13	6	19	65-70	32
19. OSC Bremerhaven	38	11	10	17	61-88	32
20. Schwarz-Weiss Essen	38	4	11	23	45-92	19

Promoted: Wacker Berlin, Viktoria Cologne, Holstein Kiel, DSC Wanne-Eickel

Top Scorers
Hrubesch (Rot-Weiss Essen) ... 42
Funkel (Bayer Uerdingen) ... 25
Mrosko (Arminia Hanover) ... 24
Mattsson (Bayer Uerdingen) ... 21
Lenz (Union Solingen) ... 19
Graul (Fortuna Cologne) ... 18
Kehr (Tennis Borussia Berlin) ... 18
Eilenfeldt (Arminia Bielefeld) ... 16
Hammes (Wattenscheid 09) ... 16
Mödrath (Fortuna Cologne) ... 16
Plücken (Union Solingen) ... 16
Stradt (Tennis Borussia Berlin) ... 16

Second Division South

Club	P	W	D	L	Goals	Pts
1. SV Darmstadt 98	38	26	6	6	90-43	58
2. 1.FC Nuremberg	38	22	9	7	75-46	53
3. FC 08 Homburg	38	20	9	9	65-45	49
4. SpVgg Bayreuth	38	22	4	12	79-50	48
5. Kickers Offenbach	38	18	10	10	88-54	46
6. SpVgg Fürth	38	19	8	11	73-42	46
7. Karlsruhe SC	38	20	5	13	76-54	45
8. SV Chio Waldhof	38	15	12	11	76-50	42
9. Wormatia Worms	38	16	10	12	63-56	42
10. Kickers Stuttgart	38	14	12	12	63-71	40
11. FV 04 Würzburg	38	13	12	13	52-53	38
12. Eintracht Trier	38	14	7	17	56-64	35
13. FC Freiburg	38	12	11	15	58-71	35
14. FC Augsburg	38	12	10	16	57-54	34
15. FSV Frankfurt	38	11	12	15	54-62	34
16. KSV Baunatal	38	13	8	17	55-80	34
17. Bayern Hof	38	13	7	18	45-62	33
18. VfR Bürstadt	38	10	5	23	48-48	25
19. Kickers Würzburg	38	4	9	25	38-93	17
20. FK Pirmasens	38	1	4	33	25-120	6

SV Chio Waldhof became SV Waldhof Mannheim

Promoted: SC Freiburg, Hanau 93, MTV Ingolstadt, Borussia Neunkirchen

Top Scorers
Günther (Karlsruhe SC) 27
Cestonaro (SV Darmstadt 98) 25
Sommerer (SpVgg Bayreuth) 25
Beichle (FC Augsburg) 21
Drexler (SV Darmstadt 98) 21
Seubert (Wormatia Worms) 21
Unger (SpVgg Fürth) 21
Heinlein (SpVgg Fürth) 18
Jordan (VfR Bürstadt) 18
Leiendecker (Eintracht Trier) 16

Third Division Champions
Baden (Nordbaden): FV 09 Weinheim
Baden (Südbaden): SC Freiburg
Bayern: 1.FC Hassfurt
Berlin: Wacker 04 Berlin
Hessen: FC Hanau 93
Mittelrhein: Viktoria Cologne
Niederrhein: Olympia Bocholt
Nord: OSV Hanover
Rheinland: TuS Neuendorf-Koblenz
Saarland: Borussia Neunkirchen
Südwest: FSV Mainz 05
Westfalen: DSC Wanne-Eickel
Württemberg: SSV Reutlingen

West German Cup
First Round
1.FC Saarbrücken 1, Bayern Munich 2
1.FC Viersen 0, Borussia Mönchengladbach 8
Alemannia Eggenstein 8, TV Horn Hamburg 0 (Horn won the original match 2-1, then played TSV 1860 Munich in the Second Round and lost 15-0. Both results were later annulled when it was discovered Horn had fielded an ineligible player.)
Arminia Hanover 0, FC Augsburg (Am.) 1
Bayer Leverkusen 5, FSV Salmrohr 0
Bremerhaven 93 3, Preussen Münster 2
BV 04 Düsseldorf 3, VfL Bad Schwartau 0
BV 08 Lüttringhausen 1, FC Freiburg 2
Concordia Hamburg 2, Bayern Hof 0
Eintracht Brunswick 10, Eintracht Nordhorn 1
Eintracht Glas-Chemie Wirges 2, DSC Wanne-Eickel 3
Eintracht Trier 3, Blaus-Weiss Wulfen 0
FC Augsburg 1, SpVgg Fürth 0
FC Konstanz 1, Eintracht Frankfurt 6
FC Normannia Gmünd 2, Fortuna Cologne 0
FC Rastatt 04, TuS Struck 1
FC St Wendel 1, Fortuna Düsseldorf 6
FC Tailfingen 3, SpVgg Neckargemünd 2
FC Villingen 0, SpVgg Bayreuth 1
FSV Ludwigshafen-Oggersheim 0, 1.FC Kaiserslautern 3
FSV Mainz 05 7, Hertha 03 Zehlendorf 1
FV 04 Würzburg 1, Jahn Regensburg 0
Göttingen 05 0, FC Schalke 04 2
Hanover 96 0, Tennis Borussia Berlin 2
Hassia Bingen 0, Kickers Stuttgart 1
Itzehoe SV 2, Borussia Brand 1
Karlsruhe SC 2, 1.FC Nuremberg 1
Kickers Offenbach 0, 1.FC Cologne 4
KSV Baunatal 2, Alemannia Aachen 3
Olympia Kirrlach 0, Bayer Uerdingen 6
OSV Hanover 2, FSV Frankfurt 5
Rot-Weiss Essen 3, VfR Oli Bürstadt 2
RSV Rehburg 1, Hertha BSC Berlin 6
Saar 05 Saarbrücken 05 1, Wacker 04 Berlin 1 aet (0-0 aet; Wacker won on penalties)
SB Heidenheim 1, FK Pirmasens 2
SC Bonn 5, Sportfreunde Eisbachtal 1
SC Gladenbach 2, SSV Elpe 1
Schleswig 06 0, Röchling Völklingen 1
SG Ellingen-Bonefeld 1, FC St Pauli 6
Sportunion Warendorf 3, FSV Hemmersdorf 1
SpVgg Bad Homburg 1, FC 08 Homburg 2
SpVgg Wirges 2, DSC Wanne-Eickel 3
SU Lichterfeld 2, Alemannia Plaidt 2 aet (1-3)
Südwest Nuremberg 1, SV Darmstadt 98 3
SV Blumenthal 1, Werder Bremen 5
SV Chio Waldhof 12, TV Lüssum 0
SV Hummelsbüttel 0, TuS Schloss Neuhaus 2
SV Sandhausen 3, Traber FC Berlin 1
TSV 1860 Munich 4, Arminia Bielefeld 2
TSV Ofterdingen 0, Hamburg SV 5
TSV Ottobrunn 0, Borussia Dortmund 9
TSV Rendsburg 0, VfL Osnabrück 1
TuRa Harksheide 1, SV Ottweiler 1 aet (1-2)
TuS Langerwehe 1, VfB Coburg 0
TuS Rosenberg 1, MSV Duisburg 11
Union Solingen 2, Schwarz-Weiss Essen 2 aet (0-2)
VfB Oldenburg 0, VfL Bochum 2
VfB Stuttgart 10, TuS Eintracht Bremen 0
VfL Wolfsburg 3, FC Bad Orb 1
VfV Hildesheim 4, TV Unterboihingen 1 aet
Viktoria 89 Berlin 2, BSV Schwenningen 3 aet
Viktoria Cologne 0, Eintracht Bad Kreuznach 2
Wattenscheid 09 1, TSV Bleidenstadt 2 aet
Westfalia Herne 6, BC Efferen 1920 1
Wuppertal SV 2, SC Herford 2 aet (0-3)

Second Round
1.FC Cologne 3, Eintracht Bad Kreuznach 1
1.FC Kaiserslautern 4, Wacker 04 Berlin 1
Bayer Leverkusen 3, FC Rastatt 04 1
Bayer Uerdingen 0, FSV Frankfurt 3
Bayern Munich 3, Eintracht Trier 1
BSV Schwenningen 4, SV Ottweiler 0
BV 04 Düsseldorf 1, Borussia Mönchengladbach 4
DSC Wanne-Eickel 3, VfL Wolfsburg 1
Eintracht Brunswick 3, Kickers Stuttgart 1
FC 08 Homburg 3, SC Herford 0
FC Alemannia Plaidt 1, SC Bonn 2
FC Schalke 04 8, TSV Bleidenstadt 1
FC St Pauli 0, VfL Bochum 3
FC Tailfingen 1, Rot-Weiss Essen 2
Fortuna Düsseldorf 3, Borussia Dortmund 1
FSV Mainz 05 1, Hamburg SV 4
Itzehoe SV 1, SpVgg Bayreuth 6
Karlsruhe SC 4, FK Pirmasens 3 aet
MSV Duisburg 3, VfB Stuttgart 0
Normannia Gmünd 1, FC Augsburg (Am.) 2
OSC Bremerhaven 0, FC Augsburg 3
Röchling Völklingen 0, Werder Bremen 4
SC Gladenbach 1, SV Sandhausen 5
Schwarz-Weiss Essen 2, Concordia Hamburg 0
SU Warendorf 1, FC Freiburg 4
SV Chio Waldhof 1, Hertha BSC Berlin 3
Tennis Borussia Berlin 1, Westfalia Herne 3
TSV 1860 Munich 7, Alemannia Eggenstein 1
TuS Langerwehe 1, FC Würzberg 04 0 aet
TuS Schloss Neuhaus 2, Eintracht Frankfurt 2 aet (0-4)
VfL Osnabrück 2, SV Darmstadt 98 1
VfV Hildesheim 3, Alemannia Aachen 0

Third Round
Bayer Leverkusen 1, Westfalia Herne 5
Borussia Mönchengladbach 3, SC Bonn 0
DSC Wanne-Eickel 0, Werder Bremen 2
FC 08 Homburg 3, Bayern Munich 1
FC Augsburg (Am.) 0, Hertha BSC Berlin 4
FC Freiburg 2, VfL Bochum 6
FC Schalke 04 1, Eintracht Frankfurt 0
Fortuna Düsseldorf 4, Rot-Weiss Essen 1
FSV Frankfurt 0, 1.FC Cologne 3
Hamburg SV 6, VfV Hildesheim 1
Karlsruhe SC 2, SpVgg Bayreuth 0
MSV Duisburg 2, 1.FC Kaiserslautern 1
Schwarz-Weiss Essen 2, BSV Schwenningen 1 aet
SV Sandhausen 0, Eintracht Brunswick 4
TSV 1860 Munich 3, FC Augsburg 0
TuS Langerwehe 2, VfL Osnabrück 0

Fourth Round
1.FC Cologne 4, Karlsruhe SC 0
Borussia Mönchengladbach 3, VfL Bochum 0
FC 08 Homburg 1, Hertha BSC Berlin 1 aet (1-4 aet)
FC Schalke 04 4, Hamburg SV 2
Fortuna Düsseldorf 3, Eintracht Brunswick 1
Schwarz-Weiss Essen 0, Westfalia Herne 0 aet (1-0)
TuS Langerwehe 1, MSV Duisburg 3
Werder Bremen 2, TSV 1860 Munich 1

Quarterfinals
1.FC Cologne 9, Schwarz-Weiss Essen 0
FC Schalke 04 1, Fortuna Düsseldorf aet (0-1)
MSV Duisburg 1, Hertha BSC Berlin 0
Werder Bremen 2, Borussia Mönchengladbach 1

Semifinals
1.FC Cologne 1, Werder Bremen 0
Fortuna Düsseldorf 4, MSV Duisburg 1

Final
in Gelsenkirchen
1.FC Cologne 2, Fortuna Düsseldorf 0

West German Internationals
7/9/77 in Helsinki 1-0 v Finland
8/10/77 in Berlin 2-1 v Italy
16/11/77 in Stuttgart 4-1 v Switzerland
14/12/77 in Dortmund 1-1 v Wales
22/2/78 in Munich 2-1 v England
8/3/78 in Frankfurt 1-0 v Soviet Union
5/4/78 in Hamburg 0-1 v Brazil
19/4/78 in Stockholm 1-3 v Sweden
1/6/78 in Buenos Aires 0-0 v Poland (WC)
6/6/78 in Cordoba 6-0 v Mexico (WC)
10/6/78 in Cordoba 0-0 v Tunisia (WC)
14/6/78 in Buenos Aires 0-0 v Italy (WC)
18/6/78 in Cordoba 2-2 v Holland (WC)
21/6/78 in Cordoba 2-3 v Austria (WC)

East German Oberliga
Club	P	W	D	L	Goals	Pts
1. Dynamo Dresden	26	21	4	1	75-18	46
2. 1.FC Magdeburg	26	15	9	2	59-19	39
3. Dynamo Berlin	26	14	6	6	38-21	34
4. Lokomotive Leipzig	26	14	5	7	63-22	33
5. Carl Zeiss Jena	26	11	7	8	41-40	29
6. FC Chemie Halle	26	10	7	9	36-32	27
7. FC Karl-Marx-Stadt	26	9	6	11	37-46	24
8. 1.FC Union Berlin	26	9	4	13	32-38	22
9. Rot-Weiss Erfurt	26	8	5	13	33-47	21

	P	W	D	L	Goals	Pts
10. Sachsenring Zwickau	26	7	7	12	22-39	21
11. Wismut Aue	26	8	3	15	34-49	19
12. Chemie Böhlen	26	7	4	15	23-63	18
13. Vorwärts Frankfurt/Oder	26	5	6	15	33-66	16
14. Wismut Gera	26	5	5	16	30-46	15

Top Scorers

Havenstein (Chemie Böhlen)	15
Schnuphase (Carl Zeiss Jena)	14
Netz (Dynamo Berlin)	13
Streich (1.FC Magdeburg)	13
Vogel (Carl Zeiss Jena)	12
Kotte (Dynamo Dresden)	11
Krostitz (Chemie Halle)	11
Kühn (Lokomotive Leipzig)	11
Dörner (Dynamo Dresden)	10
Riediger (Dynamo Berlin)	10
Vogel (Chemie Halle)	10
Weber (Dynamo Dresden)	10

Oberliga Promotion Playoff

Club	P	W	D	L	Goals	Pts
1. Stahl Riesa	8	7	1	0	27-4	15
2. Hansa Rostock	8	5	1	2	14-9	11
3. Chemie Leipzig	8	3	1	4	12-14	7
4. Vorwärts Neubrandenburg	8	1	2	5	5-17	4
5. Lokomotive Dresden	8	1	1	6	7-21	3

Second Division (Staffel A)

Club	P	W	D	L	Goals	Pts
1. Hansa Rostock	22	17	3	2	75-13	37
2. Vorwärts Stralsund	22	15	3	4	46-20	33
3. TSG Wismar	22	13	3	6	46-30	29
4. KKW Greifswald	22	10	5	7	36-30	25
5. ISG Schwerin	22	9	7	6	35-32	25
6. Dynamo Schwerin	22	9	5	8	43-27	23
7. TSG Bau Rostock	22	8	7	7	35-25	23
8. Schiffahrt/Hafen Rostock	22	8	5	9	32-32	21
9. Motor Wolgast	22	6	7	9	31-46	19
10. RB Trinwillershagen	22	5	7	10	22-40	17
11. Einheit Güstrow	22	3	2	17	21-64	8
12. Demminer VB	22	1	2	19	8-71	4

Promoted: Motor Stralsund, Veritas Wittenberge

Second Division (Staffel B)

Club	P	W	D	L	Goals	Pts
1. Vorwärts Neubrandenburg	22	14	5	3	49-7	33
2. Motor Babelsberg	22	13	6	3	48-29	32
3. Motor Eberswalde	22	11	7	4	33-17	29
4. Chemie PCK Schwedt	22	9	9	4	32-23	27
5. Stahl Eisenhüttenstadt	22	10	6	6	41-26	26
6. Post Neubrandenburg	22	9	3	10	45-34	21
7. Rotation Berlin	22	8	5	9	30-26	21
8. Stahl Hennigsdorf	22	6	9	7	43-40	21
9. Bergmann Borsig Berlin	22	7	5	10	29-48	19
10. Dynamo Fürstenwalde	22	7	4	11	32-42	18
11. Motor Hennigsdorf	22	6	3	13	25-55	15
12. Traktor Gross-Lindow	22	0	2	20	19-79	2

Promoted: NARVA Berlin, Halbleiterwerk Frankfurt/Oder, TSG Neustrelitz. Vorwärts Neubrandenburg and Post Neubrandenburg were placed in Staffel A for the following season

Second Division (Staffel C)

Club	P	W	D	L	Goals	Pts
1. Chemie Leipzig	22	14	5	3	45-15	33
2. Stahl Blankenburg	22	13	6	3	43-15	32
3. Chemie Premnitz	22	11	6	5	42-40	28
4. Chemie Buna Schkopau	22	10	6	6	38-21	26
5. Dynamo Eisleben	22	9	5	8	29-28	23
6. Chemie Wolfen	22	8	5	9	39-35	21
7. Vorwärts Dessau	22	8	5	9	30-27	21
8. Einheit Wernigerode	22	7	6	9	41-44	20
9. Stahl Brandenburg	22	6	7	9	32-28	19
10. TSG Schkeuditz	22	3	11	8	18-36	17
11. Stahl Thale	22	6	4	12	26-41	16
12. Chemie Schönebeck	22	1	6	15	18-71	8

Promoted: Motor Süd Brandenburg, Stahl NW Leipzig, Lokomotive Stendal, Fortschritt Weissenfels. Chemie Premnitz were placed in Staffel B for the following season

Second Division (Staffel D)

Club	P	W	D	L	Goals	Pts
1. Lokomotive Dresden	22	15	4	3	69-25	34
2. Energie Cottbus	22	12	7	3	34-13	31
3. Motor Werdau	22	11	7	4	45-29	29
4. Aktivist Espenhain	22	8	12	2	43-36	28
5. Aktivist Brieske-Senftenberg	22	8	10	4	44-34	26
6. Vorwärts Plauen	22	9	6	7	42-32	24
7. Fortschritt Bischofswerda	22	8	7	7	28-23	23
8. Aktivist Schwarze Pumpe	22	6	9	7	32-30	21
9. TSG Gröditz	22	7	7	8	37-47	21
10. Motor Ascota Karl-Marx-Stadt	22	3	6	13	24-48	12
11. Dynamo Lübben	22	4	2	16	17-52	10
12. Motor WAMA Görlitz	22	2	1	19	16-62	5

Promoted: TSG Lübbenau, Motor FH Karl-Marx-Stadt, Robur Zittau

Second Division (Staffel E)

Club	P	W	D	L	Goals	Pts
1. Stahl Riesa	22	18	3	1	73-15	39
2. Motor Weimar	22	12	5	5	46-32	29
3. Motor Suhl	22	11	6	5	51-29	28
4. Motor Nordhausen	22	12	3	7	50-31	27
5. Kali Werra Tiefenort	22	8	9	5	33-25	25
6. Fortschritt Weida	22	7	8	7	30-39	22
7. Chemie Zeitz	22	8	6	8	27-38	22
8. Robotron Sömmerda	22	8	3	11	39-45	19
9. Motor Hermsdorf	22	7	5	10	29-38	19
10. Landbau Bad Langensalza	22	6	6	10	30-34	18
11. Dynamo Gera	22	3	2	17	31-67	8
12. Motor Steinach	22	2	4	16	19-65	8

Promoted: Chemie IW Ilmenau, Motor Rudisleben, Chemie Schwarza

East German Cup Final
in Berlin
1.FC Magdeburg 1, Dynamo Dresden 0

East German Internationals
17/8/77 in Stockholm 1-0 v Sweden
7/9/77 in Berlin 1-0 v Scotland
24/9/77 in Vienna 1-1 v Austria (WCQ)
12/10/77 in Leipzig 1-1 v Austria (WCQ)
29/10/77 in Babelsburg 9-0 v Malta (WCQ)
16/11/77 in Izmir 2-1 v Turkey (WCQ)
8/3/78 in Karl-Marx-Stadt 3-1 v Switzerland
4/4/78 in Leipzig 0-1 v Sweden
19/4/78 in Magdeburg 0-0 v Belgium

European Cup
First Round
Vasas Budapest v Borussia Mönchengladbach .... (0-3, 1-1)
Dynamo Dresden v Halmstad BK .... (2-0, 1-2)
Second Round
Red Star Belgrade v Borussia Mönchengladbach .... (0-3, 1-5)
Liverpool v Dynamo Dresden .... (5-1, 1-2)
Quarterfinals
SW Innsbruck v Borussia Mönchengladbach .... (3-1, 0-2)
Semifinals
Borussia Mönchengladbach v Liverpool .... (2-1, 0-3)

Cup-Winners' Cup
First Round
1.FC Cologne v FC Porto .... (2-2, 0-1)
Hamburg SV v Lahden Reipas .... (8-1, 5-2)
Coleraine v Lokomotive Leipzig .... (1-4, 2-2)
Second Round
Hamburg SV v Anderlecht .... (1-2, 1-1)
Lokomotive Leipzig v Real Betis .... (1-1, 1-2)

UEFA Cup
First Round
Fiorentina v FC Schalke 04 .... (0-0, 0-3)
(First leg later awarded to Schalke 3-0 for Fiorentina's use of ineligible player)
Eintracht Frankfurt v Sliema Wanderers .... (5-0, 0-0)
Dynamo Kiev v Eintracht Brunswick .... (1-1, 0-0)
Bayern Munich v Mjöndalen IF .... (8-0, 4-0)
Odra Opole v 1.FC Magdeburg .... (1-2, 1-1)
Carl Zeiss Jena v Altay Izmir .... (5-1, 1-4)
Second Round
FC Zurich v Eintracht Frankfurt .... (0-3, 3-4)
1.FC Magdeburg v FC Schalke 04 .... (4-2, 3-1)
Start Kristiansand v Eintracht Brunswick .... (1-0, 0-4)
Bayern Munich v Marek Stanke Dimitrov .... (3-0, 0-2)
RWD Molenbeek v Carl Zeiss Jena .... (1-1, 1-1 aet)
Jena won on penalties
Third Round
Eintracht Frankfurt v Bayern Munich .... (4-0, 2-1)
PSV Eindhoven v Eintracht Brunswick .... (2-0, 2-1)
1.FC Magdeburg v Lens .... (4-0, 0-2)
Carl Zeiss Jena v Standard Liege .... (2-0, 2-1)
Quarterfinals
Eintracht Frankfurt v Grasshoppers Zurich .... (3-2, 0-1)
1.FC Magdeburg v PSV Eindhoven .... (1-0, 2-4)
Bastia v Carl Zeiss Jena .... (7-2, 2-4)

1978-79

Mächtige Maus

In the 1950s and early 1960s, Hamburg SV were the predominant team of northern Germany. In the nine seasons leading up to the formation of the Bundesliga they had put together an unbroken string of Oberliga North championships, and indeed had won that league every season since the war apart from 1955. Yet fifteen seasons of Bundesliga football had come and gone without them finishing any better than second, while other northern clubs like Werder Bremen and Eintracht Brunswick had lifted the championship plate.

In a flash of inspiration, Hamburg appointed Branko Zebec as *Trainer* in the summer of 1978. The Yugoslav had a tremendous reputation as an organiser and disciplinarian, having been the *Trainer* who had masterminded Bayern Munich's first-ever Bundesliga championship in 1969. More recently, he had transformed Eintracht Brunswick from a team of also-rans into potential championship contenders. But Zebec had a rather abrasive style which did not always meet with approval. His first pre-season training session was a rude shock for the easy-going Hamburg players. Zebec imposed strict rules and introduced the tactical revolution of zonal defence rather than man-to-man marking.

This proved to be the spark which transformed the performance of Kevin Keegan. In the previous season, the Englishman's all-action style had simply not fitted in with Hamburg's tactics, and the friction between Keegan and his teammates was exacerbated by frequent reports of the size of his monthly paycheques. This year, with the freedom to go anywhere and try anything, he inspired his side to some altogether more effective performances. Of course *Mächtige Maus* (Mighty Mouse) was not the only star in the team; there were Felix Magath, Manfred Kaltz, Rudi Kargus, Jimmy Hartwig and Horst Hrubesch. But Keegan's prodigious work-rate and determination earned him widespread admiration—not only in Germany, but throughout Europe. And at the end of the season, he was voted European Footballer of the Year.

Initially, it was 1.FC Kaiserslautern who set the pace, a team who like Hamburg had been members of the Bundesliga since its inception but had never won it. Over the summer they had replaced *Trainer* Erich Ribbeck with Karlheinz Feldkamp, who the season before had guided Arminia Bielefeld to the Second Division North championship. Feldkamp brought in Hannes Bongartz from Schalke 04 to complement a side featuring the likes of winger Benny Wendt and goalkeeper Ronnie Hellström, both Swedish internationals; striker Klaus Toppmöller; and defensive stalwarts Hans-Günter Neues and Hans-Peter Briegel. From the opening day of the season to Round 26, Lautern were never out of first place. But after a disastrous 3-1 loss at Duisburg in April, the *Roten Teufel* (Red Devils) failed to maintain their form and were overtaken: first by Hamburg, then by Stuttgart.

All three teams boasted impressive home records, but it was HSV's superior away performance which proved decisive. Hamburg scored more and conceded fewer goals than anyone else in the league. Yet all season they were matched stride-for-stride by VfB Stuttgart. The championship was decided one week before the end of the season, when Stuttgart's final home match ended in a surprising 4-1 defeat by Cologne, while Hamburg were grinding out a 0-0 draw at Arminia Bielefeld. A week later the Volksparkstadion saw scenes of wild celebration, but after an inconsequential 2-1 defeat by Bayern Munich, a pitch invasion degenerated into vandalism and hooliganism with hundreds of serious injuries. Only blind luck prevented there from being any fatalities.

The dominant force this season proved to be the weather. In all, 46 games were postponed, a record unlikely ever to be broken so long as the current two-month break is inserted into the fixtures. There was also a record nine changes of *Trainer*, with Bielefeld's Milovan Beljin the first casualty in October. Bayern's Gyula Lorant was dismissed in February and replaced by his assistant, Pal Csernai.

In an interesting feat of symmetry, the three teams who had been promoted at the beginning of the season—Bielefeld, Nuremberg, and Darmstadt—were relegated at the end of the season. Darmstadt, everyone's pre-season pick for the drop, had occupied the bottom position from their sixth match onwards, but better things were expected of Nuremberg, who had finally regained promotion nine years after becoming the first defending Bundesliga champion to be relegated.

Coming up to replace them were the two Bayer works teams, Leverkusen and Uerdingen, who had finished one-two in the Second Division North, and TSV 1860 Munich, who had again managed to pull themselves out of the Second Division South. TSV won 3-1 at home to Saarbrücken in their last match—before over 40,000—to finish a point clear of Bayreuth. At the other end FC Augsburg managed to avoid relegation by winning their final match at Hanau by the odd goal in eleven.

The West German Cup proved kind to the beaten finalists of the previous season's competition, Fortuna Düsseldorf. Drawn at home against sides no higher than the Second Division in each round up to the semis, Fortuna faced relegated Nuremberg for a place in the final and won 4-1 after extra time. The major upset had been provided by Südwest Ludwigshafen, who knocked out Kaiserslautern 2-1 mainly because Klaus Toppmöller had fluffed a 90th-minute penalty.

Düsseldorf's opposition in the final were Hertha Berlin, who had finished a disappointing fourteenth in the Bundesliga. Hertha had pipped Eintracht Brunswick in their semifinal when Jürgen Milewski scored from a rebound three minutes from time. The final proved to be something of a dour struggle which went into extra time, where an ill-judged back pass from Uwe Kliemann allowed Wolfgang Seel to score the only goal of the match. It gave Fortuna the trophy for the first time.

Düsseldorf capped a memorable year with an appearance in the Cup-Winners' Cup Final against Barcelona in Basle. Over 58,000 saw the sides finish level at 2-2 after 90 minutes but the Spanish team's cosmopolitan line-up—Neeskens, Krankl, and company—earned a memorable 4-3 victory after extra time. In the European Cup, Cologne had enjoyed a lengthy run before bowing out in the semifinal to eventual champions Nottingham Forest. The following season they poached one of Forest's players—striker Tony Woodcock.

German success in Europe didn't end there. Borussia Mönchengladbach triumphed in the UEFA Cup Final, on the strength of a 1-1 first-leg draw against Red Star before over 87,000 in Belgrade. An Alan Simonsen penalty accounted for all the scoring in the second leg as Gladbach raised the trophy for a second time. No one could claim they had an easy passage to the final; they faced difficult Austrian, Portuguese, Polish, and English sides on the way to the semifinal with Duisburg. Hertha Berlin had also reached the semifinals, making it three Bundesliga sides out of four—a feat which would be improved upon the following season.

Gladbach's league form, however, had taken an alarming dip. Champions in 1977 and runners-up in 1978, they could manage only tenth place in this season—their worst showing since their Bundesliga debut thirteen years earlier. Borussia scored fewer goals than they ever had since joining the Bundesliga, as Jupp Heynckes' retirement took its toll on the attack. *Trainer* Udo Lattek left at the end of the season to try to turn struggling Dortmund's fortunes around, and Heynckes was named as his replacement. The shadow of Hennes Weisweiler was proving difficult to live under.

Gerd Müller decided to end his fourteen-year Bundesliga career and headed for Fort Lauderdale of the North American Soccer League. He had netted a record 365 goals in 427 Bundesliga matches for Bayern Munich; in all competitive matches, he had scored over 650 times for his club. As a West German international, he found the target 68 times in 62 games—an amazing strike rate unequalled by anyone with as many caps. Berti Vogts also hung up his boots at the end of this season after fourteen years' service to Borussia Mönchengladbach and was named German Footballer of the Year.

Dynamo Berlin finished three points clear of Dynamo Dresden to win the East German League for the first of their ten consecutive championships. They did this in spite of losing their international star Lutz Eigendorf, who fled to the West in March and joined Kaiserslautern. The possibility of a double looked on, as the Berliners also reached the cup final, but an extra-time goal by Wolfgang Seguin handed that trophy to 1.FC Magdeburg.

The East German national team managed to add to its catalogue of embarrassing results by losing 2-1 in Baghdad to Iraq. West Germany's last match of the season was a friendly against Iceland in Reykjavik which they won 3-1. During the game, skipper Sepp Maier came off to give an international debut to his understudy, Harald "Toni" Schumacher. It would prove to be Maier's last appearance for his country.

Bundesliga

Club	P	W	D	L	Goals	Pts
1. Hamburg SV	34	21	7	6	78-32	49
2. VfB Stuttgart	34	20	8	6	73-34	48
3. 1.FC Kaiserslautern	34	16	11	7	62-47	43
4. Bayern Munich	34	16	8	10	69-46	40
5. Eintracht Frankfurt	34	16	7	11	50-49	39
6. 1.FC Cologne	34	13	12	9	55-47	38
7. Fortuna Dusseldorf	34	13	11	10	70-59	37
8. VfL Bochum	34	10	13	11	47-46	33
9. Eintracht Brunswick	34	10	13	11	50-55	33
10. Borussia Mönchengladbach	34	12	8	14	50-53	32
11. Werder Bremen	34	10	11	13	48-60	31
12. Borussia Dortmund	34	10	11	13	54-70	31
13. MSV Duisburg	34	12	6	16	43-56	30
14. Hertha BSC Berlin	34	9	11	14	40-50	29
15. FC Schalke 04	34	9	10	15	55-61	28
16. Arminia Bielefeld	34	9	8	17	43-56	26
17. 1.FC Nuremberg	34	8	8	18	36-67	24
18. SV Darmstadt 98	34	7	7	20	40-75	21

Top Scorers
K Allofs (Fortuna Düsseldorf) 22
Fischer (FC Schalke 04) 21
Abramczik (FC Schalke 04) 18
Keegan (Hamburg SV) 17
Toppmöller (1.FC Kaiserslautern) 17
D Hoeness (VfB Stuttgart) 16
Nickel (Eintracht Braunschweig) 16
Burgsmüller (Borussia Dortmund) 15
K-H Rummenigge (Bayern Munich) 14
Volkert (VfB Stuttgart) 14

Promotion Playoff
SpVgg Bayreuth v Bayer Uerdingen (1-1, 1-2); Uerdingen promoted to Bundesliga

Second Division North

Club	P	W	D	L	Goals	Pts
1. Bayer Leverkusen	38	24	11	3	87-34	59
2. Bayer Uerdingen	38	22	9	7	83-44	53
3. Preussen Münster	38	21	9	8	59-25	51
4. Fortuna Cologne	38	18	11	9	84-52	47
5. Westfalia Herne	38	16	11	11	65-47	43
6. FC St Pauli	38	16	11	11	56-49	43
7. Alemannia Aachen	38	14	12	12	54-47	40
8. Rot-Weiss Essen	38	14	11	13	68-62	39
9. Union Solingen	38	14	11	13	47-49	39
10. Wattenscheid 09	38	10	16	12	49-47	36
11. Tennis Borussia Berlin	38	12	12	14	58-61	36
12. Arminia Hanover	38	13	10	15	56-65	36
13. DSC Wanne-Eickel	38	11	13	14	66-66	35
14. Holstein Kiel	38	13	9	16	40-62	35
15. Hanover 96	38	9	16	13	57-68	34
16. Viktoria Cologne	38	10	12	16	53-60	32
17. Wuppertal SV	38	9	12	17	46-57	30
18. VfL Osnabrück	38	10	9	19	49-71	29
19. Rot-Weiss Lüdenscheid	38	8	6	24	49-106	22
20. Wacker 04 Berlin	38	8	5	25	33-87	21

Westfalia Herne withdrew from the Second Division before the start of the following season. FC St Pauli were relegated after their professional licence was revoked.
Promoted: OSC Bremerhaven, OSV Hanover, SC Herford, Rot-Weiss Oberhausen

Top Scorers
Mödrath (Fortuna Cologne) 28
Brücken (Bayer Leverkusen) 23
Schatzschneider (Hanover 96) 23
Schock (VfL Osnabrück) 23
Stradt (Alemannia Aachen) 23
Lüttges (Bayer Uerdingen) 22
Jürgens (Preussen Münster) 21
Beverungen (Westfalia Herne) 16
Czizewski (Viktoria Cologne) 15
Lücke (DSC Wanne-Eickel) 15
Mill (Rot-Weiss Essen) 15
Szech (Bayer Leverkusen) 15

Second Division South

Club	P	W	D	L	Goals	Pts
1. TSV 1860 Munich	38	21	11	6	75-38	53
2. SpVgg Bayreuth	38	21	10	7	86-53	52
3. Wormatia Worms	38	21	8	9	66-33	50
4. SpVgg Fürth	38	21	7	10	66-45	49
5. Karlsruhe SC	38	20	7	11	77-50	47
6. Kickers Offenbach	38	17	9	12	86-62	43
7. FC 08 Homburg	38	17	9	12	65-47	43
8. 1.FC Saarbrücken	38	15	11	12	70-58	41
9. Kickers Stuttgart	38	12	12	14	68-59	41
10. Eintracht Trier	38	12	12	14	58-57	36
11. MTV Ingolstadt	38	16	3	19	62-82	35
12. FSV Frankfurt	38	15	4	19	59-66	34
13. FC Freiburg	38	15	3	20	58-75	33
14. FV 04 Würzburg	38	13	7	18	40-62	33
15. SC Freiburg	38	11	10	17	51-75	32
16. Waldhof Mannheim	38	11	9	18	46-56	31
17. FC Hanau 93	38	11	7	20	72-98	29
18. FC Augsburg	38	11	6	21	55-89	28
19. KSV Baunatal	38	12	2	24	49-67	26
20. Borussia Neunkirchen	38	10	4	24	47-84	24

Promoted: ESV Ingolstadt, VfR Oli Bürstadt, SSV 1846 Ulm, Röchling Völklingen

Top Scorers
Kirschner (SpVgg Fürth) 33
Sommerer (SpVgg Bayreuth) 24
Allgöwer (Kickers Stuttgart) 23
Dörflinger (SC Freiburg) 20
Gerber (TSV 1860 Munich) 19
Krause (Kickers Offenbach) 19
Seubert (Wormatia Worms) 19
Künkel (1.FC Saarbrücken) 18
Bitz (Kickers Offenbach) 17
Krauth (Karlsruhe SC) 16

Third Division Champions
Baden-Württemberg: SSV 1846 Ulm
Bayern: ESV Ingolstadt
Berlin: Hertha 03 Zehlendorf
Hessen: VfR Bürstadt
Nord: OSV Hanover
Nordrhein: Rot-Weiss Oberhausen
Südwest: Röchling Völklingen
Westfalen: SC Herford

West German Cup
First Round
1.FC Kaiserslautern 7, BFC Preussen Berlin 0
1.FC Kirchheim 1, Eintracht Wirges 2
1.FC Nuremberg 4, ASV Neumarkt 0
1.FC Saarbrücken 1, SpVgg Fürth 0
Alemannia Aachen 4, FC Eislingen 1
Arminia Bielefeld 2, Hamburg SV 1 aet
ASV Burglengenfeld 1, Viktoria Cologne 4
Bayern Munich 5, SSV Glött 0
Borussia Dortmund 14, BSV Schwenningen 1
Borussia Mönchengladbach 4, Wuppertal SV 2
DSC Wanne-Eickel 2, VfR Mannheim 1
Eintracht Brunswick 2, Schwarz-Weiss Essen 0
Eintracht Trier 3, SG Fuchsmühl 1
ESV Ingolstadt 4, Viktoria Klein-Gladbach 0
FC Augsburg 4, FV Offenburg 2
FC Freiburg 6, SpVgg Neckarelz 1
FC Gütersloh 4, Eintracht Nordhorn 1
FC St Pauli 3 Bayern Hof 0 aet
FC Tailfingen 4, SV Sandhausen 3
Fortuna Cologne 2, FC Hanau 93 0
Fortuna Düsseldorf 7, Kickers Stuttgart 2
FV Würzburg 04 0, Hertha BSC Berlin 2 aet
Göttingen 05 2, FC Epe 0
Holstein Kiel 5, Saar 05 Saarbrücken 0
Karlsruhe SC 3, Eintracht Bad Kreuznach 1
KSV Baunatal 5, SV Union Essen-Frintrop 0
MSV Duisburg 4, Wattenscheid 09 3
MTV Gifhorn 0, FK Pirmasens 3
OSC Bremerhaven 0, Hanover 96 3
OSV Hanover 5, TSV Helmstedt 1
Preussen Münster 6, SV Leiwen 0
Rot-Weiss Lüdenscheid 1, 1.FC Cologne 4
Rot-Weiss Oberhausen 5, ETSV Landshut 1 aet
SC Freiburg 3, Rot-Weiss Essen 1
SC Herford 2, Kickers Würzburg 1
SC Jülich 1910 1, Kickers Offenbach 10
SC Pfullendorf 0, FC 08 Homburg 3
SG Bad Soden-Salmünster 1, VfL Neustadt/Weinstr 3
SG Ellingen-Bonefeld 3, VfB Lübeck 1
SpVgg Bad Pyrmont 1, Eintracht Frankfurt 2
SSV Dillenburg 2, FSV Frankfurt 4
Südwest Ludwigshafen 2, Concordia Hamburg 0
SuS Nord-Harrislee 0, Borussia Neunkirchen 6
SV Bliesen 2, FV Melsungen 3
SV Blumenthal 1, Fortuna Düsseldorf (Am.) 2 aet
SV Darmstadt 98 4, DJK Abenberg 1
SV Haidlfing 0, SpVgg Bayreuth 5
SV Memmelsdorf 1, 1.FC Bocholt 8
SVO Germaringen 1, VfR Oli Bürstadt 7
Tennis Borussia Berlin 2, Union Solingen 0 aet
TSV 1860 Munich 0, FC Schalke 04 5
TuS Hessisch-Oldendorf 0, Westfalia Herne 4
TuS Iserlohn 0, VfL Osnabrück 2
Union Böckingen 2, Bayer Uerdingen 8
VfB Schrecksbach 3, Arminia Hanover 5
VfB Stuttgart 12, SV Spandau 0
VfL Bochum 4, SV 08/09 Bünde 0
VfR Heilbronn 1, TuS Langerwehe 0
Victoria Hamburg 0, SSV 1846 Ulm 6
Viktoria Sindlingen 0, Bayer Leverkusen 3
Waldhof Mannheim 5, SV Börnsen 0
Werder Bremen (Am.) 1, TuS Neuendorf 1 aet (2-5)
Werder Bremen 5, SV Holzwickede 0
Wormatia Worms 4, VfB Remscheid 2

Second Round
1.FC Saarbrücken 2, Bayer Uerdingen 3
Bayern Munich 4, VfL Osnabrück 5
Borussia Mönchengladbach 6, Arminia Hanover 1
Borussia Neunkirchen 0, Borussia Dortmund 0 aet (0-2)
Eintracht Brunswick 1, SG Ellingen-Bonefeld 0
Eintracht Trier 0, 1.FC Kaiserslautern 1
Eintracht Wirges 1, Fortuna Cologne 7
FC Augsburg 1, 1.FC Nuremberg 3
FC Freiburg 2, 1.FC Bocholt 2 aet (2-3 aet)
FC Gütersloh 1, Karlsruhe SC 1 aet (0-3)
FC 08 Homburg 4, FK Pirmasens 2
FC Schalke 04 3, VfB Stuttgart 2
FC St Pauli 1, TuS Neuendorf 2
Fortuna Düsseldorf 3, VfR Heilbronn 0

Hanover 96 1, Alemannia Aachen 3
Kickers Offenbach 3, ESV Ingolstadt 0
KSV Baunatal 3, Göttingen 05 0
MSV Duisburg 3, Arminia Bielefeld 1
OSV Hanover 0, Bayer Leverkusen 3
Rot-Weiss Oberhausen 3, Fortuna Düsseldorf (Am.) 2
SC Freiburg 2, FC Tailfingen 0
SC Herford 0, Holstein Kiel 3
SpVgg Bayreuth 6, MV Melsungen 0
SSV 1846 Ulm 4, FSV Frankfurt 2
Südwest Ludwigshafen 4, Viktoria Cologne 2
SV Darmstadt 98 2, Preussen Münster 1
Tennis Borussia Berlin 3, VfR Oli Bürstadt 3 aet (0-0 aet;
Tennis Borussia won on penalties)
VfL Bochum 4, DSC Wanne-Eickel 2 aet
Waldhof Mannheim 7, VfL Neustadt/Weinstrasse 0
Werder Bremen 2, Eintracht Frankfurt 3
Westfalia Herne 1, 1.FC Cologne 3
Wormatia Worms 1, Hertha BSC Berlin 1 aet (0-2)

Third Round
1.FC Cologne 3, Eintracht Brunswick 2 aet
Bayer Leverkusen 1, SpVgg Bayreuth 0
Bayer Uerdingen 2, FC Schalke 04 1
Borussia Dortmund 6, Kickers Offenbach 1
Eintracht Frankfurt 2, KSV Baunatal 1
FC 08 Homburg 0, VfL Bochum 0 aet (0-1)
Fortuna Düsseldorf 2, Alemannia Aachen 1
Hertha BSC Berlin 2, Borussia Mönchengladbach 0
Holstein Kiel 5, Karlsruhe SC 2
MSV Duisburg 2, Waldhof Mannheim 1
Rot-Weiss Oberhausen 1, SC Freiburg 1 aet (0-0 aet; Rot-Weiss Oberhausen won on penalties)
Südwest Ludwigshafen 2, 1.FC Kaiserslautern 1
SV Darmstadt 98 1, SSV 1846 Ulm 5
Tennis Borussia Berlin 0, 1.FC Nuremberg 2
TuS Neuendorf 3, 1.FC Bocholt 1 aet
VfL Osnabrück 2, Fortuna Cologne 1

Fourth Round
1.FC Nuremberg 7, Holstein Kiel 1
Bayer Uerdingen 4, VfL Bochum 2
Borussia Dortmund 1, Eintracht Frankfurt 3
Hertha BSC Berlin 2, 1.FC Cologne 0 aet
MSV Duisburg 0, Fortuna Düsseldorf 1
Rot-Weiss Oberhausen 1, VfL Osnabrück 0
Südwest Ludwigshafen 1, SSV 1846 Ulm 1 aet (1-0)
TuS Neuendorf 1, Bayer Leverkusen 4

Quarterfinals
1.FC Nuremberg 4, Südwest Ludwigshafen 0
Eintracht Frankfurt 2, Rot-Weiss Oberhausen 1
Fortuna Düsseldorf 2, Bayer Leverkusen 1
Hertha BSC Berlin 6, Bayer Uerdingen 1

Semifinals
Fortuna Düsseldorf 4, 1.FC Nuremberg 1 aet
Hertha BSC Berlin 2, Eintracht Frankfurt 1

Final
in Hanover
Hertha BSC Berlin 0, Fortuna Düsseldorf 1 aet

West German Internationals
11/10/78 in Prague 4-3 v Czechoslovakia
15/11/78 in Frankfurt 0-0 v Hungary
Match abandoned after 59 minutes (fog)
20/12/78 in Düsseldorf 3-1 v Holland
25/2/79 in Valetta 0-0 v Malta (ECQ)
1/4/79 in Izmir 0-0 v Turkey (ECQ)
2/5/79 in Wrexham 2-0 v Wales (ECQ)
22/5/79 in Dublin 3-1 v Ireland
26/5/79 in Reykjavik 3-1 Iceland

East German Oberliga

Club	P	W	D	L	Goals	Pts
1. Dynamo Berlin	26	18	5	3	70-25	41
2. Dynamo Dresden	26	16	6	4	52-17	38
3. Carl Zeiss Jena	26	14	7	5	54-25	35
4. 1.FC Magdeburg	26	13	6	7	57-34	32
5. Lokomotive Leipzig	26	13	5	8	53-32	31
6. Chemie Halle	26	11	8	7	44-34	30
7. Rot-Weiss Erfurt	26	6	12	8	34-37	24
8. FC Karl-Marx-Stadt	26	9	6	11	27-36	24
9. Stahl Riesa	26	7	9	10	23-35	23
10. 1.FC Union Berlin	26	8	7	11	22-45	23
11. Wismut Aue	26	8	6	12	22-47	22
12. Sachsenring Zwickau	26	6	8	12	34-51	20
13. Chemie Böhlen	26	3	9	14	19-35	15
14. Hansa Rostock	26	1	4	21	17-75	6

Top Scorers
Streich (1.FC Magdeburg) 23
Riediger (Dynamo Berlin) 20
Kühn (Lokomotive Leipzig) 17
Netz (Dynamo Berlin) 16
Hoffmann (1.FC Magdeburg) 12
Heun (Rot-Weiss Erfurt) 11
Havenstein (Chemie Böhlen) 10
Lippmann (Stahl Riesa) 10
J Müller (Karl-Marx-Stadt) 10
Raab (Carl Zeiss Jena) 10

Erler (Wismut Aue) 9
Krostitz (Chemie Halle) 9
Riedel (Dynamo Dresden) 9
Terletzki (Dynamo Berlin) 9

Oberliga Promotion Playoff

Club	P	W	D	L	Goals	Pts
1. Vorwärts Frankfurt/Oder	8	7	1	0	24-6	15
2. Chemie Leipzig	8	3	3	2	11-7	9
3. Motor Suhl	8	4	1	3	14-19	9
4. Energie Cottbus	8	1	2	5	9-13	4
5. TSG Bau Rostock	8	1	1	6	8-21	3

Second Division (Staffel A)

Club	P	W	D	L	Goals	Pts
1. TSG Bau Rostock	22	16	4	2	52-23	36
2. Vorwärts Stralsund	22	12	7	3	49-22	31
3. Vorwärts Neubrandenburg	22	9	10	3	39-23	28
4. Dynamo Schwerin	22	10	7	5	47-31	27
5. TSG Wismar	22	9	5	8	33-24	23
6. Schiffahrt/Hafen Rostock	22	8	6	8	38-40	22
7. ISG Schwerin-Süd	22	6	8	8	25-27	20
8. Post Neubrandenburg	22	5	9	8	28-27	19
9. KKW Greifswald	22	6	6	10	28-29	18
10. Veritas Wittenberge	22	7	4	11	38-45	18
11. Motor Wolgast	22	2	7	13	19-50	11
12. Motor Stralsund	22	3	5	14	19-74	11

Promoted: Hydraulik Parchim, Nord Togelow, Motor WW Warnemünde. Vorwärts Neubrandenburg were placed in Staffel B for the following season

Second Division (Staffel B)

Club	P	W	D	L	Goals	Pts
1. Vorwärts Frankfurt/Oder	22	18	4	0	77-6	40
2. Stahl Eisenhüttenstadt	22	11	6	5	37-18	28
3. Rotation Berlin	22	10	8	4	34-18	28
4. Chemie Premnitz	22	8	9	5	27-26	25
5. Chemie Schwedt	22	8	7	7	34-28	23
6. Halbleiterwerk Frankfurt/Oder	22	10	3	9	30-45	23
7. Motor Babelsberg	22	8	4	10	38-34	20
8. TSG Neustrelitz	22	7	6	9	28-29	20
9. Stahl Hennigsdorf	22	7	6	9	27-35	20
10. Bergmann Borsig Berlin	22	4	8	10	17-43	16
11. NARVA Berlin	22	5	3	14	31-57	13
12. Motor Eberswalde	22	1	6	14	14-55	4

Promoted: KWO Berlin, Motor Hennigsdorf. Chemie Premnitz were placed in Staffel C for the following season

Second Division (Staffel C)

Club	P	W	D	L	Goals	Pts
1. Chemie Leipzig	22	16	3	3	61-28	35
2. Stahl Blankenburg	22	12	5	5	43-23	29
3. Chemie Buna Schkopau	22	12	4	6	38-20	28
4. Vorwärts Dessau	22	12	3	7	46-28	27
5. Chemie Wolfen	22	10	7	5	40-25	27
6. Dynamo Eisleben	22	9	5	8	40-37	23
7. Einheit Wernigerode	22	8	7	7	30-30	23
8. Stahl Brandenburg	22	8	3	11	27-33	19
9. Stahl NW Leipzig	22	6	5	11	26-38	17
10. Lokomotive Stendal	22	6	5	11	20-32	17
11. Fortschritt Weissenfels	22	6	3	13	24-50	15
12. Motor Süd Brandenburg	22	1	2	19	8-59	4

Relegation playoff: Lokomotive Stendal v Stahl NW Leipzig (1-1, 2-0); Stahl NW Leipzig relegated

Promoted: Lokomotive Halberstadt, Chemie Premnitz, Einheit Wernigerode. Stahl Brandenburg were placed in Staffel B for the following season

Second Division (Staffel D)

Club	P	W	D	L	Goals	Pts
1. Energie Cottbus	22	17	4	1	51-12	38
2. Motor Werdau	22	14	5	3	54-22	33
3. Lokomotive Dresden	22	11	7	4	39-21	29
4. Aktivist Schwarze Pumpe	22	10	6	6	33-19	26
5. Aktivist Brieske-Senftenberg	22	8	7	7	23-34	23
6. Fortschritt Bischofswerda	22	6	9	7	26-23	21
7. Vorwärts Plauen	22	6	7	9	25-31	19
8. Aktivist Espenhain	22	6	6	10	34-36	18
9. Motor FH Karl-Marx-Stadt	22	5	7	10	24-34	17
10. TSG Lübbenau	22	6	2	14	23-58	14
11. Robur Zittau	22	4	5	13	20-40	13
12. TSG Gröditz	22	4	5	13	24-46	13

Promoted: Vorwärts Kamenz, Dynamo Lübben, SG Sosa

Second Division (Staffel E)

Club	P	W	D	L	Goals	Pts
1. Motor Suhl	22	15	4	3	60-28	34
2. Motor Weimar	22	15	3	4	56-27	33
3. Wismut Gera	22	12	7	3	54-25	31
4. Kali Werra Tiefenort	22	11	6	5	36-21	28
5. Motor Nordhausen	22	10	7	5	49-29	27
6. Motor Rudisleben	22	8	7	7	37-25	23
7. Chemie Zeitz	22	8	6	8	28-34	22
8. Chemie IZ Ilmenau	22	7	6	9	26-34	20
9. Fortschritt Weida	22	6	4	12	26-37	16
10. Motor Hermsdorf	22	5	5	12	22-44	15
11. Robotron Sömmerda	22	3	5	14	23-58	11
12. Chemie Schwarza	22	0	4	18	9-64	4

Promoted: Motor Altenburg, Langenbau Bad Langensalza, WM Schmalkalden, Motor Zeulenroda. Chemie Zeitz were placed in Staffel C for the following season

East German Cup Final
in Berlin
1.FC Magdeburg 1, Dynamo Berlin 0 aet

1978-79   **127**

East German Internationals
30/8/78 in Erfurt 2-2 v Bulgaria
6/9/78 in Leipzig 2-1 v Czechoslovakia
4/10/78 in Halle 3-1 v Iceland (ECQ)
15/11/78 in Rotterdam 0-3 v Holland (ECQ)
9/2/79 in Baghdad 1-1 v Iraq
11/2/79 in Baghdad 1-2 v Iraq
28/2/79 in Burgas 0-1 v Bulgaria
28/3/79 in Budapest 0-3 v Hungary
18/4/79 in Leipzig 2-1 v Poland (ECQ)
5/5/79 in St. Gallen 2-0 v Switzerland (ECQ)
1/6/79 in Berlin 1-0 v Rumania

European Cup
First Round
1.FC Cologne v Akranes .... (4-1, 1-1)
Partizan Belgrade v Dynamo Dresden .... (2-0, 0-2 aet)
Dresden won on penalties
Second Round
1.FC Cologne v Lokomotiv Sofia .... (0-1, 0-4)
Bohemians Dublin v Dynamo Dresden .... (0-0, 0-6)
Quarterfinals
1.FC Cologne v Rangers .... (1-0, 1-1)
Austria Vienna v Dynamo Dresden .... (3-1, 0-1)
Semifinals
Nottingham Forest v 1.FC Cologne .... (3-3, 1-0)

Cup-Winners' Cup
First Round
Uni Craiova v Fortuna Düsseldorf .... (3-4, 1-1)
Valur v 1.FC Magdeburg .... (1-1, 0-4)
Second Round
Fortuna Düsseldorf v Aberdeen .... (3-0, 0-2)
1.FC Magdeburg v Ferencvaros .... (1-0, 1-2)
Quarterfinals
Fortuna Düsseldorf v Servette .... (0-0, 1-1)
1.FC Magdeburg v Banik Ostrava .... (2-1, 2-4)
Semifinals
Fortuna Düsseldorf v Banik Ostrava .... (2-1, 2-4)
Final in Basle
Barcelona 4, Fortuna Düsseldorf 3

UEFA Cup
First Round
Hertha BSC Berlin v Trakia Plovdiv .... (0-0, 2-1)
MSV Duisburg v Lech Posnan .... (5-0, 5-2)
Borussia Mönchengladbach v Sturm Graz .... (5-1, 2-1)
FC Basle v VfB Stuttgart .... (2-3, 1-4)
Dynamo Berlin v Red Star Belgrade .... (5-2, 1-4)
Carl Zeiss Jena v Lierse SK .... (1-0, 2-2)
Arsenal v Lokomotive Leipzig .... (3-0, 4-1)
Second Round
Carl Zeiss Jena v MSV Duisburg .... (0-0, 0-3 aet)
Torpedo Moscow v VfB Stuttgart .... (2-1, 0-2)
Hertha BSC Berlin v Dynamo Tblisi .... (2-0, 0-1)
Benfica v Borussia Mönchengladbach .... (0-0, 0-2 aet)
Third Round
Esbjerg v Hertha BSC Berlin .... (2-1, 0-4)
Borussia Mönchengladbach v Slask Breslau .... (1-1, 4-2)
VfB Stuttgart v Dukla Prague .... (4-1, 0-4)
Racing Strasbourg v MSV Duisburg .... (0-0, 0-4)
Quarterfinals
Hertha BSC Berlin v Dukla Prague .... (1-1, 2-1)
Honved v MSV Duisburg .... (2-3, 2-1)
Manchester City v Borussia Mönchengladbach .... (1-1, 1-3)
Semifinals
MSV Duisburg v Borussia Mönchengladbach .... (2-2, 1-4)
Red Star Belgrade v Hertha BSC Berlin .... (1-0, 1-2)
Final
Red Star Belgrade v Borussia Mönchengladbach .... (1-1, 0-1)

1979-80

Back to Bayern

Before the season even started, Bayern suffered a horrible shock when goalkeeper Sepp Maier was badly injured in a car crash on 14 July, suffering many broken bones and severe internal injuries. His illustrious career, comprising 473 Bundesliga games and 95 international caps, came to an untimely end. Only 35 years old at the time, Maier would surely have gone on to overtake Franz Beckenbauer's record total of 103 caps. In the previous fourteen years, the colourful goalkeeper had only ever missed three games for his club, making 442 consecutive league appearances, one of the most secure records in German football.

But Bayern's flamboyant Hungarian coach Pal Csernai, who had stepped up from assistant coach in January 1979, had complete faith in 20-year-old reserve keeper Walter Junghans, who stood behind a vastly experienced defence. Csernai insisted on the same tactical approach to every match, regardless of the opposition or venue. As the Bayern players became more familiar with Csernai's system they grew in confidence and, as a consequence of some consistent away results, gradually pulled ahead of title favourites Hamburg. Both teams netted over eighty goals this season, with Karl-Heinz Rummenigge and Dieter Hoeness leading the way for Bayern and Kevin Keegan topping the charts for Hamburg. In the head-to-head clashes, Hamburg came off better, winning 3-1 in the Volksparkstadion and drawing 1-1 in the Olympiastadion.

The penultimate match of the season proved to be decisive, with Hamburg away to struggling Leverkusen and Bayern facing a much tougher proposition away to third-place Stuttgart. Hamburg's thoughts were on their European Cup Final match with against Nottingham Forest four days later; they looked decidedly sloppy against Leverkusen and lost 2-0. At the same time, Bayern were putting on their best show of the year, with two goals from Udo Horsmann and one from Hoeness giving them a 3-1 win in front of a capacity 65,000 crowd at the Neckarstadion. With the final day's matches both ending as home wins, Bayern took the title by two points.

Rummenigge finished as the league's leading scorer with 26 goals—the first Bayern striker to top the charts since Gerd Müller six seasons earlier. Rummenigge was also in impressive form for the German national side, and his seven goals in eleven games helped him to be named European Footballer of the Year.

Two young players making names for themselves this season were Bernd Schuster of 1.FC Cologne and Lothar Matthäus of Borussia Mönchengladbach. Schuster, a nineteen-year-old midfielder, made his international debut against Ireland in Dublin and finished the season by collecting a winner's medal at the European Championship Final against Belgium in Italy. Matthäus had also just turned nineteen when he came on as substitute in the European Championship match against Holland and finally made the starting line-up against Brazil in Rio in March.

Eight Bundesliga teams changed their *Trainer* this season, including Werder Bremen, who got rid of Wolfgang Weber, and Cologne, who lost Hennes Weisweiler to the New York Cosmos. Bremen finished in 17th place, heavily in debt from their big-spending days of the early seventies. Nevertheless, they were destined to return the following year as champions of the Second Division North, and so have been members for all but one season in the Bundesliga.

In addition to Maier's retirement through injury, Jürgen Grabowski of Eintracht Frankfurt and Georg Schwarzenbeck of Bayern also hung up their boots for good at the end of the season. Both had made over 400 Bundesliga appearances and played over forty times for West Germany. Mönchengladbach's Norbert Ringels may have harboured thoughts of retirement after nearly severing his tongue toward the end of the season, playing the last few matches with it heavily stitched together.

The performance of Arminia Bielefeld in the Second Division North was one of the most impressive in the short history of the *Zweite Liga*. Bielefeld clinched the title with five matches left to play and scored 120 goals—an average of over three a game—whilst conceding just 31. Striker Christian Sackewitz and midfielder Norbert Eilenfeldt racked up 65 between them. The battle for second place was far less clear-cut, with Rot-Weiss Essen and Hanover 96 duelling for the playoff spot. With only goal difference separating the two sides going into the last game, Hanover lost at Herford and Essen won at Wanne-Eickel. But, for the second time in three seasons, Essen lost in the playoff and were kept out of Division One. A rejuvenated 1.FC Nuremberg clinched the Second Division South, attracting a crowd of 55,000 for their home match with second-placed Karlsruhe, which ended 1-1. Karlsruhe, scorer of 104 goals during the season, drew 43,000 for their 5-1 first-leg playoff victory over Essen and were back in the Bundesliga after a three-year absence.

SpVgg Bayreuth, a disappointing thirteenth in Division Two, pulled off the season's biggest upset in the West German Cup, beating Bayern 1-0 in their third-round tie. Oberliga Nordrhein side TuS Langerwehe embarrassed struggling Hertha BSC in the same round, holding the Berliners to a goalless draw at home before just 3,000, then winning the replay before 14,000, the winning goal coming with just two minutes left.

The quarterfinals featured three Second Division sides, including Kickers Offenbach, who had disposed of Hamburg. But Offenbach lost 5-3 in extra time to Fortuna Düsseldorf, a Klaus Allofs hat-trick in the span of six minutes doing the damage. Fortuna faced a pumped-up Dortmund side in an ill-tempered semifinal, and despite Borussia having a 10-1 advantage in corners in the first half, Allofs added two more goals to his impressive Cup total to put the home side through. This meant that Düsseldorf had reached the final for the third year running—the first team to do so since Schalke in the 1930s. Fortuna avenged their final defeat of two years earlier by beating 1.FC Cologne 2-1, with goals from Rüdiger Wenzel and Thomas Allofs.

Once again, Dynamo Berlin took the East German championship, winning all thirteen of their matches at home whilst conceding just four goals. Relegated Chemie Leipzig felt the full force of the champions' might, losing 10-0. But the country's most impressive record was amassed by Hansa Rostock, who took 43 of a possible 44 points and conceded just eight goals on the way to winning Liga Staffel A by fourteen points. Not surprisingly, they won the promotion playoff group handily and returned to the Oberliga after one season away.

Nottingham Forest beat both East and West German champions on the way to retaining the European Cup. In the quarterfinal they lost their home leg to Dynamo Berlin but managed to win the second match comfortably. In the final they came up against a Hamburg side who had retrieved a 2-0 first leg deficit against Real Madrid by winning 5-1 at the Volksparkstadion. Before 50,000 in Madrid, John Robertson's goal proved the only one that Forest needed, though Hamburg squandered a number of good chances.

The depth of talent in the Bundesliga was confirmed by the semifinal draw of the UEFA Cup: Mönchengladbach v Stuttgart, and Eintracht Frankfurt v Bayern Munich. Gladbach squeezed past VfB, while Frankfurt finished 3-3 on aggregate with Bayern before scoring twice in extra time at the Olympiastadion. The first leg of the final was a splendid contest, witnessed by 25,000 at the Bökelberg. Two goals from Christian Kulik and one from Lothar Matthäus gave Borussia a 3-2 win. But Eintracht's vital away goals, secured by Harald Karger and Bernd Hölzenbein, proved decisive in the return leg. Before 59,000 in the Waldstadion, a single goal by nineteen-year-old substitute Fred Schaub was enough to give Eintracht their first major European trophy.

West Germany came top of their European Championship qualifying group to reach the final phase in Italy, which now involved eight teams instead of four. In the group stage, the Germans beat Czechoslovakia 1-0 in a tediously dull encounter and squeezed past Holland 3-2 thanks to a Klaus Allofs hat-trick. This completed a run of twelve consecutive wins—the best in German football history—although the quality of play often paled in comparison to their more enterprising approach of the early seventies. The streak came to an end with a 0-0 draw against Greece, but West Germany still qualified for the final, where Horst Hrubesch scored a goal in each half to beat Belgium 2-1.

The East German national team had only narrowly failed to qualify for the Championships. In the vital match against Holland in Leipzig, 92,000 saw them build a 2-0 lead through Rüdiger Schnuphase and Joachim Streich, but the visitors scored three without reply to go through. East Germany had better luck in the Olympic tournament, taking the silver medal in Moscow. They beat the hosts 1-0 in the semifinals but lost by the same score to Czechoslovakia in the final.

Bundesliga

Club	P	W	D	L	Goals	Pts
1. Bayern Munich	34	22	6	6	84-33	50
2. Hamburg SV	34	20	8	6	86-35	48
3. VfB Stuttgart	34	17	7	10	75-53	41
4. 1.FC Kaiserslautern	34	18	5	11	75-53	41
5. 1.FC Cologne	34	14	9	11	72-55	37
6. Borussia Dortmund	34	14	8	12	64-56	36
7. Borussia Monchengladbach	34	12	12	10	61-60	36
8. FC Schalke 04	34	12	9	13	40-51	33
9. Eintracht Frankfurt	34	15	2	17	65-61	32
10. VfL Bochum	34	13	6	15	41-44	32
11. Fortuna Düsseldorf	34	13	6	15	62-72	32
12. Bayer Leverkusen	34	12	8	14	45-61	32
13. TSV 1860 Munich	34	10	10	14	42-53	30
14. MSV Duisburg	34	11	7	16	43-57	29
15. Bayer Uerdingen	34	12	5	17	43-61	29
16. Hertha BSC Berlin	34	11	7	16	41-61	29
17. Werder Bremen	34	11	3	20	52-93	25
18. Eintracht Brunswick	34	6	8	20	32-64	20

Top Scorers
K-H Rummenigge (Bayern Munich) 26
Hrubesch (Hamburg SV) 21
D Müller (1.FC Cologne) 21
Burgsmüller (Borussia Dortmund) 20
Nickel (Borussia Mönchengladbach) 20
Geye (1.FC Kaiserslautern) 17
K Allofs (Fortuna Düsseldorf) 16
D Hoeness (Bayern Munich) 16
Funkel (Bayer Uerdingen) 14
H Müller (VfB Stuttgart) 14

Promotion Playoffs
Karlsruhe SC v Rot-Weiss Essen (5-1, 1-3); Karlsruhe promoted to Bundesliga

Second Division North

Club	P	W	D	L	Goals	Pts
1. Arminia Bielefeld	38	30	6	2	120-31	66
2. Rot-Weiss Essen	38	24	6	8	97-54	54
3. Hanover 96	38	23	6	9	70-38	52
4. Viktoria Cologne	38	16	14	8	77-52	46
5. Wattenscheid 09	38	17	12	9	72-57	46
6. Fortuna Cologne	38	17	11	10	79-54	45
7. Alemannia Aachen	38	17	7	14	59-56	41
8. VfL Osnabrück	38	16	8	14	64-68	40
9. Union Solingen	38	13	12	13	66-55	38
10. Preussen Münster	38	13	10	15	53-59	36
11. DSC Wanne-Eickel	38	15	6	17	63-71	36
12. OSV Hanover	38	13	10	15	55-79	36
13. Tennis Borussia Berlin	38	13	9	16	57-65	35
14. Holstein Kiel	38	13	7	18	61-67	33
15. Rot-Weiss Oberhausen	38	13	7	18	46-67	33
16. Rot-Weiss Lüdenscheid	38	11	10	17	56-73	32
17. SC Herford	38	11	9	18	48-69	31
18. OSC Bremerhaven	38	10	7	21	52-79	27
19. Arminia Hanover	38	8	1	29	40-92	17
20. Wuppertal SV	38	5	6	27	35-84	16

DSC Wanne-Eickel did not participate at this level for the following season

Promoted: 1.FC Bocholt, SpVgg Erkenschwick, Göttingen 05, VfB Oldenburg

Top Scorers
Sackewitz (Arminia Bielefeld) 35
Schatzschneider (Hanover 96) 34
Eilenfeldt (Arminia Bielefeld) 30
Mödrath (Fortuna Cologne) 26
Stolzenburg (Tennis Borussia Berlin) 24
Schock (Arminia Bielefeld) 21
Hammes (Wattenscheid 09) 18
Krumbein (OSV Hanover) 18
Kunkel (Wattenscheid 09) 18
Lücke (DSC Wanne-Eickel) 17
Schonert (Viktoria Cologne) 17

Second Division South

Club	P	W	D	L	Goals	Pts
1. 1.FC Nuremberg	40	26	9	5	88-38	61
2. Karlsruhe SC	40	27	5	8	104-52	59
3. Kickers Stuttgart	40	22	8	10	94-54	52
4. SV Darmstadt 98	40	21	6	13	81-42	48
5. 1.FC Saarbrücken	40	21	5	14	69-56	47
6. SC Freiburg	40	18	10	12	68-54	46
7. SpVgg Fürth	40	17	10	13	56-51	44
8. Kickers Offenbach	40	17	9	14	78-64	43
9. FC Freiburg	40	15	13	12	78-83	43
10. Wormatia Worms	40	15	8	17	67-73	38
11. Waldhof Mannheim	40	16	6	18	57-69	38
12. FC 08 Homburg	40	13	11	16	58-62	37
13. SpVgg Bayreuth	40	16	5	19	77-82	37
14. VfR Bürstadt	40	13	11	16	57-68	37
15. Eintracht Trier	40	14	8	18	60-57	36
16. SSV 1846 Ulm	40	14	8	18	51-57	36
17. ESV Ingolstadt	40	13	8	19	57-89	34
18. FSV Frankfurt	40	13	6	21	63-97	32
19. MTV Ingolstadt	40	11	7	22	58-81	29
20. Röchling Völklingen	40	10	2	28	49-101	22
21. FV 04 Würzburg	40	6	9	25	42-82	21

Promoted: FC Augsburg, VfB Eppingen, Hessen Kassel, Borussia Neunkirchen

Top Scorers
Günther (Karlsruhe SC) 29
Krause (Kickers Offenbach) 26
Allgöwer (Kickers Stuttgart) 25
Mattern (Wormatia Worms) 20
Heck (1.FC Saarbrücken) 17
Krostina (MTV Ingolstadt) 17
Sommerer (SpVgg Bayreuth) 17
Dreher (Kickers Stuttgart) 16
Kirschner (SpVgg Fürth) 15
Künkel (1.FC Saarbrücken) 15
Nickel (Kickers Stuttgart) 15
Struth (Karlsruhe SC) 15
Wesseler (Wormatia Worms) 15

Third Division Champions
Baden-Württemberg: VfB Stuttgart (Am.)
Bayern: FC Augsburg
Berlin: BFC Preussen Berlin
Hessen: KSV Hessen Kassel
Nord: VfB Oldenburg
Nordrhein: 1.FC Bocholt
Südwest: Borussia Neunkirchen
Westfalen: SpVgg Erkenschwick

West German Cup
First Round
1.FC Bocholt 8, SV Speicher 0
1.FC Cologne 5, FSV Mainz 05 1
1.FC Kaiserslautern (Am.) 3, SV Meppen 1
1.FC Kaiserslautern 2, MSV Duisburg 0
1.FC Nuremberg 3, Eintracht Brunswick (Am.) 0
1.FC Pforzheim 10, Phönix Düdelsheim 2
Alemannia Aachen 0, Werder Bremen 1
Arminia Bielefeld 1, BFC Preussen Berlin 0
Borussia Dortmund 7, Bremen SV 0
Borussia Mönchengladbach 2, FC Biberach 1
Borussia Neunkirchen 0, Fortuna Düsseldorf 4
BV Lüttringhausen 3, SpVgg Erkenschwick 2
Eintracht Brunswick 1, Preussen Münster 0
Eintracht Frankfurt 6, BSK Neugablonz 1
Eintracht Trier 4, Wuppertal SV (Am.) 2
FC Altona 93 1, Viktoria Sindlingen 0
FC Augsburg 7, FC Wipfeld 0
FC Freiburg 2, 1.FC Saarbrücken 1
FT Geestemünde 4, SV Zeitlarn 1
FC Hanau 93 2, Wacker 04 Berlin 2 aet (1-4)
FC Östringen 1, Bayern Munich 10
FC Vilshofen 2, FV 04 Würzburg 3 aet
FSV Frankfurt 2, Viktoria Aschaffenburg 0
FV Weingarten 2, VfL Bochum 7
Hamburg SV 6, FC 08 Villingen 0
Holstein Kiel 3, OSV Hanover 2
Karlsruhe SC 5, SC Freiburg 1
Kickers Offenbach 3, Hanover 96 1
Kickers Stuttgart 3, TSV Ofterdingen 0
MTV Gifhorn 1, Bayer Leverkusen 4
Reinickendorf Füchse 4, VfB Lübeck 2
Rot-Weiss Essen 2, 1.FC Cologne (Am.) 1
SB Heidenheim 0, Hertha BSC Berlin 4
SC Bonn 4, Salamander Türkheim 0
SG Ohetal 0, KSV Baunatal 2
Sportfreunde Eisbachtal 0, FC Schalke 04 1
SpVgg Bayreuth 5, Preussen 07 Hamelin 0
SpVgg Elversberg 5, SV Heide 2 aet
SpVgg Fürth 3, BSV Weissenthurm 1
SV Geinsheim 2, DSC Wanne-Eickel 4
SV Göppingen 3, TuS Neuendorf 1
SV Heng 0, Fortuna Cologne 4
TSV 1860 Munich 5, FC St Pauli 0
TSV Ampfing 1, SV Bramfeld 2 aet
TSV Battenberg 5, SV Auersmacher 4 aet
TSV Buxtehude 0, Bayer Uerdingen 6
TuS Chlodwig Zülpich 2, ESV Ingolstadt 6
TuS Langerwehe 4, SV Hasborn 2
TuS Schloss Neuhaus 3, 1.FC Nuremberg (Am.) 2 aet
TuS Xanten 2, Arminia Hanover 1
Union Neumünster 0, Sportfreunde DJK Freiburg 2
Union Solingen 3, VfR Aalen 1
VfB 1900 Giessen 2, FC 08 Homburg 4
VfB Frohnlach 8, SV Alemannia Haibach 4 aet
VfB Gaggenau 2, SpVgg Au 2 aet (0-5)
VfB Oldenburg 1, SC Verl 2
VfL Osnabrück 3, Rot-Weiss Lüdenscheid 2 aet
VfL Wolfsburg 0, VfB Stuttgart 3
Viktoria Cologne 1, Tennis Borussia Berlin 0
Waldhof Mannheim 5, TBV Lemgo 1
Wattenscheid 09 2, MTV Ingolstadt 1
Westfalia Herne 4, SG Hagen-Vorhalle 0
Westfalia Weitmar 1, SV Darmstadt 98 2
Wuppertal SV 1, Wormatia Worms 4

Second Round
1.FC Bocholt 1, VfL Osnabrück 1 aet (2-3)
1.FC Cologne 10, FC Altona 93 0
1.FC Kaiserslautern (Am.) 2, SC Bonn 3 aet
1.FC Nuremberg 5, Bayer Leverkusen 2
Bayer Uerdingen 5, Reinickendorf Füchse 0
Borussia Mönchengladbach 4, Rot-Weiss Essen 0
DSC Wanne-Eickel 3, Kickers Offenbach 5
Eintracht Brunswick 3, Holstein Kiel 1
Eintracht Trier 4, TuS Langerwehe 0
FC Augsburg 1, Karlsruhe SC 1 aet (0-3)
FC Freiburg 1, Eintracht Frankfurt 4

FC 08 Homburg 5, FV 04 Würzburg 0
FC Schalke 04 3, KSV Baunatal 0
Fortuna Düsseldorf 2, Wacker 04 Berlin 0
FSV Frankfurt 1, Borussia Dortmund 3 aet
Kickers Stuttgart 9, VfL Frohnlach 0
SC Verl 3, SpVgg Elversberg 1
SpVgg Bayreuth 6, SpVgg Au 0
SV Darmstadt 98 4, 1.FC Kaiserslautern 0
SV Göppingen 3, FT Geestemünde 1
TSV 1860 Munich 6, 1.FC Pforzheim 1
TSV Battenberg 2, SV Bramfeld 0 aet
TuS Schloss Neuhaus 1, Fortuna Cologne 2 aet
TuS Xanten 1, Arminia Bielefeld 8
Union Solingen 3, ESV Ingolstadt 0
VfB Stuttgart 10, Wattenscheid 09 2
VfL Bochum 2, SpVgg Fürth 1
Viktoria Cologne 1, Bayern Munich 3
Waldhof Mannheim 2, Sportfreunde DJK Freiburg 2
Werder Bremen 0, Hertha BSC Berlin 2
Westfalia Herne 1, BV Lüttringhausen 4
Wormatia Worms 0, Hamburg SV 3

Third Round
1.FC Nuremberg 1, FC 08 Homburg 2
Bayer Uerdingen 2, Union Solingen 0
Borussia Dortmund 3, Arminia Bielefeld 1 aet
Eintracht Brunswick 2, VfB Stuttgart 3 aet
Eintracht Frankfurt 2, Waldhof Mannheim 0
FC Schalke 04 3, SC Bonn 1
Hertha BSC Berlin 0, TuS Langerwehe 0 aet (1-2)
Karlsruhe SC 1, Borussia Mönchengladbach 0 aet
Kickers Offenbach 2, Hamburg SV 0
SC Verl 1, Kickers Stuttgart 7
SpVgg Bayreuth 1, Bayern Munich 0
SV Darmstadt 98 7, Fortuna Cologne 2
SV Göppingen 1, Fortuna Düsseldorf 4
TSV 1860 Munich 3, BV Lüttringhausen 0
VfL Bochum 3, 1.FC Cologne 3 aet (1-2)
VfL Osnabrück 4, TSV Battenberg 0

Fourth Round
1.FC Cologne 3, SV Darmstadt 98 1
Borussia Dortmund 2, Bayer Uerdingen 1
FC 08 Homburg 1, TSV 1860 Munich 0
FC Schalke 04 2, VfL Osnabrück 0
Karlsruhe SC 3, Fortuna Düsseldorf 5
Kickers Stuttgart 2, Kickers Offenbach 5
SpVgg Bayreuth 5, TuS Langerwehe 2 aet
VfB Stuttgart 3, Eintracht Frankfurt 2

Quarterfinals
Borussia Dortmund 3, VfB Stuttgart 1
FC 08 Homburg 1, 1.FC Cologne 4

FC Schalke 04 3, SpVgg Bayreuth 1
Kickers Offenbach 2, Fortuna Düsseldorf 5 aet

Semifinals
FC Schalke 04 0, 1.FC Cologne 2
Fortuna Düsseldorf 3, Borussia Dortmund 1

Final
in Gelsenkirchen
Fortuna Düsseldorf 2, 1.FC Cologne 1

West German Internationals
12/9/79 in Berlin 2-1 v Argentina
17/10/79 in Cologne 5-1 v Wales (ECQ)
21/11/79 in Tblisi 3-1 v Soviet Union
22/12/79 in Gelsenkirchen 2-0 v Turkey (ECQ)
27/2/80 in Bremen 8-0 v Malta (ECQ)
2/4/80 in Munich 1-0 v Austria
13/5/80 in Frankfurt 3-1 v Poland
11/6/80 in Rome 1-0 v Czechoslovakia (EC)
14/6/80 in Naples 3-2 v Holland (EC)
17/6/80 in Turin 0-0 v Greece (EC)
22/6/80 in Rome 2-1 v Belgium (EC)

East German Oberliga

Club	P	W	D	L	Goals	Pts
1. Dynamo Berlin	26	20	3	3	72-16	43
2. Dynamo Dresden	26	20	2	4	65-22	42
3. Carl Zeiss Jena	26	13	6	7	41-24	32
4. 1.FC Magdeburg	26	12	6	8	45-37	30
5. Vorwärts Frankfurt/Oder	26	11	8	7	41-40	30
6. Lokomotive Leipzig	26	11	7	8	50-34	29
7. Chemie Halle	26	12	4	10	38-37	28
8. Sachsenring Zwickau	26	9	4	13	27-42	22
9. Wismut Aue	26	8	4	14	26-42	20
10. Stahl Riesa	26	5	10	11	22-53	20
11. FC Karl-Marx-Stadt	26	6	7	13	26-38	19
12. Rot-Weiss Erfurt	26	6	6	14	33-38	18
13. 1.FC Union Berlin	26	6	4	16	18-44	16
14. Chemie Leipzig	26	4	7	15	21-58	15

Top Scorers
Kühn (Lokomotive Leipzig) 21
Streich (1.FC Magdeburg) 19
Weber (Dynamo Dresden) 16
Pelka (Dynamo Berlin) 15
Riediger (Dynamo Berlin) 13
Terletzki (Dynamo Berlin) 12
Krostitz (Chemie Halle) 11
Vogel (Carl Zeiss Jena) 9
Grossmann (Lokomotive Leipzig) 8
Kotte (Dynamo Dresden) 8
Netz (Dynamo Berlin) 8
Schmuck (Dynamo Dresden) 8

Oberliga Promotion Playoff

Club	P	W	D	L	Goals	Pts
1. Hansa Rostock	8	7	0	1	20-6	14
2. Chemie Böhlen	8	3	3	2	13-12	9
3. Energie Cottbus	8	3	3	2	10-12	9
4. Wismut Gera	8	1	2	5	7-11	4
5. Dynamo Fürstenwalde	8	1	2	5	6-15	4

Second Division (Staffel A)

Club	P	W	D	L	Goals	Pts
1. Hansa Rostock	22	21	1	0	77-8	43
2. Vorwärts Stralsund	22	12	5	5	56-27	29
3. TSG Bau Rostock	22	13	3	6	60-35	29
4. ISG Schwerin-Süd	22	10	7	5	47-27	27
5. Schiffahrt/Hafen Rostock	22	10	4	8	40-28	24
6. Post Neubrandenburg	22	9	6	7	42-35	24
7. Dynamo Schwerin	22	9	3	10	39-34	21
8. TSG Wismar	22	7	6	9	31-44	20
9. KKW Greifswald	22	8	1	13	29-47	17
10. Motor WW Warnemünde	22	5	5	12	24-66	15
11. Hydraulik Parchim	22	4	3	15	20-56	11
12. Nord Torgelow	22	1	2	19	14-72	4

Promoted: Lokomotive Anklam, Veritas Wittenberge, Motor Wolgast

Second Division (Staffel B)

Club	P	W	D	L	Goals	Pts
1. Dynamo Fürstenwalde	22	12	7	3	40-16	31
2. Chemie PCK Schwedt	22	12	7	3	30-13	31
3. Vorwärts Neubrandenburg	22	7	10	5	35-28	24
4. Stahl Brandenburg	22	8	7	7	29-29	23
5. Halbleiterwerk Frankfurt/Oder	22	7	8	7	32-26	22
6. Stahl Hennigsdorf	22	9	4	9	32-34	22
7. Stahl Eisenhüttenstadt	22	7	8	7	24-29	22
8. Motor Hennigsdorf	22	6	8	8	34-47	20
9. KWO Berlin	22	7	4	11	28-33	18
10. Motor Babelsberg	22	6	6	10	21-27	18
11. Rotation Berlin	22	8	2	12	24-34	18
12. TSG Neustrelitz	22	4	7	11	16-29	15

Promoted: Bergmann Borsig Berlin, Motor Süd Brandenburg, Motor Eberswalde. Vorwärts Neubrandenburg were placed in Staffel A for the following season

Second Division (Staffel C)

Club	P	W	D	L	Goals	Pts
1. Chemie Böhlen	22	17	4	1	67-23	38
2. Vorwärts Dessau	22	13	5	4	47-30	31
3. Stahl Blankenburg	22	8	11	3	30-20	27
4. Chemie Buna Schkopau	22	9	6	7	41-25	24
5. Stahl Thale	22	7	9	6	31-27	23
6. Chemie Zeitz	22	8	5	9	31-41	21
7. Lokomotive Stendal	22	7	6	9	29-32	20
8. Dynamo Eisleben	22	7	4	11	40-42	18
9. Chemie Wolfen	22	6	6	10	28-30	18
10. Einheit Wernigerode	22	6	6	10	31-45	18
11. Chemie Premnitz	22	6	4	12	25-38	16
12. Lokomotive Halberstadt	22	4	2	16	26-73	10

Promoted: Stahl NW Leipzig, MK Sangerhausen, Chemie Schönebeck

Second Division (Staffel D)

Club	P	W	D	L	Goals	Pts
1. Energie Cottbus	22	15	4	3	49-19	34
2. Vorwärts Kamenz	22	12	8	2	39-20	32
3. Motor Werdau	22	12	4	6	42-25	28
4. Fortschritt Bischofswerda	22	11	4	7	44-27	26
5. Aktivist Espenhain	22	5	13	4	27-26	23
6. Motor FH Karl-Marx-Stadt	22	10	3	9	28-30	23
7. Aktivist Schwarze Pumpe	22	6	8	8	23-27	20
8. FSV Lokomotive Dresden	22	6	7	9	29-35	19
9. Vorwärts Plauen	22	5	8	9	29-35	18
10. Dynamo Lübben	22	5	6	11	21-40	16
11. Aktivist Brieske-Senftenberg	22	5	5	12	31-37	15
12. SG Sosa	22	3	4	15	22-63	10

Promoted: TSG Gröditz, Aufbau Krumhermersdorf, TSG Lübbenau

Second Division (Staffel E)

Club	P	W	D	L	Goals	Pts
1. Wismut Gera	22	13	6	3	55-25	32
2. Motor Weimar	22	12	7	3	56-30	31
3. Kali Werra Tiefenort	22	11	7	4	34-23	29
4. Motor Rudisleben	22	9	8	5	26-22	26
5. Fortschirtt Weida	22	7	8	7	30-28	22
6. Landbau Bad Langensalza	22	7	8	7	29-34	22
7. Motor Nordhausen	22	8	5	9	37-31	21
8. Motor Suhl	22	9	3	10	38-45	21
9. Chemie IW Ilmenau	22	7	6	9	29-21	20
10. Motor Altenburg	22	7	5	10	30-32	19
11. Motor Zeulenroda	22	6	3	13	28-55	15
12. WM Schmalkalden	22	1	4	17	13-59	6

Promoted: Motor Hermsdorf, Glückauf Sondershausen, Motor Steinach

East German Cup Final

in Berlin

Carl Zeiss Jena 3, Rot-Weiss Erfurt 1 aet

1979-80

East German Internationals
5/9/79 in Moscow 0-1 v USSR
12/9/79 in Reykjavik 3-0 v Iceland (ECQ)
26/9/79 in Chorzow 1-1 v Poland (ECQ)
13/10/79 in Berlin 5-2 v Switzerland (ECQ)
21/11/79 in Leipzig 2-3 v Holland (ECQ)
13/2/80 in Malaga 1-0 v Spain
2/4/80 in Bucharest 2-2 v Rumania
16/4/80 in Leipzig 2-0 v Greece
7/5/80 in Rostock 2-2 v USSR

European Cup
First Round
Valur Reykjavik v Hamburg SV .... (0-3, 1-2)
Dynamo Berlin v Ruch Chorzow .... (4-1, 0-0)
Second Round
Hamburg SV v Dinamo Tblisi .... (3-1, 3-2)
Dynamo Berlin v Servette Geneva .... (2-1, 2-2)
Quarterfinals
Hamburg SV v Hajduk Split .... (1-0, 2-3)
Nottingham Forest v Dynamo Berlin .... (0-1, 3-1)
Semifinals
Real Madrid v Hamburg SV .... (2-0, 1-5)
Final in Madrid
Nottingham Forest 1, Hamburg SV 0

Cup-Winners' Cup
First Round
Glasgow Rangers v Fortuna Düsseldorf .... (2-1, 0-0)
Wrexham v 1.FC Magdeburg .... (3-2, 2-5 aet)
Second Round
Arsenal v 1.FC Magdeburg .... (2-1, 2-2)

UEFA Cup
First Round
Borussia Mönchengladbach v Viking Stavanger ..... (3-0, 1-1)
Aberdeen v Eintracht Frankfurt .... (1-1, 0-1)
VfB Stuttgart v Torino .... (1-0, 1-2 aet)
FC Zurich v 1.FC Kaiserslautern .... (1-3, 1-5)
Bohemians Prague v Bayern Munich .... (0-2, 2-2)
Atlético Madrid v Dynamo Dresden .... (1-2, 0-3)
Carl Zeiss Jena v West Bromwich Albion .... (2-0, 2-1)
Second Round
Borussia Mönchengladbach v Inter Milan ...... (1-1, 3-2 aet)
Aarhus v Bayern Munich .... (1-2, 1-3)
Sporting Lisbon v 1.FC Kaiserslautern .... (1-1, 0-2)
Dinamo Bucharest v Eintracht Frankfurt .... (2-0, 0-3 aet)
Dynamo Dresden v VfB Stuttgart .... (1-1, 0-0)
Red Star Belgrade v Carl Zeiss Jena .... (3-2, 3-2)
Third Round
VTK Diosgyör v 1.FC Kaiserslautern .... (0-2, 1-6)
Grasshoppers Zurich v VfB Stuttgart .... (0-2, 0-3)
Borussia Mönchengladbach v Uni Craiova .... (2-0, 0-1)
Eintracht Frankfurt v Feyenoord .... (4-1, 0-1)
Bayern Munich v Red Star Belgrade .... (2-0, 2-3)
Quarterfinals
St. Etienne v Borussia Mönchengladbach .... (1-4, 0-2)
1.FC Kaiserslautern v Bayern Munich .... (1-0, 1-4)
VfB Stuttgart v Lokomotive Sofia .... (3-1, 1-0)
Eintracht Frankfurt v Zbrojovka Brno .... (4-1, 2-3)
Semifinals
VfB Stuttgart v Borussia Mönchengladbach .... (2-1, 0-2)
Bayern Munich v Eintracht Frankfurt .... (2-0, 1-5 aet)
Final
Borussia Mönchengladbach v Eintracht Frankfurt ... (3-2, 0-1)

1980-81

Der Kaiser returns

After three years in America, 35-year-old Franz Beckenbauer made a surprising comeback: not with Bayern Munich, but with title rivals Hamburg. HSV needed a big-name replacement for Kevin Keegan, who had returned to England after three seasons with the club. Many feared that Beckenbauer would be an embarrassment after spending so much time with the has-beens and never-wases of the North American league, but in fact he performed reasonably well and was even close to an international call-up at one time. Hamburg's real embarrassment was *Trainer* Branko Zebec, whose problems with alcohol and subsequent illnesses led to his being replaced by deputy Aleksandar Ristic in December.

Bayern skipper Paul Breitner, named West German Footballer of the Year at the end of the season, rejoined the national team after a six-year absence. Over the next two years he would add a further twenty caps to the twenty-eight he had already won. Karl-Heinz Rummenigge, who would again lead the Bundesliga in scoring, took over the captaincy of the national team from Bernard Dietz and was named European Footballer of the Year for the second time in a row.

In the league it was again Bayern and Hamburg fighting for the top spot, with the northerners three points clear at mid-season despite a 2-1 loss on their visit to Munich in October. In the return fixture in February, with Bayern four points adrift, a disastrous back-pass from Breitner was intercepted by Horst Hrubesch to put Hamburg 2-0 ahead and seemingly well on the way to the title. But a goal from Rummenigge got Bayern back into the game, and with one minute remaining Breitner made amends for his error by hitting the equaliser.

Dieter Hoeness spent a lot of the season on the injured list, but returned for Bayern's European Cup quarterfinal at Banik Ostrava, where he scored the first goal in Bayern's superb 4-2 win. The victory seemed to give a real impetus to Bayern's campaign, and they gathered points relentlessly as Hamburg began to slip. Two matches from the end of the season, the Bavarians went to arch-rivals Borussia

Mönchengladbach and came away with a 4-1 win, assuring them of the title. The final game was a celebratory stroll at home to hapless Bayer Uerdingen, the 4-0 win witnessed by over 70,000.

For the fourth straight year since gaining promotion from the Second Division, VfB Stuttgart finished in the top four, dropping just three points at home. New *Trainer* Jürgen Sundermann returned from a season away in Switzerland with Grasshoppers Zurich to replace Lothar Buchmann, who had joined Eintracht Frankfurt. The linchpins of VfB's success were the Förster brothers, Karlheinz and Bernd, both West German international defenders, and Hansi Müller, an enterprising young midfielder.

Dutch manager Rinus Michels made a bit of Bundesliga history, becoming the first Bundesliga *Trainer* not to hold a DFB coaching licence. Michels, who had spent the summer as head coach of the Los Angeles Aztecs, joined Cologne in November, soon after Karl-Heinz Heddergott was shown the door. Cologne managed to arrange this exception because of Michels' previous outstanding coaching successes. Meanwhile, MSV Duisburg, threatened by relegation, announced a change of *Trainer* but player power won a stay of execution for Friedhelm Wenzlaff as MSV climbed the table. Arminia Bielefeld had looked doomed by the turn of the year, but new *Trainer* Horst Franz encouraged an amazing improvement as Arminia overhauled three other teams to escape the drop.

It was a traumatic year for Schalke 04, whose continuous membership of the Bundesliga came to an end despite the support of fanatical crowds averaging over 27,000. Frustration spilled over into anger, with Schalke player Klaus Fischer being branded a "traitor" for his decision to join Cologne, and President Hans-Joachim Fenne receiving death threats from the more demented ranks of support. Schalke experimented with a twin-*Trainer* approach after Fahrudin Jusufi was released in May, with Rudi Assauer and Heinz Redepennig jointly occupying the hot-seat until the end of the season, but it couldn't save them from relegation.

Also going down were one-time Bundesliga champions TSV 1860 Munich, who were finding it hard to live under the long shadows now being cast over the city by the mighty Bayern. Nevertheless, their twenty-one-year-old striker Rudi Völler, who netted a hat-trick against Fortuna Düsseldorf in October, was turning a few heads, and the following season he became Division Two's top scorer with 37 goals.

Relegated the year before, Werder Bremen bounced straight back into the Bundesliga by winning the Second Division North in a gruelling 42-match campaign. Hertha Berlin had shown signs of being the likely runners-up, but with two games to go they lost a critical home contest to promotion rivals Eintracht Brunswick before nearly 69,000 in the Olympiastadion. Brunswick wound up finishing second and won the playoff to rejoin the Bundesliga after a year's absence. In the Southern Division, modest Darmstadt topped the table from the fifth match onward, as *Trainer* Werner Olk's men faced little threat all season and finished five points clear of Kickers Offenbach. This would be the last North-South split for the Division Two, as the DFB agreed to a unified twenty-team Second Division.

It was a forgettable season for clubs from Hanover in the West German Cup. Borussia Hanover were trounced 8-1 by Hanover 96 in the first round, and Second Division OSV Hanover went down 7-3 at Mönchengladbach. In the second round, Arminia Hanover lost at home to Hamburg 7-3, while Hanover 96 played out a remarkable 5-5 draw with rivals Werder Bremen, for whom Uwe Reinders equalised with almost the last kick of the match. Hanover lost the replay to a Benno Möhlmann goal.

Borussia Mönchengladbach scored an incredible 27 goals in their first four cup-ties, but had faced vastly inferior opposition each time. Paired with Kaiserslautern in the quarterfinals, they took an early lead through Wolfram Wuttke but went on to lose 3-1. The most exciting quarterfinal match saw Second Division Eintracht Brunswick pip Hamburg in extra time, Ronnie Worm scoring the winner.

Kaiserslautern scraped through to the final for the fourth time in their history—and lost for the fourth time. On this occasion they went down 3-1 to Eintracht Frankfurt in front of 71,000 at the Neckarstadion. In a match billed as Frankfurt's craft versus Lautern's graft, Eintracht took the lead when Willi Neuberger's shot was deflected past Kaiserslautern keeper Ronnie Hellström. One minute later Norbert Nachtweih played a magnificent pass to Roland Borchers for Eintracht's second and the match was effectively over. Frankfurt's South Korean import, Bum-Kun Cha, affectionately known as "Cha-Bum," added a third and Rainer Geye's last-minute goal for Lautern was a meagre consolation.

Taking his leave from the Bundesliga was 38-year-old Siegfried "Siggi" Held, who had made his debut in 1965 and appeared in 422 league matches for Dortmund, Offenbach and Uerdingen. He had earned 41 caps for West Germany.

Carl Zeiss Jena became only the second East German side to reach a European club final. Their progress in the Cup-Winners' Cup was primarily a consequence of their excellent home performances, although they received a scare by drawing 2-2 at home to Newport County. The final was held in the Düsseldorf Rheinstadion against Dynamo Tblisi, and Jena failed to respond to the big event. The local public were also less than receptive: over half of the paltry 9,000 crowd consisted of children who were admitted free of charge.

In the European Cup, Bayern thrashed Ajax at home and held the score to 1-2 in Amsterdam on the way to a semifinal meeting with Liverpool. A 0-0 stalemate at Anfield seemed a good first-leg result, but Liverpool earned a draw in Munich and went on to beat Real Madrid in the final. Hamburg suffered a humiliating loss to a Michel Platini-inspired St. Etienne in the third round of the UEFA Cup and went out.

In the East German Oberliga 621 goals were scored, the 3.41 per match average being the highest in over a quarter-century. Dynamo Berlin cantered to their third straight championship, a 2-1 loss to Vorwärts Frankfurt/Oder being the only blemish on an otherwise perfect home record. The season ended with the final appearance of Zwickau's 35-year-old goalkeeper Jürgen Croy, who retired after sixteen years of top-class football. The national team had a good year, including a 0-0 draw in Italy, but it also saw the last international appearance of Konrad Weise of Carl Zeiss Jena, who had won 86 caps over the past eleven seasons.

West Germany had stretched their unbeaten run to 23 games before they lost 2-1 to Argentina on New Year's Day in Montevideo. Worse was to come in the other match of the *Copa de Ora* competition in the form of a 4-1 hammering by Brazil. Not since the 1958 World Cup had West Germany lost by more than two goals—and that was in the third-place playoff with France, when the Germans had fielded a weakened team.

Bundesliga

Club	P	W	D	L	Goals	Pts
1. Bayern Munich	34	22	9	3	89-41	53
2. Hamburg SV	34	21	7	6	73-43	49
3. VfB Stuttgart	34	19	8	7	70-44	46
4. 1.FC Kaiserslautern	34	17	10	7	60-37	44
5. Eintracht Frankfurt	34	13	12	9	61-57	38
6. Borussia Mönchengladbach	34	15	7	12	68-64	37
7. Borussia Dortmund	34	13	9	12	69-59	35
8. 1.FC Cologne	34	12	10	12	54-55	34
9. VfL Bochum	34	9	15	10	53-45	33
10. Karlsruhe SC	34	9	14	11	56-63	32
11. Bayer Leverkusen	34	10	10	14	52-53	30
12. MSV Duisburg	34	10	9	15	45-58	29
13. Fortuna Düsseldorf	34	10	8	16	57-64	28
14. 1.FC Nuremberg	34	11	6	17	47-57	28
15. Arminia Bielefeld	34	10	6	18	46-65	26
16. TSV 1860 Munich	34	9	7	18	49-67	25
17. FC Schalke 04	34	8	7	19	43-88	23
18. Bayer Uerdingen	34	8	6	20	47-79	22

Top Scorers

K-H Rummenigge (Bayern Munich) 29
Burgsmüller (Borussia Dortmund) 27
K Allofs (Fortuna Düsseldorf) 19
Breitner (Bayern Munich) 17
Hrubesch (Hamburg SV) 17
D Müller (1.FC Cologne) 17
Pinkall (VfL Bochum) 17
Hannes (Borussia Mönchengladbach) 16
Økland (Bayer Leverkusen) 16
Schock (Arminia Bielefeld) 16

Bundesliga Promotion Playoff

Kickers Offenbach v Eintracht Brunswick (1-0, 0-2); Brunswick promoted to First Division

Second Division North

Club	P	W	D	L	Goal	Pts
1. Werder Bremen	42	30	8	4	97-33	68
2. Eintracht Brunswick	42	29	7	6	102-44	65
3. Hertha BSC Berlin*	42	31	2	9	123-42	64
4. Hanover 96*	42	20	16	6	88-49	56
5. Alemannia Aachen*	42	24	7	11	80-51	55
6. VfL Osnabrück*	42	22	8	12	76-50	52
7. Union Solingen*	42	20	10	12	76-61	50
8. Rot-Weiss Essen*	42	20	7	15	99-74	47
9. Fortuna Cologne*	42	18	10	14	83-67	46
10. Wattenscheid 09*	42	15	12	15	62-68	42
11. Viktoria Cologne*	42	14	13	15	67-79	41
12. 1.FC Bocholt	42	14	10	18	66-70	38
13. Preussen Münster	42	14	8	20	48-72	36
14. Rot-Weiss Oberhausen	42	12	11	19	59-84	35
15. VfB Oldenburg	42	12	10	20	64-89	34
16. SC Herford	42	11	10	21	48-65	32
17. Tennis Borussia Berlin	42	9	14	19	47-71	32
18. Göttingen 05	42	9	14	19	67-98	32
19. Holstein Kiel	42	12	7	23	48-81	31
20. Rot-Weiss Lüdenscheid	42	8	11	23	43-83	27
21. SpVgg Erkenschwick	42	7	8	27	46-91	22
22. OSV Hanover	42	7	5	30	41-109	19

*qualified for unified Second Division

Top Scorers

Mill (Rot-Weiss Essen) 40
Killmaier (Hertha BSC Berlin) 36
Feilzer (VfL Osnabrück) 30
Worm (Eintracht Brunswick) 30
Kostedde (Werder Bremen) 29
Schatzschneider (Hanover 96) 29
Remark (Hertha BSC Berlin) 22
Snater (Göttingen 05) 21
Krumbein (Union Solingen) 20
Lenz (Union Solingen) 20

Second Division South

Club	P	W	D	L	Goals	Pts
1. SV Darmstadt 98	38	24	7	7	85-42	55
2. Kickers Offenbach*	38	19	12	7	87-42	50
3. Kickers Stuttgart*	38	19	10	9	81-40	48
4. Hessen Kassel*	38	16	16	6	59-35	48
5. SSV 1846 Ulm	38	18	11	9	59-39	47
6. Waldhof Mannheim*	38	19	7	12	65-43	45
7. SC Freiburg*	38	16	9	13	57-50	41
8. Eintracht Trier	38	15	11	12	56-52	41
9. SpVgg Bayreuth*	38	15	9	14	60-53	39
10. FC Freiburg*	38	15	9	14	76-75	39
11. FC 08 Homburg	38	14	10	14	66-69	38
12. Wormatia Worms*	38	15	7	16	60-70	37
13. VfR Bürstadt	38	15	7	16	54-66	37
14. SpVgg Fürth	38	15	5	18	54-54	35
15. FSV Frankfurt	38	13	6	19	51-76	32
16. ESV Ingolstadt	38	14	3	21	62-92	31
17. 1.FC Saarbrücken	38	10	8	20	43-61	28
18. FC Augsburg	38	7	10	21	55-88	24
19. Borussia Neunkirchen	38	5	13	20	44-85	23
20. VfB Eppingen	38	7	8	23	44-86	22

*qualified for unified Second Division

Top Scorers

Neumann (SV Darmstadt 98) 27
Bein (Kickers Offenbach) 25
Gerber (ESV Ingolstadt) 23
Mattern (Wormatia Worms) 22
Linz (FC Freiburg) 22

1980-81

Leiendecker (Eintracht Trier) 19
Traser (1.FC Saarbrücken) 19
Demange (FC 08 Homburg) 18
Jörg (FC Augsburg) 18
Cestonaro (SV Darmstadt 98) 17
Hofmann (FSV Frankfurt) 17
Nickel (Kickers Stuttgart) 17

Third Division Champions
Baden-Württemberg: SV Sandhausen
Bayern: MTV Ingolstadt
Berlin: BFC Preussen Berlin
Hessen: Viktoria Griesheim
Nord: FC St Pauli
Nordrhein: 1.FC Cologne (Am.)
Südwest: FSV 05 Mainz
Westfalen: 1.FC Paderborn
No Oberliga clubs were promoted into the Second Division

West German Cup
First Round
1.FC Viersen 2, Karlsruhe SC 2 aet (1-2)
Alemannia Aachen 3, VfB Eppingen 0
Altas Delmenhorst 6, Blau-Weiss Wesselburen 2
Arminia Hanover 2, SpVgg Erkenschwick 1
ASC Dudweiler 0, FV 04 Würzburg 1
ASV Burglengenfeld 2, VfB Wissen 3
Bayern Munich 2, Arminia Bielefeld 0
Blau-Weiss Niederembt 1, Preussen Münster 4 aet
Borussia Mönchengladbach 7, OSV Hanover 3
Borussia Neunkirchen 1, SpVgg Bayreuth 1 aet (1-2)
Buchonia Flieden 1, ESV Ingolstadt 4
Concordia Hamburg 2, SpVgg Hamm 2 aet (2-3)
DSC Wanne-Eickel 1, SpVgg Frechen 20 3
Eintracht Brunswick 4, SC Fürstenfeldbruck 1
Eintracht Trier 0, Fortuna Düsseldorf 1
FC Augsburg 2, Wuppertal SV 0
FC Freiburg 3, VfB Bottrop 1
FC 08 Homburg 3, SG Limburgerhof 0
FC Schalke 04 2, Bayer Uerdingen 5
FSV Frankfurt 3, Röchling Völklingen 1
FSV Mainz 05 3, MTV Ingolstadt 2
FV Lauda 1, VfB Oldenburg 2 aet
Hamburg SV 11, Wormatia Worms 1
Hanover 96 8, Borussia Hanover 1
Hertha BSC Berlin 3, Holstein Kiel 1
Kickers Stuttgart 2, Rot-Weiss Lüdenscheid 0
Kickers Würzburg 2, TSV Hirschaid 1 aet
Moselfeuer Lehmen 1, Kickers Offenbach 15
MSV Duisburg 9, Wacker 04 Berlin 0
Rot-Weiss Essen 7, VfR Neuss 2
Rot-Weiss Niebüll 3, Eintracht Brunswick (Am.) 2
Rot-Weiss Oberhausen 1, FV Offenburg 0
RSV Würges 2, FC Ottering 0
SC Freiburg 4, Bremen SV 2
SC Herford 3, Eintracht Nordhorn 0
Schwarz-Weiss Essen 6, FC Neureut 0
SG 05 Pirmasens 0, TSV 1860 Munich 8
Sportfreunde Eisbachtal 1, Wattenscheid 09 3
SpVgg Ansbach 1, FSV Pfaffenhofen/Ilm 0
SpVgg Emsdetten 0, 1.FC Cologne 6
SpVgg Fürth 1, 1.FC Nuremberg 1 aet (0-3)
SV 80/09 Bünde 2, Südwest Ludwigshafen 0
SV Blumenthal 0, SC Pfullendorf 3
SV Bramfeld 2, Bayer Leverkusen 8
SV Darmstadt 98 10, FSV Hemmersdorf 0
SV Siegburg 04 2, BFC Preussen Berlin 1
TSV Gersthofen 0, OSC Bremerhaven 1
TSV Pliezhausen 0, SSV 1846 Ulm 3
TSV Plön 0, 1.FC Saarbrücken 3
TSV Röttenbach 2, Hessen Kassel 4
TuS Celle 0, Union Solingen 0 aet (0-5)
TuS Langerwehe 5, SV Stuttgart-Rot 0
TuS Neuendorf 3, SG Egelsbach 4 aet
VfB Bielefeld 1, VfB Friedrichshafen 0
VfB Gaggenau 0, Eintracht Frankfurt 3
VfB Stuttgart (Am.) 2, Borussia Dortmund 5 aet
VfB Stuttgart 4, Fortuna Cologne 0
VfL Bochum 4, SV Wilhelmshaven 1
VfL Klafeld-Geisweid 1, Rot-Weiss Frankfurt 2
VfL Osnabrück 2, Tennis Borussia Berlin 0 aet
VfR Heilbronn 0, 1.FC Kaiserslautern 3
VfR Oli Bürstadt 4, SSV Dillenburg 1 aet
Waldhof Mannheim 8, FSV Harburg 0
Werder Bremen 6, Viktoria Cologne 3 aet

Second Round
1.FC Cologne 1, SC Freiburg 1 aet (1-3)
1.FC Saarbrücken 2, FC Freiburg 2 aet (1-3)
Arminia Hanover 3, Hamburg SV 7
Atlas Delmenhorst 1, Rot-Weiss Oberhausen 0
Bayer Uerdingen 4, Wattenscheid 09 1
Bayern Munich 4, Waldhof Mannheim 2
Borussia Dortmund 3, TSV 1860 Munich 2
Eintracht Brunswick 3, Preussen Münster 1
Eintracht Frankfurt 6, VfB Friedrichshafen 0
ESV Ingolstadt 1, 1.FC Nuremberg 3
FC Augsburg 2, FSV Mainz 05 0
FC 08 Homburg 0, VfB Oldenburg 1
FSV Frankfurt 2, MSV Duisburg 0
Hanover 96 5, Werder Bremen 5 aet (0-1)
Hertha BSC Berlin 4, FV 04 Würzburg 1
Hessen Kassel 4, SpVgg Hamm 0
Karlsruhe SC 1, Alemannia Aachen 1 aet (0-1)

1980-81

Kickers Offenbach 5, Bayer Leverkusen 2
Kickers Stuttgart 13, SpVgg Ansbach 0
Kickers Würzburg 0, Fortuna Düsseldorf 2
OSC Bremerhaven 0, RSV Würges 2
Rot-Weiss Niebüll 0, Schwarz-Weiss Essen 4
SC Pfullendorf 0, SV Siegburg 04 1
SG Egelsbach 1, 1.FC Kaiserslautern 3
SpVgg Bayreuth 1, VfB Stuttgart 3
SSV 1846 Ulm 1, SC Herford 0
SV 08/09 Bünde 3, SpVgg Frechen 20 1
SV Darmstadt 98 4, VFR Oli Bürstadt 1 aet
TuS Langerwehe 1, Borussia Mönchengladbach 7
Union Solingen 1, Rot-Weiss Frankfurt 2
VfB Wissen 1, VfL Osnabrück 7
VfL Bochum 5, Rot-Weiss Essen 1

Third Round
1.FC Kaiserslautern 2, Bayern Munich 1
Alemannia Aachen 5, FC Freiburg 2
Eintracht Brunswick 3, Kickers Stuttgart 2
Eintracht Frankfurt 3, SSV 1846 Ulm 0
FC Augsburg 1, Werder Bremen 3
Fortuna Düsseldorf 3, Borussia Dortmund 0
FSV Frankfurt 1, VfL Bochum 2
Hamburg SV 11, Rot-Weiss Frankfurt 0
Hertha BSC Berlin 4, SV Darmstadt 98 1
Kickers Offenbach 1, Atlas Delmenhorst 1 aet (1-2)
RSV Würges 0, VfL Osnabrück 1
SC Freiburg 2, Hessen Kassel 1 aet
Schwarz-Weiss Essen 1, Bayer Uerdingen 2
SV 08/09 Bünde 1, Borussia Mönchengladbach 7
SV Siegburg 04 1, VfB Oldenburg 2 aet
VfB Stuttgart 2, 1.FC Nuremberg 0

Fourth Round
1.FC Kaiserslautern 3, Alemannia Aachen 0
Borussia Mönchengladbach 6, Atlas Delmenhorst 1
Eintracht Brunswick 1, SC Freiburg 0
Fortuna Düsseldorf 2, Werder Bremen 0
Hamburg SV 4, VfL Bochum 1
Hertha BSC Berlin 5, Bayer Uerdingen 1
VfB Oldenburg 4, Eintracht Frankfurt 5
VfL Osnabrück 1, VfB Stuttgart 3

Quarterfinals
1.FC Kaiserslautern 3, Borussia Mönchengladbach 1
Eintracht Brunswick 4, Hamburg SV 3 aet
Eintracht Frankfurt 2, VfB Stuttgart 1
Hertha BSC Berlin 2, Fortuna Düsseldorf 1

Semifinals
1.FC Kaiserslautern 3, Eintracht Brunswick 2
Eintracht Frankfurt 1, Hertha BSC Berlin 0

Final
in Stuttgart
Eintracht Frankfurt 3, 1.FC Kaiserslautern 1

West German Internationals
10/9/80 in Basle 3-2 v Switzerland
11/10/80 in Eindhoven 1-1 v Holland
19/11/80 in Hanover 4-1 v France
3/12/80 in Sofia 3-1 v Bulgaria (WCQ)
1/1/81 in Montevideo 1-2 v Argentina
7/1/81 in Montevideo 1-4 v Brazil
1/4/81 in Tirana 2-0 v Albania (WCQ)
29/4/81 in Hamburg 2-0 v Austria (WCQ)
19/5/81 in Stuttgart 1-2 v Brazil
24/5/81 in Lahti 4-0 v Finland (WCQ)

East German Oberliga

Club	P	W	D	L	Goals	Pts
1. Dynamo Berlin	26	17	5	4	74-31	39
2. Carl Zeiss Jena	26	16	4	6	57-29	36
3. 1.FC Magdeburg	26	15	4	7	58-35	34
4. Dynamo Dersden	26	16	2	8	49-37	34
5. Vorwärts Frankfurt/Oder	26	13	5	8	58-40	31
6. Lokomotive Leipzig	26	12	4	10	46-35	28
7. Rot-Weiss Erfurt	26	10	7	9	37-49	27
8. Chemie Halle	26	11	3	12	41-41	25
9. FC Karl-Marx-Stadt	26	6	9	11	37-54	21
10. Hansa Rostock	26	6	8	12	35-47	20
11. Sachsenring Zwickau	26	7	4	15	32-51	18
12. Wismut Aue	26	7	4	15	34-60	18
13. Stahl Riesa	26	6	5	15	38-64	17
14. Chemie Böhlen	26	5	6	15	25-48	16

Top Scorers
Streich (1.FC Magdeburg) 20
Havenstein (Chemie Böhlen) 17
Netz (Dynamo Berlin) 17
Schnuphase (Carl Zeiss Jena) 16
Conrad (Vorwärts Frankfurt/Oder) 14
Jarohs (Hansa Rostock) 13
Schulz (Dynamo Berlin) 13
Erler (Wismut Aue) 12
Krostitz (Chemie Halle) 12
Heun (Rot-Weiss Erfurt) 11
Sachse (Stahl Riesa) 11

Oberliga Promotion Playoff

Club	P	W	D	L	Goals	Pts
1. Energie Cottbus	8	5	2	1	15-7	12
2. Chemie Buna Schkopau	8	4	2	2	16-12	10
3. 1.FC Union Berlin	8	3	2	3	17-11	8
4. Schiffahrt/Hafen Rostock	8	3	1	4	15-18	7
5. Motor Suhl	8	0	3	5	9-24	3

Second Division (Staffel A)

Club	P	W	D	L	Goals	Pts
1. Schiffahrt/Hafen Rostock ...	22	15	5	2	48-20	35
2. Vorwärts Stralsund	22	15	4	3	51-13	34
3. Dynamo Schwerin	22	12	5	5	43-28	29
4. TSG Wismar	22	8	6	8	36-43	22
5. Post Neubrandenburg	22	8	5	9	35-30	21
6. ISG Schwerin-Süd	22	9	3	10	32-26	21
7. Vorwärts Neubrandenburg ..	22	8	4	10	29-32	20
8. Lokomotive Anklam	22	6	6	10	28-52	18
9. TSG Bau Rostock	22	6	5	11	28-34	17
10. Motor Wolgast	22	5	7	10	28-39	17
11. Veritas Wittenberge	22	5	7	10	24-38	17
12. KKW Greifswald	22	3	7	12	23-40	13

Promoted: Hydraulik Parchim, TSG Neustrelitz, Motor WW Warnemünde

Second Division (Staffel B)

Club	P	W	D	L	Goals	Pts
1. 1.FC Union Berlin	22	16	3	3	54-19	35
2. KWO Berlin	22	12	4	6	37-28	28
3. Dynamo Fürstenwalde	22	10	7	5	43-25	27
4. PCK Schwedt	22	9	9	4	34-19	27
5. Stahl Brandenburg	22	12	2	8	48-32	26
6. Stahl Eisenhüttenstadt	22	9	6	7	29-21	24
7. Stahl Hennigsdorf	22	9	4	9	35-36	22
8. Bergmann Borsig Berlin	22	7	7	8	32-39	21
9. Motor Hennigsdorf	22	7	5	10	42-56	19
10. Halbleiterwerk Frankfurt/Oder	22	6	4	12	23-43	16
11. Motor Eberswalde	22	5	3	14	20-41	13
12. Motor Süd Brandenburg ...	22	1	4	17	10-48	6

Promoted: EAB 47 Berlin, Stahl Finow, Motor Hennigsdorf

Second Division (Staffel C)

Club	P	W	D	L	Goals	Pts
1. Chemie Buna Schkopau	22	13	6	3	43-29	32
2. Stahl Blankenburg	22	11	7	4	34-14	29
3. Chemie Leipzig	22	10	9	3	37-26	29
4. Dynamo Eisleben	22	10	7	5	45-24	27
5. Lokomotive Stendal	22	10	7	5	27-23	27
6. Stahl Thale	22	10	6	6	33-24	26
7. Vorwärts Dessau	22	8	7	7	34-26	23
8. Stahl NW Leipzig	22	7	5	10	32-38	19
9. Chemie Zeitz	22	7	5	10	29-42	19
10. Chemie Wolfen	22	4	7	11	30-36	15
11. MK Sangerhausen	22	3	4	15	21-51	10
12. Chemie Schönebeck	22	2	4	16	20-52	8

Promoted: Motor Altenburg, Empor Halle, Einheit Wernigerode

Second Division (Staffel D)

Club	P	W	D	L	Goals	Pts
1. Energie Cottbus	22	15	6	1	47-18	36
2. TSG Gröditz	22	10	7	5	33-30	27
3. Motor Werdau	22	10	5	7	52-37	25
4. Aktivist Schwarze Pumpe ...	22	8	8	6	33-25	24
5. Aufbau Krumhermersdorf ...	22	8	6	8	36-40	22
6. Vorwärts Kamenz	22	6	8	8	33-30	20
7. Motor FH Karl-Marx-Stadt ..	22	7	6	9	31-37	20
8. Fortschritt Bischofswerda ...	22	7	6	9	22-32	20
9. Lokomotive Dresden	22	7	5	10	31-30	19
10. Vorwärts Plauen	22	5	9	8	29-31	19
11. Aktivist Espenhain	22	4	10	8	25-33	18
12. TSG Lübbenau	22	5	4	13	25-54	14

Promoted: Aktivist Brieske-Senftenberg, Motor Ascota Karl-Marx-Stadt, Robur Zittau

Second Division (Staffel E)

Club	P	W	D	L	Goals	Pts
1. Motor Suhl	22	12	5	5	36-20	29
2. Wismut Gera	22	10	8	4	42-24	28
3. Motor Nordhausen	22	9	10	3	41-25	28
4. Kali Werra Tiefenort	22	7	9	6	40-35	23
5. Motor Weimar	22	7	9	6	34-33	23
6. Glückauf Sondershausen ...	22	7	8	7	44-41	22
7. Chemie IW Ilmenau	22	6	10	6	34-31	22
8. Motor Rudisleben	22	7	7	8	34-42	21
9. Fortschritt Weida	22	6	8	8	47-39	20
10. Motor Hermsdorf	22	5	10	7	23-27	20
11. Landbau Bad Langensalza ..	22	7	4	11	31-43	18
12. Motor Steinach	22	4	2	16	32-78	10

Promoted: Motor Eisenach, WK Schmalkalden, Stahl Silbitz

East German Cup Final
in Berlin
Lokomotive Leipzig 4, Vorwärts Frankfurt/Oder 1

East German Internationals
8/10/80 in Prague 1-0 v Czechoslovakia
15/10/80 in Leipzig 0-0 v Spain
19/11/80 in Halle 2-0 v Hungary
4/4/81 in Valetta 2-1 v Malta (WCQ)
19/4/81 in Udine 0-0 v Italy
2/5/81 in Chorzow 0-1 v Poland (WCQ)
19/5/81 in Senftenberg 5-0 v Cuba

European Cup
First Round
Olympiakos v Bayern Munich .... (2-4, 0-3)
Dynamo Berlin v Apoel Nicosia .... (3-0, 1-2)
Second Round
Bayern Munich v Ajax Amsterdam .... (5-1, 1-2)
Banik Ostrava v Dynamo Berlin .... (0-0, 1-1)
Quarterfinals
Bayern Munich v Banik Ostrava .... (2-0, 4-2)
Semifinals
Liverpool v Bayern Munich .... (0-0, 1-1)

Cup-Winners' Cup
First Round
Fortuna Düsseldorf v Austria Salzburg .... (5-0, 3-0)
Roma v Carl Zeiss Jena .... (3-0, 0-4)
Second Round
Waterschei v Fortuna Düsseldorf .... (0-0, 0-1)
Carl Zeiss Jena v Valencia .... (3-1, 0-1)
Quarterfinals
Fortuna Düsseldorf v Benfica .... (2-2, 0-1)
Carl Zeiss Jena v Newport County .... (2-2, 1-0)
Semifinals
Carl Zeiss Jena v Benfica .... (2-0, 0-1)
Final in Düsseldorf
Carl Zeiss Jena 1, Dinamo Tblisi 2

UEFA Cup
First Round
Hamburg SV v FC Sarajevo .... (4-2, 3-3)
IA Akranes v 1.FC Cologne .... (0-4, 0-6)
1.FC Kaiserslautern v Anderlecht .... (1-0, 2-3)
VfB Stuttgart v Pesoporikos Larnaca .... (6-0, 4-1)
Shaktior Donetsk v Eintracht Frankfurt .... (1-0, 0-3)
Ballymena United v Vorwärts Frankfurt/Oder .... (2-1, 0-3)
1.FC Magdeburg v FK Moss .... (2-1, 3-2)
Dynamo Dresden v Napreda Krusevac .... (1-0, 1-0)
Second Round
PSV Eindhoven v Hamburg SV .... (1-1, 1-2)
1.FC Cologne v Barcelona .... (0-1, 4-0)
1.FC Kaiserslautern v Standard Liege .... (1-2, 1-2)
Utrecht v Eintracht Frankfurt .... (2-1, 1-3)
VfB Stuttgart v Vorwärts Frankfurt/Oder .... (5-1, 2-1)
Torino v 1.FC Magdeburg .... (3-1, 0-1)
FC Twente v Dynamo Dresden .... (1-1, 0-0)
Third Round
Hamburg SV v St. Etienne .... (0-5, 0-1)
Eintracht Frankfurt v Sochaux .... (4-2, 0-2)
VfB Stuttgart v 1.FC Cologne .... (3-1, 1-4 aet)
Quarterfinals
Standard Liege v 1.FC Cologne .... (0-0, 2-3)
Semifinals
Ipswich Town v 1.FC Cologne .... (1-0, 1-0)

1981-82

Happy Happel

Could anyone knock Bayern Munich off their perch at the top of the Bundesliga? At the start of the new season, few thought so. The likeliest candidate seemed to be Hamburg, who had finished the past two years as runners-up, but who had brought in a new *Trainer*, the Austrian tactician Ernst Happel, during the summer. Yet many questioned whether the team's collective nerve could withstand the pressure of expectation.

1.FC Cologne were also given an outside chance at the title. For DM2,250,000, they had obtained the services of striker Klaus Allofs from Fortuna Düsseldorf—a record fee between two Bundesliga clubs. But Allofs took a while to settle and the bulk of the goals continued to be scored by Tony Woodcock, in his third season with the club, and 21-year-old winger Pierre Littbarski.

The pace-setters of the season proved to be Bayern. With five straight wins, they compiled a record sequence of thirteen consecutive victories, stretching over two seasons. They lost 3-1 at Eintracht Brunswick to end the streak, but remained at the top for four more weeks. But by then Cologne had hit form, and after thumping Bayern 4-0 in October, they had taken over leadership of the league. At the halfway stage, Cologne had 25 points, Bayern 24, and Hamburg 23.

By February, a free-scoring Hamburg had taken over the lead. Their giant centre-forward Horst Hrubesch was wreaking havoc in opposing defences, and would go on to score 27 of his side's 95 goals—many of them coming from the innovative swerving crosses of overlapping right-back Manfred Kaltz. The ageing Franz Beckenbauer was troubled by injuries and made few appearances in his final Bundesliga season. But with Uli Stein playing consistently in goal and Felix Magath providing plenty of inspiration, Hamburg were proving to be more than Bayern's equal. When they headed to the Munich Olympiastadion in April, it was first-place HSV facing second-place Bayern. With less than half an hour to play, Bayern were leading 3-1, but Hamburg scored three times in the last twenty minutes to win 4-3.

Two of those goals had come from Hrubesch—the second on the stroke of full time. Hamburg coasted to the title, finishing three points ahead of Cologne and five ahead of Bayern.

At the bottom of the table were MSV Duisburg, who had endured a wretched season away from home, failing to win a match and leaving the Bundesliga for the first time since its creation. That left only four teams in the exclusive group of ever-presents: Hamburg, Cologne, Frankfurt and Kaiserslautern—all of whom have now managed to extend this feat to the full thirty years.

The other club to be relegated were newly-promoted Darmstadt, whose modicum of confidence had dissipated in the wake of a midseason 4-1 defeat at Bayern. Thereafter the club won just one more game. Of the other promoted clubs, Werder Bremen proved to be the most successful, finishing a very credible fifth under their new *Trainer*, Otto Rehhagel. The much-travelled Rehhagel had previously spent time in charge of 1.FC Saarbrücken, Kickers Offenbach, Borussia Dortmund, Arminia Bielefeld, Fortuna Düsseldorf, and—for a brief spell in 1976—Werder Bremen. He would go on to set a record of longevity for a single Bundesliga club, leading Werder into a thirteenth season in 1993-94.

But Bremen's season was not without its difficulties. Late in their league match with Cologne, Werder goalkeeper Dieter Burdenski was taken off with an injury, his team holding a 1-0 lead. The 21-year-old substitute goalkeeper Hermann Rülander finished the remaining thirteen minutes of play, but conceded an equaliser. Worse was to come. The following week at Frankfurt, Rülander conceded seven goals and was taken off after 78 minutes and replaced by 20-year-old Robert Frese. Frese let in two more as Werder went down 9-2. Neither Rülander nor Frese ever played in the Bundesliga again. Burdenski, who had signed from Bielefeld after their expulsion from the league in 1971-72, played on until 1988 before retiring with 478 Bundesliga appearances, a record for a goalkeeper.

The newly-unified Second Division was won by Schalke, who had overtaken Kickers Offenbach with four matches left to play and finished three points clear of the pack. Crowds at the Parkstadion were often very impressive: 35,000 for the visits of Munich 1860 and Hanover, over 40,000 to see Hertha Berlin, and 60,000 for the season-ender against Fürth. Offenbach fell apart toward the end of the season, conceding three goals in the last seventeen minutes to lose 4-1 at home to Wattenscheid in their third-to-last match. They had to settle for third place and entered the newly-created playoff between the Bundesliga's sixteenth-placed club and the Second Bundesliga's third-placed club for a place in Division One. Bayer Leverkusen retained their Bundesliga status by beating Offenbach 3-1 on aggregate.

There was also an interesting twist to the Division Two goalscoring race, where Munich 1860's Rudi Völler overtook Hanover's Dieter Schatzschneider by scoring four goals against Offenbach on the last day in a 5-2 romp. 1860 were the fourth-placed team in the Second Division, but their considerable financial problems had forced the DFB to revoke their professional licence for the following season. Consequently, 1860 were banished to the Oberliga Bayern. Völler left the sinking ship and joined Werder Bremen the following season.

The West German Cup produced few shocks or odd results, with Bayern Munich scoring twenty times in the first four rounds before Paul Breitner's brace of goals allowed them to squeeze past Werder Bremen 2-1 in the quarterfinals. SSV 1846 Ulm, left out of the new Division Two the season before, had gained a place in the quarterfinals through a series of easy draws, but lost in extra time at Bochum. Before a semifinal crowd of 45,000 in the Ruhrstadion, Bayern were a bit fortunate to beat Bochum, 2-1, thanks to a hotly-disputed penalty awarded for Karl-Heinz Rummenigge's tumble in the penalty area. Nuremberg thumped Hamburg 2-0 in the other semifinal and would have won by a greater margin were it not for Uli Stein in the HSV goal. The final was not so much a case of Bayern winning as Nuremberg throwing it away. Nuremberg had taken a 2-0 halftime lead through Reinhard Hintermaier and Werner Dressel, but Bayern scored four after the interval as the Nuremberg defence went to pieces.

Bayern could engineer no such comeback in the European Cup, where Aston Villa continued the dominance of English clubs in the competition. Peter Withe bounced the winner in off the goalpost completely against the run of play as bad luck and an inspired young substitute goalkeeper named Nigel Spink foiled Bayern.

In the Cup-Winners' Cup quarterfinals, Eintracht Frankfurt went out to Tottenham Hotspur, whilst Lokomotive Leipzig lost to eventual winners Barcelona. Kaiserslautern lost in extra time to IFK Gothenburg in the UEFA Cup, and the Swedes went on to a surprising 4-0 aggregate win over Hamburg in the final.

Pierre Littbarski scored two goals on his debut as West Germany beat Austria 3-1 in Vienna in a World Cup qualifier. The German side then beat Finland 7-1 and Albania 8-0, with skipper Rummenigge getting a hat-trick in both games, to ensure passage to Spain. West Germany's first match in the tournament was a disastrous 2-1 defeat by Algeria in Gijon. A win over Chile left them needing victory over Austria to ensure qualification for the next stage. This they achieved, but only after the most dubious of performances. After the Germans had taken an early lead through Hrubesch, both sides—assured of passage to the second phase if the scoreline stayed the same—simply went through the motions, engaging in little more than a succession of back-passes to their goalkeepers. It was perhaps the most shameful performance in World Cup history. A 0-0 draw with England and a 2-1 elimination of the host nation led to a semifinal date with France, which proved to be the most dramatic of the tournament. The French had taken a 3-1 lead before the introduction of a half-fit Rummenigge and an overhead scissors-kick equaliser from Fischer sent the game to penalties. Unfortunately, the drama was overshadowed by Toni Schumacher's infamous foul on Patrick Battiston, which swung any neutral support towards the French. The Germans, though, won on penalties. Italy beat West Germany in the final, 3-1, with all goals coming in the second half.

The West German side had established themselves as one of the world's best, but the East Germans had, as usual, failed to finish atop their World Cup qualifying group. Domestically, Dynamo Berlin lost out on the chance of the double by a penalty kick. Finishing a comfortable seven points clear of runners-up Dynamo Dresden for their fourth straight league championship, the Berliners faced Dresden in the cup final. A late equaliser by Berlin's Hans-Jürgen Riediger took the game into extra time but it ended with the score still 1-1. Dresden, having lost on penalties in the 1975 final, this time came out on top 5-4. At the end of the season, 39-year-old Eberhard Vogel had announced his retirement after a 21-year career with Karl-Marx-Stadt and Jena, having made a record 440 Oberliga appearances.

Bundesliga

Club	P	W	D	L	Goals	Pts
1. Hamburg SV	34	18	12	4	95-45	48
2. 1.FC Cologne	34	18	9	7	72-38	45
3. Bayern Munich	34	20	3	11	77-56	43
4. 1.FC Kaiserslautern	34	16	10	8	70-61	42
5. Werder Bremen	34	17	8	9	61-52	42
6. Borussia Dortmund	34	18	5	11	59-40	41
7. Borussia Mönchengladbach	34	15	10	9	61-51	40
8. Eintracht Frankfurt	34	17	3	14	83-72	37
9. VfB Stuttgart	34	13	9	12	62-55	35
10. VfL Bochum	34	12	8	14	52-51	32
11. Eintracht Brunswick	34	14	4	16	61-66	32
12. Arminia Bielefeld	34	12	6	16	46-50	30
13. 1.FC Nuremberg	34	11	6	17	53-72	28
14. Karlsruhe SC	34	9	9	16	50-68	27
15. Fortuna Düsseldorf	34	6	13	15	48-73	25
16. Bayer Leverkusen	34	9	7	18	45-72	25
17. SV Darmstadt 98	34	5	11	18	46-82	21
18. MSV Duisburg	34	8	3	23	40-77	19

Top Scorers
Hrubesch (Hamburg SV) 27
Burgsmüller (Borussia Dortmund) 22
D Hoeness (Bayern Munich) 21
Breitner (Bayern Munich) 18
Reinders (Werder Bremen) 18
Worm (Eintracht Brunswick) 17
Cestonaro (SV Darmstadt 98) 16
Littbarski (1.FC Cologne) 15
Meier (Werder Bremen) 15
Pinkall (Borussia Mönchengladbach) 15
Woodcock (1.FC Cologne) 15

First Division Playoff
Kickers Offenbach v Bayer Leverkusen (0-1, 1-2); Leverkusen remain in Division One

Second Division

Club	P	W	D	L	Goals	Pts
1. FC Schalke 04	38	19	13	6	70-35	51
2. Hertha BSC Berlin	38	20	8	10	84-47	48
3. Kickers Offenbach	38	19	8	11	70-67	46
4. TSV 1860 Munich	38	19	7	12	87-56	45
5. Hanover 96	38	19	7	12	72-52	45
6. Waldhof Mannheim	38	16	12	10	51-44	44
7. Kickers Stuttgart	38	18	7	13	76-55	43
8. Hessen Kassel	38	15	13	10	56-46	43
9. Alemannia Aachen	38	15	11	12	47-39	41
10. Fortuna Cologne	38	14	11	13	70-72	39
11. Rot-Weiss Essen	38	15	8	15	60-62	38
12. Bayer Uerdingen	38	14	10	14	47-57	38
13. VfL Osnabrück	38	14	9	15	49-59	37
14. SpVgg Fürth	38	10	15	13	61-60	35
15. SC Freiburg	38	11	12	15	49-54	34
16. Union Solingen	38	11	11	16	51-62	33
17. Wattenscheid 09	38	8	15	15	41-62	31
18. Wormatia Worms	38	8	8	22	34-74	24
19. FC Freiburg	38	7	9	22	52-88	23
20. SpVgg Bayreuth	38	7	8	23	40-76	22

TSV 1860 Munich were relegated after their professional licence was revoked

Promoted: FC Augsburg, FSV Frankfurt, BV Lüttringhausen, TuS Schloss Neuhaus.

Top Scorers
Völler (TSV 1860 Munich) 37
Schatzschneider (Hanover 96) 34
Remark (Hertha BSC Berlin) 28
Kutzop (Kickers Offenbach) 18
Lenz (Union Solingen) 18
Mödrath (Fortuna Cologne) 18
Grillemeier (Rot-Weiss Essen) 17
Mohr (Hertha BSC Berlin) 17
Täuber (Kickers Stuttgart) 16
Pallaks (Hessen Kassel) 15
Sidka (TSV 1860 Munich) 15

Third Division Champions
Baden-Württemberg: SSV 1846 Ulm
Bayern: FC Augsburg
Berlin: Tennis Borussia Berlin
Hessen: FSV Frankfurt
Nord: Werder Bremen (Am.)
Nordrhein: BV 08 Lüttringhausen
Südwest: FC 08 Homburg
Westfalen: TuS Schloss-Neuhaus

West German Cup
First Round
1.FC Cologne (Am.) 3, OSC Bremerhaven 2 aet
1.FC Hassfurt 0, 1.FC Nuremberg 2
1.FC Saarbrücken 0, Alemannia Aachen 0 aet (1-2)
Arminia Hanover 6, TSV Kappeln 1
ASC Dudweiler 0, FSV Salmrohr 0 aet (1-3)
Bayern Hof 0, Waldhof Mannheim 2
Bayern Munich 8, SC Jülich 1910 0
BFC Preussen Berlin 2, Schwarz-Weiss Essen 0
Borussia Neunkirchen 1, Preussen Münster 0
Eintracht Frankfurt 6, BSC Brunsbüttel 1
Eintracht Trier 2, FSV Frankfurt (II) 1
FC Eislingen 0, SV Darmstadt 98 3
FC 08 Homburg 1, 1.FC Kaiserslautern (Am.) 4
FC Freiburg 4, TS Woltmershausen 0

FC Gohfeld 2, FVgg 06 Kastel 1
FC Tailfingen 3, SV Ruchheim 1
FC Grone 1910 0, Borussia Dortmund 4
FC St Pauli 1, 1.FC Bocholt 2 aet
Fortuna Düsseldorf 10, SSV Überherrn 1
FSV Frankfurt 2, Witten 07 0
FV Weinheim 2, SpVgg Ludwigsburg 1 aet
FV Offenberg 3, Reinickendorf Füchse 0
Hanover 96 5, Kickers Offenbach 1
Hertha BSC Berlin 5, Bayer Leverkusen (Am.) 1
Hessen Kassel 4, FC Schalke 04 1
Holstein Kiel 3, Hermannia Kassel 2 aet
Karlsruhe SC 3, Union Solingen 0
Kickers Stuttgart 1, Hamburg SV 5
MSV Duisburg 2, 1.FC Cologne 1
Rasensport Osnabrück 1, Fortuna Cologne 2
Rot-Weiss Essen 2, OSV Hanover 0
Rot-Weiss Lüdenscheid 1, VfL Wolfsburg 2
Rot-Weiss Oberhausen 5, Tuspo Ziegenhain 3
SC Geislingen 1, VfR Oli Bürstadt 1 aet (0-4)
SC Urania Hamburg 6, VfL Hamm 4 aet
SpVgg Bayreuth 3, Bayer Uerdingen 1
SpVgg Erkenschwick 0, Bayer Leverkusen 3
SpVgg Landshut 2, Hassia Bingen 3
SSV 1846 Ulm 1, 1.FC Nuremberg (Am.) 1 aet (3-1)
SSV Dillenburg 2, Borussia Mönchengladbach 7
SV Leiwen 3, SC Herford 2 aet
SV Neckargerach 4, Kickers Würzburg 2
SV Sandhausen 3, Arminia Bielefeld 6
SV Siegburg 04, FK Pirmasens 1
Tennis Borussia Berlin 4, Post SV Regensburg 3
TSV 1860 Munich 2, SpVgg Fürth 0
TSV Marktl 0, SC Freiburg 4
TSV Nördlingen 0, VfB Oldenburg 3
TSV Rendsburg 1, Viktoria Cologne 1 aet (0-3)
TSV Röttenbach 1, SpVgg Elversberg 3
TuS Celle 4, ESV Ingolstadt 2
TuS Lörrach-Stetten 1, Wormatia Worms 2
TuS Oberwinter 2, FC Rhade 0
TuS Xanten 0, Göttingen 05 1
Union Salzgitter 2, FC Augsburg 0
VfB Eppingen 3, Hanover 96 (Am.) 1
VfB Stuttgart (Am.) 4, VfL Klafeld-Geisweid 0
VfB Stuttgart 5, FC Rastatt 0
VfL Bochum 1, 1.FC Paderborn 2
VfL Osnabrück 5, VfB Bottrop 0
Viktoria Griesheim 8, Hamburg SV (Am.) 2
Wattenscheid 09 2, TuS Iserlohn 0 aet
Werder Bremen 1, 1.FC Kaiserslautern 0
Wuppertal SV 1, Eintracht Brunswick 0

Second Round
1.FC Bocholt 2, FV Offenburg 1
1.FC Cologne (Am.) 3, Bayer Leverkusen 3 aet (0-5)
1.FC Kaiserslautern (Am.) 1, SC Urania Hamburg 3
Alemannia Aachen 2, SC Freiburg 1
Arminia Bielefeld 0, 1.FC Nuremberg 1
Bayern Munich 5, SV Neckargerach 1
Borussia Mönchengladbach 3, Arminia Hanover 1
Borussia Neunkirchen 1, Wormatia Worms 2
FC Freiburg 5, TuS Celle 1
Fortuna Düsseldorf 3, Eintracht Frankfurt 1
FSV Frankfurt 2, FC Gohfeld 0
FSV Salmrohr 0, Werder Bremen 3
FV Weinheim 1, VfL Osnabrück 3
Göttingen 05 1, Rot-Weiss Oberhausen 0 aet
Hamburg SV 2, Eintracht Trier 1
Hertha BSC Berlin 6, Viktoria Griesheim 2
Hessen Kassel 1, Fortuna Cologne 0 aet
Holstein Kiel 3, Union Salzgitter 2
Karlsruhe SC 3, Wuppertal SV 0
MSV Duisburg 3, FK Pirmasens 0
Rot-Weiss Essen 4, SV Leiwen 1
SpVgg Elversberg 7, Borussia Dortmund 4
SSV 1846 Ulm 2, VfL Wolfsburg 1
SV Darmstadt 98 4, Hassia Bingen 1
Tennis Borussia Berlin 1, VfB Oldenburg 2
TSV 1860 Munich 0, Waldhof Mannheim 1 aet
VfB Eppingen 2, BFC Preussen Berlin 0
VfB Stuttgart (Am.) 1, SpVgg Bayreuth 2
VfB Stuttgart 10, TuS Oberwinter 1
VfL Bochum 3, FC Tailfingen 1
Viktoria Cologne 1, VfR Oli Bürstadt 1 aet (0-1 aet)
Wattenscheid 09 2, Hanover 96 2 aet (0-6)

Third Round
1.FC Bocholt 3, VfR Oli Bürstadt 1
1.FC Nuremberg 2, Fortuna Düsseldorf 0
Alemannia Aachen 0, Hamburg SV 3
Bayern Munich 4, Borussia Dortmund 0
FC Freiburg 2, Holstein Kiel 0
Hanover 96 2, VfL Osnabrück 0
Hertha BSC Berlin 1, SSV 1846 Ulm 2
Hessen Kassel 1, VfL Bochum 2
MSV Duisburg 1, Karlsruhe SC 2 aet
Rot-Weiss Essen 4, Bayer Leverkusen 1
SC Urania Hamburg 1, Göttingen 05 3
SpVgg Bayreuth 2, VfB Oldenburg 0 (aet)
SV Darmstadt 98 1, Werder Bremen 3
VfB Stuttgart 0, Borussia Mönchengladbach 2
Waldhof Mannheim 3, VfB Eppingen 1
Wormatia Worms 0, FSV Frankfurt 2

Fourth Round
1.FC Bocholt 3, Göttingen 05 3 aet (2-3)
FC Freiburg 0, Bayern Munich 3
Hamburg SV 6, Karlsruhe SC 1
Hanover 96 1, 1.FC Nuremberg 3
Rot-Weiss Essen 0, Borussia Mönchengladbach 4
SSV 1846 Ulm 1, FSV Frankfurt 0
Waldhof Mannheim 1, VfL Bochum 1 aet (1-3)
Werder Bremen 2, SpVgg Bayreuth 0

Quarterfinals
1.FC Nuremberg 3, Borussia Mönchengladbach 1
Göttingen 05 2, Hamburg SV 4
VfL Bochum 3, SSV 1846 Ulm 1 aet
Werder Bremen 1, Bayern Munich 2 aet

Semifinals
1.FC Nuremberg 2, Hamburg SV 0
VfL Bochum 1, Bayern Munich 2

Final
in Frankfurt
Bayern Munich 4, 1.FC Nuremberg 2

West German Internationals
2/9/81 in Chorzow 2-0 v Poland
23/9/81 in Bochum 7-1 v Finland (WCQ)
14/10/81 in Vienna 3-1 v Austria (WCQ)
18/11/81 in Dortmund 8-0 v Albania (WCQ)
22/11/81 in Düsseldorf 4-0 v Bulgaria (WCQ)
17/2/82 in Hanover 3-1 v Portugal
21/3/82 in Rio de Janeiro 0-1 v Brazil
24/3/82 in Buenos Aires 1-1 v Argentina
14/4/82 in Cologne 2-1 v Czechoslovakia
12/5/82 in Oslo 4-2 v Norway
16/6/82 in Gijon 1-2 v Algeria (WC)
20/6/82 in Gijon 4-1 v Chile (WC)
25/6/82 in Gijon 1-0 v Austria (WC)
29/6/82 in Madrid 0-0 v England (WC)
2/7/82 in Madrid 2-1 v Spain (WC)
8/7/82 in Seville 3-3 v France aet (WC); West Germany won on penalties
11/7/82 in Madrid 1-3 v Italy (WC)

East German Oberliga

Club	P	W	D	L	Goals	Pts
1. Dynamo Berlin	26	18	5	3	74-27	41
2. Dynamo Dresden	26	15	4	7	50-24	34
3. Lokomotive Leipzig	26	13	7	6	53-29	33
4. Vorwärts Frankfurt/Oder	26	14	5	7	56-39	33
5. Carl Zeiss Jena	26	14	4	8	49-27	32
6. 1.FC Magdeburg	26	13	6	7	49-42	32
7. Rot-Weiss Erfurt	26	10	8	8	55-44	28
8. Hansa Rostock	26	9	7	10	37-40	25
9. FC Karl-Marx-Stadt	26	9	6	11	50-38	24
10. Wismut Aue	26	8	7	11	33-48	23
11. Chemie Halle	26	8	7	11	28-46	23
12. Sachsenring Zwickau	26	4	6	16	24-57	14
13. Energie Cottbus	26	3	5	18	21-62	11
14. Chemie Buna Schkopau	26	3	5	18	21-77	11

Top Scorers
Schnuphase (Carl Zeiss Jena) 19
Heun (Rot-Weiss Erfurt) 16
Pietsch (Vorwärts Frankfurt/Oder) 16
Streich (1.FC Magdeburg) 16
Minge (Dynamo Dresden) 14
Richter (Karl-Marx-Stadt) 13
Netz (Dynamo Berlin) 12
Troppa (Dynamo Berlin) 12
Busse (Rot-Weiss Erfurt) 11
Andrich (Vorwärts Frankfurt/Oder) 10
Riediger (Dynamo Berlin) 10

Oberliga Promotion Playoff

Club	P	W	D	L	Goals	Pts
1. Chemie Böhlen	8	6	1	1	16-4	13
2. 1.FC Union Berlin	8	4	3	1	11-8	11
3. Vorwärts Stralsund	8	2	3	3	7-9	7
4. Stahl Riesa	8	2	2	4	10-11	6
5. Motor Nordhausen	8	0	3	5	5-17	3

Second Division (Staffel A)

Club	P	W	D	L	Goals	Pts
1. Vorwärts Stralsund	22	15	5	2	60-20	35
2. Vorwärts Neubrandenburg	22	14	4	4	53-20	32
3. TSG Bau Rostock	22	12	6	4	49-27	30
4. ISG Schwerin-Süd	22	13	4	5	53-36	30
5. Post Neubrandenburg	22	11	6	5	45-28	28
6. Schiffahrt/Hafen Rostock	22	10	5	7	37-26	25
7. TSG Wismar	22	8	8	6	39-38	24
8. Vorwärts Schwerin	22	9	4	9	39-36	22
9. Hydraulik Parchim	22	7	1	14	34-47	15
10. Motor WW Warnemünde	22	3	3	16	25-66	9
11. Lokomotive Anklam	22	3	3	16	18-65	9
12. TSG Neustrelitz	22	2	1	19	16-59	5

Promoted: KKW Greifswald, Lok/Armaturen Prenzlau, Veritas Wittenberge

Second Division (Staffel B)

Club	P	W	D	L	Goals	Pts
1. 1.FC Union Berlin	22	15	5	2	53-17	35
2. Motor Babelsberg	22	15	2	5	64-19	32
3. Chemie PCK Schwedt	22	14	4	4	43-27	32
4. Dynamo Fürstenwalde	22	13	5	4	54-27	31
5. Stahl Brandenburg	22	12	4	6	46-38	28
6. KWO Berlin	22	10	3	9	34-29	23
7. Stahl Eisenhüttenstadt	22	7	8	7	37-32	22
8. Stahl Hennigsdorf	22	7	5	10	44-45	19
9. Bergmann Borsig Berlin	22	6	5	11	37-48	17
10. Motor Hennigsdorf	22	2	7	13	28-55	11
11. EAB 47 Berlin	22	3	4	15	23-57	10
12. Stahl Finow	22	2	0	20	15-84	4

Promoted: Rotation Berlin, Halbleiterwerk Frankfurt/Oder, Chemie Premnitz

Second Division (Staffel C)

Club	P	W	D	L	Goals	Pts
1. Chemie Böhlen	22	15	3	4	53-19	33
2. Vorwärts Dessau	22	14	5	3	45-24	33
3. Dynamo Eisleben	22	11	6	5	43-21	28
4. Chemie Leipzig	22	11	5	6	40-25	27
5. Stahl Blankenburg	22	7	8	7	26-25	22
6. Einheit Wernigerode	22	9	4	9	35-41	22
7. Lokomotive Stendal	22	5	11	6	30-31	21
8. Motor Altenburg	22	6	8	8	29-34	20
9. Stahl Thale	22	7	5	10	32-31	19
10. Stahl NW Leipzig	22	6	6	10	28-34	18
11. Chemie Zeitz	22	4	5	13	19-51	13
12. Empor Halle	22	2	4	16	19-63	8

Promoted: Chemie Markkleeberg, Motor Schönebeck, Chemie Wolfen

Second Division (Staffel D)

Club	P	W	D	L	Goals	Pts
1. Stahl Riesa	22	15	4	3	61-26	34
2. Aktivist Schwarze Pumpe	22	12	5	5	28-33	29
3. Aktivist Brieske-Senftenberg	22	11	6	5	37-28	28
4. Lokomotive Dresden	22	11	5	6	44-29	27
5. Fortschritt Bischofswerda	22	8	5	9	26-31	21
6. Motor FH Karl-Marx-Stadt	22	7	6	9	28-34	20
7. TSG Gröditz	22	6	8	8	23-34	20
8. Vorwärts Kamenz	22	5	9	8	22-30	19
9. Motor Werdau	22	7	4	11	40-37	18
10. Aufbau Krumhermersdorf	22	6	5	11	29-41	17
11. Robur Zittau	22	5	6	11	29-42	16
12. Motor Ascota Karl-Marx-Stadt	22	4	7	11	25-37	15

Promoted: Lokomotive Cottbus, Fortschritt Neustadt, Vorwärts Plauen

Second Division (Staffel E)

Club	P	W	D	L	Goals	Pts
1. Motor Nordhausen	22	17	3	2	56-16	37
2. Wismut Gera	22	15	5	2	61-16	35
3. Motor Suhl	22	15	2	5	47-20	32
4. Chemie IW Ilmenau	22	11	6	5	30-23	28
5. Motor Weimar	22	8	8	6	31-32	24
6. Kali Werra Tiefenort	22	8	6	8	26-21	22
7. Motor Rudisleben	22	5	11	6	20-22	21
8. Motor Eisenach	22	6	7	9	36-32	19
9. Fortschritt Weida	22	5	6	11	35-49	16
10. Glückauf Sondershausen	22	5	6	11	33-47	16
11. WK Schmalkalden	22	2	4	16	17-63	8
12. Stahl Silbitz	22	2	2	18	15-66	6

Relegation playoff: Fortschritt Weida v Glückauf Sondershausen (0-3, 1-4). Sondershausen remain in Staffel E.
Promoted: Motor Hermsdorf, TSG Ruhla, Motor Steinach

East German Cup Final
in Berlin
Dynamo Dresden 1, Dynamo Berlin 1 aet (Dresden won on penalties)

East German Internationals
10/10/81 in Leipzig 2-3 v Poland (WCQ)
11/11/81 in Jena 5-1 v Malta (WCQ)
26/1/82 in Natal 1-3 v Brazil
10/2/82 in Athens 1-0 v Greece
2/3/82 in Baghdad 0-0 v Iraq
14/4/82 in Leipzig 1-0 v Italy
11/5/82 in Moscow 0-1 v USSR
19/5/82 in Halmstad 2-2 v Sweden

1981-82

European Cup
Preliminary Round
St. Etienne v Dynamo Berlin .... (1-1, 0-2)
First Round
Oesters Vaexjö v Bayern Munich .... (0-1, 0-5)
Dynamo Berlin v FC Zurich .... (2-0, 1-3)
Second Round
Benfica v Bayern Munich .... (0-0, 1-4)
Dynamo Berlin v Aston Villa .... (1-2, 1-0)
Quarterfinals
Uni Craiova v Bayern Munich .... (0-2, 1-1)
Semifinals
CSKA Sofia v Bayern Munich .... (4-3, 0-4)
Final in Rotterdam
Aston Villa 1, Bayern Munich 0

Cup-Winners' Cup
Preliminary Round
Politehnica Timisoara v Lokomotive Leipzig .... (2-0, 0-5)
First Round
Eintracht Frankfurt v PAOK Salonika .... (2-0, 0-2 aet)
Frankfurt won on penalties
Swansea City v Lokomotive Leipzig .... (0-1, 1-2)
Second Round
SKA Rostov v Eintracht Frankfurt .... (1-0, 0-2)
Lokomotive Leipzig v Velez Mostar .... (1-1, 1-1 aet)
Leipzig won on penalties
Quarterfinals
Tottenham Hotspur v Eintracht Frankfurt .... (2-0, 1-2)
Lokomotive Leipzig v Barcelona .... (0-3, 2-1)

UEFA Cup
First Round
Hamburg SV v Utrecht .... (0-1, 6-3)
Hajduk Split v VfB Stuttgart .... (3-1, 2-2)
1.FC Kaiserslautern v Akademik Sofia .... (1-0, 2-1)
1.FC Magdeburg v Borussia Mönchengladbach ...... (3-1, 0-2)
Dinamo Tirana v Carl Zeiss Jena .... (1-0, 0-4)
Zenit Leningrad v Dynamo Dresden .... (1-2, 1-4)
Second Round
Bordeaux v Hamburg SV .... (2-1, 0-2)
Spartak Moscow v 1.FC Kaiserslautern .... (2-1, 0-4)
Borussia Mönchengladbach v Dundee United .... (2-0, 0-5)
Real Madrid v Carl Zeiss Jena .... (3-2, 0-0)
Feyenoord v Dynamo Dresden .... (2-1, 1-1)
Third Round
Aberdeen v Hamburg SV .... (3-2, 1-3)
SC Lokoren v 1.FC Kaiserslautern .... (1-0, 1-4)
Quarterfinals
Real Madrid v 1.FC Kaiserslautern .... (3-1, 0-5)
Hamburg SV v Xamax Neuchatel .... (3-2, 0-0)
Semifinals
1.FC Kaiserslautern v IFK Gothenburg .... (1-1, 1-2 aet)
Radnicki Nis v Hamburg SV .... (2-1, 1-5)
Final
IFK Gothenburg v Hamburg SV .... (1-0, 3-0)

1982-83

Rolff to the rescue

Just eight goals separated champions from runners-up this season, only the second time in Bundesliga history that the top two teams finished level on points. Hamburg SV picked up where they left off, stretching their unbeaten run into the new season and setting a new record of 36 consecutive games without defeat. The series ended on 24 January at the Weserstadion in Bremen, where Werder ran out 3-2 winners. And it was Bremen who were to catch up with Hamburg and provide a thrilling finish to the season.

On the last day, Werder struggled to a tense 3-2 home win over VfL Bochum, which meant that Hamburg needed both points from their match against Schalke in Gelsenkirchen. It was 1-1 until the 52nd minute when Wolfgang Rolff, who had joined HSV at the start of the season from Fortuna Cologne, surged through onto a pass from Felix Magath to beat Walter Junghans and win the championship.

By that time, Hamburg had already won the European Cup by beating the Italian giants Juventus, ending the six-year run of English domination in that competition. Rolff had done a splendid job of man-marking Michel Platini and Magath had scored the decisive goal, but it was a relatively dour contest.

Come the end of the season Rolff had established himself as one of the rising stars of the Bundesliga, teaming up with Jimmy Hartwig and Felix Magath in the Hamburg midfield to supply the goals for Horst Hrubesch and Jürgen Milewski. HSV also boasted a solid defence, with Ditmar Jakobs, Jürgen Groh, Bernd Wehmeyer, and Holger Hieronymus. They fielded a very settled team, using just seventeen players, three of whom played two matches or less. And they were well coached, with Ernst Happel's tactics of forechecking and a ruthless offside trap proving difficult for any opponent to overcome.

Bremen, though, had assembled quite a formidable squad in the two seasons since their promotion from Division Two. *Trainer* Otto Rehhagel had purchased Rudi Völler from TSV 1860 Munich, and partnered him with the rangy Frank Neubarth from Concordia Hamburg. Wolfgang Sidka, who had been Völler's teammate at 1860, came over during the summer, linking up with Benno Möhlmann, Günter Hermann and Yasuhiko Okudera in the Werder midfield.

Hamburg's triumph, and the rise of Werder, meant there was no room at the top for Bayern Munich, who could only finish fourth. Bayern replaced *Trainer* Pal Csernai toward the end of the season with assistant Reinhard Saftig. After showing patchy form, goalkeeper Walter Junghans was sold to Schalke, where netminder Norbert Nigbur's marital problems were affecting his normally reliable form. Junghans' replacement at Bayern was Jean-Marie Pfaff, the Belgian international. Pfaff's Bundesliga debut, away to Bremen, proved something of a nightmare, as he fumbled a long throw-in from Werder's Uwe Reinders into his own net for the game's only goal. A similar catastrophe—also in Bremen—would befall Frankfurt's Jürgen Pahl, who somehow contrived to throw the ball into his own net in a 3-0 defeat.

Apart from Bremen, the only other team to beat HSV all season were Arminia Bielefeld. Yet in spite of the fact that Hamburg lost just two matches, Werder managed to keep pace, dropping just two points at home (to Cologne and Düsseldorf) and ending up with 52 points—enough to have won the championship in all but three of the previous nineteen seasons.

Hamburg's reign at the top was interrupted for one week in November, after second-place Borussia Dortmund had taken on sixth-place Arminia Bielefeld at the Westfalenstadion. Bielefeld took an early lead through Frank Pagelsdorf, but soon Manfred Burgsmüller equalised for Dortmund. There was no further score until the second half—when Dortmund scored ten without reply to win 11-1. Burgsmüller wound up with five goals, and Bernd Klotz netted a hat-trick. But the following week Dortmund lost at Frankfurt—and Hamburg resumed their league leadership.

Eintracht Brunswick's new signing Lutz Eigendorf—who had fled from East Germany in March of 1979—was killed in a car crash early in the season. The circumstances of the crash were never fully explained and some still believe the East German *Stasi* had a hand in the tragedy (Eigendorf had played for the East German police team, Dynamo Berlin). Less mysteriously, Frankfurt's Willi Neuberger retired at the age of 37 after 520 Bundesliga games, including spells at Dortmund, Bremen and Wuppertal. Also bidding farewell to the Bundesliga was the outspoken Bayern midfielder Paul Breitner. Hamburg's Horst Hrubesch joined Standard Liege for the following season before re-joining the Bundesliga two years later for a short stint with Dortmund.

Waldhof Mannheim won the Second Division championship to attain Bundesliga status for the first time. Their triumph was fitting, for they had led the way most of the season, paced by the goalscoring prowess of Fritz Walter and Paul Linz and the likes of Roland Dickgiesser and Günter Sebert in defence. Kickers Offenbach, who had fallen apart in their bid for promotion the season before, made no mistake this time and gained the second spot, with Uwe Bein finishing as the club's top goalscorer.

Just one season after returning to the Bundesliga, Schalke 04 once again found relegation staring them in the face. With three matches to play, they were in sole possession of last place, one point behind Hertha Berlin and two points behind Karlsruhe. A 2-0 win over Bochum took them off the bottom, but despite a 1-0 win in

Karlsruhe. A 2-0 win over Bochum took them off the bottom, but despite a 1-0 win in Munich the following week against Bayern they wound up playing off against Second Division Bayer Uerdingen to keep their place in the top flight. Not even a return-leg crowd of 60,000 in the Gelsenkirchen Parkstadion could prevent them from losing 4-2 on aggregate, as Bayer gained promotion to Division One for the third time in nine years.

The mighty were falling in other places as well. Borussia Mönchengladbach finished a disappointing twelfth. Injuries had hampered *Trainer* Jupp Heynckes' ability to restore the club to its former glory, with Lothar Matthäus the lone ever-present in the side. But there would prove to be no end in sight to Borussia's battle against mediocrity.

Dieter Schatzschneider, who had finished second in the Division Two goalscoring race the previous season with Hanover 96, took the honours this season with 31 goals for Fortuna Cologne. He would join Hamburg the following season and then move on to Schalke a year later, before returning to Fortuna, eventually to become the Second Division's all-time leading goalscorer.

Fortuna fans will also remember this season as the one in which they nearly won the West German Cup. The competition had undergone two significant changes: just 64 teams entered the first round proper instead of 128, and any amateur team was now automatically drawn at home when paired with an opponent from the Bundesliga. The new format seemed to suit Fortuna, as well as Cologne's top side, 1.FC. Both progressed to the final, giving the event its first *Lokalderby* in history. 1.FC were drawn at home in every round and had a fairly comfortable time of things until they met VfB Stuttgart in the semifinals. There, they needed an extra-time goal from Paul Steiner to defeat VfB in an enthralling cup-tie. Fortuna had needed replays with SSV Ulm and Borussia Mönchengladbach, but they rather surprisingly had no problems in disposing of Dortmund in the other semifinal.

Of course, there could be only one site for the final: the Müngersdorf in Cologne, where 61,000 saw a single goal from Pierre Littbarski give the first division side the trophy. Fortuna, though, could count themselves rather unlucky to have lost and gave their First Division neighbours all they could handle.

It was also a banner year for Bremen's Rudi Völler, who came top of the Bundesliga goalscoring list and was voted West German Footballer of the Year. He made his international debut as a substitute in the European Championship qualifying match in Belfast, but Northern Ireland won 1-0. Another defeat, by the same score, came in a friendly in Lisbon against Portugal, which marked the last international appearance of Manfred Kaltz.

The East German national side suffered through yet another uninspiring season, failing to win any of their four European Championship qualifiers and consequently being eliminated from contention. In the Oberliga, Dynamo Berlin finished a hefty eight points clear at the top to take their fifth championship in a row, not losing a single league match all season. Vorwärts Frankfurt were runners-up, which was to prove their best-ever finish after leaving Berlin. Magdeburg enjoyed a convincing 4-0 cup final win over Karl-Marx-Stadt, with Joachim Streich scoring twice. Streich, the Oberliga's top scorer, also collected East German Footballer of the Year honours. In seven cup final appearances, Magdeburg had yet to lose. But it would prove to be their last major trophy.

Bundesliga

Club	P	W	D	L	Goals	Pts
1. Hamburg SV	34	20	12	2	79-33	52
2. Werder Bremen	34	23	6	5	76-38	52
3. VfB Stuttgart	34	20	8	6	80-47	48
4. Bayern Munich	34	17	10	7	74-33	44
5. 1.FC Cologne	34	17	9	8	69-42	43
6. 1.FC Kaiserslautern	34	14	13	7	57-44	41
7. Borussia Dortmund	34	16	7	11	78-62	39
8. Arminia Bielefeld	34	12	7	15	46-71	31
9. Fortuna Düsseldorf	34	11	8	15	63-75	30
10. Eintracht Frankfurt	34	12	5	17	48-57	29
11. Bayer Leverkusen	34	10	9	15	43-66	29
12. Borussia Mönchengladbach	34	12	4	18	64-63	28
13. VfL Bochum	34	8	12	14	43-49	28
14. 1.FC Nuremberg	34	11	6	17	44-70	28
15. Eintracht Brunswick	34	8	11	15	42-65	27
16. FC Schalke 04	34	8	6	20	48-68	22
17. Karlsruhe SC	34	7	7	20	39-86	21
18. Hertha BSC Berlin	34	5	10	19	43-67	20

Top Scorers
Völler (Werder Bremen) 23
Allgöwer (VfB Stuttgart) 21
Edvaldsson (Fortuna Düsseldorf) 21
K-H Rummenigge (Bayern Munich) 20
Hrubesch (Hamburg SV) 18
Burgsmüller (Borussia Dortmund) 17
D Hoeness (Bayern Munich) 17
Abramczik (Borussia Dortmund) 16
Littbarski (1.FC Cologne) 16
Cha (Eintracht Frankfurt) 15

First Division Playoff
Bayer Uerdingen v FC Schalke 04 (3-1, 1-1); Uerdingen promoted to Division One

Second Division

Club	P	W	D	L	Goals	Pts
1. Waldhof Mannheim	38	21	10	7	83-38	52
2. Kickers Offenbach	38	21	8	9	77-45	50
3. Bayer Uerdingen	38	19	10	9	65-44	48
4. Hessen Kassel	38	10	5	13	69-54	45
5. Kickers Stuttgart	38	18	8	12	78-51	44
6. Fortuna Cologne	38	15	13	10	76-50	43
7. SV Darmstadt 98	38	16	10	12	77-61	42
8. SC Freiburg	38	13	16	9	50-45	42
9. Alemannia Aachen	38	15	10	13	49-53	40
10. VfL Osnabrück	38	16	6	16	66-65	38
11. MSV Duisburg	38	14	9	15	55-57	37
12. Hanover 96	38	13	10	15	70-72	36
13. BV Lüttringhausen	38	13	8	17	53-76	34
14. Rot-Weiss Essen	38	12	9	17	56-60	33
15. Wattenscheid 09	38	13	7	18	59-65	33
16. Union Solingen	38	11	10	17	56-76	32
17. FC Augsburg	38	11	10	17	32-54	32
18. SpVgg Fürth	38	10	11	17	55-75	31
19. FSV Frankfurt	38	9	8	21	50-86	26
20. TuS Schloss Neuhaus	38	7	8	23	43-92	22

Top Scorers
Schatzschneider (Fortuna Cologne) 31
Mattern (SV Darmstadt 98) 21
Walter (Waldhof Mannheim) 21
Bein (Kickers Offenbach) 20
Täuber (Kickers Stuttgart) 20
Michelberger (Kickers Offenbach) 19
Dreher (Kickers Stuttgart) 18
Schäfer (Union Solingen) 18
Metzler (SpVgg Fürth) 17
Traser (Hessen Kassel) 17

Third Division Champions
Baden-Württemberg: SSV 1846 Ulm
Bayern: SpVgg Unterhaching
Berlin: SC Charlottenburg
Hessen: VfR Bürstadt
Nord: FC St Pauli
Nordrhein: Rot-Weiss Oberhausen
Südwest: 1.FC Saarbrücken
Westfalen: SV Hamm

Second Division Playoffs

Northern Group	P	W	D	L	Goals	Pts
1. Rot-Weiss Oberhausen	6	2	4	0	8-6	8
2. SC Charlottenburg	6	2	2	2	10-7	6
3. SpVgg Hamm	6	2	1	3	8-10	5
4. FC St Pauli	6	2	1	3	8-11	5

Southern Group	P	W	D	L	Goals	Pts
1. SSV 1846 Ulm	6	2	4	0	4-2	8
2. 1.FC Saarbrücken	6	2	3	1	10-10	7
3. VfR Bürstadt	6	2	1	3	10-11	5
4. SpVgg Unterhaching	6	1	2	3	9-10	4

West German Cup
First Round
1.FC Cologne 3, Bayer Uerdingen 1
1.FC Cologne (Am.) 1, FSV Mainz 05 3
Arminia Hanover 0, Eintracht Trier 2 aet
ASV Bergedorf 85 1, Bayern Munich 5 aet
Bayer Uerdingen (Am.) 0, KSV Baunatal 3
Bayern Hof 0, Arminia Bielefeld 5
Bayern Munich (Am.) 5, Werder Bremen (Am.) 3 aet
FC Ensdorf 0, Union Solingen 3

FC Freiburg 1, Rot-Weiss Lüdenscheid 1 aet (1-2)
FC Schalke 04 1, Hessen Kassel 0
Fortuna Cologne 2, SC Freiburg 0
FSV Frankfurt 3, 1.FC Kaiserslautern 2
FV Offenburg 1, Werder Bremen 4
Germania Walsrode 0, 1.FC Nuremberg 3
Hanover 96 (Am.) 2, Bayer Leverkusen 3 aet
Hanover 96 0, SV Darmstadt 98 4
Hertha 03 Zehlendorf 2, Hertha BSC Berlin 4 aet
Kickers Offenbach 1, Fortuna Düsseldorf 3 aet
MSV Duisburg 1, Hamburg SV 1 aet (0-5)
Olympia Germaringen 1, SpVgg Hamm 2
Rot-Weiss Essen 1, Borussia Dortmund 3
SpVgg Bayreuth 3, SpVgg Fürth 1
SSV 1846 Ulm 3, TuS Schloss Neuhaus 1
SV Sandhausen 1, Rot-Weiss Oberhausen 3
SV Heide 1, TSV 1860 Munich 1 aet (1-2)
VfB Stuttgart (Am.) 1, Kickers Stuttgart 5
VfB Wissen 0, Borussia Mönchengladbach 4
VfL Bochum 3, Karlsruhe SC 1
VfL Osnabrück 0, VfB Stuttgart 2
Waldhof Mannheim 2, Eintracht Frankfurt 0
Wattenscheid 09 0, Eintracht Brunswick 3
Wormatia Worms 3, Alemannia Aachen 1 aet

Second Round
1.FC Cologne 3, Bayer Leverkusen 1
Arminia Bielefeld 2, 1.FC Nuremberg 0
Eintracht Trier 1, Kickers Stuttgart 2
Eintracht Brunswick 2, Bayern Munich 0
Fortuna Düsseldorf 0, VfB Stuttgart 2
FSV Mainz 05 3, FC Schalke 04 6 aet
Hamburg SV 3, Werder Bremen 2
Rot-Weiss Oberhausen 0, Borussia Dortmund 1
Rot-Weiss Lüdenscheid 1, SV Darmstadt 98 3
SpVgg Bayreuth 0, Hertha BSC Berlin 1
SpVgg Hamm 1, VfL Bochum 1 aet (1-6)
SSV 1846 Ulm 0, Fortuna Cologne 0 aet (0-3)
TSV 1860 Munich 1, Bayern Munich (Am.) 0
Union Solingen 1, Borussia Mönchengladbach 2
Waldhof Mannheim 1, FSV Frankfurt 0
Wormatia Worms 2, KSV Baunatal 1

Third Round
1.FC Cologne 5, Kickers Stuttgart 1
Borussia Mönchengladbach 1, Waldhof Mannheim 0
Borussia Dortmund 4, SV Darmstadt 98 2
Eintracht Brunswick 1, Fortuna Cologne 2
FC Schalke 04 2, Arminia Bielefeld 2 aet (1-0)
Hertha BSC Berlin 2, Hamburg SV 1
TSV 1860 Munich 1, VfL Bochum 3
Wormatia Worms 0, VfB Stuttgart 4

Quarterfinals
1.FC Cologne 5, FC Schalke 04 0
Borussia Mönchengladbach 2, Fortuna Cologne 2 aet (1-2)
Borussia Dortmund 3, VfL Bochum 1 aet
VfB Stuttgart 2, Hertha BSC Berlin 0

Semifinals
1.FC Cologne 3, VfB Stuttgart 2 aet
Fortuna Cologne 5, Borussia Dortmund 0

Final
in Cologne
1.FC Cologne 1, Fortuna Cologne 0

West German Internationals
22/9/82 in Munich 0-0 v Belgium
13/10/82 in London 2-1 v England
17/11/82 in Belfast 0-1 v Northern Ireland (ECQ)
23/2/83 in Lisbon 0-1 v Portugal
30/3/83 in Tirana 2-1 v Albania (ECQ)
23/4/83 in Izmir 3-0 v Turkey (ECQ)
27/4/83 in Vienna 0-0 v Austria (ECQ)
7/6/83 in Luxembourg 4-2 v Yugoslavia

East German Oberliga

Club	P	W	D	L	Goals	Pts
1. Dynamo Berlin	26	20	6	0	72-22	46
2. Vorwärts Frankfurt/Oder	26	13	8	5	56-29	34
3. Carl Zeiss Jena	26	15	4	7	46-29	34
4. Lokomotive Leipzig	26	12	7	7	45-27	31
5. Rot-Weiss Erfurt	26	11	9	6	45-37	31
6. 1.FC Magdeburg	26	10	9	7	52-32	29
7. Dynamo Dresden	26	12	5	9	51-43	29
8. Hansa Rostock	26	11	6	9	38-40	28
9. FC Karl-Marx-Stadt	26	10	6	10	41-41	26
10. Wismut Aue	26	6	8	12	30-45	20
11. Chemie Halle	26	5	7	14	41-53	17
12. 1.FC Union Berlin	26	5	7	14	23-50	17
13. Chemie Böhlen	26	4	5	17	31-80	13
14. Sachsenring Zwickau	26	2	5	19	21-64	9

Top Scorers
Streich (1.FC Magdeburg) 19
Minge (Dynamo Dresden) 17
Andrich (Vorwärts Frankfurt/Oder) 16
Riediger (Dynamo Berlin) 16
Havenstein (Chemie Böhlen) 13
Schnuphase (Carl Zeiss Jena) 13
Heun (Rot-Weiss Erfurt) 12
Pastor (Chemie Halle) 12
Ernst (Dynamo Berlin) 9
Gütschow (Dynamo Dresden) 9
Quade (1.FC Union Berlin) 9

Oberliga Promotion Playoff

Club	P	W	D	L	Goals	Pts
1. Stahl Riesa	8	4	4	0	20-4	12
2. Chemie Leipzig	8	5	1	2	13-9	11
3. Stahl Brandenburg	8	3	2	3	13-9	8
4. Wismut Gera	8	3	1	4	14-17	7
5. Schiffahrt/Hafen Rostock	8	1	0	7	7-28	2

Second Division (Staffel A)

Club	P	W	D	L	Goals	Pts
1. Schiffahrt/Hafen Rostock	22	12	9	1	55-23	33
2. Vorwärts Neubrandenburg	22	13	7	2	54-26	33
3. Dynamo Schwerin	22	10	7	5	44-22	27
4. Vorwärts Stralsund	22	11	5	6	46-30	27
5. ISG Schwerin-Süd	22	7	8	7	29-32	22
6. Post Neubrandenburg	22	7	7	8	33-34	21
7. TSG Wismar	22	8	5	9	31-32	21
8. TSG Bau Rostock	22	7	6	9	37-44	20
9. Lok/Armaturen Prenzlau	22	7	6	9	32-40	20
10. Veritas Wittenberge	22	6	8	8	33-42	20
11. KKW Greifswald	22	6	2	14	24-51	14
12. Hydraulik Parchim	22	1	4	17	23-65	6

Promoted: BM Neubrandenburg, Motor Schwerin, Motor Stralsund

Second Division (Staffel B)

Club	P	W	D	L	Goals	Pts
1. Stahl Brandenburg	22	16	3	3	53-21	35
2. Dynamo Fürstenwalde	22	11	8	3	49-30	30
3. Energie Cottbus	22	11	8	3	37-30	30
4. Stahl Eisenhüttenstadt	22	11	3	8	41-34	25
5. Chemie Premnitz	22	8	7	7	37-42	23
6. Chemie PCK Schwedt	22	9	4	9	43-31	22
7. Motor Babelsberg	22	7	8	7	38-27	22
8. Stahl Hennigsdorf	22	7	7	8	44-37	21
9. Rotation Berlin	22	7	5	10	37-45	19
10. KWO Berlin	22	5	8	9	29-33	18
11. Bergmann Borsig Berlin	22	4	5	13	31-59	13
12. Halbleiterwerk Frankfurt/Oder	22	2	2	18	27-77	6

Promoted: EAB Berlin, Motor Eberswalde, Motor Süd Brandenburg

Second Division (Staffel C)

Club	P	W	D	L	Goals	Pts
1. Chemie Leipzig	22	20	1	1	43-9	41
2. Vorwärts Dessau	22	17	3	2	56-23	37
3. Chemie Buna Schkopau	22	11	8	3	45-23	30
4. Dynamo Eisleben	22	8	5	9	42-43	21
5. Stahl Thale	22	8	5	9	27-29	21
6. Chemie Markkleeberg	22	5	10	7	28-29	20
7. Einheit Wernigerode	22	5	8	9	24-37	18
8. Chemie Wolfen	22	6	5	11	29-41	17
9. Motor Schönebeck	22	5	7	10	28-43	17
10. Lokomotive Stendal	22	5	6	11	20-31	16
11. Motor Altenburg	22	6	2	14	22-44	14
12. Stahl Blankenburg	22	3	6	13	26-38	12

Promoted: Stahl NW Leipzig, Empor Tangermünde, Fortschritt Weissenfels

Second Division (Staffel D)

Club	P	W	D	L	Goals	Pts
1. Stahl Riesa	22	18	4	0	63-15	40
2. Aktivist Schwarze Pumpe	22	11	4	7	36-28	26
3. Vorwärts Kamenz	22	11	4	7	43-37	26
4. Motor FH Karl-Marx-Stadt	22	10	4	8	31-34	24
5. Aktivist Brieske-Senftenberg	22	9	5	8	28-27	23
6. Motor Wedau	22	8	5	9	33-29	21
7. Fortschritt Bischofswerda	22	8	5	9	32-29	21
8. TSG Gröditz	22	9	3	10	24-34	21
9. Lokomotive Dresden	22	5	10	7	28-28	20
10. Vorwärts Plauen	22	5	7	10	24-34	17
11. Lokomotive Cottbus	22	7	1	14	23-40	15
12. Fortschritt Neustadt	22	3	4	15	16-46	10

Promoted: Chemie Döbern, Aufbau Krumhermersdorf, Empor Tabak Dresden

Second Division (Staffel E)

Club	P	W	D	L	Goals	Pts
1. Wismut Gera	22	14	5	3	62-17	33
2. Motor Nordhausen	22	13	4	5	45-24	30
3. Motor Suhl	22	11	6	5	35-21	28
4. Chemie IW Ilmenau	22	10	7	5	31-21	27
5. Glückauf Sondershausen	22	10	6	6	51-38	26
6. Motor Rudisleben	22	9	7	6	39-28	25
7. Kali Werra Tiefenort	22	7	11	4	26-15	25
8. TSG Ruhla	22	7	6	9	25-35	20
9. Motor Weimar	22	7	5	10	31-35	19
10. Motor Hermsdorf	22	5	6	11	22-46	16
11. Motor Eisenach	22	2	7	13	21-38	11
12. Motor Steinach	22	1	2	19	13-83	4

Promoted: WK Schmalkalden, Robotron Sömmerda, Fortschritt Weida

East German Cup Final

in Berlin

1.FC Magdeburg 4, Karl-Marx-Stadt 0

East German Internationals
8/9/82 in Reykjavik 1-0 v Iceland
22/9/82 in Burgas 2-2 v Bulgaria
13/10/82 in Glasgow 0-2 v Scotland (ECQ)
17/11/82 in Karl-Marx-Stadt 4-1 v Rumania
10/2/83 in Tunis 2-0 v Tunisia
23/2/83 in Dresden 2-1 v Greece
16/3/83 in Magdeburg 3-1 v Finland
30/3/83 in Leipzig 1-2 v Belgium (ECQ)
13/4/83 in Gera 3-0 v Bulgaria
27/4/83 in Brussels 1-2 v Belgium (ECQ)
14/5/83 in Berne 0-0 v Switzerland (ECQ)
26/7/83 in Leipzig 1-3 v USSR

European Cup
First Round
Dynamo Berlin v Hamburg SV .... (1-1, 0-2)
Second Round
Hamburg SV v Olympiakos Piraeus .... (1-0, 4-0)
Quarterfinals
Dynamo Kiev v Hamburg SV .... (0-3, 2-1)
Semifinals
Real Sociedad v Hamburg SV .... (1-1, 1-2)
Final in Athens
Hamburg SV 1, Juventus 0

Cup-Winners' Cup
First Round
Torpedo Moscow v Bayern Munich .... (1-1, 0-0)
Dynamo Dresden v B1893 Copenhagen .... (3-2, 1-2)
Second Round
Tottenham Hotspur v Bayern Munich .... (1-1, 1-4)
Quarterfinals
Bayern Munich v Aberdeen .... (0-0, 2-3)

UEFA Cup
First Round
AEK Athens v 1.FC Cologne .... (0-1, 0-5)
Borussia Dortmund v Glasgow Rangers .... (0-0, 0-2)
1.FC Kaiserslautern v Trabzonspor .... (3-0, 3-0)
Vorwärts Frankfurt/Oder v Werder Bremen .... (1-3, 2-0)
Viking Stavanger v Lokomotive Leipzig .... (1-0, 2-3)
Carl Zeiss Jena v Bordeaux .... (3-1, 0-5)
Second Round
Werder Bremen v Brage IK .... (2-0, 6-2)
Glasgow Rangers v 1.FC Cologne .... (2-1, 0-5)
Napoli v 1.FC Kaiserslautern .... (1-2, 0-2)
Third Round
Seville v 1.FC Kaiserslautern .... (1-0, 0-4)
1.FC Cologne v Roma .... (1-0, 0-2)
Dundee United v Werder Bremen .... (2-1, 1-1)
Quarterfinals
1.FC Kaiserslautern v Uni Craiova .... (3-2, 0-1)

1983-84

VfB for a change

Helmut Benthaus had earned a Bundesliga championship medal as a player with 1.FC Cologne in the inaugural Bundesliga season of 1963-64. Shortly afterwards he went to Switzerland as player-coach and later manager of FC Basle, where he added seven Swiss championships and three Cup winners medals to his collection. His success south of the border linked him with several Bundesliga clubs and for a time he looked likely to take charge of Kaiserslautern. But eventually he became *Trainer* of VfB Stuttgart.

Founder members of the Bundesliga but still to be crowned champions, VfB had worked their way through a host of different *Trainers* in the hope of getting it right. The closest they had come was in 1979 when they finished second to Hamburg SV. But under Benthaus, Stuttgart finally took their first Bundesliga title—and their first German championship since 1952. This made Benthaus the most wanted *Trainer* in the land and he not only received a lucrative offer from Barcelona but was also asked by the DFB to take over from the retiring Jupp Derwall as coach of the national team. But Stuttgart refused to release him from his contract. A year later, after VfB had finished tenth, Benthaus was unceremoniously released. He spent the next few years with FC Basle before turning his back on football management.

The hub of Stuttgart's team was the Icelandic international Asgeir Sigurvinsson, who had arrived in 1982 after an indifferent season with Bayern Munich. He formed a superb four-man midfield unit with young Guido Buchwald, wily Karl Allgöwer and long-serving veteran Hermann Ohlicher. Allgöwer and Ohlicher scored plenty of goals to supplement those of striker Peter Reichert. Defensively, the team was built around brothers Karlheinz and Bernd Förster, with reliable keeper Helmut Roleder conceding just 33 goals all season.

The championship race was fierce, though, and Stuttgart were one of a number of teams capable of coming out on top. With two matches to play, three teams were level on points: VfB, Hamburg and Mönchengladbach, with Bayern close behind. But to everyone's surprise the destination of the championship was effectively settled with one match to go. Hamburg lost 2-0 at home to Frankfurt, and Mönchengladbach lost 4-1 in Dortmund. Meanwhile Ohlicher had slotted home a Bernd Förster free-kick to give Stuttgart a 2-1 win in Bremen. So suddenly VfB were two points ahead of the rest, with such a superior goal difference that the only way they could lose the title was to be beaten by five or more goals in their final match at home to Hamburg.

The season finalé, in front of a capacity crowd of 71,000 at the Neckarstadion, saw Stuttgart match HSV in every respect, and even though VfB eventually lost to a last-minute Jürgen Milewski goal, it could hardly spoil the celebrations. Mönchengladbach also won their last match to end on the same number of points as Stuttgart and Hamburg, giving the Bundesliga an unprecedented three-way tie at the top, with VfB champions on goal difference.

Goals were the name of the game this season—a record total of 1097 were scored for an average of 3.6 per game. Quite a few of them were let in by Kickers Offenbach; the 106 they conceded is second only to Tasmania Berlin in 1965-66 as the worst-ever defensive record. There was also a record number of red and yellow cards, with Michael Sziedat of Eintracht Frankfurt contributing rather more than his fair share by being sent off twice—in each of the local derbies against Offenbach. Records of a different kind were being set by the bottom club Nuremberg who went the entire season without gaining a point away from home, extending their woeful record to 29 consecutive away defeats over two seasons. They also achieved a new first by losing ten matches in a row. Meanwhile Frankfurt retained their ever-present Bundesliga status only by winning the play-off 6-1 on aggregate over Second Division MSV Duisburg.

Unexpectedly, the first managerial casualty of the season was Rinus Michels, who left Cologne of his own accord on August 23—two days before the club's first regular season match. Hannes Löhr was quickly brought in as his replacement.

Two clubs dominated the Second Bundesliga: Schalke 04 and Karlsruhe SC. With seven matches left in the season Karlsruhe overtook Schalke at the top: Hertha Berlin pumped five goals past Walter Junghans in Gelsenkirchen as Karlsruhe were winning at Lüttringhausen. That proved the critical difference in the race, with Duisburg finishing a distant third.

Oberliga Nordrhein side 1.FC Bocholt were the season's sensation in the West German Cup. They beat Brunswick in extra time in the third round and were rewarded with a quarterfinal home tie against Bayern. Before a crowd of over 16,000 at their tiny Stadion-am-Hünting, Bocholt gave their famous visitors a torrid time and only the form of Jean-Marie Pfaff in the Bayern goal allowed the Bavarians to leave town with a 2-1 victory. Karlsruhe managed not one but two spectacular comebacks in their second-round tie with Kaiserslautern. After thirteen minutes they found themselves 2-0 down but they eventually fought back to 3-3 and sent the match into extra time. Lautern then went 4-3 up but Karlsruhe again responded and won 5-4, Uwe Bühler's goal coming with a minute to go.

Both semifinals provided their fair share of excitement. At the Bökelberg, Mönchengladbach had taken a 3-1 lead over Werder Bremen after 75 minutes, but the visitors rallied to go ahead 4-3. With two minutes to play, Gladbach's Wilfried Hannes put the ball in the Bremen net, but the goal was disallowed for offside, to furious protests from the 34,500 crowd and the Borussia players. The controversy had scarcely died down when Hans-Jörg Criens again found the net for Gladbach, and this time the goal stood. Criens then scored in extra time to put Werder out.

The other semifinal proved to be a showcase for the budding talents of 18-year-old Schalke midfielder Olaf Thon. In an ebb-and-flow match against Bayern Munich, Thon scored a sublime hat-trick, his final goal coming in the dying minutes of extra time. The score at half-time was 2-3, after 90 minutes it was 4-4, and after extra time it was 6-6. Bayern won the replay, 3-2.

There was no shortage of excitement in the final, either. Frank Mill put Mönchengladbach in the lead after 33 minutes, heading in a Lothar Matthäus corner, but Wolfgang Dremmler equalised for Bayern with eight minutes left. Extra time followed, but there were no further goals, and rather than a replay, it had been decided that penalties would settle the outcome. Each side converted four of their five attempts, sending the competition into the "sudden death" phase, where Norbert Ringels' effort crashed against the post and ultimately cost Gladbach the cup.

Meanwhile, one-time Bundesliga champions Eintracht Brunswick were in dire financial straits, forcing new club president Günter Mast to introduce wage cuts and new sponsorship deals to keep the club afloat. He even proposed re-naming the club SV Jägermeister to expand their sponsorship deal with the drinks manufacturer, but the DFB vetoed the idea.

In the European Cup, defending champions Hamburg met defeat in the second round at the hands of Dinamo Bucharest, whilst Dynamo Berlin moved one stage further before losing to AS Roma, who were eventually to lose on penalties to Liverpool in the final. Dynamo Berlin were in fact the only German team to reach the quarterfinal of any of the European competitions, making this the least successful German campaign since the formation of the Bundesliga. After Dynamo's second round match at Partizan Belgrade, Falko Götz and Dirk Schlegel slipped away and headed for the West German embassy in Belgrade.

East Germany restructured its *Staffel* system at the end of this season, reverting to two regional divisions of eighteen clubs. This meant the number of Second Division clubs was cut nearly in half, but the performances of Motor Schwerin, Chemie Döbern, and WK Schmalkaden—none of whom managed to win more than one match all season—suggested this was not necessarily a bad thing.

The East German nationals won their Olympic qualifying group, but the government forced them to boycott the Los Angeles games. The absence of Eastern bloc countries allowed West Germany in through the back door, and they reached the quarterfinals before losing 5-2 to Yugoslavia.

Northern Ireland handed West Germany a 1-0 defeat in Hamburg, thus doing the double over Jupp Derwall's men in their European Championship qualifying group. But in the last qualifying match, an Albanian defender's error with ten minutes to play allowed Gerd Strack to head in a winner, and a grateful West Germany finished atop their group. In France, a draw with Portugal, a win over Rumania, and a defeat by Spain meant that Germany did not qualify for the semifinals—and that had Derwall not chose to retire, he might have been told to anyway. The new man in charge was none other than West Germany's World Cup-winning captain of 1974, Franz Beckenbauer.

Bundesliga

Club	P	W	D	L	Goals	Pts
1. VfB Stuttgart	34	19	10	5	79-33	48
2. Hamburg SV	34	21	6	7	75-36	48
3. Borussia Mönchengladbach	34	21	6	7	81-48	48
4. Bayern Munich	34	20	7	7	84-41	47
5. Werder Bremen	34	19	7	8	79-46	45
6. 1.FC Cologne	34	16	6	12	70-57	38
7. Bayer Leverkusen	34	13	8	13	50-50	34
8. Arminia Bielefeld	34	12	9	13	40-49	33
9. Eintracht Brunswick	34	13	6	15	54-69	32
10. Bayer Uerdingen	34	12	7	15	66-79	31
11. Waldhof Mannheim	34	10	11	13	45-58	31
12. 1.FC Kaiserslautern	34	12	6	16	68-69	30
13. Borussia Dortmund	34	11	8	15	54-65	30
14. Fortuna Düsseldorf	34	11	7	16	63-75	29
15. VfL Bochum	34	10	8	16	58-70	28
16. Eintracht Frankfurt	34	7	13	14	45-61	27
17. Kickers Offenbach	34	7	5	22	48-106	19
18. 1.FC Nuremberg	34	6	2	26	38-85	14

Top Scorers
K-H Rummenigge (Bayern Munich) 26
K Allofs (1.FC Cologne) 20
Mill (Borussia Mönchengladbach) 19
Schreier (VfL Bochum) 18
Völler (Werder Bremen) 18
Littbarski (1.FC Cologne) 17
Walter (Waldhof Mannheim) 16
T Allofs (1.FC Kaiserslautern) 15
Funkel (Bayer Uerdingen) 15
Schatzschneider (Hamburg SV) 15
Waas (Bayer Leverkusen) 15

First Division Playoff
MSV Duisburg v Eintracht Frankfurt (0-5, 1-1); Frankfurt remain in Division One

Second Division

Club	P	W	D	L	Goals	Pts
1. Karlsruhe SC	38	25	7	6	94-45	57
2. FC Schalke 04	38	23	9	6	95-45	55
3. MSV Duisburg	38	20	10	8	69-41	50
4. Hessen Kassel	38	20	8	10	68-39	48
5. Union Solingen	38	17	10	11	70-54	44
6. Alemannia Aachen	38	17	10	11	49-43	44
7. SC Freiburg	38	13	17	8	50-49	43
8. Kickers Stuttgart	38	13	13	12	54-52	39
9. Fortuna Cologne	38	14	10	14	66-65	38
10. 1.FC Saarbrücken	38	14	10	14	61-69	38
11. Hertha BSC Berlin	38	13	11	14	64-57	37
12. SV Darmstadt 98	38	11	13	14	48-72	35
13. SSV 1846 Ulm	38	10	12	16	58-68	32
14. Hanover 96	38	10	12	16	54-69	32
15. Wattenscheid 09	38	11	10	17	58-74	32
16. Rot-Weiss Oberhausen	38	10	11	17	51-62	31
17. Rot-Weiss Essen	38	7	15	16	48-63	29
18. SC Charlottenburg	38	10	9	19	49-68	29
19. VfL Osnabrück	38	6	6	26	46-66	29
20. BV Lüttringhausen	38	6	6	26	36-87	18

Top Scorers
Günther (Karlsruhe SC) 30
Wohlfarth (MSV Duisburg) 30
Schäfer (Union Solingen) 21
Traser (Hessen Kassel) 20
Klinsmann (Kickers Stuttgart) 19
Rombach (Alemannia Aachen) 19
Schüler (Karlsruhe SC) 19
Täuber (FC Schalke 04) 19
Löw (SC Freiburg) 17
Gaedke (SC Charlottenburg) 15
Glöde (Hertha BSC Berlin) 15
Hauck (SSV 1846 Ulm) 15
Jurgeleit (Union Solingen) 15
Kuhl (SV Darmstadt 98) 15

Third Division Champions
Baden-Württemberg: FC Freiburg
Bayern: TSV 1860 Munich
Berlin: Blau-Weiss 90 Berlin
Hessen: VfR Bürstadt
Nord: Werder Bremen (Am.)
Nordrhein: 1.FC Bocholt
Südwest: FC 08 Homburg
Westfalen: FC Gütersloh

Second Division Playoffs

Northern Group	P	W	D	L	Goals	Pts
1. Blau-Weiss 90 Berlin	8	4	3	1	13-8	11
2. FC St Pauli	8	4	3	1	12-7	11
3. 1.FC Bocholt	8	2	4	2	11-11	8
4. FC Gütersloh	8	2	2	4	14-17	6
5. SV Lurup Hamburg	8	1	2	5	13-20	4

Southern Group	P	W	D	L	Goals	Pts
1. FC 08 Homburg	6	5	1	0	15-6	11
2. VfR Bürstadt	6	3	1	2	11-8	7
3. FC Freiburg	6	1	1	4	11-15	3
4. TSV 1860 Munich	6	1	1	4	7-15	3

West German Cup
First Round
1.FC Cologne (Am.) 2, FC Gohfeld 1
Alemannia Aachen 1, VfL Bochum 0
Arminia Hanover 1, SpVgg Neu-Isenburg 2
ASV Burglengenfeld 2, KSV Baunatal 1 aet
FC Augsburg 2, SpVgg Bayreuth 1 aet
FC 08 Homburg 0, Hertha BSC Berlin 6
FC Schalke 04 3, Fortuna Düsseldorf 0
Fortuna Cologne 2, Borussia Mönchengladbach 3
FSV Frankfurt 1, Arminia Bielefeld 3
FSV Mainz 05 0, VfB Stuttgart 1
Göttingen 05 4, Eintracht Frankfurt 2
Hamburg SV 4, Borussia Dortmund 1
Hassia Bingen 4, 1.FC Bocholt 4 aet (2-3)
Hessen Kassel 0, Bayern Munich 3
MSV Duisburg 1, 1.FC Kaiserslautern 2 aet
Rot-Weiss Essen 3, Hanover 96 4
Rot-Weiss Lüdenscheid 3, SSV 1846 Ulm 2
SC Charlottenburg 2, Wattenscheid 09 1
SC Freiburg 3, Union Solingen 2
SC Herford 0, Karlsruhe SC 3
SC Pfullendorf 0, Eintracht Brunswick 7
SG Ellingen-Bonefeld 2, Holstein Kiel 3
SpVgg Fürth 2, TuS Lingen 1 aet
SV Heidingsfeld 5, SV Göppingen 1
SV Hummelsbüttel 1, Kickers Offenbach 6
SV Sandhausen 0, Bayer Uerdingen 0 aet (0-2)
TuS Schloss Neuhaus 2, BV Lüttringhausen 0
VfL Osnabrück 3, 1.FC Nuremberg 1
VfR Forst 1, 1.FC Cologne 6
Waldhof Mannheim 3, Bayer Leverkusen 1
Werder Bremen (Am.) 1, Kickers Stuttgart 3
Werder Bremen 5, SV Darmstadt 98 0

Second Round
1.FC Bocholt 3, Kickers Stuttgart 1
1.FC Cologne (Am.) 1, VfB Stuttgart 8
1.FC Cologne 6, Kickers Offenbach 2
Alemannia Aachen 1, Waldhof Mannheim 0
ASV Burglengenfeld 0, Werder Bremen 3
Borussia Mönchengladbach 3, Arminia Bielefeld 0
Eintracht Brunswick 2, VfL Osnabrück 1
FC Augsburg 0, Bayern Munich 6
Holstein Kiel 1, Bayer Uerdingen 2
Karlsruhe SC 5, 1.FC Kaiserslautern 4 aet
SC Charlottenburg 0, FC Schalke 04 3
SC Freiburg 1, Hamburg SV 4
SpVgg Fürth 1, Rot-Weiss Lüdenscheid 0
SpVgg Neu-Isenburg 0, Göttingen 05 1
SV Heidingsfeld 1, Hanover 96 3
TuS Schloss Neuhaus 0, Hertha BSC Berlin 2

Third Round
1.FC Bocholt 3, Eintracht Brunswick 1 aet
Alemannia Aachen 0, Werder Bremen 1 aet
Bayer Uerdingen 0, Bayern Munich 0 aet (0-1)
FC Schalke 04 2, Karlsruhe SC 1
Göttingen 05 0, Hertha BSC Berlin 1
Hanover 96 3, 1.FC Cologne 2
SpVgg Fürth 0, Borussia Mönchengladbach 6
VfB Stuttgart 1, Hamburg SV 1 aet (4-3)

Quarterfinals
1.FC Bocholt 1, Bayern Munich 2
Hanover 96 0, Borussia Mönchengladbach 1
Hertha BSC Berlin 3, FC Schalke 04 3 aet (0-2)
Werder Bremen 1, VfB Stuttgart 0

Semifinals
Borussia Mönchengladbach 5, Werder Bremen 4 aet
FC Schalke 04 6, Bayern Munich 6 aet (2-3)

Final
in Frankfurt
Bayern Munich 1, Borussia Mönchengladbach 1 (aet; Bayern won on penalties)

West German Internationals
7/9/83 in Budapest 1-1 v Hungary
5/10/83 in Gelsenkirchen 3-0 v Austria (ECQ)
26/10/83 in Berlin 5-1 v Turkey (ECQ)
16/11/83 in Hamburg 0-1 v Northern Ireland (ECQ)
20/11/83 in Saarbrücken 2-1 v Albania (ECQ)
15/2/84 in Varna 3-2 v Bulgaria
29/2/84 in Brussels 1-0 v Belgium
28/3/84 in Hanover 2-1 v Soviet Union
18/4/84 in Strasbourg 0-1 v France
22/5/84 in Zurich 1-0 v Italy
14/6/84 in Strasbourg 0-0 v Portugal (EC)
17/6/84 in Lens 2-1 v Rumania (EC)
20/6/84 in Paris 0-1 v Spain (EC)

East German Oberliga

Club	P	W	D	L	Goals	Pts
1. Dynamo Berlin	26	17	5	4	66-36	39
2. Dynamo Dresden	26	14	9	3	61-28	37
3. Lokomotive Leipzig	26	16	5	5	56-28	37
4. Vorwärts Frankfurt/Oder	26	13	7	6	56-36	33
5. 1.FC Magdeburg	26	12	8	6	56-33	32
6. FC Karl-Marx-Stadt	26	10	10	6	37-34	30
7. Rot-Weiss Erfurt	26	10	8	8	36-39	28
8. Wismut Aue	26	9	7	10	28-34	25
9. Hansa Rostock	26	8	8	10	32-41	24
10. Carl Zeiss Jena	26	7	6	13	50-63	20

	P	W	D	L	Goals	Pts
11. Stahl Riesa	26	7	6	13	41-55	20
12. Chemie Leipzig	26	4	6	16	21-49	14
13. 1.FC Union Berlin	26	4	6	16	27-55	14
14. Chemie Halle	26	1	9	16	32-68	11

Top Scorers

Ernst (Dynamo Berlin)	20
Minge (Dynamo Dresden)	17
Pietsch (Vorwärts Frankfurt/Oden)	17
Kühn (Lokomotive Leipzig)	15
Streich (1.FC Magdeburg)	13
Richter (Lokomotive Leipzig)	12
Mothes (Wismut Aue)	11
J Pfahl (Stahl Riesa)	11
Raab (Carl Zeiss Jena)	11
Schulz (Dynamo Berlin)	10
Steinbach (1.FC Magdeburg)	10

Oberliga Promotion Playoff

Club	P	W	D	L	Goals	Pts
1. Stahl Brandenburg	8	6	1	1	21-7	13
2. Motor Suhl	8	3	4	1	13-9	10
3. Vorwärts Dessau	8	3	1	4	18-17	7
4. Sachsenring Zwickau	8	2	1	5	11-16	5
5. Dynamo Schwerin	8	2	1	5	10-24	5

Second Division (Staffel A)

Club	P	W	D	L	Goals	Pts
1. Vorwärts Neubrandenburg	22	14	4	4	39-18	32
2. Dynamo Schwerin	22	11	6	5	51-26	28
3. Post Neubrandenburg	22	12	4	6	41-23	28
4. Schiffahrt/Hafen Rostock	22	10	6	6	40-32	26
5. Vorwärts Stralsund	22	9	7	6	40-29	25
6. TSG Bau Rostock	22	10	5	7	37-31	25
7. ISG Schwerin	22	8	7	7	42-36	23
8. Motor Stralsund	22	8	6	8	41-42	22
9. Lok/Armaturen Prenzlau	22	9	3	10	41-42	21
10. TSG Wismar	22	7	5	10	27-35	19
11. BM Neubrandenburg	22	2	6	14	33-63	10
12. Motor Schwerin	22	1	3	18	20-75	5

Second Division (Staffel B)

Club	P	W	D	L	Goals	Pts
1. Stahl Brandenburg	22	15	4	3	62-29	34
2. Motor Babelsburg	22	12	7	3	40-24	31
3. Stahl Eisenhüttenstadt	22	13	5	4	34-22	31
4. Energie Cottbus	22	12	6	4	57-26	30
5. Dynamo Fürstenwalde	22	12	5	5	44-32	29
6. Rotation Berlin	22	10	7	5	41-24	27
7. Chemie PCK Schwedt	22	10	4	8	47-31	24
8. Chemie Premnitz	22	7	4	11	20-36	18
9. Stahl Hennigsdorf	22	4	4	14	36-55	12
10. EAB 47 Berlin	22	4	4	14	24-53	12
11. Motor Eberswalde	22	4	2	16	24-60	10
12. Motor Süd Brandenburg	22	2	2	18	22-59	6

Second Division (Staffel C)

Club	P	W	D	L	Goals	Pts
1. Vorwärts Dessau	22	13	6	3	56-24	32
2. Chemie Böhlen	22	10	8	4	48-30	28
3. Chemie Wolfen	22	9	8	5	44-28	26
4. Dynamo Eisleben	22	10	6	6	37-27	26
5. Chemie Markkleeberg	22	7	11	4	36-22	25
6. Chemie Buna Schkopau	22	9	7	6	39-30	25
7. Stahl NW Leipzig	22	6	10	6	41-41	22
8. Einheit Wernigerode	22	9	4	9	32-33	22
9. Fortschritt Weissenfels	22	7	2	13	42-47	16
10. Stahl Thale	22	4	8	10	23-33	16
11. Motor Schönebeck	22	5	6	11	33-58	16
12. Empor Tangermünde	22	4	2	16	18-76	10

Second Division (Staffel D)

Club	P	W	D	L	Goals	Pts
1. Sachsenring Zwickau	22	15	4	3	63-21	34
2. Aktivist Schwarze Pumpe	22	11	6	5	42-23	28
3. Aufbau Krumhermersdorf	22	10	8	4	40-26	28
4. Fortschritt Bischofswerda	22	11	4	7	47-39	26
5. Aktivist Brieske-Senftenberg	22	11	4	7	34-30	26
6. Motor FH Karl-Marx-Stadt	22	8	9	5	37-23	25
7. TSG Gröditz	22	10	5	7	37-28	25
8. Lokomotive Dresden	22	10	3	9	40-37	23
9. Empor Tabak Dresden	22	5	5	12	24-36	15
10. Vorwärts Kamenz	22	5	5	12	29-44	15
11. Motor Werdau	22	4	4	14	16-49	12
12. Chemie Döbern	22	1	5	16	13-66	7

1983-84

Second Division (Staffel E)

Club	P	W	D	L	Goals	Pts
1. Motor Suhl	22	14	3	5	36-21	31
2. Motor Nordhausen	22	11	8	3	30-15	30
3. Glückauf Sondershausen	22	12	5	5	34-18	29
4. Robotron Sömmerda	22	11	5	6	32-22	27
5. Kali Werra Tiefenort	22	10	7	5	25-19	27
6. Wismut Gera	22	10	6	6	31-26	26
7. Motor Rudisleben	22	8	4	10	25-28	20
8. Motor Weimar	22	6	7	9	24-25	19
9. Chemie IW Ilmenau	22	6	6	10	18-26	18
10. TSG Ruhla	22	5	7	10	17-27	17
11. Fortschritt Weida	22	5	4	13	18-33	14
12. WK Schmalkaden	22	1	4	17	12-42	6

The Second Division was re-structured into two "Staffeln" for the following season, with the top six finishers in each of the five "Staffeln" qualifying. Vorwärts Neubrandenburg did not participate at this level and were replaced by ISG Schwerin.
Also promoted: Dynamo Berlin II, Dynamo Dresden II, Vorwärts Frankfurt/Oder II, Rot-Weiss Erfurt II, Carl Zeiss Jena II, Motor Grimma.

East German Cup Final
in Berlin
Dynamo Dresden 2, Dynamo Berlin 1

East German Internationals
24/8/83 in Bucharest 0-1 v Rumania
12/10/83 in Berlin 3-0 v Switzerland (ECQ)
16/11/83 in Halle 2-1 v Scotland (ECQ)
15/2/84 in Athens 3-1 v Greece
28/3/84 in Erfurt 2-1 v Czechoslovakia

European Cup
First Round
Hamburg SV received a bye
Dynamo Berlin v Jeunesse D'Esch .... (4-1, 2-0)
Second Round
Dinamo Bucharest v Hamburg SV .... (3-0, 2-3)
Dynamo Berlin v Partizan Belgrade .... (2-0, 0-1)
Quarterfinals
Roma v Dynamo Berlin .... (3-0, 1-2)

Cup-Winners' Cup
Preliminary Round
Swansea City v 1.FC Magdeburg .... (1-1, 0-1)
First Round
Wacker Innsbruck v 1.FC Cologne .... (1-0, 1-7)
1.FC Magdeburg v Barcelona .... (1-5, 0-2)
Second Round
Ujpest Dozsa v 1.FC Cologne .... (3-1, 2-4)

UEFA Cup
First Round
1.FC Kaiserslautern v Watford .... (3-1, 0-3)
Anorthosis Larnaca v Bayern Munich .... (0-1, 0-10)
VfB Stuttgart v Levsky Spartak .... (1-1, 0-1)
Werder Bremen v Malmö FF .... (1-1, 2-1)
IB Vestmannaeyar v Carl Zeiss Jena .... (0-0, 0-3)
Nottingham Forest v Vorwärts Frankfurt/Oder ...... (2-0, 1-0)
Bordeaux v Lokomotive Leipzig .... (2-3, 0-4)
Second Round
Lokomotive Leipzig v Werder Bremen .... (1-0, 1-1)
PAOK Saloniki v Bayern Munich .... (0-0, 0-0 aet)
Bayern won on penalties
Sparta Rotterdam v Carl Zeiss Jena .... (3-2, 1-1)
Third Round
Bayern Munich v Tottenham Hotspur .... (1-0, 0-2)
Sturm Graz v Lokomotive Leipzig .... (2-0, 0-1)

1984-85

Germany's Wembley

With Bayern Munich netting eleven million marks from Inter Milan for Karl-Heinz Rummenigge, they could well afford the two million mark-plus outlay needed to acquire Lothar Matthäus from Borussia Mönchengladbach. The 26-cap Matthäus had played 162 Bundesliga games for Gladbach but jumped at the chance to join Bayern, candidly expressing his belief that they were more likely to be in the race for honours than his current club. The trickiest part of his contract negotiations was to ensure he could continue wearing Puma boots when the rest of the team had to wear Adidas. Another player on the move was Hans-Peter Briegel, leaving Kaiserslautern for Italian side Verona, with whom he went on to win a championship medal in his very first season.

Bayern already had plenty of talent and experience in their team—Sören Lerby, Klaus Augenthaler, Dieter Hoeness and the rest—but lacked a little imagination and unpredictability. Whilst this deficiency was partially addressed by the acquisition of Matthäus, further assistance came in the form an 18-year-old unknown who had just joined the Bayern ranks from local rivals 1860—Ludwig Kögl. For the first few matches Kögl watched from the bench as his team got off to a winning start, but as the away match in Bielefeld drifted towards a 1-1 draw, *Trainer* Udo Lattek decided it was time to give the youngster his debut. And it paid off—Kögl created goals for Norbert Nachtweih and Matthäus to clinch a valuable win. Kögl was only in the starting line-up thirteen times that season, but he came on as a substitute fourteen times, and his left-wing wizardry even earned him an invitation to travel with the West German national squad to a four-team tournament in Mexico.

Bayern and Werder Bremen spent virtually the entire season neck-and-neck at the top of the table, with Rudi Völler enjoying another prolific year for high-scoring Werder. Meanwhile Matthäus missed several matches because of injury and because he had been sent off twice—once in the Bundesliga and once in the Cup-Winners' Cup.

Matthäus's snubbing of his former club won him no friends in Mönchengladbach and the Gladbach-Bayern confrontation scheduled for 10 November took on an added sense of rivalry. Come the day of the match, though, there was only one problem. The Gladbach squad was stranded in Poland, fog-bound at a Warsaw airport after their UEFA Cup match with Widzew Lodz. The game wound up being replayed on December 10, and Gladbach won 3-2.

The tension surrounding the title race continued until the very last day of the season, with Bayern leading Bremen by two points. Bayern were away to already-doomed Eintracht Brunswick, where in the second half Kögl put Hoeness through to score the only goal of the game and clinch the championship. At the same time Bremen were going down 2-0 in Dortmund to give Bayern a rather flattering four-point margin at the top.

Both teams' success was due in no small part to their formidable home records. Werder had gone through the season unbeaten at the Weser Stadion, while Bayern's only home defeat was on 6th October when they went down 2-1 to Waldhof Mannheim. Mannheim enjoyed an exceptionally good season and but for a 2-1 loss in Leverkusen in their last match would have earned themselves an unprecedented UEFA Cup berth.

Mönchengladbach wound up finishing fourth, and even managed a 10-0 win over Brunswick. This was the sixth occasion that a Bundesliga match had gone into double figures—and Gladbach had done it on four of them. Brunswick's fifteen defeats away from home and paltry 39 goals scored ensured them of a miserable season. *Trainer* Aleksandar Ristic was sacked in April after a 2-0 home loss to Leverkusen, but the club picked up just four more points from their remaining seven matches under new boss Heinz Patzig and finished at the foot of the table. The next-to-bottom club, Karlsruhe, were seven points adrift and their *Trainer* Werner Olk resigned in March.

Arminia Bielefeld were the other condemned team. They won their final match, at home to Uerdingen, but all the other teams threatened with relegation won, too. Consequently, Arminia's goal difference of -15 turned out to be two goals worse than that of fifteenth-placed Düsseldorf and they had to face the playoff.

The Second Division promotion race was one of the most exciting in history. Hessen Kassel had topped the table for most of the latter half of the season, and going into their last match were one point ahead of second-placed Nuremberg. The fixture list, though, had dramatically pitted Nuremberg at home to Kassel in the season finale, and 56,339 saw goals from Dieter Eckstein and Thomas Brunner give the home side victory and the division championship. As a result, Kassel lost not only the top spot, but also any chance they had of promotion, finishing fourth. Hanover 96 stole second place, winning their last match 2-0 at home to Hertha Berlin in front of 60,000. At the bottom Kickers Offenbach, who two seasons earlier had been a First Division side, were relegated to the Oberliga Hessen.

From this season onwards, the German Cup Final was held in the Berlin Olympiastadion. The DFB, keenly aware of the recent lack of top-level football available to the denizens of West Berlin, were soon to turn the Olympiastadion into a sort of German Wembley. Perhaps this acted as some sort of incentive to the struggling Oberliga Baden-Württemberg side SC Geislingen, for they created two of the season's biggest upsets, knocking out Hamburg in the first round and Kickers Offenbach in the next. Second Division Union Solingen went all the way to the quarterfinals, where a crowd of 13,000 wasn't enough to keep them from losing to Mönchengladbach, 2-1.

The competition brought varying levels of success for the two teams supported by the Bayer chemical firm. Bayer Leverkusen got through their first three rounds without conceding a goal, but then lost 3-1 to Bayern Munich in the quarterfinals. Bayer Uerdingen went all the way to the final for the first time in their history, squeezing past Second Division 1.FC Saarbrücken in a somewhat lifeless semifinal.

Bayern had needed an extra-time penalty from Sören Lerby and some nifty goalkeeping from Jean-Marie Pfaff to get past Mönchengladbach in their semifinal, and provided the opposition on Uerdingen's big day. A crowd of 70,000 saw Bayer seize a rare moment of glory with a convincing 2-1 win. Dieter Hoeness put Bayern 1-0 up after just eight minutes, but Horst Feilzer equalised for Bayer moments later. Uerdingen had a goal disallowed for offside just before halftime and it was left to Wolfgang Schäfer to score the winner on 67 minutes.

There was a strong sense of *deja vu* about the East German season. In the Oberliga, Dynamo Berlin captured yet another championship, with Dynamo Dresden second, and Lokomotive Leipzig third—exactly the same order as the previous season. The champions amassed an Oberliga record 90 goals, with Rainer Ernst, Frank Pastor, and Andreas Thom accounting for two-thirds of them. Bottom club Motor Suhl proved particularly generous to the champions, losing 8-0 at home and 6-0 away in their two league encounters. The only blemish on Dynamo's otherwise perfect home record came in a 2-1 loss to Dynamo Dresden.

The cup final was also a repeat of last year's all-Dynamo affair, with Dresden again bettering Berlin by one goal. Like the previous season, Dresden held a two-goal advantage until the final few minutes of the match, and again 48,000 were in attendance at the Stadion der Weltjugend. But the Second Division had a significantly different look about it. The five *Staffeln* had been truncated back into two, with sides like Empor Tabak Dresden and Lokomotive/Armaturen Prenzlau left trailing in its wake. There were clear-cut winners in each Staffel, with Union Berlin and Sachsenring Zwickau each five points clear at the top.

The East German national team equalled their worst-ever defeat when they lost 4-1 to Denmark in Copenhagen. Bryan Robson's late goal for England proved the difference when the two teams met at Wembley, which proved to be the last between the two nations. It was a significant occasion for Joachim Streich, who became the first East German to earn 100 caps. Streich retired at the end of the season after sixteen years of top-level football with Rostock and Magdeburg. His 378 Oberliga appearances yielded a record 229 goals, and he was also to go down in East German footballing history as their most-capped player (102), and top goalscorer (55). Streich had been voted East German Footballer of the Year twice and had four times led the Oberliga in scoring.

West Germany put together a series of five straight wins in their World Cup qualifying group to put them well on the way to Mexico. But they ended the season with a series of poor performances during a mini-tournament there. The following year, though, their fortunes in that country would improve considerably.

Bundesliga

Club	P	W	D	L	Goals	Pts
1. Bayern Munich	34	21	8	5	79-38	50
2. Werder Bremen	34	18	10	6	87-51	46
3. 1.FC Cologne	34	18	4	12	69-66	40
4. Borussia Mönchengladbach	34	15	9	10	77-53	39
5. Hamburg SV	34	14	9	11	58-49	37
6. Waldhof Mannheim	34	13	11	10	47-50	37
7. Bayer Uerdingen	34	14	8	12	57-52	36
8. FC Schalke 04	34	13	8	13	63-62	34
9. VfL Bochum	34	12	10	12	52-54	34
10. VfB Stuttgart	34	14	5	15	79-59	33
11. 1.FC Kaiserslautern	34	11	11	12	56-60	33
12. Eintracht Frankfurt	34	10	12	12	62-67	32
13. Bayer Leverkusen	34	9	13	12	52-54	31
14. Borussia Dortmund	34	13	4	17	51-65	30
15. Fortuna Düsseldorf	34	10	9	15	53-66	29
16. Arminia Bielefeld	34	8	13	13	46-61	29
17. Karlsruhe SC	34	5	12	17	47-88	22
18. Eintracht Brunswick	34	9	2	23	39-79	20

Top Scorers
K Allofs (1.FC Cologne) 26
Völler (Werder Bremen) 25
Allgöwer (VfB Stuttgart) 19
T Allofs (1.FC Kaiserslautern) 19
Reich (Arminia Bielefeld) 18
Täuber (FC Schalke 04) 18
Thiele (Fortuna Düsseldorf) 17
Fischer (VfL Bochum) 16
Littbarski (1.FC Cologne) 16
Matthäus (Bayern Munich) 16
Mill (Borussia Mönchengladbach) 16

Bundesliga Playoff
1.FC Saarbrücken v Arminia Bielefeld (2-0, 1-1); Saarbrücken promoted to Division One

Second Division

Club	P	W	D	L	Goals	Pts
1. 1.FC Nuremberg	38	23	4	11	71-45	50
2. Hanover 96	38	18	14	6	79-58	50
3. 1.FC Saarbrücken	38	21	7	10	70-41	49
4. Hessen Kassel	38	20	9	9	72-48	49
5. Alemannia Aachen	38	18	10	10	60-46	43
6. Union Solingen	38	18	5	15	64-70	41
7. Blau-Weiss 90 Berlin	38	15	9	14	66-56	39
8. SC Freiburg	38	14	10	14	45-49	38
9. Kickers Stuttgart	38	14	9	15	51-49	37
10. Wattenscheid 09	38	14	8	16	61-68	36
11. Fortuna Cologne	38	14	8	16	58-67	36
12. Rot-Weiss Oberhausen	38	13	9	16	64-70	35
13. MSV Duisburg	38	12	11	15	56-63	35
14. Hertha BSC Berlin	38	10	15	13	50-59	35
15. SV Darmstadt 98	38	13	9	16	52-64	35
16. FC 08 Homburg	38	13	8	17	57-58	34
17. FC St Pauli	38	11	11	16	48-59	33
18. VfR Bürstadt	38	12	7	19	48-56	31
19. Kickers Offenbach	38	10	12	16	43-56	30
20. SSV 1846 Ulm	38	5	12	21	48-81	22

Kickers Offenbach two points deducted

Top Scorers
Burgsmüller (Oberhausen) 29
Pascal Notthoff (MSV Duisburg) 17
Dannenberg (Kickers Stuttgart) 16
Blättel (1.FC Saarbrücken) 15
Höfer (Kickers Offenbach) 15
Bunk (Blau-Weiss 90 Berlin) 14
Gaedke (Blau-Weiss 90 Berlin) 14
Grillemeier (Hertha BSC Berlin) 14
Gue (Hanover 96) 14
Knauf (Hessen Kassel) 14
Kuhl (SV Darmstadt 98) 14
Kurtenbach (Fortuna Cologne) 14

Third Division Champions
Baden-Württemberg: SV Sandhausen
Bayern: SpVgg Bayreuth
Berlin: Tennis Borussia Berlin
Hessen: Viktoria Aschaffenburg
Nord: VfL Osnabrück
Nordrhein: Rot-Weiss Essen
Südwest: FSV Salmrohr
Westfalen: SC Eintracht Hamm

Second Division Playoffs

Northern Group	P	W	D	L	Goals	Pts
1. VfL Osnabrück	8	7	0	1	18-5	14
2. Tennis Borussia Berlin	8	4	1	3	12-12	9
3. Rot-Weiss Essen	8	3	1	4	18-15	7
4. SC Eintracht Hamm	8	2	2	4	10-18	6
5. SV Hummelsbüttel	8	2	0	6	10-18	4

Southern Group	P	W	D	L	Goals	Pts
1. SpVgg Bayreuth	6	4	0	2	10-12	8
2. Viktoria Aschaffenburg	6	3	1	2	14-9	7
3. FSV Salmrohr	6	3	0	3	11-11	6
4. SV Sandhausen	6	1	1	4	10-13	3

West German Cup
First Round
1.FC Cologne 8, Kickers Stuttgart 0
1.FC Nuremberg (Am.) 1, SW Ludwigshafen 0
1.FC Paderborn 1, Hanover 96 4
Arminia Bielefeld 1, 1.FC Nuremberg 3 aet
ASC Dudweiler 1, Borussia Dortmund 5
Bayer Leverkusen 5, 1.FC Kaiserslautern 0
Bayern Munich (Am.) 3, Wattenscheid 09 5
Borussia Mönchengladbach 4, Blau-Weiss 90 Berlin 1
BV Lüttringhausen 0, Bayern Munich 1
Eintracht Brunswick 1, Eintracht Frankfurt 3
Eintracht Haiger 2, CSC 03 Kassel 1 aet
FC Altona 93 2, Eintracht Trier 1
Fortuna Cologne 2, MSV Duisburg 2 aet (2-2 aet; Cologne won on penalties)
Fortuna Düsseldorf 2, SSV 1846 Ulm 0
FV 08 Duisburg 1, Waldhof Mannheim 4
Hertha BSC Berlin 1, Hessen Kassel 0
Olympia Bocholt 1, FC Schalke 04 3
OSC Bremerhaven 0, Werder Bremen 4
Rot-Weiss Essen 1, 1.FC Saarbrücken 2
SC Charlottenburg 1, Karlsruhe SC 3 aet
SC Geislingen 2, Hamburg SV 0
SC Herford 2, Kickers Offenbach 3
SC Jülich 1910 2, FC Rastatt 1
SpVgg Bayreuth 7, SV Mettlach 0
SV Darmstadt 98 3, SC Freiburg 0
SV Schwetzingen 1, Alemannia Aachen 2
TSV Havelse 2, VfL Bochum 2 aet (0-4)
TSV Ofterdingen 0, VfL Bochum (Am.) 1
VfB Oldenburg 1, Bayer Uerdingen 6
VfB Stuttgart 5, Rot-Weiss Oberhausen 4
VfL Kellinghusen 1, Union Solingen 4
VfL Osnabrück 1, TSV Friesen Hänigsen 5 aet

Second Round
1.FC Nuremberg (Am.) 0, SC Jülich 1910 3
1.FC Saarbrücken 4, 1.FC Nuremberg 1
Alemannia Aachen 3, VfL Bochum 0
Bayer Uerdingen 2, Fortuna Düsseldorf 1
Borussia Dortmund 1, FC Schalke 04 1 aet (2-3)
Borussia Mönchengladbach 4, Eintracht Frankfurt 2 aet
Eintracht Haiger 1, Karlsruhe SC 0 aet
FC Altona 93 0, Bayer Leverkusen 3
Hanover 96 2, 1.FC Cologne 1
Hertha BSC Berlin 4, Fortuna Cologne 3 aet
SC Geislingen 4, Kickers Offenbach 2
SpVgg Bayreuth 1, Union Solingen 2

TSV Friesen Hänigsen 0, Bayern Munich 8
VfL Bochum (Am.) 1, VfB Stuttgart 2
Wattenscheid 09 0, Waldhof Mannheim 4
Werder Bremen 5, SV Darmstadt 98 0

Third Round
Alemannia Aachen 0, Borussia Mönchengladbach 2
Bayern Munich 1, Waldhof Mannheim 0
Eintracht Haiger 0, Union Solingen 8
Hanover 96 1, FC Schalke 04 0
Hertha BSC Berlin 0, Bayer Leverkusen 4
SC Geislingen 0, Bayer Uerdingen 2
SC Jülich 1910 2, Werder Bremen 4
VfB Stuttgart 0, 1.FC Saarbrücken 0 aet (2-2 aet; Saarbrücken won on penalties)

Quarterfinals
1.FC Saarbrücken 1, Hanover 96 0
Bayer Uerdingen 2, Werder Bremen 1
Bayer Leverkusen 1, Bayern Munich 3
Union Solingen 1, Borussia Mönchengladbach 2

Semifinals
1.FC Saarbrücken 0, Bayer Uerdingen 1
Bayern Munich 1, Borussia Mönchengladbach 0 aet

Final
in Berlin
Bayer Uerdingen 2, Bayern Munich 1

West German Internationals
12/9/84 in Düsseldorf 1-3 v Argentina
17/10/84 in Cologne 2-0 v Sweden (WCQ)
16/12/84 in Valetta 3-2 v Malta (WCQ)
29/1/85 in Hamburg 0-1 v Hungary
24/2/85 in Lisbon 2-1 v Portugal (WCQ)
27/3/85 in Saarbrücken 6-0 v Malta (WCQ)
17/4/85 in Augsburg 4-1 v Bulgaria
30/4/85 in Prague 5-1 v Czechoslovakia (WCQ)
12/6/85 in Mexico City 0-3 v England
15/6/85 in Mexico City 0-2 v Mexico

East German Oberliga

Club	P	W	D	L	Goals	Pts
1. Dynamo Berlin	26	20	4	2	90-28	44
2. Dynamo Dresden	26	15	8	3	69-34	38
3. Lokomotive Leipzig	26	17	4	5	55-26	38
4. Wismut Aue	26	12	8	6	38-33	32
5. 1.FC Magdeburg	26	11	9	6	53-35	31
6. Rot-Weiss Erfurt	26	10	10	6	47-39	30
7. Carl Zeiss Jena	26	9	7	10	36-27	25
8. Vorwärts Frankfurt/Oder	26	7	8	11	41-38	22
9. FC Karl-Marx-Stadt	26	7	7	12	39-48	21
10. Hansa Rostock	26	6	9	11	37-51	21
11. Stahl Brandenburg	26	5	10	11	25-39	20
12. Stahl Riesa	26	6	8	12	29-55	20
13. Chemie Leipzig	26	4	9	13	26-56	17
14. Motor Suhl	26	1	3	22	16-92	5

Top Scorers

Ernst (Dynamo Berlin)	24
Pastor (Dynamo Berlin)	22
Streich (1.FC Magdeburg)	18
Gütschow (Dynamo Dresden)	17
Thom (Dynamo Berlin)	14
Kuhlee (Vorwärts Frankfurt/Oder)	13
Mothes (Wismut Aue)	13
Weidemann (Rot-Weiss Erfurt)	12
Glowatzky (Karl-Marx-Stadt)	11
Minge (Dynamo Dresden)	11
Persigehl (Karl-Marx-Stadt)	11

Second Division (Staffel A)

Club	P	W	D	L	Goals	Pts
1. 1.FC Union Berlin	34	21	8	5	81-29	50
2. Stahl Eisenhüttenstadt	34	18	9	7	72-42	45
3. Motor Babelsberg	34	17	10	7	50-36	44
4. Energie Cottbus	34	17	8	9	60-36	42
5. Rotation Berlin	34	14	13	7	61-41	41
6. Dynamo Fürstenwalde	34	16	8	10	60-53	40
7. Vorwärts Stralsund	34	15	9	10	53-45	39
8. Dynamo Berlin II	34	13	10	11	64-48	36
9. Aktivist Schwarze Pumpe	34	15	6	13	41-43	36
10. Vorwärts Frankfurt/Oder II	34	13	7	14	57-52	33
11. Aktivist Brieske-Senftenberg	34	11	11	12	43-45	33
12. Post Neubrandenburg	34	10	10	14	35-37	30
13. Chemie Buna Schkopau	34	9	11	14	34-51	29
14. Dynamo Schwerin	34	7	12	15	33-50	26
15. TSG Bau Rostock	34	8	9	17	38-61	25
16. Schiffahrt/Hafen Rostock	34	5	12	17	30-60	22
17. ISG Schwerin	34	7	7	20	35-80	21
18. Chemie Wolfen	34	7	6	21	31-69	20

Promoted: KKW Greifswald, Stahl Hettstedt, Lok/Armaturen Prenzlau. Chemie Buna Schkopau were placed in Staffel B for the following season

Second Division (Staffel B)

Club	P	W	D	L	Goals	Pts
1. Sachsenring Zwickau	34	24	6	4	73-27	54
2. Chemie Halle	34	19	11	4	77-30	49
3. Dynamo Dresden II	34	19	9	6	71-39	47
4. Chemie Böhlen	34	17	10	7	57-42	44
5. Fortschritt Bischofswerda	34	15	12	7	58-41	42
6. Vorwärts Dessau	34	12	10	12	50-48	34
7. Motor Nordhausen	34	10	14	10	35-41	34
8. Chemie Markkleeberg	34	12	9	13	52-49	33
9. Wismut Gera	34	11	9	14	52-45	31
10. Carl Zeiss Jena II	34	12	7	15	48-52	31
11. Motor FH Karl-Marx-Stadt	34	11	9	14	39-46	31
12. Rot-Weiss Erfurt II	34	11	9	14	43-61	31
13. Glückauf Sondershausen	34	10	11	13	39-57	31
14. Motor Grimma	34	9	12	13	42-61	30
15. Dynamo Eisleben	34	10	9	15	44-53	29
16. Aufbau Krumhermersdorf	34	8	10	16	31-58	26
17. Kali Werra Tiefenort	34	7	8	19	29-54	22
18. Robotron Sömmerda	34	3	7	24	30-66	13

Promoted: Wismut Aue II, Chemie Ilmenau, Motor Weimar. Vorwärts Dessau were placed in Staffel A for the following season

East German Cup Final

in Berlin
Dynamo Dresden 3, Dynamo Berlin 2

East German Internationals

11/8/84 in Berlin 1-1 v Mexico
29/8/84 in Gera 2-1 v Rumania
12/9/84 in Zwickau 1-0 v Greece
12/9/84 in London 0-1 v England
10/10/84 in Aue 5-2 v Algeria
20/10/84 in Leipzig 2-3 v Yugoslavia (WCQ)
17/11/84 in Esch 5-0 v Luxembourg (WCQ)
8/12/84 in Paris 0-2 v France (WCQ)
29/1/85 in Montevideo 0-3 v Uruguay
6/2/85 in Guayaquil 3-2 v Ecuador
13/3/85 in Batna 1-1 v Algeria
6/4/85 in Sofia 0-1 v Bulgaria (WCQ)
17/4/85 in Frankfurt/Oder 1-0 v Norway
8/5/85 in Copenhagen 1-4 v Denmark
18/5/85 in Babelsberg 3-1 v Luxembourg (WCQ)

European Cup
First Round
Levski Spartak Sofia v VfB Stuttgart .... (1-1, 2-2)
Aberdeen v Dynamo Berlin .... (2-1, 1-2 aet)
Dynamo won on penalties
Second Round
Dynamo Berlin v FK Austria .... (3-3, 1-2)

Cup-Winners' Cup
First Round
Bayern Munich v FK Moss .... (4-1, 2-1)
Malmö FF v Dynamo Dresden .... (2-0, 1-4)
Second Round
Bayern Munich v Trakia Plovdiv .... (4-1, 0-2)
Dynamo Dresden v Metz .... (3-1, 0-0)
Quarterfinals
Bayern Munich v Roma .... (2-0, 2-1)
Dynamo Dresden v Rapid Vienna .... (3-0, 0-5)
Semifinals
Bayern Munich v Everton .... (0-0, 1-3)

UEFA Cup
First Round
Dukla Banska v Borussia Mönchengladbach .... (2-3, 1-4)
Anderlecht v Werder Bremen .... (1-0, 1-2)
1.FC Cologne v Pogon Stettin .... (2-1, 1-0)
Southampton v Hamburg SV .... (0-0, 0-2)
Lokomotive Leipzig v Lilleström SK .... (7-0, 0-3)
Vorwärts Frankfurt/Oder v PSV Eindhoven .... (2-0, 0-3)
Second Round
Standard Liege v 1.FC Cologne .... (0-2, 1-2)
Borussia Mönchengladbach v Widzew Lodz .... (3-2, 0-1)
Hamburg SV v CSKA Sofia .... (4-0, 2-1)
Lokomotive Leipzig v Spartak Moscow .... (1-1, 0-2)
Third Round
Spartak Moscow v 1.FC Cologne .... (1-0, 0-2)
Hamburg SV v Inter Milan .... (2-1, 0-1)
Quarterfinals
Inter Milan v 1.FC Cologne .... (1-0, 3-1)

1985-86

Saved by the post

Werder Bremen started the season so well that they seemed certain to collect their first Bundesliga title for 21 years. They remained favourites despite losing 3-1 to Bayern at the Olympic Stadium shortly before Christmas, although the worst blow was losing striker Rudi Völler for a lengthy period, the victim of a challenge from Bayern's Klaus Augenthaler. By the midway stage of the season, Werder had rifled in fifty goals and topped the table; Bayern were three points behind in third place.

With four games remaining Werder's lead over Bayern had stretched to four points, but second-place Mönchengladbach had dropped to third. When Bremen played host to Bayern in the penultimate round of the season, their lead had shrunk to two points but they could clinch the championship by winning the game. Bayern had clearly come to the Weserstadion looking for a draw and with the score 0-0 going into the last minute they seemed likely to get it. As Rudi Völler and Sören Lerby engaged in one last challenge for possession, the ball bounced up and hit Lerby on the hand—and the referee showed no hesitation in pointing to the penalty spot. Werder defender Michael Kutzop seemed the ideal man to take the kick—after all, he had never missed a penalty before. Kutzop strode up . . . and blasted his spot-kick against the post. So near, and yet so far; the match was effectively over, and now the title race would go to the very last game.

Werder still led by two points and needed a only draw from their visit to VfB Stuttgart, assuming that Bayern made no mistake at home to Mönchengladbach. Indeed, Bayern crushed Borussia, 6-0. With 38 minutes left to play, though, Werder were 2-0 behind and laying siege to the Stuttgart goal. But all they wound up with was a 79th minute consolation goal from Manfred Burgsmüller which was no consolation at all. So Bayern had finished level on points with Bremen, but ahead of them on goal difference. The championship had been well and truly stolen.

Mönchengladbach had to settle for fourth place in the end, as Karlheinz Feldkamp's Bayer Uerdingen won ten of their last twelve matches, and drew the other two, to finish third. In spite of the previous season's West German Cup triumph, Uerdingen were expected by most to finish no better than mid-table. Though they conceded more goals than thirteen other teams in the league, and were handicapped by a heavy backlog of fixtures, Uerdingen enjoyed their best-ever finish in the Bundesliga. Feldkamp would stay one more season at the club before moving to Eintracht Frankfurt, who in this season removed Dietrich Weise as *Trainer* on the way to a dismal fifteenth place finish.

Uerdingen's most remarkable achievement came in a Cup-Winners' Cup quarterfinal tie against Dynamo Dresden. Down 2-0 from the first leg in East Germany, Bayer found themselves 3-1 down early in the second half of the second leg. But a Wolfgang Funkel penalty and a Dynamo own-goal levelled the scores on the night—and four further Uerdingen goals gave them an incredible 7-5 come-from-behind aggregate win.

Most teams were managing with the services of only one or two *Trainers*, but Hanover 96 went through four and still finished the season by going seventeen games without a win, ending up in eighteenth place. Back in November, after an excellent 3-1 away win at Eintracht Frankfurt, they had sacked their *Trainer* Werner Biskup for allegedly turning up to work drunk. Caretaker coach Jürgen Rynio took charge for a few weeks before Jörg Berger was handed the reins, but Berger was replaced after only two months by Helmut Kalthoff. Hanover also set an all-time Bundesliga record by conceding 17 penalties over the course of the season.

A week beforehand, Dortmund had dismissed Pal Csernai for guiding Borussia to a sixteenth-place finish. Reinhard Saftig was named as Csernai's replacement, just as he had been at Bayern three seasons earlier. Dortmund had now changed their *Trainer* sixteen times in the twelve seasons since regaining promotion to the Bundesliga, yet they had never finished higher than fourth.

This year's Second Division table had a strange look, with rank outsiders Homburg and Blau-Weiss Berlin filling the top two spots to make it into the Bundesliga for the first time (and not for very long). It was a fitting reward for tiny Homburg, a footballing outpost midway between Saarbrücken and Kaiserslautern, who had turned in consistently good performances throughout their long spell in the Second Division. Even stranger was the look at the bottom of the table: Hertha Berlin and MSV Duisburg were relegated into the amateur leagues, and Eintracht Brunswick only narrowly avoided the same fate. Duisburg, once capable of attracting gates over 20,000 to their Wedau Stadion, were now struggling to pull in four-figure crowds and drew just 600 for their final home match of the season.

Third-place Fortuna Cologne managed to miss promotion to the first division by just twenty seconds. In their play-off series against Dortmund, they won at home 2-0 before 44,000 and were only 2-1 down in the return leg until Jürgen Wegmann equalised for Borussia less than half a minute before the referee blew for full time. The contest therefore went to a third match—and a deflated Fortuna gave up seven second half-goals to lose 8-0.

In the West German Cup, Eintracht Trier kept holders Bayer Uerdingen to a 0-0 draw at their own Moselstadion, then sensationally knocked them out with three second half goals before just 3,000 in Krefeld. VfB Stuttgart managed to reach the final in spite of a particularly difficult passage. They faced Brunswick, Nuremberg, Bremen, and Schalke before meeting Dortmund in the semifinal. SV Sandhausen of the Oberliga Baden-Württemberg had a considerably easier draw and managed to reach the quarterfinals before losing to Dortmund.

Both semifinals were one-sided affairs, with 40,000 seeing Stuttgart blow out Dortmund in the Neckarstadion and Bayern Munich facing little resistance from Waldhof Mannheim in front of 37,000 in Waldhof's second home of Ludwigshafen. Stuttgart were forced to call up reserve goalkeeper Armin Jäger for the final and Bayern made his afternoon a misery with an emphatic 5-2 win. VfB reacted to Jäger's showing by transferring him to neighbours Kickers Stuttgart for the following season—for whom he would play in the next cup final.

In the UEFA Cup, Cologne strung together a sequence of good results to reach the final, where they met Real Madrid. The Spaniards had needed a last-minute strike to get past Mönchengladbach on away goals in the third round. Cologne, still desperate to add a European trophy to their list of honours, lost the first match heavily and never recovered. Only 21,000 saw the return leg—played in Berlin owing to UEFA's displeasure with rowdy Cologne fans earlier in the competition—and goals from Klaus Allofs and Ralf Geilenkirchen provided a consolation victory.

Once again Dynamo Berlin were the team to beat in East German football, and although their points total of 34 was their lowest since their string of Oberliga championships began, they still finished unbeaten at home and two points clear of the field. Runners-up Lokomotive Leipzig set the highest-ever score for a East German Cup Final by overwhelming Union Berlin 5-1, with Hans Richter getting a hat-trick. The season ended with the final appearance of Dresden sweeper Hans-Jürgen Dörner after a 17-year career. The top league goalscorer was Union Berlin's Ralf Strässer, but his meagre total of fourteen goals from 26 games was the lowest ever needed to win the honour.

East Germany's national side came third in their World Cup qualifying group and were out of the running for a place in Mexico despite home wins over France and Bulgaria, both of whom went instead. A string of four consecutive defeats ended yet another bleak international season. Meanwhile the West German team was displaying a distinct lack of confidence. They lost their first-ever World Cup qualifying match, at home to Portugal, and endured a sequence of six games without a win, their worst since the war. Nevertheless, they managed to qualify. They started poorly in Mexico yet still reached the knock-out phase. There, a late goal from a Matthäus free kick gave them a win over Morocco, and penalties were needed to beat Mexico in the quarterfinals. In the semifinal, Völler and Andy Brehme scored in a win over France, and so despite looking decidedly pedestrian, West Germany had once again reached the final of the World Cup.

And once again, they lost. Argentina, inspired by Diego Maradona, overcame goals from Rummenigge and Völler to win one of the more dramatic finals of recent times, 3-2. The match marked the end of an era, as the national team underwent a wholesale restructure. Karl-Heinz Rummenigge, Karlheinz Förster, Hans-Peter Briegel, Felix Magath, Ditmar Jakobs, Norbert Eder, and Dieter Hoeness all had made their last international appearances. A new West German side would emerge—one which would return from the next competition as world champions.

Bundesliga

Club	P	W	D	L	Goals	Pts
1. Bayern Munich	34	21	7	6	82-31	49
2. Werder Bremen	34	20	9	5	83-41	49
3. Bayer Uerdingen	34	19	7	8	63-60	45
4. Borussia Mönchengladbach	34	15	12	7	65-51	42
5. VfB Stuttgart	34	17	7	10	69-45	41
6. Bayer Leverkusen	34	15	10	9	63-51	40
7. Hamburg SV	34	17	5	12	52-35	39
8. Waldhof Mannheim	34	11	11	12	41-44	33
9. VfL Bochum	34	14	4	16	55-57	32
10. FC Schalke 04	34	11	8	15	53-58	30
11. 1.FC Kaiserslautern	34	10	10	14	49-54	30
12. 1.FC Nuremberg	34	12	5	17	51-54	29
13. 1.FC Cologne	34	9	11	14	46-59	29
14. Fortuna Düsseldorf	34	11	7	16	54-78	29
15. Eintracht Frankfurt	34	7	14	13	35-49	28
16. Borussia Dortmund	34	10	8	16	49-65	28
17. 1.FC Saarbrücken	34	6	9	19	39-68	21
18. Hanover 96	34	5	8	21	43-92	18

Top Scorers
Kuntz (VfL Bochum) 22
Allgöwer (VfB Stuttgart) 21
Neubarth (Werder Bremen) 20
Cha (Bayer Leverkusen) 17
T Allofs (1.FC Kaiserslautern) 16
Klinsmann (VfB Stuttgart) 16
Täuber (FC Schalke 04) 16
D Hoeness (Bayern Munich) 15
Remark (Waldhof Mannheim) 14
Waas (Bayer Leverkusen) 14
Wegmann (Borussia Dortmund) 14

First Division Playoff
Fortuna Cologne v Borussia Dortmund (2-0, 1-3, 0-8); Dortmund remain in Division One

Second Division

Club	P	W	D	L	Goals	Pts
1. FC 08 Homburg	38	20	9	9	75-42	49
2. Blau-Weiss 90 Berlin	38	17	13	8	76-48	47
3. Fortuna Cologne	38	19	8	11	64-52	46
4. Arminia Bielefeld	38	18	9	11	60-47	45
5. Hessen Kassel	38	19	6	13	58-47	44
6. Kickers Stuttgart	38	17	9	12	73-55	43
7. Karlsruhe SC	38	17	9	12	64-50	43
8. Alemannia Aachen	38	15	13	10	56-45	43
9. Wattenscheid 09	38	17	9	12	63-56	43
10. SV Darmstadt 98	38	16	9	13	63-57	41
11. Rot-Weiss Oberhausen	38	12	13	13	61-60	37
12. Eintracht Brunswick	38	13	10	15	65-62	36
13. Viktoria Aschaffenburg	38	15	5	18	57-59	35
14. VfL Osnabrück	38	11	13	14	48-57	35
15. Union Solingen	38	10	14	14	48-64	34
16. SC Freiburg	38	12	9	17	54-62	33
17. Hertha BSC Berlin	38	8	15	15	50-62	31
18. SpVgg Bayreuth	38	11	9	18	40-73	31
19. Tennis Borussia Berlin	38	10	9	19	48-73	29
20. MSV Duisburg	38	5	5	28	34-86	15

Top Scorers
Bunk (Blau-Weiss 90 Berlin) 26
Linz (VfL Osnabrück) 22
Tschiskale (Wattenscheid 09) 22
Grabosch (Fortuna Cologne) 19
Sane (SC Freiburg) 18
Tobolik (Viktoria Aschaffenburg) 18
Labbadia (SV Darmstadt 98) 17
Mattern (Blau-Weiss 90 Berlin) 15
Merkle (Kickers Stuttgart) 15
Allievi (Wattenscheid 09) 14
Brandts (Alemannia Aachen) 14
Jurgeleit (Union Solingen) 14
Kohn (Arminia Bielefeld) 14
Künast (Karlsruhe SC) 14

Third Division Champions
Baden-Württemberg: SSV 1846 Ulm
Bayern: SpVgg Landshut
Berlin: SC Charlottenburg
Hessen: Kickers Offenbach
Nord: FC St Pauli
Nordrhein: Rot-Weiss Essen
Südwest: Wormatia Worms
Westfalen: ASC Schöppingen

Second Division Playoffs

Northern Group	P	W	D	L	Goals	Pts
1. FC St Pauli	8	5	2	1	16-8	12
2. Rot-Weiss Essen	8	5	2	1	16-12	11
3. SC Charlottenburg	8	3	3	2	16-9	9
4. VfB Oldenburg	8	2	1	5	12-18	5
5. ASC Schöppingen	8	1	1	6	8-21	3

Southern Group	P	W	D	L	Goals	Pts
1. SSV 1846 Ulm	6	3	2	1	11-7	8
2. FSV Salmrohr	6	3	2	1	10-7	8
3. Kickers Offenbach	6	1	5	0	11-8	7
4. TSV 1860 Munich	6	0	1	5	4-14	1

West German Cup
First Round
1.FC Achterberg 0, VfL Osnabrück 2
1.FC Kaiserslautern 3, Eintracht Frankfurt 1
Alemannia Aachen 1, Tennis Borussia Berlin 0
Blau-Weiss 90 Berlin 3, Fortuna Cologne 0
Borussia Neunkirchen 3, Rot-Weiss Oberhausen 2
Bremen SV 1, MSV Duisburg 3
Eintracht Trier 3, Karlsruhe SC 0
FC Altona 93 2, Fortuna Düsseldorf 3 aet
FC Erbach 2, SC Birkenfeld 1
FC St Pauli 2, Arminia Bielefeld 0 aet
FC Wangen 2, SV Darmstadt 98 1
FV Ebingen 2, 1.FC Nuremberg 7
Göttingen 05 1, 1.FC Saarbrücken 6
Hanover 96 3 SC Freiburg 1
Hertha BSC Berlin 2, Bayer Leverkusen 5
Kickers Offenbach 1, Bayern Munich 3
Kickers Stuttgart 3, FC 08 Homburg 3 aet (1-4)
SC Neukirchen 2, Borussia Dortmund 9
Sportfreunde Eisbachtal 1, FC Schalke 04 2
SpVgg Ansbach 0, Waldhof Mannheim 3
SpVgg Plattling 2, Itzehoe SV 0
SV Sandhausen 1, Union Solingen 0
SV Weil 0, Werder Bremen 7
TSV 1860 Munich 2, 1.FC Cologne 4
TuS Paderborn-Neuhaus 5, 1.FC Cologne (Am.) 3
VfB Stuttgart 6, Eintracht Brunswick 3
VfL Bochum 3, Hamburg SV 2
VfL Erp 1, SSV 1846 Ulm 2
VfR Bürstadt 1, Bayer Uerdingen 3
VfR Langelsheim 2, DSC Wanne-Eickel 5
Wattenscheid 09 2, Borussia Mönchengladbach 5
Wuppertal SV 2, Hessen Kassel 3

Second Round
1.FC Kaiserslautern 4, 1.FC Cologne 1 aet
1.FC Nuremberg 0, VfB Stuttgart 1
1.FC Saarbrücken 2, Bayern Munich 3
Alemannia Aachen 4, MSV Duisburg 3 aet
Borussia Neunkirchen 1, FC 08 Homburg 3
DSC Wanne-Eickel 0, Werder Bremen 4
Eintracht Trier 0, Bayer Uerdingen 0 aet (3-0)
FC Erbach 0, Blau-Weiss 90 Berlin 1
FC Schalke 04 3, Borussia Mönchengladbach 1
Fortuna Düsseldorf 1, VfL Bochum 1 aet (2-2 aet; Bochum won on penalties)
Hanover 96 2, Hessen Kassel 1
SpVgg Plattling 0, Bayer Leverkusen 2
SSV 1846 Ulm 5, FC St Pauli 2
SV Sandhausen 4, FC Wangen 1
TuS Paderborn-Neuhaus 2, Borussia Dortmund 4
Waldhof Mannheim 4, VfL Osnabrück 1

Third Round
Alemannia Aachen 1, FC Schalke 04 2 aet
Eintracht Trier 1, Bayer Leverkusen 3 aet
FC 08 Homburg 1, Borussia Dortmund 3 aet
SSV 1846 Ulm 3, 1.FC Kaiserslautern 4 aet
SV Sandhausen 3, Blau-Weiss 90 Berlin 2
VfB Stuttgart 3, Werder Bremen 0
VfL Bochum 1, Bayern Munich 1 aet (0-2)
Waldhof Mannheim 5, Hanover 96 1

Quarterfinals
1.FC Kaiserslautern 0, Bayern Munich 3
Bayer Leverkusen 0, Waldhof Mannheim 1
SV Sandhausen 1, Borussia Dortmund 3
VfB Stuttgart 6, FC Schalke 04 2

Semifinals
VfB Stuttgart 4, Borussia Dortmund 1
Waldhof Mannheim 0, Bayern Munich 2

Final
in Berlin
Bayern Munich 5, VfB Stuttgart 2

West German Internationals
28/8/85 in Moscow 0-1 v Soviet Union
25/9/85 in Stockholm 2-2 v Sweden (WCQ)
16/10/85 in Stuttgart 0-1 v Portugal (WCQ)
17/11/85 in Munich 2-2 v Czechoslovakia (WCQ)
5/2/86 in Avellino 2-1 v Italy
12/3/86 in Frankfurt 2-0 v Brazil
9/4/86 in Basle 1-0 v Switzerland
11/5/86 in Bochum 1-1 v Yugoslavia
14/5/86 in Dortmund 3-1 v Holland
4/6/86 in Queretaro 1-1 v Uruguay (WC)
8/6/86 in Queretaro 2-1 v Scotland (WC)
13/6/86 in Queretaro 0-2 v Denmark (WC)
17/6/86 in Monterrey 1-0 v Morocco (WC)
21/6/86 in Monterrey 0-0 v Mexico aet (WC); West Germany won on penalties
25/6/86 in Guadalajara 2-0 v France (WC)
29/6/86 in Mexico City 2-3 v Argentina (WC)

East German Oberliga

Club	P	W	D	L	Goals	Pts
1. Dynamo Berlin	26	12	10	4	46-31	34
2. Lokomotive Leipzig	26	12	8	6	33-22	32
3. Carl Zeiss Jena	26	9	13	4	32-18	31
4. 1.FC Magdeburg	26	9	11	6	39-33	29
5. Stahl Brandenburg	26	10	9	7	27-23	29
6. Dynamo Dresden	26	10	8	8	40-39	28
7. 1.FC Union Berlin	26	9	9	8	32-31	27
8. FC Karl-Marx-Stadt	26	9	8	9	33-32	26
9. Vorwärts Frankfurt/Oder	26	8	9	9	37-35	25
10. Rot-Weiss Erfurt	26	6	12	8	41-34	24
11. Wismut Aue	26	7	10	9	31-40	24
12. Stahl Riesa	26	7	8	11	27-36	22
13. Hansa Rostock	26	7	6	13	31-46	20
14. Sachsenring Zwickau	26	2	9	15	27-56	13

Top Scorers

Strässer (1.FC Union Berlin) 14
Raab (Carl Zeiss Jena) 12
Pastor (Dynamo Berlin) 11
Schnürer (Vorwärts Frankfurt/Oder) .. 11
Mothes (Wismut Aue) 10
Thom (Dynamo Berlin) 10
Busse (Rot-Weiss Erfurt) 9
Minge (Dynamo Dresden) 9
Glowatzky (Karl-Marx-Stadt) 8
Kühn (Lokomotive Leipzig) 8
Sammer (Dynamo Dresden) 8
Schlünz (Hansa Rostock) 8

Second Division (Staffel A)

Club	P	W	D	L	Goals	Pts
1. Dynamo Berlin II	34	18	10	6	58-35	46
2. Energie Cottbus	34	20	5	9	53-30	45
3. Chemie Leipzig	34	16	11	7	58-36	43
4. Vorwärts Stralsund	34	17	6	11	54-39	40
5. Vorwärts Dessau	34	16	7	11	64-53	39
6. KKW Greifswald	34	14	7	13	42-45	35
7. Vorwärts Frankfurt/Oder II	34	12	10	12	52-43	34
8. Motor Babelsberg	34	12	10	12	62-58	34
9. Rotation Berlin	34	12	10	12	47-43	34
10. Stahl Eisenhüttenstadt	34	12	10	12	53-52	34
11. Aktivist Schwarze Pumpe	34	13	8	13	39-40	34
12. Lok/Armaturen Prenzlau	34	13	8	13	37-43	34
13. Dynamo Schwerin	34	11	11	12	61-54	33
14. Dynamo Fürstenwalde	34	10	11	13	54-48	31
15. Post Neubrandenburg	34	11	9	14	39-54	31
16. Aktivist Brieske-Senftenberg	34	10	8	16	32-53	28
17. Stahl Hettstedt	34	7	6	21	31-72	20
18. TSG Bau Rostock	34	4	9	21	28-63	17

Energie Cottbus, not Dynamo Berlin II, were promoted to the First Division
Promoted: Chemie Guben, Motor Ludwigsfelde, Schiffahrt/Hafen Rostock, ISG Schwerin. Aktivist Schwarze Pumpe were placed in Staffel B for the following season

Second Division (Staffel B)

Club	P	W	D	L	Goals	Pts
1. Fortschritt Bischofswerda	34	23	6	5	61-23	52
2. Chemie Halle	34	22	3	9	85-36	47
3. Chemie Böhlen	34	16	7	11	59-44	39
4. Motor Grimma	34	15	8	11	43-39	38
5. Carl Zeiss Jena II	34	14	10	10	45-45	38
6. Dynamo Dresden II	34	14	9	11	57-50	37
7. Dynamo Eisleben	34	13	10	11	42-45	36
8. Glückauf Sondershausen	34	13	8	13	50-53	34
9. Motor Weimar	34	11	11	12	38-39	33
10. Motor Nordhausen	34	11	11	12	40-45	33
11. Chemie Buna Schkopau	34	11	10	13	35-38	32
12. Wismut Gera	34	13	6	15	46-51	32
13. Chemie Markkleeberg	34	10	11	13	51-53	31
14. Motor Suhl	34	12	7	15	38-52	31
15. Chemie Ilmenau	34	8	12	14	40-51	28
16. Rot-Weiss Erfurt II	34	10	8	16	41-57	28
17. Motor FH Karl-Marx-Stadt	34	9	8	17	31-44	26
18. Wismut Aue II	34	4	9	21	37-66	17

Promoted: Motor Schönebeck, Kali Werra Tiefenort

East German Cup Final
in Berlin
Lokomotive Leipzig 5, 1.FC Union Berlin 1

East German Internationals

14/8/85 in Oslo 1-0 v Norway
11/9/85 in Leipzig 2-0 v France (WCQ)
28/9/85 in Belgrade 2-1 v Yugoslavia (WCQ)
16/10/85 in Glasgow 0-0 v Scotland
16/11/85 in Karl-Marx-Stadt 2-1 v Bulgaria (WCQ)
15/2/86 in San Jose (USA) 2-1 v Mexico
19/2/86 in Braga 3-1 v Portugal
12/3/86 in Leipzig 0-1 v Holland
26/3/86 in Athens 0-2 v Greece
8/4/86 in Goiana 0-3 v Brazil
23/4/86 in Nitra 0-2 v Czechoslovakia

European Cup
First Round
Gornik Zabrze v Bayern Munich .... (1-2, 1-4)
Dynamo Berlin v FK Austria Vienna .... (0-2, 1-2)
Second Round
Bayern Munich v FK Austria Vienna .... (4-2, 3-3)
Quarterfinals
Bayern Munich v Anderlecht .... (2-1, 0-2)

Cup-Winners' Cup
First Round
Zurrieq v Bayer Uerdingen .... (0-3, 0-9)
CS Brugge v Dynamo Dresden .... (3-2, 1-2)
Second Round
Bayer Uerdingen v Galatasaray .... (2-0, 1-1)
HJK Helsinki v Dynamo Dresden .... (1-0, 2-7)
Quarterfinals
Dynamo Dresden v Bayer Uerdingen .... (2-0, 3-7)
Semifinals
Atlético Madrid v Bayer Uerdingen .... (1-0, 3-2)

UEFA Cup
First Round
1.FC Cologne v Sporting Gijon .... (0-0, 2-1)
Chernomoretz Odessa v Werder Bremen .... (2-1, 2-3)
Borussia Mönchengladbach v Lech Posnan .... (1-1, 2-0)
Sparta Rotterdam v Hamburg SV .... (2-0, 0-2 aet)
Sparta won on penalties
Wismut Aue v Dnepr Dnepropetrovsk .... (1-3, 1-2)
Coleraine v Lokomotive Leipzig .... (1-1, 0-5)
Second Round
1.FC Cologne v Bohemians Prague .... (4-0, 4-2)
Sparta Rotterdam v Borussia Mönchengladbach ...... (1-1, 1-5)
AC Milan v Lokomotive Leipzig .... (2-0, 1-3)
Third Round
Hammarby IF v 1.FC Cologne .... (2-1, 1-3)
Borussia Mönchengladbach v Real Madrid .... (5-1, 0-4)
Quarterfinals
Sporting Lisbon v 1.FC Cologne .... (1-1, 0-2)
Semifinals
1.FC Cologne v Waregem .... (4-0, 3-3)
Final
Real Madrid v 1.FC Cologne .... (5-1, 0-2)

1986-87

Disappointed champions

This was a season of farewells. Ernst Happel left Hamburg after six successful years to return to Austria. Udo Lattek completed a hat-trick of titles at Bayern Munich before moving to 1.FC Cologne as technical director. Rudi Völler left Werder Bremen after five years to play in Italy, and Dieter Hoeness retired after eight seasons at Bayern.

Another farewell was organised rather more hastily. After the World Cup, the national team goalkeeper, Toni Schumacher, wrote a book which—among other things—detailed the seamier activities of the West German squad over the summer. The "revelations" resulted in him being banned by the DFB from further international appearances. He had gained 76 German caps over seven years. In addition, Schumacher was also released by his club, 1.FC Cologne. Bodo Illgner quickly replaced Schumacher between the sticks at Cologne, but the national team replacement was not so readily decided. Second-choice netminder Uli Stein had been sent home in disgrace from the World Cup after having made crude remarks about national team boss Franz Beckenbauer, so the relatively inexperienced Eike Immel suddenly found himself the new number one.

Controversy would prove no stranger to Stein. In a 2-1 cup win at Augsburg, he had been sent off for hurling insults at the referee. In the German Super Cup match between Hamburg and Bayern, the curtain-raiser to the 1987-88 season, the Bavarians' new signing Jürgen Wegmann had just put his team 2-1 ahead in the 87th minute when Stein punched him. He was sent off, of course, but by this time Hamburg's patience had worn thin and they asked him to find another club.

Hamburg's participation in the Super Cup had been ensured by winning the West German Cup. They encountered only one First Division side throughout the competition—Borussia Mönchengladbach—but the real highlight of their run was a 6-0 pasting of local rivals St Pauli. Hamburg's opponents in the final were Second Division Kickers Stuttgart, who took a shock lead after twelve minutes through Kurt

Kurtenbach. Dietmar Beiersdorfer levelled the score three minutes later, but it took a Manfred Kaltz free kick with just two minutes to play to give HSV victory. An own goal from Nils Schlotterbeck in the last minute served only to distort the scoreline.

There had been the odd surprise in earlier rounds of the competition. BVL Remscheid emphatically disposed of 1.FC Kaiserslautern in the first round with three unanswered second-half goals, and Second Division Alemannia Aachen eliminated Werder Bremen after 240 minutes of scoreless football, winning 7-6 on penalties. Ironically, Werder keeper Dieter Burdenski missed the decisive one.

Hamburg had reached the semifinal with more than a little bit of luck. A 1-0 fourth-round victory over Darmstadt was achieved only through a last-minute goal from Manfred Kastl. And in the semifinal against Mönchengladbach, Kastl repeated the feat by heading a cross from Frank Schmöller against the post and then chesting in the rebound. Kickers Stuttgart had beaten Frankfurt 3-1 in the quarterfinal, aided by Wlodzimierz Smolarek's sending off in the sixth minute. They played their semifinal against a Fortuna Düsseldorf side so out-of-form one could scarcely imagine how the club had managed to get so far in the competition.

Many Bundesliga clubs were faced with major personnel changes. Andy Brehme was a newcomer to Bayern, having arrived during the summer after five years with Kaiserslautern. Frank Mill had moved from Mönchengladbach to Dortmund, and Polish international Miroslav Okonski signed for Hamburg. Goalkeepers had also been on the move in the close season: Immel from Dortmund to Stuttgart, Andy Köpke from Hertha BSC to Nuremberg, and Oliver Reck from Kickers Offenbach to Bremen.

Although Hamburg and Bayer Leverkusen managed to keep pace initially, Bayern marched inexorably towards their tenth German championship to overtake the nine wins of 1.FC Nuremberg. But Bayern, of course, had collected nine of their ten titles within a twenty-year period, whereas Nuremberg had taken only one since the formation of the Bundesliga. Bayern lost just one match all season, a shock 3-0 home defeat by Leverkusen. On their travels, they won at Düsseldorf, Stuttgart, Bochum, Nuremberg, Mönchengladbach and Hamburg and drew the other eleven—the only undefeated away record in the history of the league.

Despite their superb domestic form, the celebrations in Munich were somewhat muted, even when Bayern had wrapped up the title after a 2-2 home draw with Uerdingen with three weeks of the season still to go. This was because ten days previously Bayern had suffered such bitter disappointment in the European Cup Final in Vienna. Their path to the final wasn't far from reading like a Who's Who of European Football; PSV Eindhoven, FK Austria, Anderlecht, and Real Madrid all found their quest for glory ending in Munich. Desperate to regain a trophy they had last claimed eleven years earlier, Bayern faced the Portugese champions FC Porto in the final before a crowd of 59,000 predominantly German fans in Vienna. Despite leading 1-0 at half time, with Ludwig Kögl having an inspired match on the wing, Bayern let in two goals after the interval and lost.

Mönchengladbach was the team showing the best form towards the end of the season. They won their last ten games, catapulting them from twelfth to third in the league. Uwe Rahn scored fourteen times over this period to pinch the top goalscorer's trophy from Fritz Walter, who was in his last year with Waldhof Mannheim. Borussia Dortmund enjoyed something of a renaissance, qualifying for a

UEFA Cup spot after finishing third from bottom the season before. The new scoring duo of Mill and Norbert Dickel accounted for over half the club's goals; gates at the Westfalenstadion increased by nearly 10,000 a match.

The previous season's runners-up Werder Bremen slipped down the table, mainly due to a poor away record. Goals were proving somewhat harder for them to come by now that Völler had left for Italy. In the Weserstadion Bremen extended their unbeaten run to 43 games over a period of two and a half years before entertaining Mönchengladbach on 28th March—and losing 7-1.

Gladbach also put seven past Waldhof Mannheim, but the side most accustomed to letting in goals was Blau-Weiss 90 Berlin, who were playing their first season in the Bundesliga. They suffered a run of 21 consecutive games without a win and finished bottom by some distance. After spending the next five years in Division Two, Blau-Weiss's financial problems were to result in their being refused a professional licence. The club were forced to disband and in 1992 re-formed as Blau-Weiss 92. The other newly-promoted side, FC Homburg, did comparatively well to finish sixteenth, although *Trainer* Fritz Fuchs was the first managerial casualty of the way, being dismissed after just two matches. Udo Klug held the post for most of the season, but after being crushed 6-0 by Bremen with five matches to play, Homburg asked assistant Gerd Schwickert to finish the season. The club did manage to stave off what seemed inevitable by winning the play-off games against St. Pauli and remained in the Bundesliga for another year, although their points total of 21 remains the lowest for any team not to be relegated.

Hanover 96 bounced straight back into the top flight by winning the Second Division championship, four points clear of Karlsruhe. They had led virtually all season and even a 5-5 draw with bottom club Salmrohr on the last day did not affect the outcome. (Hanover played their reserve goalkeeper in an outfield position in that match and had led 4-0 at one stage). At the start of the season, Karlsruhe had replaced *Trainer* Lothar Buchmann with a 36-year-old scout for Borussia Mönchengladbach, Winfried Schäfer, who would go on to become one of the longest-serving one-club *Trainers* in Bundesliga history. At the bottom, Eintracht Brunswick failed to heed the warning signals of the season before and were relegated to the Oberliga North. Hessen Kassel, who had finished fourth two seasons ago and a respectable fifth the previous season, also were relegated.

The West German national team played only five times this season, their quietest year in the Bundesliga era. Meanwhile, the East German team played seven matches without registering a goal. They broke their duck in Chemnitz, with goals from Andreas Thom and Ulf Kirsten giving them victory against Iceland. There was better news from the East German Under-18s, who won the European Championship, beating Italy in the final.

As Dynamo Berlin marched relentlessly to yet another East German championship, focus shifted towards Lokomotive Leipzig, who became only the third East German side to reach a major European final. In the Cup-Winners' Cup they needed penalties to get past Bordeaux in the semifinals, and in the final in Athens, they went down to a first-half goal from Ajax Amsterdam's Marco van Basten. Leipzig had to be content with a 4-1 win in the East German Cup Final, their last major honour to date.

Bundesliga

Club	P	W	D	L	Goals	Pts
1. Bayern Munich	34	20	13	1	67-31	53
2. Hamburg SV	34	19	9	6	69-37	47
3. Borussia Mönchengladbach	34	18	7	9	74-44	43
4. Borussia Dortmund	34	15	10	9	70-50	40
5. Werder Bremen	34	17	6	11	65-54	40
6. Bayer Leverkusen	34	16	7	11	56-38	39
7. 1.FC Kaiserslautern	34	15	7	12	64-51	37
8. Bayer Uerdingen	34	12	11	11	51-49	35
9. 1.FC Nuremberg	34	12	11	11	62-62	35
10. 1.FC Cologne	34	13	9	12	50-53	35
11. VfL Bochum	34	9	14	11	52-44	32
12. VfB Stuttgart	34	13	6	15	55-49	32
13. FC Schalke 04	34	12	8	14	50-58	32
14. Waldhof Mannheim	34	10	8	16	52-71	28
15. Eintracht Frankfurt	34	8	9	17	42-53	25
16. FC 08 Homburg	34	6	9	19	33-79	21
17. Fortuna Düsseldorf	34	7	6	21	42-91	20
18. Blau-Weiss 90 Berlin	34	3	12	19	36-76	18

Top Scorers
Rahn (Borussia Mönchengladbach) 24
Walter (Waldhof Mannheim) 23
Völler (Werder Bremen) 22
Dickel (Borussia Dortmund) 20
Hartmann (1.FC Kaiserslautern) 17
Mill (Borussia Dortmund) 17
Klinsmann (VfB Stuttgart) 16
Kohr (1.FC Kaiserslautern) 16
Waas (Bayer Leverkusen) 15
K Allofs (1.FC Cologne) 14
Andersen (1.FC Nuremberg) 14
Matthäus (Bayern Munich) 14
Schreier (Bayer Leverkusen) 14
Wuttke (1.FC Kaiserslautern) 14
Zorc (Borussia Dortmund) 14

First Division Playoff
FC 08 Homburg v FC St Pauli (3-1, 1-2); Homburg remain in Division One

Second Division

Club	P	W	D	L	Goals	Pts
1. Hanover 96	38	23	10	5	86-48	56
2. Karlsruhe SC	38	22	8	8	79-49	52
3. FC St Pauli	38	19	11	8	63-45	49
4. SV Darmstadt 98	38	20	7	11	72-48	47
5. Alemannia Aachen	38	18	10	10	55-36	46
6. VfL Osnabrück	38	18	8	12	69-66	44
7. Kickers Stuttgart	38	18	6	14	72-55	42
8. SC Freiburg	38	13	13	12	59-56	39
9. Arminia Bielefeld	38	12	14	12	58-55	38
10. Rot-Weiss Essen	38	14	10	14	70-69	38
11. Wattenscheid 09	38	12	14	12	59-66	38
12. Union Solingen	38	13	9	16	61-65	35
13. SSV 1846 Ulm	38	13	9	16	55-63	35
14. Fortuna Cologne	38	10	15	13	51-66	35
15. 1.FC Saarbrücken	38	10	14	14	53-71	34
16. Rot-Weiss Oberhausen	38	13	7	18	52-55	33
17. Eintracht Brunswick	38	11	10	17	52-47	32
18. Viktoria Aschaffenburg	38	5	14	19	47-72	24
19. Hessen Kassel	38	6	10	22	40-75	22
20. FSV Salmrohr	38	4	13	21	48-94	21

Top Scorers
Reich (Hanover 96) 26
Linz (VfL Osnabrück) 20
Labbadia (SV Darmstadt 98) 18
Schütterle (Karlsruhe SC) 18
Gries (Alemannia Aachen) 17
Heitkamp (Rot-Weiss Essen) 17
Löw (SC Freiburg) 17
Sane (SC Freiburg) 17
Kurtenbach (Kickers Stuttgart) 16
Tschiskale (Wattenscheid 09) 16

Third Division Champions
Baden-Württemberg: SV Sandhausen
Bayern: SpVgg Bayreuth
Berlin: Hertha BSC Berlin
Hessen: Kickers Offenbach
Nord: SV Meppen
Nordrhein: BVL 08 Remscheid
Südwest: Eintracht Trier
Westfalen: SpVgg Erkenschwick

Second Division Playoffs

Northern Group	P	W	D	L	Goals	Pts
1. BVL 08 Remscheid	8	3	4	1	11-5	10
2. SV Meppen	8	2	6	0	13-10	6
3. Hertha BSC Berlin	8	3	3	2	11-10	9
4. SpVgg Erkenschwick	8	1	4	3	7-12	6
5. Arminia Hanover	8	0	5	3	10-15	5

Southern Group	P	W	D	L	Goals	Pts
1. Kickers Offenbach	6	3	1	2	13-7	7
2. SpVgg Bayreuth	6	3	1	2	10-11	7
3. Eintracht Trier	6	3	0	3	9-8	6
4. SV Sandhausen	6	2	0	4	6-12	4

West German Cup
First Round
Bayer Leverkusen 6, VfL Osnabrück 0
Bayer Uerdingen 6, VfB Stuttgart 4 aet
Blau-Weiss Friedrichstadt 1, Hassia Bingen 0
Bremen SV 1, Hessen Kassel 1 aet (1-1 aet; Bremen won on penalties)
BVL 08 Remscheid 3, 1.FC Kaiserslautern 0
DSC Wanne-Eickel 2, Blau-Weiss 90 Berlin 4
Eintracht Frankfurt 3, Eintracht Brunswick 1
FC Amberg 0, Borussia Mönchengladbach 7
FC Emmendingen 0, 1.FC Cologne 4
FSV Frankfurt 2, 1.FC Nuremberg 8
FSV Mainz 05 1, FC Schalke 04 0
Hamburg SV 3, Union Solingen 0
Hertha BSC Berlin 1, Bayern Munich 2
Rot-Weiss Lüdenscheid 2, 1.FC Saarbrücken 4 aet
Rot-Weiss Oberhausen 1, Borussia Dortmund 3
SC Charlottenburg 0, SV Darmstadt 98 3
SKV Mörfelden 0, Borussia Neunkirchen 3
SpVgg Bayreuth 0, Wattenscheid 09 3 aet
SV Meppen 1, MSV Duisburg 2
SV Sandhausen 0, Fortuna Cologne 1
Tennis Borussia Berlin 0, Kickers Stuttgart 5
TSG Giengen 1, Hanover 96 3
TSV 1860 Munich 1, FC Augsburg 5 aet
TSV Stelingen 1, Arminia Bielefeld 5
VfL Bochum 1, FC St Pauli 2
VfL Hamm 1, FC Gütersloh 1 aet (2-2 aet; Gütersloh won on penalties)
VfL Wolfsburg 2, Karlsruhe SC 2 aet (1-4)
VfR Aalen 0, Fortuna Düsseldorf 2
Viktoria Aschaffenburg 1, Waldhof Mannheim 2
Viktoria Cologne 2, SC Freiburg 5
Viktoria Goch 0, FC 08 Homburg 3
Werder Bremen 0, Alemannia Aachen 0 aet (0-0 aet; Aachen won on penalties)

Second Round
1.FC Cologne 3, Waldhof Mannheim 1
Alemannia Aachen 4, 1.FC Saarbrücken 0
Arminia Bielefeld 0, Karlsruhe SC 2
Bayer Uerdingen 3, 1.FC Nuremberg 2
Blau-Weiss Friedrichstadt 1, SV Darmstadt 98 2
Borussia Mönchengladbach 6, Borussia Dortmund 1
Borussia Neunkirchen 2, Kickers Stuttgart 3
Bremen SV 0, FC St Pauli 3
BVL Remscheid 3, Hanover 96 3 aet (1-2)
FC Augsburg 1, Hamburg SV 2
FC Gütersloh 0, Blau-Weiss 90 Berlin 5
FC 08 Homburg 1, Bayern Munich 3
Fortuna Cologne 1, SC Freiburg 1 aet (2-1)
Fortuna Düsseldorf 2, Bayer Leverkusen 1 aet
FSV Mainz 05 0, Eintracht Frankfurt 1 aet
MSV Duisburg 1, Wattenscheid 09 1 aet (1-2)

Third Round
Alemannia Aachen 0, Borussia Mönchengladbach 2 aet
Bayer Uerdingen 3, 1.FC Cologne 1
Blau-Weiss 90 Berlin 1, Karlsruhe SC 2
Fortuna Cologne 0, SV Darmstadt 98 2 aet
Fortuna Düsseldorf 3, Bayern Munich 0
Hamburg SV 6, FC St Pauli 0
Kickers Stuttgart 2, Hanover 96 0
Wattenscheid 09 1, Eintracht Frankfurt 3

Quarterfinals
Borussia Mönchengladbach 9, Bayer Uerdingen 2
Fortuna Düsseldorf 1, Karlsruhe SC 0
Kickers Stuttgart 3, Eintracht Frankfurt 1
SV Darmstadt 98 0, Hamburg SV 1

Semifinals
Hamburg SV 1, Borussia Mönchengladbach 0
Kickers Stuttgart 3, Fortuna Düsseldorf 0

Final
in Berlin
Hamburg SV 3, Kickers Stuttgart 1

West German Internationals
24/9/86 in Copenhagen 2-0 v Denmark
15/10/86 in Hanover 2-2 v Spain
29/10/86 in Vienna 1-4 v Austria
25/3/87 in Tel Aviv 2-0 v Israel
18/4/87 in Cologne 0-0 v Italy

East German Oberliga

Club	P	W	D	L	Goals	Pts
1. Dynamo Berlin	26	19	4	3	59-20	42
2. Dynamo Dresden	26	13	10	3	52-24	36
3. Lokomotive Leipzig	26	13	8	5	34-22	34
4. Wismut Aue	26	12	8	6	40-26	32
5. 1.FC Magdeburg	26	11	6	9	42-32	28
6. Carl Zeiss Jena	26	10	8	8	32-31	28
7. Rot-Weiss Erfurt	26	7	10	9	33-33	24
8. FC Karl-Marx-Stadt	26	6	12	8	27-34	24
9. Stahl Brandenburg	26	7	9	10	27-34	23
10. Vorwärts Frankfurt/Oder	26	6	9	11	23-32	21
11. 1.FC Union Berlin	26	6	7	13	26-52	19
12. Stahl Riesa	26	6	6	14	29-39	18
13. Energie Cottbus	26	7	4	15	19-45	18
14. Fortschritt Bischofswerda	26	6	5	15	25-44	17

Top Scorers

Pastor (Dynamo Berlin) 17
J Pfahl (Stahl Riesa) 15
Minge (Dynamo Dresden) 14
Backs (Dynamo Berlin) 12
Kirsten (Dynamo Dresden) 11
Thom (Dynamo Berlin) 11
Heun (Rot-Weiss Erfurt) 10
Halata (1.FC Magdeburg) 9
Bittner (Wismut Aue) 8
Mothes (Wismut Aue) 8
Wuckel (1.FC Magdeburg) 8

Second Division (Staffel A)

Club	P	W	D	L	Goals	Pts
1. Hansa Rostock	34	26	6	2	89-25	58
2. Dynamo Fürstenwalde	34	16	9	9	66-49	41
3. Vorwärts Dessau	34	18	5	11	64-47	41
4. Vorwärts Stralsund	34	14	12	8	42-29	40
5. Dynamo Berlin II	34	13	13	8	65-53	39
6. Vorwärts Frankfurt/Oder II	34	14	9	11	58-53	37
7. Stahl Eisenhüttenstadt	34	11	13	10	46-44	35
8. Motor Babelsberg	34	13	9	12	61-64	35
9. KKW Greifswald	34	11	13	10	46-50	35
10. Chemie Leipzig	34	13	7	4	43-51	33
11. Dynamo Schwerin	34	9	14	11	60-62	32
12. Rotation Berlin	34	11	10	13	48-59	32
13. Lok/Armaturen Prenzlau	34	11	9	14	52-55	31
14. Motor Ludwigsfelde	34	8	14	12	35-46	30
15. Post Neubrandenburg	34	7	15	12	42-51	29
16. ISG Schwerin	34	7	10	17	50-70	24
17. Schiffahrt/Hafen Rostock	34	5	13	16	38-58	23
18. Chemie Guben	34	5	7	22	38-77	17

Promoted: Aktivist Brieske-Senftenberg, Hansa Rostock II, Lokomotive Stendal. Lokomotove/Armaturen Prenzlau were replaced by Motor Prenzlau. Vorwärts Dessau and Chemie Leipzig were placed in Staffel B for the following season

Second Division (Staffel B)

Club	P	W	D	L	Goals	Pts
1. Chemie Halle	34	21	11	2	63-28	53
2. Sachsenring Zwickau	34	21	6	7	64-26	48
3. Chemie Böhlen	34	16	12	6	48-26	44
4. Aktivist Schwarze Pumpe	34	16	9	9	48-35	41
5. Motor Nordhausen	34	13	11	10	54-45	37
6. Motor Schönebeck	34	12	13	9	40-37	37
7. Chemie Buna Schkopau	34	13	10	11	46-44	38
8. Wismut Gera	34	12	11	11	51-45	35
9. Motor Grimma	34	13	7	14	43-54	33
10. Chemie Markkleeberg	34	9	14	11	44-42	32
11. Motor Suhl	34	11	10	13	38-39	32
12. Dynamo Dresden II	34	10	10	14	42-50	30
13. Motor Weimar	34	8	14	12	32-45	30
14. Carl Zeiss Jena II	34	10	9	15	27-46	29
15. Kali Werra Tiefenort	34	8	10	16	32-47	26
16. Dynamo Eisleben	34	7	10	17	26-57	24
17. Glückauf Sondershausen	34	6	11	17	39-47	23
18. Chemie Ilmenau	34	7	8	19	28-50	22

Promoted: Robotron Sömmerda, Stahl Thale, Fortschritt Weida. Aktivist Schwarze Pumpe and Motor Schönebeck were placed in Staffel A for the following season

East German Cup Final
in Berlin
Lokomotive Leipzig 4, Hansa Rostock 1

East German Internationals
20/8/86 in Lahti 0-1 v Finland
10/9/86 in Leipzig 0-1 v Denmark
24/9/86 in Oslo 0-0 v Norway (ECQ)
29/10/86 in Karl-Marx-Stadt 2-0 v Iceland (ECQ)
19/11/86 in Leipzig 0-0 v France (ECQ)
25/3/87 in Istanbul 1-3 v Turkey
29/4/87 in Kiev 0-2 v USSR (ECQ)
13/5/87 in Brandenburg 2-0 v Czechoslovakia
3/6/87 in Reykjavik 6-0 v Iceland (ECQ)
28/7/87 in Leipzig 0-0 v Hungary

European Cup
First Round
PSV Eindhoven v Bayern Munich .... (0-2, 0-0)
Orgryte Gothenburg v Dynamo Berlin .... (2-3, 1-4)
Second Round
Bayern Munich v FK Austria Vienna .... (2-0, 1-1)
Brondby v Dynamo Berlin .... (2-1, 1-1)
Quarterfinals
Bayern Munich v Anderlecht .... (5-0, 2-2)
Semifinals
Bayern Munich v Real Madrid .... (4-1, 0-1)
Final in Vienna
FC Porto 2, Bayern Munich 1

Cup-Winners' Cup
First Round
VfB Stuttgart v Spartak Trnava .... (1-0, 0-0)
Glentoran v Lokomotive Leipzig .... (1-1, 0-2)
Second Round
Torpedo Moscow v VfB Stuttgart .... (2-0, 5-3)
Rapid Vienna v Lokomotive Leipzig .... (1-1, 1-2 aet)
Quarterfinals
Lokomotive Leipzig v Sion .... (2-0, 0-0)
Semifinals
Bordeaux v Lokomotive Leipzig .... (0-1, 1-0 aet)
Leipzig won on penalties
Final in Athens
Ajax Amsterdam 1, Lokomotive Leipzig 0

UEFA Cup
First Round
Atlético Madrid v Werder Bremen .... (2-0, 1-2 aet)
Kalmar FF v Bayer Leverkusen .... (1-4, 0-3)
Bayer Uerdingen v Carl Zeiss Jena .... (3-0, 4-0)
Borussia Mönchengladbach v Partizan Belgrade ..... (1-0, 3-1)
Athletic Bilbao v 1.FC Magdeburg .... (2-0, 0-1)
Coleraine v Stahl Brandenburg .... (1-1, 0-1)
Second Round
Widzew Lodz v Bayer Uerdingen .... (0-0, 0-2)
Borussia Mönchengladbach v Feyenoord .... (5-1, 2-0)
Dukla Prague v Bayer Leverkusen .... (0-0, 1-1)
IFK Gothenburg v Stahl Brandenburg .... (2-0, 1-1)
Third Round
Bayer Uerdingen v Barcelona .... (0-2, 0-2)
Glasgow Rangers v Borussia Mönchengladbach ..... (1-1, 0-0)
Quarterfinals
Borussia Mönchengladbach v Vitoria Guimaraes ..... (3-0, 2-2)
Semifinals
Dundee United v Borussia Mönchengladbach .... (0-0, 2-0)

1987-88

A dream fulfilled

Before the 1992-93 season, Bayer Leverkusen were known to football trivia enthusiasts as the one club with a European trophy to its name but no domestic title. Though they had spent the last nine consecutive seasons in the Bundesliga, Leverkusen could hardly be considered part of German football's elite. They had never finished any higher than sixth place, never appeared in a German Cup Final, and their average home gates hovered around 10,000. Yet being a "works team" for the mighty Bayer chemical conglomerate, they had wealthy backers prepared to invest heavily in their quest for success. Under Erich Ribbeck, Leverkusen progressed from thirteenth place in 1985 to sixth place in 1987 and qualified for the UEFA Cup.

Bayer despatched Feyenoord and Barcelona on their way to the semifinal, as Werder Bremen were reaching the same stage by beating Dynamo Tblisi and Verona. The two Bundesliga clubs were then drawn against each other in the semifinal, with Leverkusen scoring the only goal in 180 minutes of play to go through. In the first leg of the final in Barcelona, Español built up a comprehensive 3-0 lead but Leverkusen staged a marvellous fight-back in the second half of the home leg, with goals from Falko Götz and their imports, the Brazilian Tita and the South Korean Bum-Kun Cha. After extra time proved inconclusive, the outcome was decided on spot-kicks, and Bayer won 3-2, despite going 2-0 behind. Leverkusen managed another credible sixth-place finish in the Bundesliga, but it was somewhat inconsequential in light of their surprising European triumph.

Bayern Munich were once again the team to beat in the Bundesliga, and their challengers were expected to be Hamburg, Stuttgart, and Bremen. Werder handed over DM1.2 million to relegated Blau-Weiss Berlin for striker Karl-Heinz Riedle, seeing him as a much-needed replacement for Rudi Völler. Their other major signing was the combative Uli Borowka, acquired from Mönchengladbach for DM1.6 million. Stuttgart spent a bundle on Waldhof Mannheim's Maurizio Gaudino and Fritz Walter. Pierre Littbarski returned to the Bundesliga after a disastrous season with Racing Paris, and it was his Cologne side who set the pace by going undefeated in their first twelve games.

The two controversial goalkeepers from the previous season found new employers. Time had healed all wounds as far as Schalke 04 were concerned and they obtained the services of the outcast Toni Schumacher, while Uli Stein, instructed to pack his bags by Hamburg SV, moved to Eintracht Frankfurt.

Although Bremen were ahead by the mid-season break, the biggest shock for Cologne was the departure of father-figure Udo Lattek, who decided to take up a job as columnist for a sports magazine. Bremen gradually extended their lead at the top, with goalkeeper Oliver Reck at one stage going a record 641 minutes without conceding a goal. Werder scored five against Schalke, Stuttgart and Uerdingen, and the only match they lost at home was the last of the season, a local derby with Hamburg—after they had been presented with the championship trophy.

Two years after the penalty drama against Bayern which had effectively decided the championship, Bremen had made amends by beating the Bavarians 3-2. Riedle scored twice, and the other goal, fittingly, was a penalty. On May 3 Werder wrapped up the title, winning 1-0 in Frankfurt with three matches left in hand.

At last, Werder *Trainer* Otto Rehhagel's dream had been fulfilled: he had won the ultimate prize in West German football. As a player, he had appeared for Hertha Berlin on the very first day of the league in August 1963. He went on to make over 200 Bundesliga appearances for Hertha and Kaiserslautern. His first coaching appointment was at 1.FC Saarbrücken, but he soon became one of the most frequent passengers on the managerial merry-go-round. In 1981 he took over at Werder—for the second time—and has remained there ever since, becoming the longest-serving *Trainer* in Bundesliga history.

Eintracht Frankfurt managed to make significant improvements in their away form, which bolstered their final league placing. A 3-1 win at Leverkusen on August 26 ended a record run of 32 successive journeys without a win, and just eleven points from a possible 64. By the end of November Waldhof Mannheim had equalled this unenviable feat, in their case with only eight points from 64 before they won 1-0 in Dortmund.

After 552 games, Schalke's Klaus Fichtel, at 43 the oldest player ever to have appeared in the Bundesliga by some four years, announced his retirement. He made his last appearance on May 21, in a 4-1 loss to Bremen. Schalke had gone through yet another very poor season, suffering an 8-1 beating at the hands of Bayern, and as Fichtel bowed out, so did Schalke—relegated for the third time in seven years.

Almost inevitably, Homburg were the other club to go down. The club went through three *Trainers*, three goalkeepers, and 25 field players, all to no avail. The fight to avoid the play-off spot was intense, with an 88th minute goal from Karlsruhe's Arno Glesius condemning Mannheim to sixteenth position. The play-off was a marathon affair, with Mannheim being held 4-4 on aggregate by SV Darmstadt and then 0-0 after extra time in the replay, before retaining their status through nothing more than a penalty shoot-out.

The top two teams in the Second Division were Kickers Stuttgart and FC St. Pauli. Kickers had led the way from virtually the start of the season, but St. Pauli had been pushed hard by Wattenscheid, Düsseldorf, and Darmstadt, and gained promotion only through an exceptionally strong finish. Wattenscheid missed out on the playoff spot when they could only draw at Saarbrücken in their last match and Darmstadt won at Osnabrück. So the following season the cities of Stuttgart and Hamburg would both boast two first division teams—and once again Berlin would have none. The city of Bielefeld would have no team in either Division One or Division Two. Arminia, a First Division club two seasons ago, finished rock-bottom of the Second and dropped into the Oberliga Westfalen.

The most memorable West German Cup tie was a second round match at Wolfsburg. Werder Bremen were cruising to a comfortable 4-1 victory with just six minutes to go, when Wolfsburg grabbed what appeared to be a consolation goal. In the 89th minute, Werder were still 4-2 up—but amazingly, Wolfsburg scored twice before the final whistle to force extra time. With Michel Kutzop having been shown the red card, a short-handed Werder managed to see off Wolfsburg courtesy of Frank Ordenewitz's strike in the 101st minute.

Bremen were eventually eliminated in one of the semifinals by Eintracht Frankfurt. VfL Bochum drew defending champions Hamburg in the other, and caught them on an off day. Andrzej Iwan's second goal for Bochum summed up HSV's performance: the ball slipped from keeper Jupp Koitka's grasp and trickled through his legs, much to the delight of the 31,000 in the Ruhrstadion. The final was decided on a 25-yard free kick by the star of the match, the Hungarian international Lajos Detari, who scored with nine minutes left. Frankfurt collected their fourth West German Cup, keeping the Bochum trophy cabinet bare for yet another season.

If familiarity breeds contempt, then Dynamo Berlin's triumph in the East Germany Oberliga was a major source of abhorrence. This was their tenth consecutive title, a record unsurpassed in modern European league history. Dynamo also won the cup—surprisingly, for the first time since 1959—but needed extra time and a goal from Thomas Doll to secure the double. Despite total success in domestic competitions, Dynamo once again failed in the early stages of the European Cup, going out to Bordeaux in the first round. Indeed, of their ten appearances in the competition, only twice had they made it past the second round. At the other end of the table, it was revealed that Wismut Aue's general manager Werner Lorenz had offered 1.FC Magdeburg players a "five-figure sum" in exchange for a few vital points in the battle against relegation.

The East German national side had a mixed season, typified by a 2-1 defeat in Morocco and a 1-0 win in France. In their Olympic qualifying group, East Germany finished second to Italy and did not go to Seoul, and in their European Championship group they came second to the Soviet Union and did not qualify there, either. Meanwhile the West German Olympic team won five and drew two of their eight qualifiers to go through.

As hosts, the full West German team automatically qualified for the European Championships, and wins over Denmark and Spain followed a draw with Italy and took them through to the semifinal. There, they went down 2-1 to eventual champions Holland at the Volksparkstadion in Hamburg. The Germans were angered by the Netherlands' Frank Rijkaard pretending to wipe his backside with an opponent's shirt after the match, but the Holland/West Germany rivalry was becoming one of the most fierce in European football. And it would not be the last controversial incident Rijkaard would find himself involved in against the Germans.

Bundesliga

Club	P	W	D	L	Goals	Pts
1. Werder Bremen	34	22	8	4	61-22	52
2. Bayern Munich	34	22	4	8	83-45	48
3. 1.FC Cologne	34	18	12	4	57-28	48
4. VfB Stuttgart	34	16	8	10	69-49	40
5. 1.FC Nuremberg	34	13	11	10	44-40	37
6. Hamburg SV	34	13	11	10	63-68	37
7. Borussia Mönchengladbach	34	14	5	15	55-53	33
8. Bayer Leverkusen	34	10	12	12	53-60	32
9. Eintracht Frankfurt	34	10	11	13	51-50	31
10. Hanover 96	34	12	7	15	59-60	31
11. Bayer Uerdingen	34	11	9	14	59-61	31
12. VfL Bochum	34	10	10	14	47-51	30
13. Borussia Dortmund	34	9	11	14	51-54	29
14. 1.FC Kaiserslautern	34	11	7	16	53-62	29
15. Karlsruhe SC	34	9	11	14	37-55	29
16. Waldhof Mannheim	34	7	14	13	35-50	28
17. FC 08 Homburg	34	7	10	17	37-70	24
18. FC Schalke 04	34	8	7	19	48-84	23

Top Scorers
Klinsmann (VfB Stuttgart) 19
Riedle (Werder Bremen) 18
Matthäus (Bayern Munich) 17
Reich (Hanover 96) 17
Kohr (1.FC Kaiserslautern) 16
Walter (VfB Stuttgart) 16
Eckstein (1.FC Nuremberg) 15
Ordenewitz (Werder Bremen) 15
Thon (FC Schalke 04) 14
Kuntz (Bayer Uerdingen) 13
Leifeld (VfL Bochum) 13
Povlsen (1.FC Cologne) 13
Wegmann (Bayern Munich) 13
Zorc (Borussia Dortmund) 13

First Division Playoff
SV Darmstadt 98 v Waldhof Mannheim (3-2, 1-2, 0-0 aet); Mannheim won third match on penalties to remain in Division One

Division Two

Club	P	W	D	L	Goals	Pts
1. Kickers Stuttgart	38	19	13	6	89-49	51
2. FC St Pauli	38	19	11	8	65-38	49
3. SV Darmstadt 98	38	16	15	7	48-32	47
4. Wattenscheid 09	38	18	11	9	62-48	47
5. Fortuna Düsseldorf	38	20	6	12	63-38	46
6. Alemannia Aachen	38	17	12	9	60-45	46
7. Blau-Weiss 90 Berlin	38	16	11	11	65-48	43
8. Kickers Offenbach	38	13	13	12	56-49	39
9. VfL Osnabrück	38	13	12	13	47-47	38
10. SC Freiburg	38	13	12	13	61-63	38
11. Rot-Weiss Essen	38	11	12	15	53-60	34
12. Fortuna Cologne	38	15	4	19	58-67	34
13. 1.FC Saarbrücken	38	12	10	16	57-67	34
14. SV Meppen	38	12	10	16	55-72	34
15. Union Solingen	38	12	10	16	48-65	34
16. Rot-Weiss Oberhausen	38	13	7	18	48-54	33
17. SpVgg Bayreuth	38	14	5	19	55-66	33
18. BVL Remscheid	38	11	7	20	54-74	29
19. SSV 1846 Ulm	38	12	5	21	51-75	29
20. Arminia Bielefeld	38	6	10	22	29-67	22

Rot-Weiss Oberhausen were relegated after their professional licence was revoked, allowing SpVgg Bayreuth to remain in Division Two

Top Scorers
Sane (SC Freiburg) 21
Gries (Alemannia Aachen) 19
Kremer (BVL Remscheid) 18
Steubing (SSV 1846 Ulm) 17
Zander (FC St Pauli) 17
Grabosch (Kickers Stuttgart) 16
D Müller (Kickers Offenbach) 16
Schlumberger (Blau-Weiss 90 Berlin) 16
Wenzel (FC St Pauli) 16
Glöde (VfL Osnabrück) 15

Third Division Champions
Baden-Württemberg: FV 09 Weinheim
Bayern: SpVgg Unterhaching
Berlin: Hertha BSC Berlin
Hessen: Viktoria Aschaffenburg
Nord: Eintracht Brunswick
Nordrhein: MSV Duisburg
Südwest: FSV 05 Mainz
Westfalen: Preussen Münster

Second Division Playoffs

Northern Group

	P	W	D	L	Goals	Pts
1. Hertha BSC Berlin	8	5	1	2	19-12	11
2. Eintracht Brunswick	8	5	1	2	12-8	11
3. MSV Duisburg	8	4	2	2	19-13	10
4. Preussen Münster	8	1	2	5	10-18	4
5. VfL Wolfsburg	8	1	2	5	13-22	4

Southern Group

	P	W	D	L	Goals	Pts
1. FSV Mainz 05	6	4	1	1	17-9	9
2. Viktoria Aschaffenburg	6	3	2	1	9-8	8
3. SpVgg Unterhaching	6	1	2	3	8-12	4
4. FV 09 Weinheim	6	1	1	4	5-10	3

1987-88

West German Cup

First Round
1.FC Cologne 3, VfB Stuttgart 0
1.FC Kaiserslautern 3, Waldhof Mannheim 1 aet
1.FC Pforzheim 3, 1.FC Saarbrücken 2
Arminia Bielefeld 1, SC Freiburg 4 aet
Borussia Mönchengladbach 2, Bayer Leverkusen 1 aet
Concordia Hamburg 3, SpVgg Erkenschwick 0
Eintracht Brunswick 2, 1.FC Nuremberg 3
Eintracht Frankfurt 3, FC Schalke 04 2
FC St Pauli 0, Blau-Weiss 90 Berlin 3 aet
FSV Salmrohr 2, VfL Osnabrück 0
FV Offenburg 3, Borussia Dortmund 3 aet (0-5)
Hamburg SV 3, FC 08 Homburg 0
KSV Baunatal 1, SSV 1846 Ulm 1 aet (1-2)
Preussen Münster 1, Rot-Weiss Oberhausen 1 aet (2-0)
Rot-Weiss Essen 1, Bayern Munich 3
RSV Würges 0, Fortuna Düsseldorf 3
Südwest Ludwigshafen 1, Fortuna Cologne 6
SV Heidingsfeld 1, Bayer Uerdingen 2
SV St. Ingbert 0, Union Solingen 2
TSV Verden 0, Werder Bremen 4
TSV Vestenbergsreuth 0, SV Darmstadt 98 4
TuS Paderborn-Neuhaus 0, Kickers Stuttgart 5
VfB Dillingen 0, TSG Giengen 1
VfB Lübeck 1, Schwarz-Weiss Essen 2
VfB Oldenburg 0, VfL Bochum 0 aet (1-4)
VfL Hamm 2, Hessen Kassel 7
VfL Wolfsburg 3, Hanover 96 0
VfR Aachen-Forst 0, Karlsruhe SC 5
VfR Aalen 1, Alemannia Aachen 2
Viktoria Aschaffenburg 4, Wattenscheid 09 0
Viktoria Cologne 1, Hertha BSC Berlin 3
Werder Bremen (Am.) 5, MTV Ingolstadt 1

Second Round
1.FC Kaiserslautern 4, Blau-Weiss 90 Berlin 3
1.FC Pforzheim 2, Concordia Hamburg 0
Borussia Mönchengladbach 2, Bayern Munich 2 aet (2-3 aet)
Eintracht Frankfurt 3, SSV 1846 Ulm 0
Fortuna Cologne 1, SC Freiburg 0
FSV Salmrohr 0, Borussia Dortmund 1
Hertha BSC Berlin 1, Bayer Uerdingen 2
Hessen Kassel 3, Kickers Stuttgart 1
Karlsruhe SC 1, 1.FC Nuremberg 1 aet (1-2)
Preussen Münster 2, Alemannia Aachen 2 aet (1-0)
Schwarz-Weiss Essen 1, SV Darmstadt 98 0
TSG Giengen 1, VfL Bochum 2 aet
Union Solingen 1, Fortuna Düsseldorf 2
VfL Wolfsburg 4, Werder Bremen 5 aet
Viktoria Aschaffenburg 1, 1.FC Cologne 0
Werder Bremen (Am.) 1, Hamburg SV 3

Third Round
1.FC Kaiserslautern 1, Hamburg SV 2
1.FC Pforzheim 1, Werder Bremen 1 aet (1-3)
Bayer Uerdingen 3, Borussia Dortmund 3 aet (2-1)
Bayern Munich 3, 1.FC Nuremberg 1
Fortuna Düsseldorf 0, Eintracht Frankfurt 1
Hessen Kassel 0, Viktoria Aschaffenburg 1
Preussen Münster 2, Fortuna Cologne 3
Schwarz-Weiss Essen 0, VfL Bochum 1

Quarterfinals
Eintracht Frankfurt 4, Bayer Uerdingen 2
Hamburg SV 2, Bayern Munich 1
VfL Bochum 4, Fortuna Cologne 1
Viktoria Aschaffenburg 1, Werder Bremen 3

Semifinals
VfL Bochum 2, Hamburg SV 0
Werder Bremen 0, Eintracht Frankfurt 1

Final
in Berlin
Eintracht Frankfurt 1, VfL Bochum 0

West German Internationals
12/8/87 in Berlin 2-1 v France
9/9/87 in Düsseldorf 3-1 v England
23/9/87 in Hamburg 1-0 v Denmark
13/10/87 in Gelsenkirchen 1-1 v Sweden
18/11/87 in Budapest 0-0 v Hungary
12/12/87 in Brasilia 1-1 v Brazil
16/12/87 in Buenos Aires 0-1 v Argentina
31/3/88 in Berlin 1-1 v Sweden aet; Sweden won on penalties
2/4/88 in Berlin 1-0 v Argentina
27/4/88 in Kaiserslautern 1-0 v Switzerland
4/6/88 in Bremen 1-1 v Yugoslavia
10/6/88 in Düsseldorf 1-1 v Italy (EC)
14/6/88 in Gelsenkirchen 2-0 v Denmark (EC)
17/6/88 in Munich 2-0 v Spain (EC)
21/6/88 in Hamburg 1-2 v Holland (EC)

East German Oberliga

Club	P	W	D	L	Goals	Pts
1. Dynamo Berlin	26	15	7	4	59-30	37
2. Lokomotive Leipzig	26	14	9	3	42-21	37
3. Dynamo Dresden	26	12	9	5	47-24	33
4. Stahl Brandenburg	26	12	5	9	44-37	29
5. Chemie Halle	26	7	12	7	33-33	26
6. Carl Zeiss Jena	26	8	10	8	28-29	26
7. 1.FC Magdeburg	26	9	7	10	34-33	25
8. FC Karl-Marx-Stadt	26	8	9	9	40-45	25
9. Hansa Rostock	26	7	9	10	42-49	23
10. Wismut Aue	26	8	7	11	24-34	23
11. 1.FC Union Berlin	26	7	8	11	35-54	22
12. Rot-Weiss Erfurt	26	8	5	13	40-49	21
13. Vorwärts Frankfurt/Oder	26	6	9	11	33-43	21
14. Stahl Riesa	26	3	10	13	23-43	16

Top Scorers

Thom (Dynamo Berlin)	20
Heun (Rot-Weiss Erfurt)	15
J Pfahl (Stahl Riesa)	13
Ernst (Dynamo Berlin)	12
Richter (Karl-Marx-Stadt)	12
Seier (1.FC Union Berlin)	12
Doll (Dynamo Berlin)	11
Wuckel (1.FC Magdeburg)	10
Glowatzky (Karl-Marx-Stadt)	9
Gütschow (Dynamo Dresden)	9
Jeske (Stahl Brandenburg)	9
Schnürer (Vorwärts Frankfurt/Oder)	9

Second Division (Staffel A)

Club	P	W	D	L	Goals	Pts
1. Energie Cottbus	34	20	10	4	69-24	50
2. Rotation Berlin	34	17	10	7	55-34	44
3. Dynamo Berlin II	34	17	9	8	63-49	43
4. Motor Ludwigsfelde	34	18	5	11	51-35	41
5. Aktivist Brieske Senftenberg	34	13	11	10	49-44	37
6. Post Neubrandenburg	34	12	13	9	49-47	37
7. KKW Greifswald	34	15	4	15	56-55	34
8. Dynamo Schwerin	34	10	14	10	50-60	34
9. Dynamo Fürstenwalde	34	10	13	11	44-54	33
10. Vorwärts Stralsund	34	12	8	14	41-52	32
11. Motor Babelsberg	34	12	7	15	49-49	31
12. Aktivist Schwarze Pumpe	34	8	15	11	38-38	31
13. Motor Schönebeck	34	12	7	15	45-51	31
14. Vorwärts Frankfurt/Oder II	34	11	6	17	60-65	28
15. Stahl Eisenhüttenstadt	34	9	10	15	36-35	28
16. Lokomotive Stendal	34	11	5	18	36-58	27
17. Motor Prenzlau	34	8	10	16	40-54	26
18. Hansa Rostock II	34	7	11	16	40-57	25

Promoted: KWO Berlin, Stahl Hennigsdorf, Schiffahrt/Hafen Rostock. Vorwärts Frankfurt/Oder II did not play at this level in the following season.

Second Division (Staffel B)

Club	P	W	D	L	Goals	Pts
1. Sachsenring Zwickau	34	20	10	4	66-34	50
2. Stahl Thale	34	14	14	6	57-40	42
3. Vorwärts Dessau	34	15	12	7	52-38	42
4. Dynamo Dresden II	34	16	9	9	57-35	41
5. Fortschritt Bischofswerda	34	15	11	8	58-41	41
6. Chemie Leipzig	34	16	9	9	40-33	41
7. Chemie Buna Schkopau	34	12	15	7	49-43	39
8. Chemie Markkleeberg	34	12	11	11	53-50	35
9. Wismut Gera	34	10	14	10	47-41	34
10. Motor Suhl	34	11	11	12	38-43	33
11. Robotron Sömmerda	34	12	8	14	47-50	32
12. Motor Grimma	34	10	10	14	41-54	30
13. Chemie Böhlen	34	8	13	13	36-43	29
14. Motor Weimar	34	9	10	15	36-52	28
15. Motor Nordhausen	34	7	13	14	39-47	27
16. Fortschritt Weida	34	10	7	17	40-54	27
17. Kali Werra Tiefenort	34	8	10	16	40-56	26
18. Carl Zeiss Jena II	34	4	7	23	29-71	15

Promoted: Aktivist Borna, Dynamo Eisleben, Motor FH Karl-Marx-Stadt

East German Cup Final
in Berlin
Dynamo Berlin 2, Carl Zeiss Jena 0

East German Internationals

19/8/87 in Lubin 0-2 v Poland
23/9/87 in Gera 2-0 v Tunisia
10/10/87 in Berlin 1-1 v USSR (ECQ)
28/10/87 in Magdeburg 3-1 v Norway
18/11/87 in Paris 1-0 v France (ECQ)
27/1/88 in Valencia 0-0 v Spain
2/3/88 in Mohammedia 1-2 v Morocco
30/3/88 in Halle 3-3 v Rumania
13/4/88 in Burgas 1-1 v Bulgaria

European Cup
First Round
Bayern Munich v CSKA Sofia .... (4-0, 1-0)
Bordeaux v Dynamo Berlin .... (2-0, 2-0)
Second Round
Xamax Neuchatel v Bayern Munich .... (2-1, 0-2)
Quarterfinals
Bayern Munich v Real Madrid .... (3-2, 0-2)

Cup-Winners' Cup
First Round
Avenir Beggen v Hamburg SV .... (0-5, 0-3)
Lokomotive Leipzig v Marseilles .... (0-0, 0-1)
Second Round
Hamburg SV v Ajax Amsterdam .... (0-1, 0-2)

UEFA Cup
First Round
Borussia Mönchengladbach v Español .... (0-1, 1-4)
Glasgow Celtic v Borussia Dortmund .... (2-1, 0-2)
Mjöndalen IF v Werder Bremen .... (0-5, 1-0)
Austria Vienna v Bayer Leverkusen .... (0-0, 1-5)
Spartak Moscow v Dynamo Dresden .... (3-0, 0-1)
Wismut Aue v Valur Reykjavik .... (0-0, 1-1)
Second Round
Borussia Dortmund v Velez Mostar .... (2-0, 1-2)
Spartak Moscow v Werder Bremen .... (4-1, 2-6 aet)
Toulouse v Bayer Leverkusen .... (1-1, 0-1)
Wismut Aue v Flamurtari Vlora .... (1-0, 0-2)
Third Round
Feyenoord v Bayer Leverkusen .... (2-2, 0-1)
Werder Bremen v Dynamo Tbilisi .... (2-1, 1-1)
Borussia Dortmund v FC Bruges .... (3-0, 0-5 aet)
Quarterfinals
Bayer Leverkusen v Barcelona .... (0-0, 1-0)
Verona v Werder Bremen .... (0-1, 1-1)
Semifinal
Bayer Leverkusen v Werder Bremen .... (1-0, 0-0)
Final
Español v Bayer Leverkusen .... (3-0, 0-3 aet)
Leverkusen won on penalties

1988-89

Dutch treat?

With their first trophy of any consequence tucked away in the cabinet, an ambitious Bayer Leverkusen had put a considerable amount of money and effort into luring Rinus Michels back into the Bundesliga, in the hope that he could build on the club's UEFA Cup success of the previous season. When *Trainer* Erich Ribbeck, who had brought the club the only honours it had ever known, decided to become General Manager at Hamburg, Bayer brought in their new man. But early in the season, Leverkusen were dumped out of the UEFA Cup, and in the Bundesliga they could do little more than founder in mid-table. Michels came under a lot of criticism for chopping and changing his team at will yet never seeming to come up with the right combination. So in April, after less than a season in charge, he was given his marching orders and assistant Jürgen Gelsdorf assumed control.

After Jupp Heynckes had finished his successful playing career, he put himself through the tough DFB coaching scheme to gain his *Trainer*'s licence. In 1979 he took over at Borussia Mönchengladbach and stayed in charge for eight years, leading them through six European campaigns—though never the Bundesliga title. So when Bayern Munich offered him the opportunity to take over from Udo Lattek in 1987, Heynckes accepted. Having lost out to Werder Bremen in his first season with Munich, and having then lost Lothar Matthäus and Andreas Brehme to Inter Milan, Heynckes took advantage of Bayern's considerable buying power to bring in Roland Grahammer and Stefan Reuter from Nuremberg, Olaf Thon from relegated Schalke and Sweden's Johnny Ekström from Italian club Empoli.

The changes made all the difference. Grahammer and the defence conceded just 26 goals all season. Up front, Jürgen Wegmann and Roland Wohlfarth combined for 30 of Bayern's league-leading 67 goals. Bayern once again became the most feared team in the country, going through the first 22 games of the season undefeated before finally losing at Mönchengladbach. Bayern's closest rivals were Bremen and 1.FC Cologne, both of whom eventually came into contention after recovering from poor starts. Thomas Hässler was emerging as a new star in a Cologne team which went thirteen matches without defeat, Jürgen Kohler anchoring the defence and Thomas Allofs scoring the goals. Defending champions Werder fielded a side virtually unchanged from the year before. Karlheinz Riedle and Frank Neubarth proved a useful striking partnership, and the sweeper, Norwegian international Rune Bratseth, was the pick of the Bundesliga's current crop of imports.

The season built up to an exciting climax, with Bayern due to visit Cologne two weeks before the end. Cologne had only managed a draw in Hanover and were now two points behind Bayern. Shortly before the big game, Cologne *Trainer* Christoph Daum appeared on a television sports programme and completely lost his composure, bursting into a tirade of insults against Heynckes. Bayern were not short of motivation on the day, and 60,000 saw a hat-trick by Roland Wohlfarth give the Bavarians a 3-1 win and their eleventh championship.

Cologne lost their last match of the season at Mannheim to finish five points behind Bayern. Still, Daum had reasons to be cheerful: not since winning the league in 1978 had the club enjoyed a higher finish. Bremen took third place, the seventh consecutive season Otto Rehhagel's team had earned a place in the top five.

Mönchengladbach needed to beat HSV in their last match to qualify for the UEFA Cup, but lost 4-0 and finished sixth. In November their midfielder Christian Hochstätter had been hit in the eye with a firework thrown from the terraces during Borussia's 3-1 loss at Karlsruhe. The DFB, though, ordered the match to be replayed at a neutral site, and so later in the season Gladbach faced KSC for a third time, in Heilbronn. They scored in the third minute of injury time to secure a 2-2 draw.

The surprise of the Bundesliga was newly-promoted FC St. Pauli, who finished comfortably in mid-table, playing before packed crowds of frenzied fans at their cramped but quaint Millerntor ground. The club had averaged around 11,000 in the previous season's promotion-clinching campaign, but now crowds had swelled to over 20,000—fourth-best in the league, and technically in excess of the ground's capacity (their home match against Hamburg was moved to the Volksparkstadion and attracted over 60,000).

Hanover 96 finished bottom by quite some distance, but above them a remarkable series of results meant that no less than four clubs had finished level on points in places fourteen to seventeen. As a consequence of goal difference, Nuremberg (-18) and VfL Bochum (-20) retained their status, Eintracht Frankfurt (-23) faced the ordeal of a play-off and Stuttgart Kickers (-27) were consigned to relegation. Frankfurt edged out Saarbrücken 3-2 on aggregate to maintain—barely—their ever-present record of Bundesliga membership.

Fortuna Düsseldorf regained a place in the First Division behind the sharp-shooting of Sven Demandt, whose 35 goals put him well in front of his divisional rivals. Fortuna won their last six matches to climb from fourth place to first. Homburg claimed second place and a hasty return to the top flight, despite having dismissed yet another *Trainer*, Slobodan Cendic, late in the season. But the oddest match of the season was in Cologne, where Fortuna hosted Wattenscheid in a crucial promotion battle. An 86th minute winner from Stefan Emmerling gave Wattenscheid a bizarre 6-5 victory. Fortuna had been at or near the top of the division for most of the season, but when their top scorer Uwe Fuchs broke his arm their hopes faded.

The battle to avoid relegation was incredibly tight, with only three points separating all nine clubs in the lower half of the league. Amongst those escaping the jaws of amateur football by the skin of their collective teeth were Schalke 04, Hertha Berlin, Rot-Weiss Essen, and Kickers Offenbach. MSV Duisburg came out of the amateur leagues, winning the Oberliga Nordrhein comfortably, but Oberliga Baden-Württemberg table-toppers SSV Reutlingen were given quite a scare. On the last day of the season, second-place 1.FC Pforzheim won 8-0 against VfL Neckarau to finish level with Reutlingen on points. Reutlingen needed to win a hastily-arranged playoff to advance to the promotion round.

Dortmund and Bremen reached the final of the West German Cup. Dortmund's semifinal match with VfB Stuttgart had been action-packed, but ill-tempered: three players were sent off and five others booked as Dortmund won 2-0. Bremen faced Bayer Leverkusen, who missed enough good chances to win handsomely before succumbing to a Dieter Eilts goal with three minutes left.

The final produced some very attractive football, most of it coming from Dortmund. Karlheinz Riedle gave Werder the lead on the quarter-hour, but Werder were unable to build on their lead. Two goals from Norbert Dickel, one from Frank Mill, and one from Michael Lusch gave Borussia their first West German Cup since 1965. The new star in Dortmund's side was Andreas Möller, a 21 year-old midfielder who was attracting more than a cursory glance from a few Italian clubs.

The East German season's major talking point was Dynamo Dresden's Oberliga championship, which ended Dynamo Berlin's astonishing run of ten consecutive titles. Dresden finished eight points clear, with Torsten Gütschow taking top goalscoring honours, and Andreas Trautmann named East German Footballer of the Year. The East German season's most remarkable turnaround was managed by Stahl Eisenhüttenstadt in *Liga Staffel A*. The previous year, just one point had separated them from relegation. This season, they finished top of their division—by scoring one goal more than second-place Dynamo Fürstenwalde—and joined the top flight for only the second time in their history. But interest in the national team was on the wane. Only 11,000 were in Cottbus to see the game with Poland, and a mere 6,500 turned up in Berlin for the visit of Greece. This was hardly surprising, as the East Germans won only one of their five World Cup qualifying matches and stood virtually no chance of making it to Italy.

At the Seoul Olympics in September, West Germany progressed to the semifinal but lost to Brazil on penalties after a 1-1 draw. The Germans beat Italy 3-0 to take the bronze medal. Frank Mill captained a side which included Uwe Kamps, Wolfram Wuttke, Michael Schulz, Jürgen Klinsmann and Thomas Hässler.

Three German teams reached the semifinals of the UEFA Cup this year, but the odd team out, Napoli, walked away with the honours, beating Bayern and then Stuttgart for the trophy. Attendance broke all records for a European final: 81,000 in Naples and 67,000 in Stuttgart. Napoli won the home leg thanks to a bit of Diego Maradona's hand-ball "magic" and some curious refereeing decisions, but emerged worthy winners after an impressive 3-3 draw in the Neckarstadion. In the European Cup, Dynamo Berlin registered a 3-0 win in the home leg against Werder Bremen, but went 5-0 down at the Weserstadion. Werder put out Glasgow Celtic on the way to a semifinal meeting with AC Milan, where a dubious penalty proved the difference between the two sides.

Bundesliga

Club	P	W	D	L	Goals	Pts
1. Bayern Munich	34	19	12	3	67-26	50
2. 1.FC Cologne	34	18	9	7	58-30	45
3. Werder Bremen	34	18	8	8	55-32	44
4. Hamburg SV	34	17	9	8	60-36	43
5. VfB Stuttgart	34	16	7	11	58-49	39
6. Borussia Mönchengladbach	34	12	14	8	44-43	38
7. Borussia Dortmund	34	12	13	9	56-40	37
8. Bayer Leverkusen	34	10	14	10	45-44	34
9. 1.FC Kaiserslautern	34	10	13	11	47-44	33
10. FC St Pauli	34	9	14	11	41-42	32
11. Karlsruhe SC	34	12	8	14	48-51	32
12. Waldhof Mannheim	34	10	11	13	43-52	31
13. Bayer Uerdingen	34	10	11	13	50-60	31
14. 1.FC Nuremberg	34	8	10	16	36-54	26
15. VfL Bochum	34	9	8	17	37-57	26
16. Eintracht Frankfurt	34	8	10	16	30-53	26
17. Kickers Stuttgart	34	10	6	18	41-68	26
18. Hanover 96	34	4	11	19	36-71	19

Top Scorers
K Allofs (1.FC Cologne) 17
Wohlfarth (Bayern Munich) 17
Bein (Hamburg SV) 15
Criens (Borussia Mönchengladbach) 13
Klinsmann (VfB Stuttgart) 13
Kohr (1.FC Kaiserslautern) 13
Kuntz (Bayer Uerdingen) 13
Leifeld (VfL Bochum) 13
Neubarth (Werder Bremen) 13
Riedle (Werder Bremen) 13
Walter (VfB Stuttgart) 13
Wegmann (Bayern Munich) 13

First Division Playoff
Eintracht Frankfurt v 1.FC Saarbrücken (2-0, 1-2); Frankfurt remain in Division One

Second Division

Club	P	W	D	L	Goals	Pts
1. Fortuna Düsseldorf	38	19	11	8	85-52	49
2. FC 08 Homburg	38	18	11	9	55-36	47
3. 1.FC Saarbrücken	38	17	12	9	53-43	46
4. Fortuna Cologne	38	20	5	13	80-57	45
5. SC Freiburg	38	17	8	13	66-52	42
6. Wattenscheid 09	38	17	8	13	68-58	42
7. Alemannia Aachen	38	17	7	14	58-55	41
8. Blau-Weiss 90 Berlin	38	15	11	12	56-54	41
9. Eintracht Brunswick	38	12	14	12	43-43	38
10. SV Meppen	38	12	13	13	55-54	37
11. SV Darmstadt 98	38	16	5	17	56-57	37
12. FC Schalke 04	38	13	10	15	58-51	36
13. Hertha BSC Berlin	38	11	14	13	45-44	36
14. VfL Osnabrück	38	13	10	15	58-66	36
15. Kickers Offenbach	38	14	7	17	51-53	36
16. Rot-Weiss Essen	38	13	9	16	54-60	35
17. SpVgg Bayreuth	38	12	10	16	52-60	34
18. Viktoria Aschaffenburg	38	12	10	16	47-60	34
19. FSV Mainz 05	38	8	13	17	44-76	29
20. Union Solingen	38	6	8	24	24-77	20

Kickers Offenbach were refused a professional licence for the following season, allowing SpVgg Bayreuth to remain in Division Two

Top Scorers
Demandt (Fortuna Düsseldorf) 35
Fuchs (Fortuna Cologne) 22
Haub (Viktoria Aschaffenburg) 16
Anderbrügge (FC Schalke 04) 15
Tschiskale (Wattenscheid 09) 15
Wolff (SpVgg Bayreuth) 15
Eichenauer (SV Darmstadt 98) 14
Sendscheid (Alemannia Aachen) 13
Gries (Alemannia Aachen/Hertha Berlin) 12
Pförtner (Fortuna Cologne) 12
Van der Pütten (SV Meppen) 12

Third Division Champions
Baden-Württemberg: SSV Reutlingen
Bayern: SpVgg Unterhaching
Berlin: Reinickendorf Füchse
Hessen: Hessen Kassel
Nord: TSV Havelse
Nordrhein: MSV Duisburg
Südwest: SV Edenkoben
Westfalen: Preussen Münster

Second Division Playoffs

Northern Group

	P	W	D	L	Goals	Pts
1. MSV Duisburg	8	4	3	1	16-8	11
2. Preussen Münster	8	4	2	2	10-7	6
3. Göttingen 05	8	4	1	3	16-11	9
4. Reinickendorf Füchse	8	3	0	5	15-19	6
5. TSV Havelse	8	1	2	5	5-17	4

Southern Group

	P	W	D	L	Goals	Pts
1. Hessen Kassel	6	3	2	1	12-5	8
2. SpVgg Unterhaching	6	3	1	2	9-11	7
3. SSV Reutlingen	6	3	0	3	9-8	6
4. SV Edenkoben	6	1	1	4	3-9	3

West German Cup
First Round
1.FC Cologne 6, SV Darmstadt 98 1
1.FC Kaiserslautern 2, FC St Pauli 1
Arminia Bielefeld 0, VfL Bochum 0 aet (1-4 aet)
Bayern Munich 11, Blau-Weiss 90 Berlin 2
Borussia Dortmund 6, Eintracht Brunswick 0
BSC Erlangen 0, Bayer Leverkusen 5
BVL 08 Remscheid 2, SpVgg Landshut 3
FC Augsburg 1, Alemannia Aachen 4
FC Bitburg 1, Saar 05 Saarbrücken 3
FC Schalke 04 1, Borussia Mönchengladbach 1 aet (2-1)
Fortuna Cologne 1, Fortuna Düsseldorf 0
FSV Salmrohr 2, SC Freiburg 0
Germania Dörnigheim 0, SpVgg Bayreuth 5
Karlsruhe SC 2, Kickers Stuttgart 1
MSV Duisburg 3, Hamburg SV 5 aet
SG Düren 99 1, Kickers Offenbach 3
SKG Heidelberg 1, Waldhof Mannheim 3
SSV Reutlingen 2, Sportfreunde Hamborn 07 1
SSV 1846 Ulm 1, 1.FC Nuremberg 4
STV Horst-Emscher 0, Union Solingen 0 aet (1-5)
SV Meiendorf 0, TSV Osterholz-Tenever 1
SV Meppen 1, Bayer Uerdingen 2
SV Ottfingen 0, VfB Stuttgart 5
TBV Lemgo 0, FC 08 Homburg 4
TSV Verden 1, Rot-Weiss Essen 2
Türkiyemspor Berlin 0, FC Emmendingen 2
TuS Hoisdorf 3, Rot-Weiss Oberhausen 0
VfL Kirchheim/Teck 1, SV Wehen 2
VfL Wolfsburg 1, Eintracht Frankfurt 1 aet (1-6)
Wattenscheid 09 1, VfL Osnabrück 1 aet (1-2)
Werder Bremen 4, Hanover 96 1
Wormatia Worms 1, 1.FC Saarbrücken 3

Second Round
1.FC Cologne 1, Waldhof Mannheim 2
1.FC Kaiserslautern 5, Kickers Offenbach 0
1.FC Nuremberg 1, Karlsruhe SC 1 aet (0-1)
Bayer Uerdingen 5, Eintracht Frankfurt 4 aet
Borussia Dortmund 2, FC 08 Homburg 1
FC Emmendingen 1, SV Wehen 3
FSV Salmrohr 0, 1.FC Saarbrücken 1 aet
Saar 05 Saarbrücken 3, FC Schalke 04 3 aet (1-7)
SpVgg Landshut 1, Alemannia Aachen 2
SSV Reutlingen 1, Rot-Weiss Essen 1 aet (1-3)
TSV Osterholz-Tenever 0, Bayer Leverkusen 6
TuS Hoisdorf 0, Bayern Munich 4
Union Solingen 2, Fortuna Cologne 2 aet (2-5)
VfB Stuttgart 3, VfL Bochum 2 aet
VfL Osnabrück 0, Hamburg SV 1
Werder Bremen 6, SpVgg Bayreuth 1

Third Round
Alemannia Aachen 1, Bayer Uerdingen 4
Bayer Leverkusen 5, Waldhof Mannheim 2
Bayern Munich 3, Karlsruhe SC 4
FC Schalke 04 2, Borussia Dortmund 3
Hamburg SV 3, Rot-Weiss Essen 1
SV Wehen 2, 1.FC Kaiserslautern 3
VfB Stuttgart 2, 1.FC Saarbrücken 0 aet
Werder Bremen 3, Fortuna Cologne 1 aet

Quarterfinals
Bayer Leverkusen 2, Bayer Uerdingen 0
Borussia Dortmund 1, Karlsruhe SC 0
Hamburg SV 0, Werder Bremen 1
VfB Stuttgart 4, 1.FC Kaiserslautern 0

Semifinals
Bayer Leverkusen 1, Werder Bremen 2
Borussia Dortmund 2, VfB Stuttgart 0

Final
in Berlin
Borussia Dortmund 4, Werder Bremen 1

West German Internationals
31/8/88 in Helsinki 4-0 v Finland (WCQ)
21/9/88 in Düsseldorf 1-0 v Soviet Union
19/10/88 in Munich 0-0 v Holland (WCQ)
22/3/89 in Sofia 2-1 v Bulgaria
26/4/89 in Rotterdam 1-1 v Holland (WCQ)
31/5/89 in Cardiff 0-0 v Wales (WCQ)

East German Oberliga

Club	P	W	D	L	Goals	Pts
1. Dynamo Dresden	26	16	8	2	61-26	40
2. Dynamo Berlin	26	12	8	6	51-32	32
3. FC Karl-Marx-Stadt	26	12	6	8	38-36	30
4. Hansa Rostock	26	12	5	9	34-31	29
5. Lokomotive Leipzig	26	11	6	9	39-26	28
6. 1.FC Magdeburg	26	11	6	9	35-30	28
7. Wismut Aue	26	10	8	8	35-35	28
8. Carl Zeiss Jena	26	11	5	10	35-24	27
9. Chemie Halle	26	8	9	9	36-38	25
10. Energie Cottbus	26	9	5	12	29-41	23
11. Stahl Brandenburg	26	9	4	13	36-43	22
12. Rot-Weiss Erfurt	26	9	3	14	27-39	21
13. Sachsenring Zwickau	26	6	4	16	25-49	16
14. 1.FC Union Berlin	26	5	5	16	22-53	15

Top Scorers

Gütschow (Dynamo Dresden) 17
Kirsten (Dynamo Dresden) 14
Doll (Dynamo Berlin) 13
Thom (Dynamo Berlin) 13
Marschall (Lokomotive Leipzig) 12
Halata (Lokomotive Leipzig) 11
Wuckel (1.FC Magdeburg) 11
Jeske (Stahl Brandenburg) 10
Raab (Carl Zeiss Jena) 10
Röhrich (Hansa Rostock) 10
Sander (Energie Cottbus) 10

Second Division (Staffel A)

Club	P	W	D	L	Goals	Pts
1. Stahl Eisenhüttenstadt	34	16	12	6	57-32	44
2. Dynamo Fürstenwalde	34	16	12	6	56-32	44
3. Vorwärts Frankfurt/Oder	34	16	11	7	59-33	43
4. Dynamo Berlin II	34	15	13	6	49-31	43
5. Aktivist Schwarze Pumpe	34	15	11	8	47-35	41
6. Rotation Berlin	34	13	12	9	43-32	38
7. Schiffahrt/Hafen Rostock	34	14	8	12	43-42	36
8. Vorwärts Stralsund	34	12	9	13	39-38	33
9. Dynamo Schwerin	34	11	11	12	34-41	33
10. Motor Schönebeck	34	9	15	10	35-43	33
11. Post Neubrandenburg	34	9	14	11	46-53	32
12. KKW Greifswald	34	11	9	11	45-47	31
13. Motor Ludwigsfelde	34	12	7	15	31-42	31
14. KWO Berlin	34	8	13	13	37-41	29
15. Stahl Hennigsdorf	34	10	9	15	32-46	29
16. Aktivist Brieske-Senftenberg	34	9	8	17	35-59	26
17. Motor Babelsberg	34	6	12	16	30-55	24
18. Lokomotive Stendal	34	8	6	20	38-53	22

Promoted: Bergmann Borsig Berlin, Chemie Guben, Lokomotive Prenzlau, Chemie Velten. Vorwärts Stralsund were replaced by Motor Stralsund. Dynamo Berlin II did not participate at this level in the following season.

Second Division (Staffel B)

Club	P	W	D	L	Goals	Pts
1. Fortschritt Bischofswerda	34	17	13	4	71-34	47
2. Vorwärts Dessau	34	16	10	8	51-26	42
3. Motor Suhl	34	17	8	9	51-36	42
4. Robotron Sömmerda	34	15	9	10	40-36	39
5. Wismut Gera	34	13	12	9	60-58	38
6. Chemie Leipzig	34	16	6	12	49-47	38
7. Chemie Böhlen	34	14	8	12	39-35	36
8. Chemie Markkleeberg	34	10	14	10	49-46	34
9. Dynamo Dresden II	34	12	9	13	54-53	33
10. Dynamo Eisleben	34	10	13	11	41-43	33
11. Stahl Riesa	34	12	9	13	42-45	33
12. Chemie Buna Schkopau	34	11	10	13	53-59	32
13. Motor Weimar	34	10	11	13	41-46	31
14. Stahl Thale	34	10	11	13	35-43	31
15. Motor FH Karl-Marx-Stadt	34	10	9	15	46-50	29
16. Motor Nordhausen	34	11	6	17	37-49	28
17. Aktivist Borna	34	7	13	14	36-51	27
18. Motor Grimma	34	6	7	21	45-82	19

Promoted: DKK Krumhermersdorf, TSG Meissen, Union Mühlhausen

East German Cup Final

in Berlin
Dynamo Berlin 1, Karl-Marx-Stadt 0

East German Internationals

31/8/88 in Berlin 1-0 v Greece
21/9/88 in Cottbus 1-2 v Poland
29/10/88 in Berlin 2-0 v Iceland (WCQ)
30/11/88 in Istanbul 1-3 v Turkey (WCQ)
13/2/89 in Cairo 4-0 v Egypt
8/3/89 in Athens 2-3 v Greece
22/3/89 in Dresden 1-1 v Finland
12/4/89 in Magdeburg 0-2 v Turkey (WCQ)
26/4/89 in Kiev 0-3 v USSR (WCQ)
20/5/89 in Leipzig 1-1 v Austria (WCQ)

European Cup
First Round
Dynamo Berlin v Werder Bremen .... (3-0, 0-5)
Second Round
Glasgow Celtic v Werder Bremen .... (0-1, 0-0)
Quarterfinals
Werder Bremen v AC Milan .... (0-0, 0-1)

Cup-Winners' Cup
First Round
Grasshopppers Zurich v Eintracht Frankfurt .... (0-0, 0-1)
Carl Zeiss Jena v SC Krems .... (5-0, 0-1)
Second Round
Eintracht Frankfurt v Sakaryaspor .... (3-1, 3-0)
FC Jena v Sampdoria .... (1-1, 1-3)
Quarterfinals
Eintracht Frankfurt v Mechelen .... (0-0, 0-1)

UEFA Cup
First Round
FC Antwerp v 1.FC Cologne .... (2-4, 1-2)
Roma v 1.FC Nuremberg .... (1-2, 3-1)
Bayer Leverkusen v Belenenses .... (0-1, 0-1)
VfB Stuttgart v Banyasz Tatabanya .... (2-0, 1-2)
Bayern Munich v Legia Warsaw .... (3-1, 7-3)
Aarau v Lokomotive Lepizig .... (0-3, 0-4)
Aberdeen v Dynamo Dresden .... (0-0, 0-2)
Second Round
1.FC Cologne v Glasgow Rangers .... (2-0, 1-1)
Dynamo Zagreb v VfB Stuttgart .... (1-3, 1-1)
Bayern Munich v Dunajska Streda .... (3-1, 2-0)
Lokomotive Leipzig v Napoli .... (1-1, 0-2)
Dynamo Dresden v SW Waregem .... (4-1, 1-2)
Third Round
Real Sociedad v 1.FC Cologne .... (1-0, 2-2)
FC Groningen v VfB Stuttgart .... (1-3, 0-2)
Bayern Munich v Inter Milan .... (0-2, 3-1)
Dynamo Dresden v Roma .... (2-0, 2-0)
Quarterfinals
VfB Stuttgart v Real Sociedad .... (1-0, 0-1 aet)
Stuttgart won on penalties
Heart of Midlothian v Bayern Munich .... (1-0, 0-2)
Victoria Bucharest v Dynamo Dresden .... (1-1, 0-4)
Semifinals
VfB Stuttgart v Dynamo Dresden .... (1-0, 1-1)
Napoli v Bayern Munich .... (2-0, 2-2)
Final
Napoli v VfB Stuttgart .... (2-1, 3-3)

1989-90

Bayern's eleven

On November 9, 1989 the East German government decided to open the border with the West. The infamous Berlin Wall was knocked down and the German nation had taken its first steps toward reunification. Although it would be another season before the full effect of change would be felt on the football pitch, in December the first official transfer of a player from East to West Germany took place, when Dynamo Berlin striker Andreas Thom joined Bayer Leverkusen for DM3.6 million. Dynamo were one of several East German clubs to change their name over the course of the season, and were now known as FC Berlin.

Bayern Munich had already become the most successful team in West Germany, and this season would see them add to their impressive array of honours by winning the Bundesliga for a record eleventh time. Bayern were one of a number of clubs involved in major pre-season transfers, acquiring Manfred Schwabl from Nuremberg and Jürgen Kohler from 1.FC Cologne. Elsewhere, Jürgen Klinsmann left VfB Stuttgart for Inter Milan, Uwe Bein moved from Hamburg to Frankfurt, Kaiserslautern obtained Stefan Kuntz from Uerdingen and Bruno Labbadia from Hamburg, and New Zealand international Wynton Rufer came to Werder Bremen from Grasshoppers Zurich. But it was Bayer Leverkusen who perhaps got the best deal when they signed the Brazilian fullback Jorginho from Flamengo.

Having spent several seasons at the wrong end of the Bundesliga, Eintracht Frankfurt showed considerable improvement under *Trainer* Jörg Berger. After six matches they led the table, never to drop further than fourth all season. Norwegian Jörn Andersen scored eighteen goals and became the first foreigner to be crowned Bundesliga goalscoring champion. Eintracht were consistent away from home and usually managed a draw, but did win at Bremen and Cologne. Their cause was aided by a lack of injuries, four players being ever-present all season and three others missing just one game each. The most reliable players included Manfred Binz, Ralf Falkenmeyer, Stefan Studer and Karl-Heinz Körbel, who by the end of the season had overtaken Manfred Kaltz as the player with the most Bundesliga appearances: 569. Frankfurt also headed the fair play table, with no red cards and the lowest number of bookings. Hamburg's Dietmar Beiersdorfer, on the other hand, preferred a different approach: he was booked no fewer than twelve times in 31 games. Overall there were a record 966 cautions—or an average of over three per match.

The season also produced a quite bizarre injury, which Hamburg's Ditmar Jakobs had the misfortune of suffering in a match at Werder Bremen. After making a sliding goal-line clearance, Jakobs impaled himself on one of the hooks securing the net to the goal. The game was held up for nearly half an hour as paramedics extricated him, and the accident forced him to miss most of the season.

At the midway point, Cologne, Bayern and Leverkusen were neck-and-neck, and over a period of ten weeks the league leadership changed hands ten times. But once Bayern got their noses in front after twenty games, they gradually pulled away from their rivals. Frankfurt had worked their way up to third place, and when the two teams met in Munich in March, over 70,000 saw Thomas Strunz take advantage of a defensive error to score the game's only goal. It gave Bayern both points and a decisive lead at the top of the table. From there they coasted to the championship. As Bayern were confirmed as national champions for a record twelfth time (they had won their first in 1932 and added eleven more in the Bundesliga), skipper Klaus Augenthaler picked up a record seventh championship medal.

Borussia Dortmund continued their progress under Horst Köppel. After a mediocre start, they put together a twenty-match unbeaten run, ending in a 3-0 loss at Bayern in the last game of the season, amidst the home crowd's celebrations. Dortmund's average attendance of 37,000 was the highest in the league, bettering even Bayern's. Meanwhile at the bottom Mönchengladbach avoided the possibility of relegation only by winning at Uerdingen in their last match. That left Bochum in sixteenth place and facing Saarbrücken in the playoffs, which they won.

Kaiserslautern were staring relegation in the face with only twelve games remaining when they sacked *Trainer* Gerd Roggensack and appointed the well-travelled Karl-Heinz Feldkamp, who had just returned from Egypt. It proved a wise move, for under Feldkamp's stewardship, Lautern finally won the West German Cup—after four previous appearances in the final. Werder Bremen, on the other hand, lost out for the second year running. Two goals from Bruno Labbadia and one from Stefan Kuntz put Kaiserslautern 3-0 up after half an hour, and although Frank Neubarth and Manfred Burgsmüller cut the deficit to 3-2, Lautern were worthy winners. It was Feldkamp's third cup success with as many clubs; he had also led Uerdingen (1986) and Frankfurt (1988) to the honour.

There was a mad scramble at the bottom of the table which not unexpectedly resulted in Homburg's second stint in the Bundesliga lasting just one season. More surprisingly, Waldhof Mannheim, who had sat comfortably in mid-table for much of the season, failed to win any of their last twelve games and also found themselves back in Division Two.

Kickers Offenbach were left to think what might have been. Relegated from the Division Two the season before, they finished third in the Oberliga Hessen and missed out on the promotion playoffs. Earlier, they had knocked Mönchengladbach out of the cup but then lost to Kaiserslautern in the next round by a solitary goal.

Second Division Schalke's crowds averaged over 27,000—some 14,000 better than anyone else—but they finished their season weakly and had to settle for fifth place. Hertha Berlin claimed the top spot to return to the Bundesliga for the first time since 1983. Wattenscheid's lethal strike force of Uwe Tschiskale and Maurice Banach propelled them to a runners-up position, earning Wattenscheid Bundesliga status for the first time. Once again Saarbrücken were saddled with playing off for a promotion spot.

At the bottom, SpVgg Bayreuth finally succeeded in being relegated. They had finished in a relegation spot in each of the previous two years but gained a reprieve when higher-placed clubs were refused a professional licence due to financial problems (Rot-Weiss Oberhausen in 1988, Kickers Offenbach in 1989). This time Bayreuth finished 18th and fate could not save them from the Oberliga Bayern.

Retiring from professional football at the end of the season was 40-year-old Manfred Burgsmüller of Werder Bremen, after a career which included stints at Rot-Weiss Essen, Borussia Dortmund and 1.FC Nuremberg. With 214 goals, he had worked his way up to fourth place on the all-time list of Bundesliga goalscorers.

In the European competitions, the Bundesliga fared well in the UEFA Cup, again boasting two of the semifinalists. But both Cologne and Bremen went out to Italian opposition to set up an all-Serie A final. Bayern Munich came close to victory in their semifinal encounter with AC Milan, but lost out after conceding a sloppy extra-time goal in front of 73,000 at home.

Dynamo Dresden won the East German Oberliga again, but only on goal difference from Karl-Marx-Stadt. They compiled an incredible away record of one win, eleven draws, and one defeat. Dresden also completed the double for the third time, beating struggling Second Division side PSV (formerly Dynamo) Schwerin in the cup final before a crowd of just 5,750. Ulf Kirsten scored the decisive goal six minutes from the end. League gates were plummeting, with the average of 8,303 being the lowest in the 41-year history of the Oberliga. The East German national side won only three of their eight World Cup qualifying matches, and two of those were against Iceland. Not surprisingly, they once again did not qualify.

Though suffering just one defeat in fourteen internationals and qualifying for Italia '90 the West German side were not terribly impressive in the run-up to the World Cup. But in their initial group matches in Italy, they finished in first place through emphatic wins over Yugoslavia and the United Arab Emirates and a draw with Colombia. In the next phase, they avenged their 1988 European Championship semifinal defeat by beating Holland 2-1. Rudi Völler was sent off after being spat at by the Netherlands' Frank Rijkaard but Jürgen Klinsmann scored one and set up the other to put Germany through to the quarterfinals. There, they scraped through against Czechoslovakia to set up a semifinal clash with England. Neither 90 minutes of play nor extra time could separate the two evenly-matched teams, but the Germans held their nerves in the penalty shoot-out to go through.

The final in Rome was a horrendous anti-climax, with Argentina contributing nothing in terms of football and West Germany relying on histrionics and gamesmanship. A dubious penalty settled the result, with Andy Brehme the goalscorer. West Germany had now reached the final of the last three World Cups. Pierre Littbarski, who had helped them to reach each of them, retired from international football after picking up his medal, having earned 73 caps.

Bundesliga

Club	P	W	D	L	Goals	Pts
1. Bayern Munich	34	19	11	4	64-28	49
2. 1.FC Cologne	34	17	9	8	54-44	43
3. Eintracht Frankfurt	34	15	11	8	61-40	41
4. Borussia Dortmund	34	15	11	8	51-35	41
5. Bayer Leverkusen	34	12	15	7	40-32	39
6. VfB Stuttgart	34	15	6	13	53-47	36
7. Werder Bremen	34	10	14	10	49-41	34
8. 1.FC Nuremberg	34	11	11	12	42-46	33
9. Fortuna Düsseldorf	34	10	12	12	41-41	32
10. Karlsruhe SC	34	10	12	12	32-39	32
11. Hamburg SV	34	13	5	16	39-46	31
12. 1.FC Kaiserslautern	34	10	11	13	42-55	31
13. FC St Pauli	34	9	13	12	31-46	31
14. Bayer Uerdingen	34	10	10	14	41-48	30
15. Borussia Mönchengladbach	34	11	8	15	37-45	30
16. VfL Bochum	34	11	7	16	44-53	29
17. Waldhof Mannheim	34	10	6	18	36-53	26
18. FC 08 Homburg	34	8	8	18	33-51	24

Top Scorers

Andersen (Eintracht Frankfurt)	18
Kuntz (1.FC Kaiserslautern)	15
Wohlfarth (Bayern Munich)	13
Walter (VfB Stuttgart)	13
Götz (1.FC Cologne)	11
Criens (Borussia Mönchengladbach)	10
Freiler (Waldhof Mannheim)	10
Furtok (Hamburg SV)	10
Golke (FC St Pauli)	10
Leifeld (VfL Bochum)	10
McInally (Bayern Munich)	10
Möller (Borussia Dortmund)	10
Rufer (Werder Bremen)	10
Zorc (Borussia Dortmund)	10

First Division Playoff
1.FC Saarbrücken v VfL Bochum (0-1, 1-1); Bochum remain in Division One

Second Division

Club	P	W	D	L	Goals	Pts
1. Hertha BSC Berlin	38	22	9	7	65-39	53
2. Wattenscheid 09	38	21	9	8	70-35	51
3. 1.FC Saarbrücken	38	15	16	7	58-33	46
4. Kickers Stuttgart	38	19	7	12	68-48	45
5. FC Schalke 04	38	16	11	11	69-51	43
6. Rot-Weiss Essen	38	15	12	11	49-46	42
7. Eintracht Brunswick	38	15	9	14	55-51	39
8. Hanover 96	38	12	14	12	53-43	38
9. Blau-Weiss 90 Berlin	38	12	13	13	46-52	37
10. MSV Duisburg	38	11	15	12	50-58	37
11. SV Meppen	38	10	16	12	47-57	36
12. Preussen Münster	38	13	10	15	45-65	36
13. SC Freiburg	38	11	12	15	53-52	34
14. Fortuna Cologne	38	9	16	13	48-60	34
15. VfL Osnabrück	38	12	9	17	58-69	33
16. SV Darmstadt 98	38	10	13	15	43-55	33
17. Hessen Kassel	38	13	7	18	35-64	33
18. SpVgg Bayreuth	38	11	9	18	54-59	31
19. Alemannia Aachen	38	11	8	19	52-63	30
20. SpVgg Unterhaching	38	7	15	16	43-61	29

Top Scorers

Banach (Wattenscheid 09)	22
Tschiskale (Wattenscheid 09)	19
Glöde (VfL Osnabrück)	18
Gries (Hertha BSC Berlin)	18
Schüler (Kickers Stuttgart)	18
Sendscheid (FC Schalke 04)	18
Yeboah (1.FC Saarbrücken)	17
Kober (MSV Duisburg)	16
Borodjuk (FC Schalke 04)	16
Bolzek (Fortuna Cologne)	15

Third Division Champions:

Baden-Württemberg: Karlsruhe SC (Am.)
Bayern: Schweinfurt 05
Berlin: Reinickendorf Füchse
Hessen: Rot-Weiss Frankfurt
Nord: VfB Oldenburg
Nordrhein: Wuppertal SV
Südwest: FSV Mainz 05
Westfalen: Arminia Bielefeld

Second Division Playoffs

Northern Group	P	W	D	L	Goals	Pts
1. VfB Oldenburg	8	5	2	1	19-8	12
2. TSV Havelse	8	5	2	1	19-15	12
3. Arminia Bielefeld	8	3	3	2	16-11	9
4. Wuppertal SV	8	2	0	6	11-21	4
5. Reinickendorf Füchse	8	1	1	6	8-18	3

Southern Group	P	W	D	L	Goals	Pts
1. FSV Mainz 05	6	4	0	2	10-6	8
2. Schweinfurt 05	6	3	2	1	7-4	8
3. SSV Reutlingen	6	3	1	2	11-8	7
4. Rot-Weiss Frankfurt	6	0	1	5	3-13	1

West German Cup

First Round
1.FC Pforzheim 4, SpVgg Bayreuth 1
1.FC Saarbrücken 3, SV Meppen 1
Arminia Hanover 2, FC 08 Homburg 1
Bayer Leverkusen (Am.) 0, 1.FC Kaiserslautern 1
Borussia Dortmund 3, Fortuna Cologne 0
Eintracht Frankfurt 0, Bayern Munich 1
FC St Pauli 1, Werder Bremen 2
FC Wangen 0, SV Darmstadt 98 3
FC Gütersloh 1, Hertha BSC Berlin 1 aet (1-0)
FSV Salmrohr 1, TuS Hoisdorf 3
FSV Mainz 05 2, Alemannia Aachen 0
Hamburg SV 2, MSV Duisburg 4
Hanover 96 0, Borussia Mönchengladbach 3
Hertha 03 Zehlendorf 0, 1.FC Nuremberg 4
Kickers Offenbach 2, Bayer Uerdingen 1
Rot-Weiss Essen 1, Wattenscheid 09 2
Rot-Weiss Frankfurt 0, Waldhof Mannheim 1
SC Jülich 1910 2, Blau-Weiss 90 Berlin 2 aet (0-1)
SC Geislingen 0, TSV 1860 Munich 3
Schweinfurt 05 1, FC Altona 93 0
SpVgg Plattling 1, Fortuna Düsseldorf 2 aet
SV Edenkoben 1, Saar 05 Saarbrücken 2
SV Langenau 0, Kickers Stuttgart 6
SV Wiesbaden 0, VfL Bochum 2
TSG Pfeddersheim 2, VfB Gaggenau 0
Union Solingen 1, SC Freiburg 3 aet
VfL Bückeburg 0, Eintracht Brunswick 2
VfL Osnabrück 3, FC Schalke 04 1 aet
VfL Wolfsburg 1, VfB Stuttgart 3
VfR Sölde 0, 1.FC Cologne 3
Viktoria Aschaffenburg 2, Karlsruhe SC 6
Werder Bremen (Am.) 1, Bayer Leverkusen 4

Second Round
1.FC Pforzheim 1, VfL Bochum 0
Arminia Hanover 2, 1.FC Cologne 4
Bayern Munich 2, Waldhof Mannheim 0
Borussia Dortmund 2, Eintracht Brunswick 3
Borussia Mönchengladbach 4, 1.FC Nuremberg 1
FC Gütersloh 0, VfB Stuttgart 2 aet
Fortuna Düsseldorf 4, 1.FC Saarbrücken 0
FSV Mainz 05 1, 1.FC Kaiserslautern 3
Kickers Stuttgart 2, Werder Bremen 3
SC Freiburg 1, Karlsruhe SC 2
Schweinfurt 05 4, Blau-Weiss 90 Berlin 2
SV Edenkoben 1, MSV Duisburg 2 aet
SV Darmstadt 98 1, Bayer Leverkusen 0
TSG Pfeddersheim 1, Kickers Offenbach 3
TuS Hoisdorf 0, TSV 1860 Munich 2
Wattenscheid 09 0, VfL Osnabrück 2

Third Round
1.FC Kaiserslautern 2, 1.FC Cologne 1
1.FC Pforzheim 1, Fortuna Düsseldorf 3
Kickers Offenbach 1, Borussia Mönchengladbach 0 aet
MSV Duisburg 4, SV Darmstadt 98 1
Schweinfurt 05 0, Eintracht Brunswick 2
TSV 1860 Munich 1, Werder Bremen 2
VfB Stuttgart 3, Bayern Munich 0
VfL Osnabrück 0, Karlsruhe SC 2

Quarterfinals
1.FC Kaiserslautern 3, Fortuna Düsseldorf 1
Eintracht Brunswick 3, VfL Osnabrück 2
Kickers Offenbach 1, MSV Duisburg 1 aet (1-0)
Werder Bremen 3, VfB Stuttgart 0

Semifinals
Kickers Offenbach 0, 1.FC Kaiserslautern 1
Werder Bremen 2, Eintracht Brunswick 0

Final
in Berlin
1.FC Kaiserslautern 3, Werder Bremen 2

West German Internationals
6/9/89 in Dublin 1-1 v Ireland
4/10/89 in Dortmund 6-1 v Finland (WCQ)
15/11/89 in Cologne 2-1 v Wales (WCQ)
28/2/90 in Montpellier 1-2 v France
25/4/90 in Stuttgart 3-3 v Uruguay
26/5/90 in Düsseldorf 1-0 v Czechoslovakia
30/5/90 in Gelsenkirchen 1-0 v Denmark
10/6/90 in Milan 4-1 v Yugoslavia (WC)
15/6/90 in Milan 5-1 v United Arab Emirates (WC)
19/6/90 in Milan 1-1 v Colombia (WC)
24/6/90 in Milan 2-1 v Holland (WC)
1/7/90 in Milan 1-0 v Czechoslovakia (WC)
4/7/90 in Turin 1-1 v England aet (WC); West Germany won on penalties
8/7/90 in Rome 1-0 v Argentina (WC)

East German Oberliga

Club	P	W	D	L	Goals	Pts
1. Dynamo Dresden	26	12	12	2	47-26	36
2. FC Karl-Marx-Stadt	26	13	10	3	35-20	36
3. 1.FC Magdeburg	26	13	8	5	39-22	34
4. FC Berlin	26	9	12	5	38-35	30
5. Carl Zeiss Jena	26	11	8	7	29-27	30
6. Hansa Rostock	26	9	9	8	38-33	27
7. Energie Cottbus	26	10	7	9	36-37	27
8. Lokomotive Leipzig	26	9	7	10	34-33	25
9. Chemie Halle	26	8	8	10	38-38	24
10. Stahl Brandenburg	26	6	12	8	35-37	24
11. Rot-Weiss Erfurt	26	5	9	12	29-40	19
12. Stahl Eisenhüttenstadt	26	2	14	10	22-31	18
13. Wismut Aue	26	5	8	13	25-36	18
14. Fortschritt Bischofswerda	26	7	2	17	22-52	16

Top Scorers
Gütschow (Dynamo Dresden) 18
Heidrich (Karl-Marx-Stadt) 12
Rösler (1.FC Magdeburg) 11
Wuckel (1.FC Magdeburg) 11
Kirsten (Dynamo Dresden) 10
Sammer (Dynamo Dresden) 10
Sander (Energie Cottbus) 10
Schülbe (Chemie Halle) 9
Doll (FC Berlin) 8
Jarohs (Hansa Rostock) 8
Jeske (Stahl Brandenburg) 8

Second Division (Staffel A)

Club	P	W	D	L	Goals	Pts
1. Vorwärts Frankfurt/Oder	34	22	9	3	80-30	53
2. 1.FC Union Berlin	34	18	11	5	57-20	47
3. Rotation Berlin	34	17	6	11	71-54	40
4. Chemie Velten	34	14	12	8	58-41	40
5. Aktivist Schwarze Pumpe	34	14	12	8	55-40	40
6. KKW Greifswald	34	13	10	11	47-40	36
7. Schiffahrt/Hafen Rostock	34	11	11	12	41-34	33
8. Bergmann Borsig Berlin	34	12	9	13	44-53	33
9. Post Neubrandenburg	34	10	12	12	47-45	32
10. Motor Stralsund	34	10	12	12	49-56	32
11. Chemie Guben	34	12	7	15	46-45	31
12. KWO Berlin	34	10	10	14	40-51	30
13. Dynamo Fürstenwalde	34	7	16	11	44-55	30
14. PSV Schwerin	34	10	10	14	40-51	30
15. Stahl Hennigsdorf	34	9	12	13	31-47	30
16. Lokomotive Prenzlau	34	8	11	15	45-61	27
17. Motor Ludwigsfelde	34	9	9	19	37-59	27
18. Motor Schönebeck	34	6	9	19	26-73	21

Promoted: Fortschritt Bischofswerda, Aktivist Brieske-Senftenberg, Motor Eberswalde. Dynamo Fürstenwalde, KWO Berlin, and Chemie Velten did not participate at this level in the following season.

Second Division (Staffel B)

Club	P	W	D	L	Goals	Pts
1. Chemie Böhlen	34	22	7	5	77-35	51
2. Chemie Leipzig	34	15	9	10	47-36	39
3. Stahl Riesa	34	13	12	6	49-38	38
4. FSV Zwickau	34	14	10	10	51-49	38
5. Dessau 89	34	14	10	10	48-50	38
6. Stahl Thale	34	13	11	10	48-47	37
7. TSG Meissen	34	15	6	13	45-43	36
8. Robotron Sömmerda	34	11	13	10	41-36	35
9. Motor Suhl	34	10	14	10	42-39	34
10. Motor FH Karl-Marx-Stadt	34	12	10	12	46-46	34
11. Wismut Gera	34	10	13	11	46-49	33
12. Motor Weimar	34	11	11	11	41-50	33
13. Chemie Ilmenau	34	10	11	13	34-39	31
14. Chemie Buna Schkopau	34	10	10	14	51-59	30
15. MSV Eisleben	34	9	10	15	48-51	28
16. DKK Krumhermersdorf	34	8	12	14	36-53	28
17. TSG Markkleeberg	34	8	11	15	40-46	27
18. Union Mühlhausen	34	8	6	20	38-62	22

Promoted: BSV Borna, Wacker Nordhausen, Kali Werra Tiefenort, 1.FC Markkleeberg. Chemie Böhlen, Chemie Buna Schkopau, and MSV Eisleben did not participate at this level in the following season. Chemie Leipzig were promoted to Division One.

East German Cup Final
in Berlin
Dynamo Dresden 2, PSV Schwerin 1

East German Internationals
23/8/89 in Erfurt 1-1 v Bulgaria
6/9/89 in Reykjavik 3-0 v Iceland (WCQ)
8/10/89 in Karl-Marx-Stadt 2-1 v USSR (WCQ)
25/10/89 in Valletta 4-0 v Malta
15/11/89 in Vienna 0-3 v Austria (WCQ)
24/1/90 in Kuwait 0-3 v France
26/1/90 in Kuwait 2-1 v Kuwait
29/3/90 in Berlin 3-2 v USA
11/4/90 in Karl-Marx-Stadt 2-0 v Egypt
25/4/90 in Glasgow 1-0 v Scotland
13/5/90 in Rio de Janeiro 3-3 v Brazil

European Cup
First Round
Glasgow Rangers v Bayern Munich .... (1-3, 0-0)
Dynamo Dresden v AEK Athens .... (1-0, 3-5)
Second Round
Bayern Munich v Nentori Tirana .... (3-1, 3-0)
Quarterfinals
Bayern Munich v PSV Eindhoven .... (2-1, 1-0)
Semifinals
AC Milan v Bayern Munich .... (1-0, 1-2 aet)

Cup-Winners' Cup
First Round
Besiktas v Borussia Dortmund .... (0-1, 1-2)
Valur Reykjavik v Dynamo Berlin .... (1-2, 1-2)
Second Round
Borussia Dortmund v Sampdoria .... (1-1, 0-2)
Monaco v Dynamo Berlin .... (0-0, 1-1 aet)

UEFA Cup
First Round
VfB Stuttgart v Feyenoord .... (2-0, 1-2)
1.FC Cologne v Plastika Nitra .... (4-1, 1-0)
Örgryte Gothenburg v Hamburg SV .... (1-2, 1-5)
Lilleström v Werder Bremen .... (1-3, 0-2)
Karl-Marx-Stadt v Boavista .... (1-0, 2-2)
Hansa Rostock v Banik Ostrava .... (2-3, 0-4)
Second Round
Zenit Leningrad v VfB Stuttgart .... (0-1, 0-5)
1.FC Cologne v Spartak Moscow .... (3-1, 0-0)
Real Zaragoza v Hamburg SV .... (1-0, 0-2 aet)
Werder Bremen v Austria Vienna .... (5-0, 0-2)
Sion v Karl-Marx-Stadt .... (2-1, 1-4)
Third Round
FC Antwerp v VfB Stuttgart .... (1-0, 1-1)
Red Star Belgrade v 1.FC Cologne .... (2-0, 0-3)
Hamburg SV v FC Porto .... (1-0, 1-2)
Napoli v Werder Bremen .... (2-3, 1-5)
Juventus v Karl-Marx-Stadt .... (2-1, 1-0)
Quarterfinals
1.FC Cologne v FC Antwerp .... (2-0, 0-0)
FC Liege v Werder Bremen .... (1-4, 2-0)
Semifinals
Juventus v 1.FC Cologne .... (3-2, 0-0)
Werder Bremen v Fiorentina .... (1-1, 0-0)

1990-91

East meets West

The German nation was officially reunified on October 3, 1990. Amongst all the changes the new country was faced with, a decision needed to be made as to how to re-structure its professional football system. With so many aspects of East German society being overtaken by the way of the west, the Bundesliga never looked threatened, but how would it integrate with its eastern counterpart? Just how many East German clubs, for example, were good enough for the Bundesliga?

It was decided that the top two East German teams would go straight into the following season's Bundesliga and the next six would join the Second Division. But many East German players could not wait another year and joined western clubs, some at bargain prices. Bayer Leverkusen plucked Ulf Kirsten from Dynamo Dresden and Andreas Thom from Dynamo Berlin. Thom's teammate Thomas Doll joined Hamburg SV and Kirsten's teammate Matthias Sammer went to VfB Stuttgart. Meanwhile, the best West German players continued to be snapped up by Italian clubs: Thomas Hässler left Cologne for Juventus for DM15.5 million and Karlheinz Riedle moved from Bremen to Lazio for DM13 million.

With East Germany's communist regime deposed, questions regarding Dynamo Berlin's domination of the East German league began to surface. Being the team of the East German secret police, Dynamo's chief patron was none other than Erich Mielke, the head of the *Stasi*. Evidence came to light that referees had manipulated results in deference to the power Mielke wielded, suggesting that many of Dynamo's titles had not been earned but rigged.

In addition to having questions asked about their past, Dynamo, now known as FC Berlin, faced further problems as a large (and ironically right-wing) hooligan element attached itself to the club. In their match with Sachsen Leipzig in October 1990, riots broke out which resulted in the controversial fatal shooting of a Dynamo fan by police. Elsewhere, crowd problems in Dresden forced the referee to abandon the European Cup quarterfinal tie between Dynamo Dresden and Red Star Belgrade with the score at 1-1. UEFA awarded the Yugoslavian champions a 3-0 victory, and they would go on to lift the trophy.

Karlheinz Feldkamp brought seven new players into his Kaiserslautern squad to add to the four new arrivals from the previous season, but still made a profit by selling sweeper Franco Foda to Leverkusen. This meant that only five of his 24-strong squad had been with the club more than two years. Kaiserslautern had been in continuous membership of the Bundesliga since its formation and had finished in every single position from third to sixteenth. But they had last won the German championship in 1953, and in recent years their ever-present status looked under threat. The Fritz-Walter-Stadion on the Betzenberg, though, was still feared by visiting teams, with its fanatical supporters crowded right up to the touchlines on steeply-banked terracing. And this proved to be Kaiserslautern's season. Up to the two-thirds stage, they had been swapping leadership of the league with Bayern Munich and Werder Bremen. But in Round 22, Kaiserslautern played host to Bayern in a crucial match, and goals from Demir Hotic and Stefan Kuntz gave them a 2-1 win. The next week Bayern lost at home to struggling Düsseldorf and Lautern found themselves three points ahead. Fan support was phenomenal: despite Kaiserslautern's comparatively small population and its rather isolated geographical position, nearly every home match was attracting a crowd of over 30,000.

In Round 25, Bayern and Werder Bremen shared the points in a 1-1 draw. All three top sides dropped unexpected points, and Bremen fell out of the reckoning by drawing six matches out of seven and then losing 2-1 to Kaiserslautern. So with two games remaining, Kaiserslautern were four points ahead of Bayern. They needed only one point to take the title and, being unbeaten at home all season, looked certain to defeat lowly Borussia Mönchengladbach. But as the crowd celebrated prematurely, the Kaiserslautern players went to pieces and gave up three goals. A last-minute flourish made the final score 3-2, but Bayern had won in Nuremberg to close the gap to two points—and the Munich side had a far better goal difference. Bayern finished the season at home to relegated Uerdingen, whilst Lautern had to travel to seventh-placed Cologne, who were still striving for a UEFA Cup spot.

There were ten-mile traffic jams on the motorways leading to Cologne as the entire population of Kaiserslautern seemed to head for the showdown on the Rhine. The tension turned to celebration as Kaiserslautern scored goal after goal and coasted to a 6-2 win, Bernhard Winkler scoring twice. As the news filtered through to Munich, the disappointed Bayern players laboured to a 2-2 draw, and the Red Devils won the title by a deceptively wide three-point margin.

There had been further misery for the Bavarians earlier in the season. FV Weinheim of the Oberliga Baden-Württemberg created the shock of the West German Cup by knocking Bayern out in the first round, thanks to a goal from Thomas Schwechheimer. SpVgg Fürth, playing in a division lower than Weinheim, created nearly as big an upset with a 3-1 win over Dortmund, and in the second round, FC Remscheid of the Oberliga Nordrhein dismissed Mönchengladbach.

The semifinal tie between Cologne and MSV Duisburg produced the intriguing spectacle of a player grateful for being sent off. Cologne took advantage of the fact that Duisburg's strike force had been decimated through injury and won the game 3-0, but the main talking point had been the exploits of Cologne's striker Frank Ordenewitz. Ordenewitz, the recipient of the FIFA Fair Play Award in 1988, had received a yellow card early in the game, which took him over the disciplinary limit and ruled him out of any place in the final. With three minutes left to play, though, Ordenewitz was sent off for kicking the ball away, to the unabashed delight of Cologne *Trainer* Christoph Daum. Through a peculiar loophole, Ordenewitz appeared to have ensured his place in the final, as the more immediate red-card suspension would expire in time for a rendezvous with his old Werder teammates in Berlin. Eventually the DFB decided to bend the rules a bit and wound up suspending Ordenewitz from the final anyway.

With or without Ordenewitz, Cologne had reached the final for a record tenth time, whilst Bremen were there for the third year in a row. A speculative shot from Dieter Eilts was cancelled out by Maurice Banach's 62nd-minute effort and extra time had to be played. But no further goals were scored, and Werder took the trophy 4-3 on penalties. The 24-year-old Banach would be killed in a automobile accident later that year.

Meanwhile in Division Two, two famous clubs won promotion back into the Bundesliga: Schalke 04 and MSV Duisburg. Schalke had somewhat controversially lured *Trainer* Aleksandar Ristic away from First Division Düsseldorf early in the new year and wound up being crowned Second Division champions, clinching promotion with a 2-1 win over Fortuna Cologne before 55,000. Duisburg, promoted from the Oberliga Nordrhein at the beginning of the previous season, didn't lose a match at home. Financial difficulties were threatening the status of two other sides in the division. Rot-Weiss Essen's were too severe for the DFB's liking, and they were relegated from Division Two; debt-riddled FSV Mainz 05 survived that punishment, but their play suggested a similar fate was just a matter of time. Meanwhile once-mighty TSV 1860 Munich regained entry into professional football by gaining promotion to the Second Division from the Oberliga Bayern.

Karl-Heinz Körbel ended a nineteen-year career with his one-and-only Bundesliga club, Eintracht Frankfurt, by setting a new league record of 602 appearances. It would have been 603, but "Faithful Charly" had collected four yellow cards over the season and was suspended from playing in his club's season finale. Rules are rules, said the DFB—Frank Ordenewitz excepted, of course—and Körbel was forced to view his farewell match from the touchlines. Still, 40,000 fans turned up to bid him *auf Wiedersehen* and saw Frankfurt beat Stuttgart 4-0.

In East Germany, the final season of the renamed *Nordost Fussball Verband Oberliga* was surprisingly won by Hansa Rostock. Dynamo Dresden finished second to clinch the other spot in the Bundesliga. Rot-Weiss Erfurt, Chemie Halle, FC Chemnitz (formerly Karl-Marx-Stadt) and Carl Zeiss Jena qualified for Division Two, but once-proud 1.FC Magdeburg found themselves consigned to the amateur leagues. The East German national side played its 293rd and last game in Brussels on September 12, with Matthias Sammer netting both goals in a 2-0 win over Belgium. They finished on an unbeaten run of six games, and their all-time record was a reasonably impressive 138 wins, 69 draws, and 86 defeats. Yet they had only managed to qualify for one World Cup. A planned East Germany/West Germany farewell match was called off because of fears of crowd trouble. The first united German team took on Switzerland in Stuttgart and won 4-0. Sammer was the only eastern player in the starting line-up, although Andreas Thom came on as substitute and scored one of the goals.

Bundesliga

Club	P	W	D	L	Goals	Pts
1. 1.FC Kaiserslautern	34	19	10	5	72-45	48
2. Bayern Munich	34	18	9	7	74-41	45
3. Werder Bremen	34	15	14	6	46-29	42
4. Eintracht Frankfurt	34	15	10	9	63-40	40
5. Hamburg SV	34	16	8	10	60-38	40
6. VfB Stuttgart	34	14	10	10	57-44	38
7. 1.FC Cologne	34	13	11	10	50-43	37
8. Bayer Leverkusen	34	11	13	10	47-46	35
9. Borussia Mönchengladbach	34	9	17	8	49-54	35
10. Borussia Dortmund	34	10	14	10	46-57	34
11. Wattenscheid 09	34	9	15	10	42-51	33
12. Fortuna Düsseldorf	34	11	10	13	40-49	32
13. Karlsruhe SC	34	8	15	11	46-52	31
14. VfL Bochum	34	9	11	14	50-52	29
15. 1.FC Nuremberg	34	10	9	15	40-54	29
16. FC St Pauli	34	6	15	13	33-53	27
17. Bayer Uerdingen	34	5	13	16	34-54	23
18. Hertha BSC Berlin	34	3	8	23	37-84	14

Top Scorers
Wohlfarth (Bayern Munich) 21
Furtok (Hamburg SV) 20
Möller (Eintracht Frankfurt) 16
Allofs (Fortuna Düsseldorf) 15
Rufer (Werder Bremen) 15
Banach (1.FC Cologne) 14
Sane (Wattenscheid 09) 13
Criens (Borussia Mönchengladbach) 12
Walter (VfB Stuttgart) 12
Kirsten (Bayer Leverkusen) 11
Kohn (VfL Bochum) 11
Kuntz (1.FC Kaiserslautern) 11
Nando (Hamburg SV) 11
Sammer (VfB Stuttgart) 11
Schütterle (Karlsruhe SC) 11

First Division Playoff
FC St Pauli v Kickers Stuttgart (1-1, 1-1, 1-3); Kickers promoted to Division One

Second Division

Club	P	W	D	L	Goals	Pts
1. FC Schalke 04	38	23	11	4	64-29	57
2. MSV Duisburg	38	21	11	6	70-34	53
3. Kickers Stuttgart	38	21	9	8	63-32	51
4. FC 08 Homburg	38	16	13	9	42-37	45
5. 1.FC Saarbrücken	38	15	14	9	47-30	44
6. Blau-Weiss 90 Berlin	38	12	20	6	55-42	44
7. Waldhof Mannheim	38	15	12	11	60-47	42
8. FSV Mainz 05	38	14	13	11	45-52	41
9. SC Freiburg	38	15	10	13	54-48	40
10. Hanover 96	38	12	14	12	49-49	38
11. Fortuna Cologne	38	11	15	12	51-53	37
12. VfB Oldenburg	38	10	16	12	58-53	36
13. Eintracht Brunswick	38	12	11	15	53-52	35
14. VfL Osnabrück	38	12	11	15	51-55	35
15. Rot-Weiss Essen	38	12	10	16	49-52	34
16. SV Meppen	38	10	14	14	35-42	34
17. SV Darmstadt 98	38	10	13	15	46-54	33
18. Preussen Münster	38	8	13	17	35-59	29
19. TSV Havelse	38	6	7	25	44-82	19
20. Schweinfurt 05	38	2	9	27	26-95	13

Rot-Weiss Essen were relegated after their professional licence was revoked

Top Scorers
Tönnies (MSV Duisburg) 29
Marin (Kickers Stuttgart) 22
Adler (Blau-Weiss 90 Berlin) 21
Heisig (Hanover 96) 17
Schlotterbeck (SC Freiburg) 16
Aden (Eintracht Brunswick) 14
Capocchiano (TSV Havelse) 14
Borodjuk (FC Schalke 04) 13
Eichenauer (SV Darmstadt 98) 13
Moutas (Kickers Stuttgart) 13
Wolff (Waldhof Mannheim) 13

Third Division Champions:
Baden-Württemberg: 1.FC Pforzheim
Bayern: TSV 1860 Munich
Berlin: Tennis Borussia Berlin
Hessen: Hessen Kassel
Nord: VfL Wolfsburg
Nordrhein: FC Remscheid
Südwest: Borussia Neunkirchen
Westfalen: SC Verl

Second Division Playoff

Northern Group

	P	W	D	L	Goals	Pts
1. FC Remscheid	8	5	3	0	16-5	13
2. VfL Wolfsburg	8	4	1	3	15-14	9
3. Göttingen 05	8	3	2	3	14-12	8
4. SC Verl	8	3	2	3	15-17	8
5. Tennis Borussia Berlin	8	1	0	7	6-18	2

Southern Group

	P	W	D	L	Goals	Pts
1. TSV 1860 Munich	6	3	3	0	11-5	9
2. Hessen Kassel	6	2	3	1	8-6	7
3. 1.FC Pforzheim	6	2	1	3	8-11	5
4. Borussia Neunkirchen	6	0	3	3	5-10	3

West German Cup
First Round
Alemannia Aachen 0, Bayer Uerdingen 1 aet
ASC Shöppingen 1, Eintracht Frankfurt 2
Borussia Neunkirchen 2, Fortuna Düsseldorf 3 aet
DSC Wanne-Eickel 1, Hertha BSC Berlin 3
Eintracht Haiger 1, Borussia Mönchengladbach 2
Eintracht Trier 0, VfB Stuttgart 1
FC Miltach 1, 1.FC Nuremberg 3
FC Remscheid 3, Fortuna Cologne 2 aet
FC Wangen 1, Rot-Weiss Essen 2
FSV Frankfurt 3, Preussen Münster 4 aet
FV 09 Weinheim 1, Bayern Munich 0
Göttingen 05 0, Hamburg SV 4
Hessen Kassel 1, FC 08 Homburg 0
Kickers Stuttgart 4, SV Darmstadt 98 0
Kilia Kiel 1, FC St Pauli 4
SC Pfullendorf 0, MSV Duisburg 2
SpVgg Bayreuth 0, Blau-Weiss 90 Berlin 3
SpVgg Fürth 3, Borussia Dortmund 1
SpVgg Unterhaching 0, FC Schalke 04 1
SpVgg Weiden 1, Werder Bremen 2
SSV Reutlingen 3, Karlsruhe SC 6 aet
Südwest Ludwigshafen 1, 1.FC Kaiserslautern 7
SV Hilden-Nord 2, SC Freiburg 1 aet
SV Ludweiler 0, SV Meppen 3
Teutonia Waltrop 0, Eintracht Brunswick 1
Türkiyemspor Berlin 2, 1.FC Saarbrücken 6
TuS Bersenbrück 0, Hanover 96 4
VfL Wolfsburg 1, 1.FC Cologne 6
Victoria Hamburg 0, Bayer Leverkusen 5
Viktoria Cologne 2, VfL Osnabrück 4
Waldhof Mannheim 3, VfL Bochum 2
Werder Bremen (Am.) 1, Wattenscheid 09 3

Second Round
1.FC Kaiserslautern 1, 1.FC Cologne 2
Bayer Leverkusen 0, Bayer Uerdingen 1
Eintracht Frankfurt 0, 1.FC Nuremberg 0 aet (2-0 aet)
FC Remscheid 1, Borussia Mönchengladbach 0
FC Schalke 04 4, Eintracht Brunswick 0
Fortuna Düsseldorf 0, Blau-Weiss 90 Berlin 0 aet (0-1)
FV 09 Weinheim 1, Rot-Weiss Essen 3
Hanover 96 0, Hamburg SV 0 aet (1-2)
Hertha BSC Berlin 1, MSV Duisburg 2
Hessen Kassel 3, Kickers Stuttgart 2
Karlsruhe SC 0, VfB Stuttgart 2
SpVgg Fürth 0, 1.FC Saarbrücken 1
SV Hilden-Nord 0, Preussen Münster 4
SV Meppen 2, Waldhof Mannheim 0
VfL Osnabrück 1, Wattenscheid 09 2 aet
Werder Bremen 2, FC St Pauli 0

Third Round
1.FC Cologne 1, SV Meppen 0

1.FC Saarbrücken 0, Eintracht Frankfurt 0 aet (2-3 aet)
Bayer Uerdingen 4, Rot-Weiss Essen 2 aet
FC Remscheid 2, Hessen Kassel 3 aet
Hamburg SV 1, Wattenscheid 09 2
MSV Duisburg 3, Blau-Weiss 90 Berlin 2 aet
Preussen Münster 0, VfB Stuttgart 1
Werder Bremen 3, FC Schalke 04 1

Quarterfinals
1.FC Cologne 1, VfB Stuttgart 0 aet
Bayer Uerdingen 1, MSV Duisburg 4
Eintracht Frankfurt 3, Wattenscheid 09 1
Hessen Kassel 0, Werder Bremen 2

Semifinals
Eintracht Frankfurt 2, Werder Bremen 2 aet (3-6)
MSV Duisburg 0, 1.FC Cologne 0 aet (0-3)

Final
in Berlin
Werder Bremen 1, 1.FC Cologne 1 aet (Werder won on penalties)

West German Internationals
29/8/90 in Lisbon 1-1 v Portugal
10/10/90 in Stockholm 3-1 v Sweden
31/10/90 in Luxembourg 3-2 v Luxembourg (ECQ)
19/12/90 in Stuttgart 4-0 v Switzerland
27/3/91 in Frankfurt 2-1 v Soviet Union
1/5/91 in Hanover 1-0 v Belgium (ECQ)
5/6/91 in Cardiff 0-1 v Wales (ECQ)

East German Oberliga

Club	P	W	D	L	Goals	Pts
1. Hansa Rostock	26	13	9	4	44-25	35
2. Dynamo Dresden	26	12	8	8	48-28	32
3. Rot-Weiss Erfurt	26	11	9	6	30-26	31
4. Chemie Halle	26	10	9	7	40-31	29
5. FC Chemnitz	26	9	11	6	24-23	29
6. Carl Zeiss Jena	26	12	4	10	41-36	28
7. Lokomotive Leipzig	26	10	8	8	37-33	28
8. Stahl Brandenburg	26	9	9	8	34-31	27
9. Stahl Eisenhüttenstadt	26	7	12	7	29-25	26
10. 1.FC Magdeburg	26	9	8	9	34-32	26
11. FC Berlin	26	7	8	11	25-39	22
12. FC Sachsen Leipzig	26	6	10	10	23-38	22
13. Energie Cottbus	26	3	10	13	21-38	16
14. Victoria 91 Frankfurt	26	4	5	17	29-54	13

The top two clubs were admitted into the Bundesliga. The next six clubs were admitted into the Second Division. The bottom two clubs were placed in the Oberliga Nordost, leaving the remaining four clubs to play off against the two East German Second Division champions for a place in the Second Division.

Top Scorers
Gütschow (Dynamo Dresden) 20
Schülbe (Chemie Halle) 13
Fuchs (Hansa Rostock) 11
Laessig (1.FC Magdeburg) 10
Klee (Carl Zeiss Jena) 9
Romstedt (Rot-Weiss Erfurt) 9
Löhnert (Stahl Eisenhüttenstadt) 8
Rische (Lokomotive Leipzig) 8
Rösler (1.FC Magdeburg/Dynamo Dresden) .. 8
Peschke (Carl Zeiss Jena) 7
Raab (Carl Zeiss Jena) 7
Weichert (Hansa Rostock) 7

Second Division (Staffel A)

Club	P	W	D	L	Goals	Pts
1. 1.FC Union Berlin	30	16	10	4	68-30	42
2. Chemie Guben	30	15	11	4	53-36	41
3. Rotation Berlin	30	17	5	8	64-38	39
4. Fortschritt Bischofswerda	30	16	7	7	45-27	39
5. Bergmann Borsig Berlin	30	14	10	6	60-36	38
6. Post Neubrandenburg	30	13	9	8	47-37	35
7. Aktivist Schwarze Pumpe	30	12	10	8	45-35	34
8. Lokomotive Altmark Stendal	30	10	12	8	36-31	32
9. Stahl Hennigsdorf	30	12	8	10	48-47	32
10. Aktivist Brieske-Senftenberg	30	8	15	7	34-35	31
11. SC Griefswald	30	10	9	11	37-42	29
12. Hafen Rostock	30	6	11	13	21-38	23
13. Rot-Weiss Prenzlau	30	5	11	14	36-54	21
14. Motor Eberswalde	30	6	9	15	31-51	21
15. PSV Schwerin	30	8	4	18	43-75	20
16. TSV 1860 Stralsund	30	1	1	28	14-70	3

TSV Stralsund disbanded midway through the season. All return matches were awarded to opponents as 2-0 victories.

Second Division (Staffel B)

Club	P	W	D	L	Goals	Pts
1. FSV Zwickau	30	20	6	4	77-27	46
2. Wismut Aue	30	18	10	2	73-24	46
3. Stahl Thale	30	12	15	3	44-23	39
4. Chemnitz SV 51	30	16	7	7	54-40	39
5. Soemtron Sömmerda	30	12	11	7	50-35	35
6. Wismut Gera	30	10	13	7	54-35	33
7. 1.FC Markkleeberg	30	13	7	10	36-28	33
8. TSG Meissen	30	13	6	11	37-35	32
9. BSV Borna	30	11	9	10	45-44	31
10. Motor Weimar	30	9	9	12	45-44	27
11. Stahl Riesa	30	9	9	12	32-40	27
12. 1.SV Suhl 06	30	8	10	12	26-39	26
13. Wacker Nordhausen	30	6	11	13	29-42	23
14. Anhalt Dessau	30	8	5	17	39-50	21
15. Kali Werra Tiefenort	30	7	5	18	38-90	19
16. Germania Ilmenau	30	0	3	27	16-99	3

Second Division Playoff

Group 1	P	W	D	L	Goals	Pts
1. Stahl Brandenburg	6	4	1	1	9-6	9
2. FC Berlin	6	3	2	1	10-5	8
3. 1.FC Union Berlin	6	2	1	3	5-7	5
4. 1.FC Magdeburg	6	0	2	4	6-12	2

Group 2	P	W	D	L	Goals	Pts
1. Lokomotive Leipzig	6	4	2	0	11-0	10
2. Stahl Eisenhüttenstadt	6	3	2	1	8-6	8
3. FSV Zwickau	6	1	2	3	5-9	4
4. Sachsen Leipzig	6	1	0	5	3-13	2

East German Cup Final
in Berlin
Hansa Rostock 1, Stahl Eisenhüttenstadt 0

East German International
13/9/90 in Brussels 2-0 v Belgium

European Cup
First Round
Apoel Nicosia v Bayern Munich .... (2-3, 0-4)
Union Luxembourg v Dynamo Dresden .... (1-3, 0-3)
Second Round
Bayern Munich v CSKA Sofia .... (4-0, 3-0)
Dynamo Dresden v Malmö FF .... (1-1, 1-1 aet)
Dresden won on penalties
Quarterfinals
Bayern Munich v FC Porto .... (1-1, 2-0)
Red Star Belgrade v Dynamo Dresden .... (3-0, 2-1)
Second leg abandoned, awarded to Red Star 3-0
Semifinals
Bayern Munich v Red Star Belgrade .... (1-2, 2-2)

Cup-Winners' Cup
First Round
1.FC Kaiserslautern v Sampdoria .... (1-0, 0-2)
PSV Schwerin v Austria Vienna .... (0-2, 0-0)

UEFA Cup
First Round
Brondby v Eintracht Frankfurt .... (5-0, 1-4)
Borussia Dortmund v FC Chemnitz .... (2-0, 2-0)
IFK Norrköping v 1.FC Cologne .... (0-0, 1-3)
Bayer Leverkusen v Twente Entschede ... (1-0, 1-1 aet)
1.FC Magdeburg v PS Rovaniemi .... (0-0, 1-0)
Second Round
Uni Craiova v Borussia Dortmund .... (0-3, 0-1)
1.FC Cologne v Inter Bratislava .... (0-1, 2-0)
GKS Katowice v Bayer Leverkusen .... (1-2, 0-4)
1.FC Magdeburg v Bordeaux .... (0-1, 0-1)
Third Round
Anderlecht v Borussia Dortmund .... (1-0, 1-2)
Brondby v Bayer Leverkusen .... (3-0, 0-0)

1991-92

Photo finish

Once again, some of the top German talent left for Italy: Stefan Reuter and Jürgen Kohler went to Juventus, and Thomas Doll joined Lazio. Andy Möller, though, was not quite sure how many teams he had signed for and stayed at Frankfurt for another year.

The Bundesliga had been extended to twenty clubs for one season to accommodate two East German clubs. One of them, Hansa Rostock, started superbly, and led the league after seven games. But they soon fell away in quite dramatic fashion and wound up being relegated. The other, Dynamo Dresden, were hampered by a weak start, but they managed to preserve their new-found status with a couple of critical victories toward season's end.

The championship was a three-team race which was not resolved until the final whistle of the final match. Unexpectedly, Bayern Munich were not one of the sides challenging for the title. In fact, they finished with their worst league showing since 1978. And their troubles were not confined to the Bundesliga: they could only scrape past Cork City in the UEFA Cup, and were ripped apart in the following round by Danish part-timers B1903 Copenhagen. Jupp Heynckes had been sacked as *Trainer* after two ignominious defeats: a German Cup exit at home to Homburg, and a 4-1 home loss to relegation candidates Kickers Stuttgart. He was replaced by Danish international Sören Lerby, who fared no better, and in March the experienced Erich Ribbeck was brought in an attempt to salvage something from the season. Meanwhile, Bayern midfielder Stefan Effenberg's arrogant pronouncements in the media led to him being booed and whistled by fans in every stadium in Germany—even when playing for the national side—before his strong-running midfield performances won grudging appreciation.

After Rostock began to crack, Frankfurt took over at the top with Dortmund and Stuttgart pressing hard. Defending champions Kaiserslautern were never far behind but could not close the gap. Dragoslav Stepanovic, an extrovert Yugoslavian, had taken over as Frankfurt *Trainer* midway through the previous season and made minor changes to personnel but major changes to attitude and tactics. Midfielders Andy Möller and Uwe Bein were the linchpins of the team's new-found success.

Dortmund had appointed a new *Trainer,* Ottmar Hitzfeld, and had made a shrewd acquisition by paying Bayer Uerdingen just DM400,000 for the services of Swiss striker Stephane Chapuisat. (Chapuisat signed for Dortmund the following season, for which Borussia coughed up an additional DM2.6 million.) Thomas Helmer enjoyed a superb season in defence, and Chapuisat received sterling support from Flemming Povlsen and Michael Rummenigge up front. Local youngster Stefan Klos claimed the goalkeeper's jersey from "Teddy" de Beer and quickly established himself as one of the league's safest netminders. Meanwhile in Stuttgart the talkative Christoph Daum was basing his team around three reliable players: defender Guido Buchwald, midfielder Matthias Sammer and striker Fritz Walter. Walter won the goalscoring title, Buchwald was a mainstay in the German national team, and Sammer was snapped up by Inter Milan at the end of the season.

Had Dortmund produced better performances in their clashes with their two rivals at the top, they would surely have won the title. They could only manage draws in the two home matches and were trounced 4-2 at Stuttgart and 3-0 at Frankfurt. Frankfurt won their top-of-the-table clash 2-1 in Stuttgart and drew 1-1 in the return match, but dropped some surprising points at home, drawing with the likes of Düsseldorf and Wattenscheid. Come the day of the 38th and final round of the lengthy season, Frankfurt were in first place, Stuttgart in second and Dortmund in third—all on fifty points apiece.

The final fixtures paired Rostock with Frankfurt, Leverkusen with Stuttgart, and Duisburg with Dortmund. Ten minutes into the Duisburg match, Chapuisat put Dortmund ahead. After twenty minutes of the Leverkusen game, Stuttgart's Slobodan Dubajic stumbled and fell onto the ball and Leverkusen converted the resulting penalty. Three minutes later Leverkusen's Andreas Thom chipped the ball over Eike Immel but Günter Schäfer made a spectacular goal-line clearance to keep Stuttgart in the game. Then Stuttgart winger Ludwig Kögl broke through and was brought down on the edge of the penalty area. Stuttgart were awarded a spot-kick and Fritz Walter equalised.

Midway through the second half Frankfurt conceded a goal but soon equalised. Dortmund remained in the driving seat as the clocks ticked round to the last five minutes, so Frankfurt and Stuttgart threw caution to the wind and attacked furiously. With four minutes remaining in Leverkusen, Kögl centred from the left and Buchwald was in the right place to head VfB into a 2-1 lead. Was there still time for Frankfurt to do the same and snatch the title? As Eintracht pushed everyone forward in injury time, Rostock broke away, and Stefan Böger put the ball into an empty net. It was all over. Right at the death of the season, VfB Stuttgart had snatched their second Bundesliga championship.

Four clubs were relegated from Division One, including Duisburg, who had only gained promotion the season before. It was quite a scramble, with no fewer than nine clubs involved with just two matches to play. Wattenscheid, everyone's favourites for the drop, kept themselves afloat by scoring a credible number of goals, and gaining 1-1 draws away to the league's top four clubs. They needed to beat Gladbach in their last match to be assured of staying up—and did, 3-2.

The Second Division had a rather contrived look about it. The infusion of East German sides necessitated a return to the old north-south format, but in addition the season was split into two halves. First there was a qualification phase, after which the two divisions of twelve clubs were split into an upper half and a lower half to determine the relegation and promotion places. When it all was over, Bayer Uerdingen had edged out VfB Oldenburg for the promotion place in the north, and Saarbrücken had finished comfortably in front in the south. Most East German sides struggled and Brandenburg, Halle, and Rot-Weiss Erfurt were relegated.

Although there was no playoff for a place in the First Division there was plenty of playing off at the bottom of the table. This provided Fortuna Cologne with a lucky break. Financial problems had forced Blau-Weiss Berlin out of Division Two, and so spared Fortuna from automatic relegation. Fortuna responded by winning their playoff group, keeping Munich 1860 and TSV Havelse in the amateur leagues.

Starting with this season, the DFB decided to do away with replays in the West German Cup; if teams were still level after 90 minutes, there would be extra time and, if needed, penalties to decide a winner. Second Division Hanover 96 provided the competition's major surprise, knocking out Bochum, Dortmund, Uerdingen, Karlsruhe, and—before a semifinal crowd of 57,000 in the Niedersachsenstadion—Werder Bremen. In the final they beat Mönchengladbach on penalties after a palling 0-0 draw. The hero of the day, not surprisingly, was their goalkeeper, Jörg Sievers. *Trainer* Michael Lorkowski celebrated Hanover's first major domestic honour since 1955 by leaving for St. Pauli.

Going out on penalties may have been heartbreaking for Gladbach supporters, but Kaiserslautern's exit in the European Cup was equally as traumatic. Having lost 2-0 in Barcelona, they stormed to a magnificent 3-0 lead at the Betzenberg with two goals from Demir Hotic and one from Bjarne Goldbaek. But a last-minute breakaway goal from Barça's Bakero saw Lautern eliminated on the away goals rule. The Spanish champions qualified for the lucrative new "Champions League" format and walked off with the trophy.

Werder Bremen had some close shaves—most notably in a snowstorm in Turkey against Galatasaray and in a barrage of coins and beer cans in Bruges—but they managed to reach the final of the Cup-Winners' Cup in Lisbon. There, before an appallingly small crowd of 5,000, they beat Monaco on the strength of goals from Wynton Rufer and Klaus Allofs. It was the first major European competition won by a Bundesliga side since Leverkusen's UEFA Cup win in 1988, and Werder's first-ever taste of European glory.

The unified German national team atoned for their slip-up in Wales the season before by winning the return fixture 4-1 and finishing at the top of their European Championship qualifying group. In the first match of the championships in Sweden, a disappointing 1-1 draw with the Commonwealth of Independent States (the former Soviet Union), skipper Rudi Völler was injured and ruled out for the remainder of the tournament. A 2-0 win over Scotland and a 3-1 defeat by Holland saw the Germans scrape through to the semifinals. There, they beat Sweden 3-2 with Karl-Heinz Riedle and Thomas Hässler getting the goals. But in the final, they came up against a vastly-underrated Danish side who had only qualified for the Championships because of the political instability in Yugoslavia. The Danes embarrassed the favoured Germans with a deserved 2-0 win.

Bundesliga

Club	P	W	D	L	Goals	Pts
1. VfB Stuttgart	38	21	10	7	62-32	52
2. Borussia Dortmund	38	20	12	6	66-47	52
3. Eintracht Frankfurt	38	18	14	6	76-41	50
4. 1.FC Cologne	38	13	18	7	58-41	44
5. 1.FC Kaiserslautern	38	17	10	11	58-42	44
6. Bayer Leverkusen	38	15	13	10	53-39	43
7. 1.FC Nuremberg	38	18	7	13	54-51	43
8. Karlsruhe SC	38	16	9	13	48-50	41
9. Werder Bremen	38	11	16	11	44-45	38
10. Bayern Munich	38	13	10	15	59-61	36
11. FC Schalke 04	38	11	12	15	45-45	34
12. Hamburg SV	38	9	16	13	32-43	34
13. Borussia Mönchengladbach	38	10	14	14	37-49	34
14. Dynamo Dresden	38	12	10	16	34-50	34
15. VfL Bochum	38	10	13	15	38-55	33
16. Wattenscheid 09	38	9	14	15	50-60	32
17. Kickers Stuttgart	38	10	11	17	53-64	31
18. Hansa Rostock	38	10	11	17	43-55	31
19. MSV Duisburg	38	7	16	15	43-55	30
20. Fortuna Düsseldorf	38	6	12	20	41-46	24

Top Scorers
Walter (VfB Stuttgart) 22
Chapuisat (Borussia Dortmund) 20
Wohlfarth (Bayern Munich) 17
Yeboah (Eintracht Frankfurt) 15
Sippel (Eintracht Frankfurt) 14
Marin (Kickers Stuttgart) 13
Spies (Hansa Rostock) 13
Tönnies (MSV Duisburg) 13
Bode (Werder Bremen) 12
Eckstein (1.FC Nuremberg) 12
Kirsten (Bayer Leverkusen) 12
Möller (Eintracht Frankfurt) 12
Moutas (Kickers Stuttgart) 12

Second Division North

Top half

	P	W	D	L	Goals	Pts
1. Bayer Uerdingen	32	15	9	8	47-29	39
2. VfB Oldenburg	32	12	14	6	56-39	38
3. Hertha BSC Berlin	32	13	9	10	46-41	35
4. FC St Pauli	32	13	9	10	40-38	35
5. Hanover 96	32	10	14	8	34-37	34
6. SV Meppen	32	10	10	12	36-37	30

Bottom half

	P	W	D	L	Goals	Pts
1. Eintracht Brunswick	32	12	9	11	54-48	33
2. FC Remscheid	32	8	15	9	39-38	31
3. VfL Osnabrück	32	10	11	11	45-54	31
4. Blau-Weiss 90 Berlin	32	11	8	13	41-50	30
5. Fortuna Cologne	32	8	9	15	39-50	25
6. Stahl Brandenburg	32	8	7	17	37-53	23

Blau-Weiss 90 Berlin' were automatically relegated after their professional licence was revoked; their place in the Second Division playoff was taken by Fortuna Cologne

Top Scorers
Drulak (VfB Oldenburg) 21
Sailer (FC St Pauli) 15
Klaus (VfL Osnabrück) 14
Aden (Eintracht Brunswick) 13
Holze (Eintracht Brunswick) 12
Gries (Hertha BSC Berlin) 11
Lünsmann (Hertha BSC Berlin) 11
Pröpper (FC Remscheid) 11
Wollitz (VfL Osnabrück) 11
Belanov (Eintracht Brunswick) 10
Linke (VfB Oldenburg) 10

Second Division South

Top half

	P	W	D	L	Goals	Pts
1. 1.FC Saarbrücken	32	15	12	15	52-30	42
2. Waldhof Mannheim	32	12	14	6	44-31	38
3. SC Freiburg	32	13	11	8	52-41	37
4. FC Chemnitz	32	12	12	8	35-30	36
5. Carl Zeiss Jena	32	12	9	11	39-36	33
6. FC 08 Homburg	32	10	12	10	41-36	32

Bottom half

	P	W	D	L	Goals	Pts
1. VfB Leipzig	32	10	11	11	42-42	31
2. SV Darmstadt 98	32	11	9	12	41-49	31
3. FSV Mainz 05	32	9	12	11	39-38	30
4. TSV 1860 Munich	32	8	14	10	31-32	30
5. FC Halle	32	7	13	12	35-47	27
6. Rot-Weiss Erfurt	32	5	7	20	36-75	17

Top Scorers
Preetz (1.FC Saarbrücken) 17
Heidrich (FC Chemnitz) 12
Fincke (SC Freiburg) 11
Hobsch (VfB Leipzig) 11
Jurgeleit (FC 08 Homburg) 11
Spies (SC Freiburg) 11
Schüler (1.FC Saarbrücken) 10
Turowski (VfB Leipzig) 10
Weiss (SV Darmstadt 98) 10
Hayer (FSV Mainz 05) 9
Wolff (Waldhof Mannheim) 9

Third Division Champions:
Baden-Württemberg: SSV Reutlingen
Bayern: SpVgg Unterhaching
Hessen: Viktoria Aschaffenburg
Nord: VfL Wolfsburg
Nordost (Nord): FC Berlin
Nordost (Mitte): 1.FC Union Berlin
Nordost (Süd): FSV Zwickau
Nordrhein: Wuppertal SV
Südwest: FSV Salmrohr
Westfalen: Preussen Münster

Second Division Playoff

Group 1	P	W	D	L	Goals	Pts
1. Fortuna Cologne	4	3	1	0	9-3	7
2. TSV 1860 Munich	4	1	1	2	2-6	3
3. TSV Havelse	4	0	2	2	2-4	2

Group 2	P	W	D	L	Goals	Pts
1. VfL Wolfsburg	6	5	0	1	15-7	10
2. FSV Zwickau	6	4	0	2	17-11	8
3. FC Berlin	6	2	0	4	9-8	4
4. 1.FC Union Berlin	6	1	0	5	6-21	2

Group 3	P	W	D	L	Goals	Pts
1. Wuppertal SV	4	4	0	0	11-4	8
2. FSV Salmrohr	4	1	1	2	3-6	3
3. Preussen Münster	4	0	1	3	4-8	1

Group 4	P	W	D	L	Goals	Pts
1. SpVgg Unterhaching	4	2	2	0	4-1	6
2. SSV Reutlingen	4	1	2	1	4-4	4
3. Viktoria Aschaffenburg	4	0	2	2	3-6	2

West German Cup
First Round
Arminia Bielefeld 1, FSV Mainz 05 0
Blau-Weiss Parchim 1, Stahl Eisenhüttenstadt 0
Borussia Dortmund (Am.) 2, 1.FC Saarbrücken 5
Bremen SV 0, Fortuna Cologne 7
ESV Lokomotive Cottbus 0, VfB Oldenburg 3
FC Berlin 0, SC Freiburg 2
FC Freiburg 3, FC Chemnitz 1
Karlsruhe SC (Am.) 1, SV Meppen 0
Marathon 02 Berlin 0, Hanover 96 7
Preussen Münster 1, VfL Osnabrück 2
SC Greifswald 2, Stahl Brandenburg 2 aet (Greifswald won on penalties)
SC Jülich 1910 2, Hertha BSC Berlin 1
SC Neukirchen 1, FC Halle 3
Schweinfurt 05 1, Waldhof Mannheim 6
SpVgg Glas-Chemie Wirges 1, FC 08 Homburg 6
SpVgg Zschopau 2, Rot-Weiss Hasborn 3 aet
SpVgg Unterhaching 0, Bayer Uerdingen 0 aet (Uerdingen won on penalties)
SpVgg Ludwigsburg 3, Eintracht Brunswick 2
SpVgg Weiden 1, SV Darmstadt 98 2 aet
SpVgg Fürth 1, Carl Zeiss Jena 0
SV 1910 Kahla 1, Rot-Weiss Erfurt 4
Türkiyemspor Berlin 2, Blau-Weiss 90 Berlin 1
Viktoria Herxheim 2, FC St Pauli 3 aet
Wismut Aue 2, VfB Leipzig 4 aet

Second Round
Arminia Bielefeld 0, Borussia Dortmund 2
Arminia Hanover 1, SC Jülich 1910 5
Bayern Munich 2, FC 08 Homburg 4 aet
Bergmann-Borsig Berlin 2, SC Freiburg 1
Blau-Gelb Berlin 0, VfB Leipzig 5
Borussia Mönchengladbach 2, Wattenscheid 09 0
Eintracht Trier 0, Bayer Leverkusen 2
FC Freiburg 3, Karlsruhe SC (Am.) 2
FC Remscheid 2, VfB Oldenburg 0
Fortuna Düsseldorf 2, FC St Pauli 1
Hamburg SV (Am.) 1, FC Halle 0
Hansa Rostock 3, SV Darmstadt 98 1
Holstein Kiel 1, Bayer Uerdingen 2
MSV Duisburg 0, 1.FC Kaiserslautern 2 aet
Rot-Weiss Erfurt 2, FC Schalke 04 1
Rot-Weiss Essen 0, Karlsruhe SC 2
Rot-Weiss Hasborn 1, VfL Osnabrück 1 aet (Hasborn won on penalties)
Rot-Weiss Wernigerode 0, 1.FC Cologne 4
SC 08 Bamberg 4, 1.FC Saarbrücken 1
SC Greifswald 0, Dynamo Dresden 2
SpVgg Brakel 0, Fortuna Cologne 3
SpVgg Fürth 0, Waldhof Mannheim 3
SpVgg Ludwigsburg 1, Eintracht Frankfurt 6
SSV Reutlingen 4, TSV Krähenwinkel 1
TSG Backnang 1, 1.SV Suhl 06 3
TSV Havelse 1, 1.FC Nuremberg 1 aet (Havelse won on penalties)
Türkiyemspor Berlin 0, Kickers Stuttgart 4

VfL Bochum 2, Hanover 96 3
VfL Wolfsburg 4, Viktoria Aschaffenburg 3 aet
Viktoria Cologne 2, Blau-Weiss Parchim 0
Werder Bremen (Am.) 1, VfB Stuttgart 5
Werder Bremen 3, Hamburg SV 1

Third Round
1.SV Suhl 06 0, Dynamo Dresden 5
Bayer Leverkusen 2, 1.FC Cologne 0
Borussia Dortmund 2, Hanover 96 3
Eintracht Frankfurt 0, Karlsruhe SC 1
FC Freiburg 1, Rot-Weiss Hasborn 0
FC 08 Homburg 0, 1.FC Kaiserslautern 0 aet (Kaiserslautern won on penalties)
FC Remscheid 1, Bayer Uerdingen 3
Fortuna Cologne 5, Hansa Rostock 3 aet
Fortuna Düsseldorf 1, Werder Bremen 3
Hamburg SV (Am.) 2, Bergmann-Borsig Berlin 2 aet (Hamburg won on penalties)
Kickers Stuttgart 3, VfB Leipzig 1 aet
SC 08 Bamberg 4, TSV Havelse 0
SC Jülich 1910 0, Borussia Mönchengladbach 1
SSV Reutlingen 3, Rot-Weiss Erfurt 1
VfL Wolfsburg 1, VfB Stuttgart 3
Viktoria Cologne 1, Waldhof Mannheim 0

Fourth Round
Borussia Mönchengladbach 2, Fortuna Cologne 0
FC Freiburg 1, VfB Stuttgart 6
Hamburg SV (Am.) 0, Karlsruhe SC 1
Hanover 96 1, Bayer Uerdingen 0
SC 08 Bamberg 0, 1.FC Kaiserslautern 1
SSV Reutlingen 2, Bayer Leverkusen 3 aet
Viktoria Cologne 1, Kickers Stuttgart 2 aet
Werder Bremen 4, Dynamo Dresden 1

Quarterfinals
Bayer Leverkusen 1, VfB Stuttgart 0 aet
Borussia Mönchengladbach 2, Kickers Stuttgart 0
Hanover 96 1, Karlsruhe SC 0
Werder Bremen 2, 1.FC Kaiserslautern 0

Semifinals
Borussia Mönchengladbach 2, Bayer Leverkusen 2 aet (Mönchengladbach won on penalties)
Hanover 96 1, Werder Bremen 1 aet (Hanover won on penalties)

Final
in Berlin
Hanover 96 0, Werder Bremen 0 aet (Hanover won on penalties)

German Internationals
11/9/91 in London 1-0 v England
16/10/91 in Nuremberg 4-1 v Wales (ECQ)
20/11/91 in Brussels 1-0 v Belgium (ECQ)
18/12/91 in Leverkusen 4-0 v Luxembourg (ECQ)
25/3/92 in Turin 0-1 v Italy
22/4/92 in Prague 1-1 v Czechoslovakia
30/5/92 in Gelsenkirchen 1-0 v Turkey
2/6/92 in Bremen 1-1 v Northern Ireland
12/6/92 in Norrköping 1-1 v CIS (EC)
15/6/92 in Norrköping 2-0 v Scotland (EC)
18/6/92 in Gothenburg 1-3 v Holland (EC)
21/6/92 in Stockholm 3-2 v Sweden (EC)
26/6/92 in Gothenburg 0-2 v Denmark (EC)

European Cup
First Round
1.FC Kaiserslautern v Etar Tarnovo .... (2-0, 1-1)
Barcelona v Hansa Rostock .... (3-0, 0-1)
Second Round
Barcelona v 1.FC Kaiserslautern .... (2-0, 1-3)

Cup-Winners' Cup
First Round
Stahl Eisenhüttenstadt v Galatasaray .... (1-2, 0-3)
FC Bacau v Werder Bremen .... (0-6, 0-5)
Second Round
Werder Bremen v Ferencvaros .... (3-2, 1-0)
Quarterfinals
Werder Bremen v Galatasaray .... (2-1, 0-0)
Semifinals
FC Brugge v Werder Bremen .... (1-0, 0-2)
Final in Lisbon
Werder Bremen 2, Monaco 0

UEFA Cup
First Round
Hamburg SV v Gornik Zabrze .... (1-1, 3-0)
Cork City v Bayern Munich .... (1-1, 0-2)
Eintracht Frankfurt v Spora Luxembourg .... (6-1, 5-0)
VfB Stuttgart v Pecsi Munkas .... (4-1, 2-2)
FC Halle v Torpedo Moscow .... (2-1, 0-3)
FC Gronigen v Rot-Weiss Erfurt .... (0-1, 0-1)
Second Round
Hamburg SV v CSKA Sofia .... (2-0, 4-1)
B1903 Copenhagen v Bayern Munich .... (6-2, 0-1)
AA Gent v Eintracht Frankfurt .... (0-0, 1-0)
Osasuna v VfB Stuttgart .... (0-0, 3-2)
Rot-Weiss Erfurt v Ajax Amsterdam .... (1-2, 0-3)
Third Round
Hamburg SV v Sigma Olmütz .... (1-2, 1-4)

1992-93

Amateur dramatics

This was a memorable season for the German Cup—not only because it was celebrating its 50th year but because, for the first time, an amateur side had managed to reach the final. Whilst Hertha BSC Berlin's Second Division side reflected on another mediocre season in Division Two, their amateur counterparts from the Oberliga Nordost-Mitte found themselves in the Olympiastadion on cup final day, playing Bayer Leverkusen before a crowd of over 76,000.

No one was quite sure how or why Hertha managed to go as far as they had. They were essentially a group of very young local players who had hardly set the third division alight. Although they had benefited from a few lucky draws, particularly in the early rounds, they proved their worth by toppling both the holders, Hanover 96, and first-division 1.FC Nuremberg in the competition. *Trainer* Jochen Ziegert maintained that a certain degree of his team's success was down to regular visits to a local pizzeria, where players stuffed themselves full of carbohydrate-rich pasta.

But perhaps the single most important factor was the semifinal draw, which pitted Leverkusen against Eintracht Frankfurt and thus gave Hertha the far easier task of facing mid-table Second Division side Chemnitz. Before over 56,000 in Berlin—or five hundred times as many people who had watched the amateurs' league match against SV Thale a few days earlier—Hertha took a 2-0 lead, then hung on for dear life as an embarrassed Chemnitz threw everything they had into attack.

Not surprisingly, though, the cup final proved to be something of an anticlimax, as Leverkusen took control of the match from the outset. They had to wait until the 77th minute for Ulf Kirsten to head them into the lead, but it proved to be the game's only goal. Leverkusen thus had finally claimed their first domestic trophy, five years after winning their first European one.

This was a season in which Bayern Munich were expected to find their feet again and re-assert their domination over the Bundesliga. They made a plethora of heavyweight close-season purchases, including Borussia Dortmund's international defender Thomas Helmer, Bayer Leverkusen's Brazilian international Jorginho, precocious midfielder Mehmet Scholl from Karlsruhe, and Wattenscheid's star midfielder Markus Schupp. Early in the season, Bayern's midfield was further shored up by the return of German national team captain Lothar Matthäus, who had been in dispute with Inter Milan.

With a steadier defence, and plenty of ideas emanating from midfield, Bayern swept to the top of the table after the first match and occupied first place for almost the entire season. But off the pitch, things were not going so smoothly. A number of very public internal squabbles—particularly between Matthäus and Bayern general manager Uli Hoeness—began to attract more and more attention. Inevitably, team morale slumped. Instead of pulling away from the field, Bayern began to struggle, particularly away from home where they failed to win any of their last eight matches. Eventually their comfortable lead at the top of the table had dissipated.

Coming up from behind were Werder Bremen, who had also made a few key acquisitions. Austrian international midfielder Andy Herzog was purchased from Rapid Vienna, while Dietmar Beiersdorfer left Hamburg SV to partner the Norwegian Rune Bratseth in central defence. After the winter break, VfB Leipzig's Bernd Hobsch, riding high at the top of the Second Division goalscoring charts, arrived to give an added dimension to the Werder attack. Unlike at Bayern, morale was no problem, and although Bremen also struggled on their late-season travels, they still were picking up enough points to worry the league leaders.

In late April, Bayern travelled to the Weserstadion to face Bremen in what was being billed as the match of the season. Despite scoring the first goal, Bayern fell apart and wound up losing 4-1. Though still top of the table, they had lost an important psychological battle. Four matches later, Bayern went to Karlsruhe and, in perhaps the turning point of the season, were soundly beaten, 4-2.

With two matches left, the Bavarians took on relegation-threatened VfL Bochum at the Olympiastadion whilst Werder hosted their northern rivals Hamburg. As the afternoon unfolded it became apparent that Bayern were going to win comfortably, but Bremen stepped into high gear, eventually trouncing a disinterested HSV 5-0. When the final whistle blew in Munich, the hosts winning 3-1, Werder had overtaken Bayern at the top—by one goal. Once again, the fate of the championship would not be decided until the last match of the season.

Bayern had the unenviable task of finishing their season before a capacity crowd of 70,000 at the Parkstadion in Gelsenkirchen against Schalke 04. Schalke had replaced the renowned *Trainer* Udo Lattek with former St. Pauli and Dynamo Dresden boss Helmut Schulte, but it didn't prevent them from going through yet another indifferent season. Nevertheless, Schalke, like the rest of the Bundesliga, knew that Bayern were no invincible force. Bremen visited Stuttgart to take on the defending champions, who were experiencing a similarly disappointing campaign. VfB had also found team unity an elusive quality, with several players expressing in no uncertain terms their dislike for general manager Dieter Hoeness, the brother of Uli. Bayern could only draw 3-3 with Schalke, and so Bremen's 3-0 victory over a languid Stuttgart earned them their third Bundesliga championship.

Despite their shortcomings in the league, Bayern were a big hit at the gate, and attendance at the Olympiastadion exceeded 45,600 a game—the second-highest Bundesliga average ever. Dortmund's figure was over 40,000 and five other teams—Stuttgart, Kaiserslautern, Schalke, Cologne, and Nuremberg—averaged over 25,000. German football enjoyed its best season at the turnstiles in fifteen years. Perhaps the weather had something to do with it: for the first time in Bundesliga history, not a single match had been postponed!

The race to become goalscoring champion was clouded in controversy after Eintracht Frankfurt had mistakenly played four foreigners at the same time for a few minutes of their match against the bottom club Bayer Uerdingen. Frankfurt had won the match, 5-2 with Anthony Yeboah scoring four. But Uerdingen protested and the DFB decided to award the match to Uerdingen, 2-0. Yeboah's big day was not to be ignored, though: his goals would count in the record books, and so he became the first player ever to score four times for his side in a 2-0 defeat. Kirsten, whose season's output of 20 goals for Leverkusen made him joint top scorer with Yeboah, did not mind sharing the honours with the powerful Ghanaian striker.

This was not an isolated incident. Stuttgart exposed their ignorance of the somewhat confusing rules surrounding foreign players—and it cost them their place in the European Cup. VfB thought they had beaten Leeds United on away goals until a fair-minded German journalist pointed out that the entry of Croatian Jovo Siminic late into the second leg meant that VfB had finished the match with four foreigners on the pitch. UEFA awarded Leeds the match 3-0, meaning the clubs were now level on aggregate, and since no extra time or penalties had been staged, ordered a third match to be played in Barcelona. In a near-empty Bernabeu Stadium, the English champions won 2-1 to advance.

A more professional performance was fashioned by Dortmund, who reached the UEFA Cup Final before becoming unstuck against Juventus and a former player of theirs, midfielder Andy Möller. Borussia had needed penalties to beat Auxerre in the semifinals, but had looked impressive against their previous three opponents.

The customary *Trainer* merry-go-round showed little sign of abating. The most controversial change was at Leverkusen, where Reinhard Saftig had—in addition to leading Bayer to a place in the cup final—kept his side in the top five almost all season. That wasn't good enough for general manager Rainer Calmund, though, who in mid-season poached Dragoslav Stepanovic from Frankfurt.

Newly-promoted 1.FC Saarbrücken started their return to the Bundesliga brightly, paced by the goalscoring efforts of their American striker, Eric Wynalda. But by the end of the season, they had plummeted into last place with a display of attacking impotence unrivalled in the history of league, failing to score a single goal in over sixteen straight hours of league play. Joining Saarbrücken and Uerdingen in relegation were Bochum, whose fans' faith in the club's traditional ability to stage last-minute recoveries led to them nicknaming their team "the unrelegatable." Bochum still clung to the possibility of staying up, as a DFB investigation exposed a number of improper financial practices at Dresden which threatened to see Dynamo relegated in their place. But a week after the season concluded, it was decided that Dresden's penalty would be to start the following season with four fewer points than the rest of the field. Many viewed this with some cynicism, suggesting that the DFB only allowed Dresden to stay up because the Bundesliga would be without a representative from the former East Germany.

It was a marathon Second Division season, with the 24 clubs each playing 46 matches. The season started in July, and proved to be one of the first tests of FIFA's new back-pass law. On opening day a number of players attempted to circumvent the rule by dropping to one knee and shunting the ball back to the goalkeeper—but FIFA intervened, declaring it as contrary to the spirit of the Laws of the Game. SC Freiburg stormed to the Second Division championship with an entertaining display of positive football, earning them promotion to the Bundesliga for the very first time. Much of the club's success was attributed to *Trainer* Volker Finke, who had shrewdly assembled a "dream team" of talented if little-known players which included Martin Braun, Max Heidenreich, Andreas Zeyer, Uwe Spies and even an Albanian international, Altin Rraklli.

MSV Duisburg finished runners-up, but third place was not decided until the last day, when VfB Leipzig beat FSV Mainz 05 before a home crowd of 38,000 to claim the final promotion spot ahead of Waldhof Mannheim. It was a bittersweet triumph for *Trainer* Jürgen Sundermann, who earlier in the season had signed a contract for the following season—with Mannheim.

In an effort to reduce the size of the Second Division for the following season, seven clubs were relegated to the Oberliga. Among the casualties were Fortuna Düsseldorf, who had lured Alexander Ristic back in a forlorn effort to keep the club out of the amateur leagues. Fortuna thus suffered the ignominy of being relegated from the first division to the third in successive seasons.

Rot-Weiss Essen, TSV 1860 Munich, and Union Berlin won their respective Second Division promotion playoff groups, but one of the ten Oberliga champions was not able to participate. Sachsen Leipzig won the Oberliga Nordost-Mitte on goal difference from Fortschritt Bischofswerda, but failed in the relatively simple task of applying for a professional licence in time. Bischofswerda took their place, but finished a distant third behind the two Berlin clubs. Tennis Borussia Berlin, who had gone through the entire Oberliga Nordost-Nord campaign without losing a match, failed to keep this streak alive in the playoffs, but gained entry through the back door when Union were found to have forged a letter from their bank assuring their financial solvency. (Union in fact had no financial worries, but were struggling to meet the DFB's deadline for their professional licence application and decided to cut corners.)

The national team avenged their European Championship Final defeat by beating Denmark in Copenhagen. The visit of Ghana attracted a large crowd to Bochum's Ruhrstadion, and despite being 1-0 down halfway through the second half, the Germans won 6-1. They also won a four-team tournament in the United States over the summer.

Bundesliga

Club	P	W	D	L	Goals	Pts
1. Werder Bremen	34	19	10	5	63-30	48
2. Bayern Munich	34	18	11	5	74-45	47
3. Eintracht Frankfurt	34	15	12	7	56-39	42
4. Borussia Dortmund	34	18	5	11	61-43	41
5. Bayer Leverkusen	34	14	12	8	64-45	40
6. Karlsruhe SC	34	14	11	9	60-54	39
7. VfB Stuttgart	34	12	12	10	56-50	36
8. 1.FC Kaiserslautern	34	13	9	12	50-40	35
9. Borussia Mönchengladbach	34	13	9	12	59-59	35
10. FC Schalke 04	34	11	12	11	42-43	34
11. Hamburg SV	34	8	15	11	42-44	31
12. 1.FC Cologne	34	12	4	18	41-51	28
13. 1.FC Nuremberg	34	10	8	16	30-47	28
14. Wattenscheid 09	34	10	8	16	46-67	28
15. Dynamo Dresden	34	7	13	14	32-49	27
16. VfL Bochum	34	8	10	16	45-52	26
17. Bayer Uerdingen	34	7	10	17	35-64	24
18. 1.FC Saarbrücken	34	5	13	16	37-71	23

Top Scorers

Kirsten (Bayer Leverkusen)	20
Yeboah (Eintracht Frankfurt)	20
Rufer (Werder Bremen)	17
Chapuisat (Borussia Dortmund)	15
Thom (Bayer Leverkusen)	13
Walter (VfB Stuttgart)	13
Wegmann (VfL Bochum)	13
Kirjakov (Karlsruhe SC)	11
Labbadia (Bayern Munich)	11
Anderbrügge (FC Schalke 04)	10
Bender (Karlsruhe SC)	10
Dahlin (Borussia Mönchengladbach)	10
Eckstein (Eintracht Frankfurt)	10
Herzog (Werder Bremen)	10
Krieg (Karlsruhe SC)	10
Knup (VfB Stuttgart)	10
Pflipsen (Borussia Mönchengladbach)	10
Sammer (Borussia Dortmund)	10
Schmitt (Eintracht Frankfurt)	10
Witeczek (1.FC Kaiserslautern)	10
Zorc (Borussia Dortmund)	10

Second Division

Club	P	W	D	L	Goals	Pts
1. SC Freiburg	46	27	11	8	102-57	65
2. MSV Duisburg	46	23	14	9	65-40	60
3. VfB Leipzig	46	22	14	10	66-45	58
4. Waldhof Mannheim	46	21	13	12	66-53	55
5. Hertha BSC Berlin	46	19	15	12	82-55	53
6. Fortuna Cologne	46	19	12	15	56-44	50
7. FC Chemnitz	46	19	12	15	64-56	50
8. Carl Zeiss Jena	46	19	12	15	66-59	50
9. Hanover 96	46	16	16	14	60-60	48
10. SV Meppen	46	15	17	14	41-43	47
11. Hansa Rostock	46	17	12	17	54-52	46
12. FSV Mainz 05	46	17	12	17	54-48	46
13. Wuppertal SV	46	16	13	17	55-50	45
14. VfL Wolfsburg	46	16	13	17	65-69	45
15. Kickers Stuttgart	46	15	13	18	60-59	43
16. FC 08 Homburg	46	13	17	16	50-53	43
17. FC St Pauli	46	12	19	15	47-52	43
18. SpVgg Unterhaching	46	15	12	19	58-67	42
19. Eintracht Brunswick	46	15	11	20	65-73	41
20. VfL Osnabrück	46	14	13	19	63-72	41
21. Fortuna Düsseldorf	46	11	12	23	45-65	34
22. VfB Oldenburg	46	12	10	24	57-90	34
23. FC Remscheid	46	9	15	23	50-83	33
24. SV Darmstadt 98	46	9	14	23	43-79	32

Top Scorers

Reich (VfL Wolfsburg)	27
Gries (Hertha BSC Berlin)	23
Aden (Eintracht Brunswick)	19
Drulak (VfB Oldenburg)	19
Hubner (FC 08 Homburg)	18
Akpoborie (Carl Zeiss Jena)	17
Heidrich (FC Chemnitz)	17
Preetz (MSV Duisburg)	17
Tönnies (Wuppertal SV)	17
Rraklli (FC Freiburg)	16
Hobsch (VfB Leipzig)	15
Braun (FC Freiburg)	15

Second Division Playoffs

Group 1

	P	W	D	L	Goals	Pts
1. 1.FC Union Berlin	4	3	0	1	7-5	6
2. Tennis Borussia Berlin	4	2	0	2	8-5	4
3. FV 08 Bischofswerda	4	1	0	3	3-8	2

Union Berlin were refused a professional licence, so Tennis Borussia took their place in Division Two

Group 2

	P	W	D	L	Goals	Pts
1. Rot-Weiss Essen	6	4	2	0	15-4	10
2. Preussen Münster	6	3	1	2	8-9	7
3. Eintracht Trier	6	1	2	3	3-8	4
4. VfL Herzlake	6	0	2	4	2-7	3

Group 3

	P	W	D	L	Goals	Pts
1. TSV 1860 Munich	6	2	4	0	8-5	8
2. SSV 1846 Ulm	6	2	3	1	7-7	7
3. Kickers Offenbach	6	1	4	1	5-4	6
4. SC Norderstedt	6	0	3	3	5-9	3

Third Division Champions
Baden-Württemberg: SSV 1846 Ulm
Bayern: TSV 1860 Munich
Hessen: Kickers Offenbach
Nord: VfL Herzlake
Nordost (Mitte): 1.FC Union Berlin
Nordost (Nord): Tennis Borussia Berlin
Nordost (Süd): Sachsen Leipzig
Nordrhein: Rot-Weiss Essen
Südwest: Eintracht Trier
Westfalen: Preussen Münster

German Cup
First Round
ASV Bergedorf 85 1, Bayer Leverkusen 3
Bayer Leverkusen (Am.) 2, Hamburg SV 2 aet (Hamburg SV won on penalties)
Borussia Neunkirchen 0, Bayern Munich 6
FC Gundelfingen 0, Bayer Uerdingen 1
FC Halle 1, Borussia Dortmund 4
Fortuna Düsseldorf (Am.) 1, Borussia Mönchengladbach 2
FSV Salmrohr 2, Wattenscheid 09 0
Göttingen 05 1, FC Schalke 04 3
Jahn Regensburg 2, VfB Lübeck 1
Kickers Emden 1, 1.FC Saarbrücken 5
OT Bremen 1, 1.FC Nuremberg 7
SC Jülich 1910 1, Werder Bremen 5 aet
SK Lüneburg 0, Karlsruhe SC 3
Sportfreunde Siegen 0, VfB Stuttgart 6
SpVgg Fürth 0, VfL Bochum 2
Stahl Brandenburg 0, 1.FC Kaiserslautern 2
SV Wehen 2, Eintracht Frankfurt 3
TSV 1860 Munich 1, Dynamo Dresden 2
Wacker Nordhausen 0, 1.FC Cologne 8

Second Round
Bayer Leverkusen 1, 1.FC Kaiserslautern 0
Borussia Dortmund 2, Bayern Munich 2 aet (Dortmund won on penalties)
Carl Zeiss Jena 2, 1.FC Saarbrücken 1
Dynamo Dresden 2, VfB Leipzig 3
FC Freiburg 0, FSV Mainz 05 3
FC Remscheid 2, SV Darmstadt 98 1
FC St Pauli 2, 1.FC Nuremberg 3 aet
Fortuna Cologne 0, SV Meppen 1
FSV Altmark Stendal 0, FSV Salmrohr 2
FV Bischofswerda 3, VfB Oldenburg 2
Hansa Rostock 2, VfB Stuttgart 0 aet
Hertha BSC Berlin (Am.) 3, SGK Heidelberg 0
Karlsruhe SC 4, Hamburg SV 2
Kickers Stuttgart 1, FC Chemnitz 2
MSV Duisburg 0, 1. FC Cologne 0 aet (Duisburg won on penalties)
Rot-Weiss Erfurt 0, Bayer Uerdingen 0 aet (Uerdingen won on penalties)
Rot-Weiss Essen 2, FC Schalke 04 0
Rot-Weiss Frankfurt 3, Waldhof Mannheim 4
SC 08 Bamberg 1, Eintracht Frankfurt 3
SC Freiburg 2, Hertha BSC Berlin 4
Sportfreunde Ricklingen 5, SC Verl 4 aet
SpVgg Bad Homburg 1, Eintracht Brunswick 5
SpVgg Beckum 0, Werder Bremen 7
SpVgg Plattling 2, Jahn Regensburg 1
SSV 1846 Ulm 2, Post Neubrandenburg 1
Stahl Eisenhüttenstadt 1, Wuppertal SV 1 aet (Eisenhüttenstadt won on penalties)
TuS Hoppstädten 0, VfR Heilbronn 3
VfL Bochum 1, Hanover 96 2
VfR Aalen 1, FC 08 Homburg 2
Viktoria Aschaffenburg 0, VfL Osnabrück 6
Werder Bremen (Am.) 1, Borussia Mönchengladbach 2
Wormatia Worms 2, Fortuna Düsseldorf 4

Third Round
1.FC Nuremberg 5, FC Remscheid 2 aet
Bayer Uerdingen 0, Hanover 96 1
Eintracht Frankfurt 4, Waldhof Mannheim 1 aet
Fortuna Düsseldorf 2, Hansa Rostock 2 aet (Düsseldorf won on penalties)
FSV Salmrohr 0, FC 08 Homburg 1
FV Bischofswerda 0, Karlsruhe SC 1 aet
Hertha BSC Berlin (Am.) 4, VfB Leipzig 2
MSV Duisburg 3, Eintracht Brunswick 1
Rot-Weiss Essen 3, Stahl Eisenhüttenstadt 2
Sportfreunde Ricklingen 0, FC Chemnitz 2
SpVgg Plattling 1, Carl Zeiss Jena 3
SSV 1846 Ulm 1, Borussia Dortmund 3
SV Meppen 2, Hertha BSC Berlin 4 aet
VfL Osnabrück 4, Borussia Mönchengladbach 1
VfR Heilbronn 0, Bayer Leverkusen 2
Werder Bremen 3, FSV Mainz 05 1

Fourth Round
Bayer Leverkusen 1, Hertha BSC Berlin 0
Carl Zeiss Jena 3, MSV Duisburg 2 aet
Eintracht Frankfurt 2, VfL Osnabrück 1
FC 08 Homburg 0, 1.FC Nuremberg 0 aet (Nuremberg won on penalties)
Fortuna Düsseldorf 0, Karlsruhe SC 1
Hertha BSC Berlin (Am.) 4, Hanover 96 3
Rot-Weiss Essen 0, FC Chemnitz 1
Werder Bremen 2, Borussia Dortmund 0

Quarterfinals
Carl Zeiss Jena 0, Bayer Leverkusen 2
FC Chemnitz 2, Werder Bremen 1 aet
Hertha BSC Berlin (Am.) 2, 1.FC Nuremberg 1
Karlsruhe SC 1, Eintracht Frankfurt 1 aet (Frankfurt won on penalties)

Semifinals
Eintracht Frankfurt 0, Bayer Leverkusen 3
Hertha BSC Berlin (Am.) 2, FC Chemnitz 1

Final
in Berlin
Bayer Leverkusen 1, Hertha BSC Berlin (Am.) 0

German Internationals
9/9/92 in Copenhagen 2-1 v Denmark
14/10/92 in Dresden 1-1 v Mexico
18/11/92 in Nuremberg 0-0 v Austria
16/12/92 in Porto Alegre 1-3 v Brazil
20/12/92 in Montevideo 4-1 v Uruguay
24/3/93 in Glasgow 1-0 v Scotland
14/4/93 in Bochum 6-1 v Ghana
10/6/93 in Washington DC 3-3 v Brazil
13/6/93 in Chicago 4-3 v U.S.A.
19/6/93 in Pontiac 2-1 v England

European Cup
First Round
VfB Stuttgart v Leeds United .... (3-0, 1-4)
Second leg awarded to Leeds 3-0 because of Stuttgart's use of an ineligible player. This necessitated a third match, played in Barcelona, which Leeds won 2-1.

Cup-Winners' Cup
First Round
Werder Bremen v Hanover 96 .... (3-1, 1-2)
Second Round
Werder Bremen v Sparta Prague .... (2-3, 0-1)

UEFA Cup
First Round
Fram Reykjavik v 1.FC Kaiserslautern .... (0-3, 0-4)
Floriana v Borussia Dortmund .... (0-1, 2-7)
1.FC Cologne v Glasgow Celtic .... (2-0, 0-3)
Widzew Lodz v Eintracht Frankfurt .... (2-2, 0-9)
Second Round
Borussia Dortmund v Glasgow Celtic .... (1-0, 2-1)
1.FC Kaiserslautern v Sheffield Wednesday .... (3-1, 2-2)
Eintracht Frankfurt v Galatasaray .... (0-0, 0-1)
Third Round
Ajax Amsterdam v 1.FC Kaiserslautern .... (2-0, 1-0)
Borussia Dortmund v Real Zaragoza .... (3-1, 1-2)
Quarterfinals
Roma v Borussia Dortmund .... (1-0, 0-2)
Semifinals
Borussia Dortmund v Auxerre .... (2-0, 0-2 aet)
Dortmund won on penalties
Final
Borussia Dortmund v Juventus .... (1-3, 0-3)

Bibliography

Books
25 Jahre Bundesliga. Sport und Spiel Verlag, 1988.
Becker, Friedebert. *Europa Pokal 1969*. Copress Verlag, 1969.
Chronik der 2. Fussball-Bundesliga 1974-1989. Sport und Spiel Verlag, 1989.
Die Deutsche Pokal Geschichte, 1935-1988. Sport und Spiel Verlag, 1988.
Friedemann, Horst. *Sparwasser und Mauerblümchen*. Klartext Verlag, 1991.
Grüne, Hardy. *Who's Who des Deutschen Fussballs Band 2: Deutsche Vereine von 1902-1992*. Kasseler Sport Verlag, 1992.
Inglis, Simon. *The Football Grounds of Europe*. Collins Willow, 1990.
Kicker Almanach. Olympia-Verlag, various years.
Molenaar, Hans. *Europa Cup 1971/72*. De Boekerij, 1972.
Rippon, Anton. *European Cup*. Mirror Books, 1980.
Rothman's Football Yearbook. Queen Anne Press, various years.
Rowlinson, John, and Motson, John. *The European Cup, 1955-1980*. Queen Anne Press, 1980.
Simon, Günter. *Fussball Informativ*. Sportverlag Berlin, 1985.

Periodicals
Fussball Sport Extra. Deutscher Sportverlag, various years.
Fussball Woche. Sportverlag GmbH, various years.
Kicker Bundesliga Sonderheften. Olympia-Verlag, various years.
Kicker Spezial: 20 Jahre Bundesliga. Olympia-Verlag, 1983.
Kicker Spezial: 25 Jahre Bundesliga. Olympia-Verlag, 1988.
Kicker Spezial: 30 Jahre Bundesliga. Olympia-Verlag, 1993.

The Author

Dave Wangerin was born and raised in the American midwest, but moved to Britain in 1987 when the incongruity of being a football fan and living in the United States became too much for him to bear.

An occasional contributor to *When Saturday Comes* and other half-decent publications, he also edits the obscure German football fanzine *Elfmeter* which he helped start in 1988. He is often found in the Witton Lane Stand at Villa Park with his wife Nicola.

ADVERTISEMENT

And now, a few words about

ELFMETER

A British Look at German Football

For over five years, millions of German football fans have turned to ELFMETER for news and information about the Bundesliga. (Okay, maybe not millions. But we're new to advertising.)

ELFMETER is dedicated exclusively to German football. A fairly weighty subject, we're sure you'd agree. It's written—in English—by fans, for fans. It's not very expensive, it doesn't weigh a lot, and most issues don't contain too many spelling mistakes. And above all, it doesn't take itself too seriously.

ELFMETER
A British Look at German Football
Issue 24   75p
Werder snatch the title
All's well that ends well?

The 1992/93 season in review
with reports from Bremen, München, Berlin, Leverkusen, Münster, and, er, Unterhaching

To join the millions of fans . . . er, the very large number of fans . . . who have helped to make ELFMETER Britain's top-selling German football publication, just fill in the coupon below, and send it with a stamped, addressed envelope (overseas three IRCs) to the address below.

To: *Elfmeter*, 16 Mallory Road, Perton, Staffordshire WV6 7XN

Okay, here's my SAE. Send me a sample *Elfmeter*.

Name: _____

Address: _____

Postcode: _____

Is this the first you've ever heard of *Elfmeter*? Yes ☐   No ☐